Idle Talk

NEW PERSPECTIVES ON CHINESE CULTURE AND SOCIETY

A series sponsored by the American Council of Learned Societies and made possible through a grant from the Chiang Ching-kuo Foundation for International Scholarly Exchange

1. Joan Judge and Hu Ying, eds., *Beyond Exemplar Tales: Women's Biography in Chinese History*
2. David A. Palmer and Xun Liu, eds., *Daoism in the Twentieth Century: Between Eternity and Modernity*
3. Joshua A. Fogel, ed., *The Role of Japan in Modern Chinese Art*
4. Thomas S. Mullaney, James Leibold, Stéphane Gros, and Eric Vanden Bussche, eds., *Critical Han Studies: The History, Representation, and Identity of China's Majority*
5. Jack W. Chen and David Schaberg, eds., *Idle Talk: Gossip and Anecdote in Traditional China*

Idle Talk

Gossip and Anecdote in Traditional China

EDITED BY JACK W. CHEN
AND DAVID SCHABERG

Global, Area, and International Archive
University of California Press
BERKELEY   LOS ANGELES   LONDON

The Global, Area, and International Archive (GAIA) is an initiative of the Institute of International Studies, University of California, Berkeley, in partnership with the University of California Press, the California Digital Library, and international research programs across the University of California system.

University of California Press, one of the most distinguished university presses in the United States, enriches lives around the world by advancing scholarship in the humanities, social sciences, and natural sciences. Its activities are supported by the UC Press Foundation and by philanthropic contributions from individuals and institutions. For more information, visit www.ucpress.edu.

University of California Press
Berkeley and Los Angeles, California

University of California Press, Ltd.
London, England

© 2014 by The Regents of the University of California

Library of Congress Cataloging-in-Publication Data

A catalog record for this book is available from the Library of Congress.

ISBN: 978-0-520-28977-2

23 22 21 20 19 18 17 16 15 14
10 9 8 7 6 5 4 3 2 1

To our sons:
Damien Heller-Chen
Milo Lei Schaberg
Rafe Lei Schaberg

Contents

Acknowledgments   ix

    INTRODUCTION   1
    Jack W. Chen

1. WORD OF MOUTH AND THE SOURCES OF WESTERN
   HAN HISTORY   17
   David Schaberg

2. TALES FROM BORDERLAND: ANECDOTES IN
   EARLY MEDIEVAL CHINA   38
   Xiaofei Tian

3. KNOWING MEN AND BEING KNOWN: GOSSIP AND
   SOCIAL NETWORKS IN THE *SHISHUO XINYU*   55
   Jack W. Chen

4. ORAL SOURCES AND WRITTEN ACCOUNTS:
   AUTHORITY IN TANG TALES   71
   Sarah M. Allen

5. I READ THEY SAID HE SANG WHAT HE WROTE: ORALITY,
   WRITING, AND GOSSIP IN TANG POETRY ANECDOTES   88
   Graham Sanders

6. GOSSIP, ANECDOTE, AND LITERARY HISTORY:
   REPRESENTATIONS OF THE YUANHE ERA IN
   TANG ANECDOTE COLLECTIONS   107
   Anna M. Shields

7. SHEN KUO CHATS WITH INK STONE AND
   WRITING BRUSH   132
   Ronald Egan

8. MEN, WOMEN, AND GOSSIP IN SONG CHINA   154
   Beverly Bossler

9. GLYPHOMANTIC DREAM ANECDOTES   178
   Richard E. Strassberg

10. THE RETRIBUTORY POWER OF GOSSIP IN *THE
    STORY OF THE STONE*   194
    Dore J. Levy

    POSTFACE: "BELIEVE IT OR NOT"   217
    Stephen Owen

    Bibliography   225

    Contributors   239

    Index   241

Acknowledgments

Of the ten chapters included here, nine were originally presented at an international conference entitled, "Gossip, Anecdote, and Occasion in Traditional China," held in May 2008 at UCLA. The editors would like to thank the American Council of Learned Societies and the Chiang Ching-kuo Foundation, which generously supported the conference and provided a publishing subvention. We would also like to thank the Center for Chinese Studies at UCLA, our home department of Asian Languages & Cultures, and the UCLA College of Letters and Science, for their additional support and encouragement.

A number of papers presented at the conference could not be included in the present volume, but we are very grateful to Cheng Yu-yu, Michael Fuller, Mark Halperin, David R. Knechtges, Lee Fong-mao, Liu Yuan-ju, Andrew Miller, and Scott L. Waugh, as their participation greatly enriched both that occasion and the resulting volume. We would additionally like to single out Richard Gunde and Nathaniel K. Isaacson whose assistance made the conference possible, and Brian Bernards, Matthew Cochran, Maura Dykstra, David Hull, Tim Lee, and Hanmo Zhang, who graciously chaired the panels. The external reviewer provided insightful comments, which have strengthened the resulting volume. Finally, as with all things, we are grateful to our families for their understanding and patience.

Introduction
Jack W. Chen

Let me begin with an anecdote, though one of a more modern vintage than the others discussed in this volume. On International Women's Day (March 8) in 1935, the silent-film actress Ruan Lingyu 阮玲玉 added barbiturates to her congee, wrote two suicide notes, and then died of an overdose at the young age of twenty-four.¹ The first note, which bore no particular addressee, blamed her estranged common-law husband Zhang Damin 張達民 for his cruelty and vindictiveness. During their time together, Zhang Damin had gambled away much of their money, and once Ruan fell in love with the Cantonese tea merchant Tang Jishan 湯季珊, Zhang demanded financial support, threatening to report Ruan for adultery. She agreed to pay him one hundred *yuan* a month, though this turned out not to be enough. Zhang repeatedly sought more money, threatening to go to the newspapers if Ruan did not agree to his demands. Tang Jishan opposed her continuing attempts to placate Zhang and in a fit of rage, slapped her across the face. Zhang decided to sue both Ruan and Tang in court and to slander Ruan in the tabloid newspapers.

Despairing that public opinion would favor Zhang and realizing that life with Tang was also problematic, the actress decided to end her life. In one of the notes, she wrote:

> Alas! So what can I do? I keep thinking it over, and all I can think of is death. Alas! My death—how is it worth lamenting? Still, it's just that I'm afraid gossip is something to be feared—gossip is something to be feared.
> 唉! 那有甚麻法子想呢? 想之又想, 惟有一死了之罷。唉! 我一死何足惜, 不過還是怕人言可畏, 人言可畏罷了。²

And yet, while she feared the savaging of public opinion in her last days, the public would turn out in the tens of thousands at her funeral procession to mourn her death.

This tragic story is an anecdote about gossip, one that simultaneously demonstrates how gossip may become anecdote. To be sure, gossip and anecdote are not the same, though they are frequently related. While gossip is commonly defined as "idle talk," that is, talk without productive value or factual reliability, anecdotes are usually understood as short, interesting narratives, told for amusement or to display wit. However, scholars have in recent years offered more complex definitions of both terms and set aside moralistic concerns, emphasizing how gossip and anecdote function within social communities. For example, the social psychologists Nicholas DiFonzo and Prashant Bordia describe gossip as "evaluative social talk about individuals . . . that arises in the context of social network formation, change, and maintenance . . . [and that fulfills] a variety of essential social network functions including entertainment, maintaining group cohesiveness, establishing, changing and maintaining group norms, group power structure and group membership."³ Similarly, anecdotes, whatever their narrative interest, may also serve to bring about social cohesion. As the literary scholar Malina Stefanovska has written, "Telling anecdotes served as a means of tightening the community and drawing its boundaries through the exchange of rumors and news" and through their "oral circulation, which undoubtedly preceded any written versions, delineated groups of shared interests, channels of communication, and elective affinities."⁴ In this way, both gossip and anecdote are constitutive of, and constituted by, local structures of social organization and relationality—which is to say, the interpersonal networks that manifest themselves throughout society.

To return to Ruan Lingyu, this is a tale of gossip that points beyond the simple fact of gossipy scandal to the question of how tales of gossip are produced and circulated within society. Not long after her suicide, Lu Xun 魯迅 (1881–1936) would write an essay entitled, "On 'Gossip Is Something to Be Feared'" 論《人言可畏》, in which he attacked the Shanghai tabloid industry for its role in provoking Ruan's death.⁵ Lu Xun, who otherwise had little good to say about gossip, makes a particularly telling point in his essay on the affair:

> If some malicious crone in Shanghai's streets and alleys hears that some neighbor's second wife has a strange man coming and going, she'll be overjoyed to talk about it, but if it's in regard to a wife in Gansu having an affair or whoever in Xinjiang is getting married again, then she won't even want to hear about it.
>
> 上海的街頭巷尾的老虔婆，一知道近鄰的阿二嫂家有野男人出入，津津樂道，但如果對她講甘肅的誰在偷漢，新疆的誰在再嫁，她就不要聽了。⁶

What Lu Xun perceives is that gossip and its anecdotes are always a product of particular communities, taking place only within a restricted social economy, a local network of participants, who all know (however distantly) the object of the gossip. That is, one can participate in gossip only if one belongs to the social network through which the gossip circulates—a tautological condition that might also be expressed by saying that gossip and the network along which it travels are mutually constitutive, that gossip in a sense creates the network along which it is circulated.

What is perhaps most striking about the Ruan Lingyu anecdote—and the reason why I have chosen to begin with it—is how it demonstrates the intertextual resonances of gossip within the history of Chinese literature and culture. The proverb "gossip is something to be feared," which can be translated more literally as "people's talk is to be feared," has its origins in the poem "Zhongzi Please" 將仲子 (Poem 76) from the *Shijing* 詩經 (Classic of poetry). In the poem, the (female) speaker beseeches her paramour not to make public the nature of their relationship, first pointing out how her parents' and brothers' words are to be feared, and then concluding with the general statement, "That people talk a lot, / This also can be feared" 人之多言，亦可畏也.[7] The poetic speaker is aware of how knowledge of their trysts will travel beyond the confines of the household and become part of the sphere of public talk that constitutes their community. This public sphere of talk is no less manifest in rural village life than it is in urban celebrity culture. Even though Ruan Lingyu may have been more free to choose her lovers than a woman was in the late Zhou dynasty, she was nonetheless equally vulnerable to the force of public opinion. Indeed, in some ways, Ruan Lingyu may have been even more vulnerable—as a famous actress, she was a product of celebrity culture in the first place.

While similar examples of gossip and anecdote may be found in abundance within the literary and historical writings of traditional China, there has heretofore been little scholarly attention to how gossip and anecdote have shaped literary and historical narratives. At best, gossip and anecdote were considered supplementary to serious literary and historical scholarship, and at worst, they were considered unreliable and slanderous sources of misinformation. Yet a perusal of the dynastic histories—the officially sanctioned, grand narratives of imperial China *par excellence*—reveals just how the historiographers of each dynasty have relied on the use of anecdotes, gossip, and other largely unverifiable sources. Such materials permeate not only the biographical accounts (*liezhuan* 列傳), but also the imperial annals (*benji* 本紀), providing illustrative examples—or sometimes simply titillating details—in the descriptions of state affairs and the lives of leading families and individuals.⁸

Gossip and anecdote embodied tensions between public and private knowledge, between reliable and unreliable sources of information. Over time, writings incorporating such materials would include such diverse genres as anomaly accounts and marvelous tales (*zhiguai chuanqi* 志怪傳奇), miscellanies and private accounts (variously known as *biji* 筆記 and *zalu* 雜錄, among other terms), and so-called unofficial or secret histories (*waishi* 外史 and *neizhuan* 內傳). Genres such as travelogues, gazetteers, and geographic works also made use of gossip and anecdotes by way of filling out the details of the regions and places under discussion and adding local flavor to the accounts. For some historians and scholars, the use of such materials occasioned alarm, but for most, the pleasures of recounting interesting tidbits outweighed the risks of deviating from the strictly factual, moralizing dictates of classical Confucian historiographic standards. Moreover, certain works, such as the *Zhenguan zhengyao* 貞觀政要 (Essentials of government during the Zhenguan reign), were compiled as exemplary anecdotal histories that demonstrated good government in hopes of providing models for a less ideal or moral age.⁹

It should be noted that there is no single term for gossip within either classical or modern Chinese, though terms such as *xianhua* 閒話 ("idle talk"), *xiantan* 閒談 ("idle conversations"), and *liuyan* 流言 ("rumor") are often used. Often the presence of gossip is simply evoked by reference to communal speech, such as the terms *renyan* 人言 and *shiyan* 世言, or to the hearing (*wen* 聞) and transmission (*chuan* 傳) of such speech. Anecdotes are variously referred to as *yishi* 逸事 or 軼事 ("uncollected matters"), *yiwen* 遺聞 ("uncollected news"), or sometimes simply *gushi* 故事 ("old tales"). From these terms, one can clearly see an emphasis on the oral nature of gossip, which is passed on by word of mouth and as such belongs vaguely to the discursive community, rather than to the individual. There is also the acknowledgment of gossip as something that takes place as a leisure-time activity and as a nonproductive form of communication. When the terms for anecdote may also reflect an oral situation, there is additionally a sense that they represent items of interest that are not integrated into larger narrative structures, but are dispersed or freely circulating, necessitating the work of an editor or compiler who will collate them in a publishable form.

The essays gathered in this volume constitute a first attempt to define, describe, and analyze the place of gossip and anecdote within Chinese literary and cultural history. Organized in a chronological manner, from the Han to the Qing, the essays provide a kind of anecdotal history of traditional literary and historical genres, from official to unofficial historiography, from dream anecdotes to *The Story of the Stone*. It should be noted that the essays are not meant to comprise a strictly defined literary history of anecdote and gossip, but rather, to serve as an overview of a long-neglected topic in Chinese literary and historical studies and to suggest new avenues of research.

The place of gossip and anecdote within official historiography is the very subject undertaken by David Schaberg in chapter 1. Schaberg provides a new perspective on the two works that would inaugurate the tradition of official dynastic historiography in China—the *Shiji* 史記 (Records of the historian) and the *Hanshu* 漢書 (History of the Han dynasty)—by showing how the two major histories of the Western Han are informed by gossip about the affairs of the imperial family and anecdotes of palace life. There is no question that archival sources for the Han would not include the kind of information that Sima Qian 司馬遷 (ca. 145–ca. 86 BCE) and Ban Gu 班固 (32–92 CE) regularly interwove into their historical narratives. However, at the same time, while such supplementary materials can no longer be verified in contemporaneous sources, their appearance in the two histories was not met with any ostensible criticism or outcry regarding their truthfulness. The problematic nature of Sima Qian's and Ban Gu's sources is, in fact, acknowledged by the two historians in the course of relating hearsay and oral report, though they implicitly defend their choices to utilize hearsay and oral report by appeal to the larger world of public opinion, which serves as an indirect proof of reliability.

There is here an interesting demonstration of the epistemology of gossip. What Schaberg shows is how the objects of public opinion are always the last to discover what people are saying about them. That is, gossip gravitates around those in positions of authority, not least of all because those in positions of authority are usually the ones who set the gossip into motion in the first place, but they are also paradoxically the last to know how the gossip portrays them. If gossip is information about a secret that escapes the domains of private knowledge to become public knowledge, it is also the case that this public knowledge is often hidden from those who have the most intimate experience of the secret in the first place.

In chapter 2, Tian Xiaofei directly examines the nature and function of anecdote through a series of readings drawn from dynastic history, anecdotal collections, poetic exposition, and travel writing. Anecdotes, as Tian discusses, may either support or disrupt larger narratives; they serve to exemplify character and plot, and thus must be deployed with care. How one interprets and understands an anecdote is also something that the composer of a narrative must manage, adding affirming phrases such as "all marveled at this"—or leaving them out. However, for collections such as the famed *Shishuo xinyu* 世說新語 (*A New Account of Tales of the World*), with its systematic categorization of behaviors and topics, there is another level to the management of anecdotal interpretation. Tian shows how one anecdote might lend itself to multiple readings, as the same story is presented under three different categories, each one emphasizing a different aspect of the same basic plot.

While anecdotes may serve as rhetorical illustrations of character, Tian goes on to argue that anecdotes simultaneously have a vested interest in the personal and in the representation of the personal. Turning to a comparison between a poetic exposition on a military campaign and a prose account of the same occasion, she shows how unspoken generic rules help to fashion what is represented and what is omitted. The personal anecdote, she notes, has no place in the poetic exposition, but often serves to anchor the prose account in subjective experience, binding that travel narrative to a specific perspective and thus creating a sense of cohesion—and anticipating the sustained subjective accounts found in certain later fiction. She concludes her piece with a discussion of the well-known anecdote about encountering a fan in Faxian's *Foguo ji* 佛國記 (*A Record of Buddhistic Kingdoms*), which highlights a poignant moment of personal longing within the otherwise dry travelogue.

It is to the world of the *Shishuo xinyu* that I return in chapter 3, taking up the question of social knowledge and the economy of reputation that underlies much of the anecdotal collection. I connect the *Shishuo xinyu*'s interest in reputation (*zhiming* 知名) to the longstanding political concern with "knowing men" (*zhiren* 知人), tracing the issue from the *Shangshu* 尚書 (Esteemed documents) and *Lüshi chunqiu* 呂氏春秋 (Annals of Lü Buwei) to the Eastern Han *Renwu zhi* 人物志 (Treatise on personalities). For these texts, "knowing men" is the sovereign's responsibility, since it is the sovereign who is tasked with the identification of individual talents and the proper employment of his subjects. I show how the *Shishuo xinyu* reenvisions the political act of "knowing men" by situating it within the construction of social networks and relationships. To be able to know and use another's abilities is to gain influence within society, both in terms of gaining a reputation for discerning judgment and in terms of reconfiguring the networks to one's own advantage.

However, much of the *Shishuo xinyu* is concerned with the *manner* in which these judgments of men are made, not just with the actual judgments themselves. Earlier readings of the collection have emphasized themes of aesthetic cultivation and social detachment in the making of judgments; what I show is how such virtuosic acts of discernment inform a discursive agonistics and a consciousness of differentials of social capital within the community. The anecdotes that transmit these judgments are themselves a form of gossip, pointing back to a world of social talk and social intercourse. I conclude with an examination of one figure known for his ability to *zhiren*: Chu Pou 褚裒 (303–49), an eminent official who would become father-in-law to Emperor Kang 康帝 (r. 342–44) of the Eastern Jin. In two anecdotes on the *non*-recognition of Chu Pou, what emerges is the way in which the names of the eminent circulate among the social networks and are preserved within the anecdotes that comprise the *Shishuo xinyu*.

Sarah M. Allen, in chapter 4, turns to the world of classical tales (often identified as *chuanqi* 傳奇, "transmitted marvels," or simply as *xiaoshuo* 小說, "fiction") in the eighth and ninth centuries. Allen discusses the problem of how such stories establish narrative authority when there are different, competing versions of a given event or when there is simply skepticism about the improbability of a reported event. For the latter situation, the narrator may turn to someone with inside knowledge, one who has first-hand experience of the event and can confirm that the story is indeed as related in the narrative. This is how the implausible event in the story "The Severed Soul" ("Lihun ji" 離魂記), in which a woman's soul leaves her body and experiences a life of its own, is resolved. Similarly, when a narrative takes up not a private or localized occurrence, but one that can be falsified within publicly known or circulated historical records, then the narrative must produce a witness to the event who will address the discrepancies between the narrative and the historical accounts. Allen provides readings of three such stories: "Yao Hong" 姚泓, in which a green-feathered creature is revealed to be the last ruler of the fifth-century Later Qin; "Biography of Shangqing" ("Shangqing zhuan" 上清傳), in which a palace maid explains to the emperor the truth behind the rivalry and plotting between two major court officials; and finally, "The Ancient Inscription from the Liang Datong Period" ("Liang Datong guming ji" 梁大同古銘記), in which the erudition of an unjustly forgotten scholar is rediscovered and brought back into public knowledge. In each of these tales, reliance on officially accepted textual accounts turns out to be insufficient, necessitating the oral reports of eyewitnesses or other figures who have intimate knowledge of the true facts of the matter.

A historiography based upon the archive of written records may be subject to political pressures and interests, thus excluding marginal voices (such as that of a maid) who would have a more comprehensive and unbiased perspective on events but lack the channels through which to testify. What Allen shows is how a world of oral report and inside knowledge, a world of gossip, serves to destabilize the claimed authority of officially recognized textual evidence. The empire of the text, in other words, coexists with communities of talk, and from the perspective of Tang tales, it is the communities of talk that take epistemic precedence.

Tang dynasty communities of talk are also examined by Graham Sanders in chapter 5, though here from the perspective of anecdotes about poetry. Sanders notes that there is often a tension between proximate and distant accounts, with the former claiming authority based on temporal closeness to the event and the latter based on a critical deliberation possible only with temporal remove. This sets up an epistemological quandary similar to the problem of oral reports versus written accounts discussed by Sarah Allen, and indeed may articulate one central question for an examination of anecdotal literature. For the basis of his chapter, Sanders takes up one particularly complex anecdote from a late ninth-century collection, the *Yunxi youyi* 雲谿友議 (Friendly conversations at Cloudy Creek), compiled by Fan Shu 范攄 (fl. ca. 877). The anecdote is structured in three parts: the first segment deals with an encounter between the scholar Li She 李涉 (fl. 827–35) and a group of bandits whose leader recognizes him by literary reputation and asks for a poem; the second with a failed later meeting between the two men and an encounter with a former concubine of a now-deceased friend; and the last, years after Li She's death, with a young scholar who meets an old man who turns out to be none other than the bandit leader.

Poems are composed and recited in the course of the anecdote, the most important of which is the poem presented by Li She to the bandit, which the young scholar chants at the end. As Sanders points out, the longstanding belief that poems are nonfictional evocations of a historical occasion anchors the anecdotal framework for the poems related in the course of the story. This allows the compiler of the anecdote collection to make his own comment on the reliability of the story, revealing that he once met the young scholar of the last segment and that the young scholar showed him the handwritten poem composed by Li She for the bandit. And equally important, the presence of the evidential poem allows anecdote to pass from a condition of mere gossip to fact, suggesting that Fan Shu is transmitting not merely an item of narrative interest, but a verifiable historical account.

It is with the question of how historiography and anecdote relate that Anna M. Shields begins her essay in chapter 6. Shields discusses anecdotal representations of the Yuanhe 元和 reign period (806–20) within three Tang anecdote collections: the *Tang guoshi bu* 唐國史補 (Supplement to the Tang history of the state) of Li Zhao 李肇 (d. after 829), the *Yinhua lu* 因話錄 (Records of hearsay) of Zhao Lin 趙璘 (803–after 868), and the *Tang zhiyan* 唐摭言 (Collected sayings from the Tang) of Wang Dingbao 王定保 (870–940). The significance of the Yuanhe reign (with the understanding that "Yuanhe" as a cultural moment is temporally broader than the political reign) may be found in cultural debates over the nature of literary writing by figures active during this time, such as Han Yu 韓愈 (768–824), Yuan Zhen 元稹 (779–831), and Bai Juyi 白居易 (772–846). Shared claims of innovation (*xin* 新) and strangeness (*guai* 怪) that Yuanhe authors claimed as normative values of literature promoted the notion of a "Yuanhe style" 元和體. By the Song dynasty, the Yuanhe was remembered as a watershed moment, one whose literary reformations would be influential for writers such as Ouyang Xiu 歐陽修 (1007–72) and Su Shi 蘇軾 (1037–1101).

However, it is with an eye to understanding the significance of Yuanhe era literary history for the Tang, rather than in terms of its influence on the Song, that Shields examines anecdotes and comments from the *Guoshi bu*, *Yinhua lu*, and *Tang zhiyan*. Within these three texts, Shields shows three very different constructions of the same literary era. Not only are prominent figures such as Han Yu and Bai Juyi represented here in ways that differ from their later receptions, but their shifting evaluations reveal how literary and cultural histories are discontinuous and complex processes, reflecting ideological concerns and perspectival limitations that are smoothed out over the decades. Shields takes care to note that anecdotal sources for literary history are no more genuine or authentic than official historiographies, yet the anecdotes do provide the possibility of hearing contemporary assessments, reflective of individual sensibilities, that are occluded within the monumental records compiled at the state's command.

It is a very different kind of anecdote that Ronald Egan examines in chapter 7, in his essay on Shen Kuo 沈括 (1031–95) and his *biji* 筆記

("brush jottings") collection, the *Mengxi bitan* 夢溪筆談 (Chatting with my writing brush at Dreams Creek). Shen's table of contents, translated by Egan, shows a broad set of topics that includes court ritual procedures, literature and music, artisans and their techniques, jokes, and strange events. Shen Kuo then clarifies how he has conceived his collection, noting that he is less interested in the gossip that derives from elite social networks than in rustic conversations and back-alley hearsay. While the preface is accurate insofar as the *Mengxi bitan* is surprisingly light on matters involving high-ranking historical figures, what Egan calls attention to is how the preface misleads the reader by casting the rest of its contents in terms of conventional gossip from city and country.

There is, in fact, nothing conventional about what Shen Kuo includes in his work. Egan draws upon four topics, drawn from across the various chapters in Shen's classification of the text, to show the breadth of what is found in the *Mengxi bitan*. First, Egan discusses Shen's interest in relating information about socially invisible segments of traditional society, from well-diggers and builders to the inventor of movable type, Bi Sheng 畢昇 (d. 1051). Second, he turns to Shen's fascination with scientific knowledge and the writer's own experimentations with astronomy, uranography, and optics. Third, he takes up anecdotes about peculiar figures, including both eccentrics of social rank or standing, like his neighbor Shi Yannian 石延年, and those, like the wizard Xu 許, who are marginal to society. Fourth and last, he takes up those anecdotes that show how conventional knowledge and morality are insufficient for a clear understanding of the world, or may run contrary to how the world actually operates. Examples here include (once again) Shi Yannian, who dies only when the emperor, concerned for his health, orders the man to stop drinking alcohol, as well as a long bipartite anecdote in which an act of mercy is rewarded in one case but causes disaster in the other.

These anecdotes and other miscellaneous bits of information are not what is normally understood to be gossip, but as Egan points out, they open windows upon the vast networks of knowledge that are rarely acknowledged in traditional Chinese sources. The baseness of his subjects points to the central significance of "talk," which would have been the primary means by which Shen Kuo could have gathered his information and composed this *biji*—certainly there would have been few written records upon which he could have relied. Moreover, the popularity and wide circulation of *Mengxi bitan* would have ensured that the oral informants of Shen Kuo's work would be remembered in a textual medium, one that translated ephemeral, local knowledge into the anecdotal currency of a reading public.

The subject that Beverly Bossler discusses in chapter 8—the status of courtesans as represented in anecdotal literature—is one that resonates both with the treatment of socially marginal figures found in Egan's essay and with the nature of unofficial historiography discussed by Shields. As Bossler notes, whereas official historiographic sources focus almost exclusively on male homosocial relationships (most often in elite social circles), the unofficial nature of anecdotal sources allows for perspectives on how courtesans participated in elite networks. She begins by discussing the social significance of the banquet, which offered elite men a chance to display status and wealth, not to mention cultural sophistication. As certain anecdotes show, courtesans were often present for such occasions, and they took direct part in the social negotiations of status as well, lavishing attention on those worthy to receive it and ignoring those of lesser rank. However, the social prestige and material wealth amassed by leading courtesans, as depicted in other anecdotes, could lead to government confiscations of property in times of economic or political duress. And while a grand reputation might elevate a courtesan in the eyes of her admirers, it could not bring her or her offspring the kind of legal protection an official wife would enjoy.

However, the social representation of courtesans, as Bossler shows, has much to do with their idealization within literary culture. Poems and songs about the grace and beauty of courtesans established conventions both in terms of descriptive rhetoric and in terms of emotional or behavioral mappings. The courtesan as object of romance is what is produced by elite men in their poetic fantasies, and it is difficult, as she argues, to clearly perceive the reality beyond the conventions. Indeed, one of the central problems caused by romantic idealization is how it obscures the domestic lives of many private courtesans. Bossler shows how anecdotes speak both to the emotional complexity of the relationships between courtesans and the elite men they served, which stood in uneasy relationship to the legal codifications of official marriages, and to the conventional romantic thematizations, which stressed temporariness and parting. While Bossler discusses how there is historical evidence that courtesans and female entertainers in some cases were afforded certain liberties and privileges, or treated as wives in all but name, she ends by noting the limitations of anecdotal sources for accurate representations of courtesans during the Song.

If one aspect of the private lives of public men is discussed by Bossler, then it is another aspect—the private realm of dreaming—that Richard E. Strassberg takes up in chapter 9. The focus of Strassberg's essay is the glyphomantic tradition of dream interpretation, which treats dreams as picture-puzzles not unlike the rebus-based dream analyses of Freud in his *Interpretation of Dreams*. In dream-based glyphomancy, either the dream includes a glyph (character) that must be interpreted, or the components of the dream are themselves revealed to comprise a glyph or glyphs. Strassberg examines anecdotes about dreams and their interpretation from early medieval China through to the late imperial period, drawing on historiographical texts, philosophical sources, and novel-length fiction. He sets these anecdotes within the Ming and Qing traditions of dream interpretation, as represented by figures such as Chen Shiyuan 陳士元 (1516–97) and Cheng Xing 程省 (fl. mid-17th cent.), both of whom attempted to systematize principles of oneiric exegesis.

As Strassberg shows, the relationship between the private and the public within anecdotes about dreams and dream interpretation is complicated: dreams take place within the private space of an individual mind, but their meanings often have very public consequences. Dreams are in and of themselves esoteric and opaque—even to the dreamer him- or herself—requiring interpretation by a skilled reader of dreams, so that the private symbology of dream logic may be translated into the public spaces of common language. Of course, once the dream and its interpretation are cast in anecdotal form, the dream is already made public (in a sense, published), revealing the dream as a kind of secret or occult history, one that is given to one individual and yet may be read and understood by others.

Finally, in chapter 10, Dore J. Levy takes up the question of gossip directly by examining how social talk functions within the imagined world of the great Qing dynasty novel, *Honglou meng* 紅樓夢 (*A Dream of Red Mansions*), perhaps better known to the Anglophone world as *The Story of the Stone* (David Hawkes's translation of its alternate title, *Shitou ji* 石頭記). As Levy shows, the world described in *Story of the Stone* is a closed society, though one in which gossip and rumor often take the place of true knowledge. Unlike the economy of reputation found in the *Shishuo xinyu*, in which there is public consensus and judgment of the worth of its participants, what governs the world of the Rongguo 榮國 and Ningguo 寧國 mansions is an absence of such shared information. The news that travels through the mansions often cannot be confirmed, though the characters treat the news as true, leading them at times to make rash or ill-informed decisions. Yet, as Levy demonstrates, it is precisely the circulation and reception of gossip upon which the plot of the novel—on both its cosmic and domestic levels—turns. For *Story of the Stone*, gossip is never merely idle chitchat; the social exchange of talk takes on karmic significance, bringing the central characters of the novel closer to their fates.

It is fitting to conclude on a cosmic note, one that shows how social talk may link the private spaces of the household to more exalted realms. Gossip and anecdote are often considered marginal forms of discourse, but they pervade society and culture, serving on the one hand as the ordinary hum of daily conversation, but, on the other, as the unacknowledged building blocks from which official histories and public reputations are constructed. In an earlier period, a study of gossip and its related forms of social talk might have resulted in the kind of argument put forward by the philosopher Henry Lanz, who attempted to show that "gossip is not merely a ludicrous weakness chiefly confined to the idle portion of the fair sex, but a social force, an intricate mechanism through which the organized forces of evil gain access to various departments of human life."[10] Lanz connected the act of gossiping to the diabolical schemes of the Devil himself, arguing that idle gossip constituted a metaphysical assault against moral seriousness insofar as gossip represented the telling of malicious untruths and the creation of ugly fictions.

We may now smile at the antiquated sexism of Lanz's polemic or the sanctimony with which he launches his critique, but Lanz nevertheless treats gossip as something serious and worthy of analysis. A more congenial view of gossip may be found in a statement by Truman Capote:

> What I say is that *all* literature is gossip, certainly all prose-narrative literature. What in God's green earth is *Anna Karenina* or *War and Peace* or *Madame Bovary* if not gossip? Or Jane Austen? Or Proust? Gossip is the absolute exchange of human communication. It can be two ladies at the back fence or Tolstoy writing *War and Peace*.[11]

To this one might add Oscar Wilde's famous aphorism, "History is merely gossip," originally from his play *Lady Windermere's Fan*.[12] Of course, both Capote and Wilde are making hyperbolic claims for gossip with the intent of shocking such moral arbiters as Professor Lanz. One might further quibble with how the two writers are defining a form of social talk that cannot simply be equated with discursive domains as vast as "literature" or "history." Nevertheless, the two statements anticipate the contemporary reevaluation of how gossip—and its attendant form of anecdote—both participate within the textual forms of a society's central traditions and also precondition how the central traditions are themselves constituted. What is transmitted within the cultural memory as "literature" and "history" was once the subject of social talk, and it is through the process of such talk that the tradition comes to take shape. Reputation—whether it be that of an unfortunate actress, a celebrated poem, or a member of the social elite—is first traded along the networks of a community and only afterwards is set down within a culture's written archives and historical records. To put it another way, if, as Capote and Wilde respectively claim, literature and history may be considered gossip, then perhaps one might respond that gossip may, in turn, also be considered literature and history.

The ten chapters included here, along with the postface by Stephen Owen, speak to the central role of "idle talk" throughout the Chinese tradition. While the collection is organized along chronological lines, the chapters also possess certain thematic commonalities, whether it be the relationship between official and unofficial historiography (Schaberg in chapter 1, Shields in chapter 6, Egan in chapter 7, Bossler in chapter 8); the place of anecdote in literary history and cultural memory (Tian in chapter 2, Strassberg in chapter 9); or the world of orality and the influence of social talk (Chen in chapter 3, Allen in chapter 4, Sanders in chapter 5, and Levy in chapter 10). What, in the end, this collection seeks to provide is an introduction to an as-yet unmapped territory by providing a range of different methodologies and subjects, spread across the history of traditional China, in the hope of spurring future research on this neglected topic.

NOTES

1. For this account of Ruan Lingyu's suicide, I have drawn on the discussions found in Michael G. Chang, "The Good, the Bad, and the Beautiful: Movie Actresses and Public Discourse in Shanghai, 1920s–1930s," in *Cinema and Urban Culture in Shanghai, 1922–1943*, ed. Yingjin Zhang (Stanford: Stanford University Press, 1999), 155–57; and Richard J. Meyer, *Ruan Ling-yu: The Goddess of Shanghai* (Hong Kong: Hong Kong University Press, 2005), 52–56.

2. From Zhongguo dianyingjia xiehui dianyingshi yanjiubu 中國電影家協會電影史研究部, ed., *Ruan Lingyu* 阮玲玉 (Beijing: Zhongguo dianying chubanshe, 1985), 12.

3. DiFonzo and Bordia, *Rumor Psychology: Social and Organizational Approaches* (Washington, D.C.: American Psychological Association, 2007), 19.

4. Malina Stefanovska, "Exemplary or Singular? The Anecdote in Historical Narrative," *SubStance* 118 (2009): 17.

5. In *Lu Xun quanji* 魯迅全集 (Beijing: Renmin wenxue chubanshe, 2005), 6:343–46. Also see the translation of the complete essay in Yang Xianyi and Gladys Yang, trans., *Lu Xun: Selected Works* (Beijing: Foreign Languages Press, 1980), 4:194–97.

6. *Lu Xun quanji*, 6:344.

7. In Cheng Junying 程俊英 and Jiang Jianyuan 蔣見元, eds., *Shijing zhuxi* 詩經注析 (Beijing: Zhonghua shuju, 1991), 15.223. For translations of the complete poem, see Arthur Waley, trans., *The Book of Songs*, rev. ed., ed. Joseph R. Allen (New York: Grove Press, 1996), 65; and Stephen Owen, ed. and trans., *An Anthology of Chinese Literature: Beginnings to 1911* (New York: W. W. Norton & Company, 1996), 46.

8. On this, see my "Blank Spaces and Secret Histories: Questions of Historiographic Epistemology in Medieval China," *Journal of Asian Studies* 69, no. 4 (Nov. 2010): 1071–91.

9. Wu Jing 吳兢 (670–749), comp., *Zhenguan zhengyao* 貞觀政要 (Shanghai: Shanghai guji chubanshe, 1978).

10. Henry Lanz, "Metaphysics of Gossip," *International Journal of Ethics* 46, no. 4 (Jul. 1936): 492.

11. Beverly Gary Kempton, "Books: Truman Capote," *Playboy* 23, no. 12 (Dec. 1976): 47. This is reprinted in M. Thomas Inge, ed., *Truman Capote: Interviews* (Jackson, Miss.: University of Mississippi Press, 1987), 336–38.

12. In *Complete Works of Oscar Wilde* (London: HarperCollins, 1994), 451.

1   Word of Mouth and the Sources of Western Han History
David Schaberg

> *Fama, malum qua non aliud velocius ullum;*
> *mobilitate viget, viresque adquirit eundo*
> —Vergil, *Aeneid* 4.174–75

Just as dirt is matter out of place, gossip is poorly distributed knowledge.¹ In colloquial English, one can ask to hear "the dirt" on someone not only because one's dirt is something to hide, but also because the material in question is thought to have escaped from wherever it was well contained and to have been scattered about where it does not belong. Gossip and rumor also tend to reflect concentrations of power, in that they thrive especially around individuals and institutions whose deeds have the farthest-reaching effects on the people around them and whose secret motivations therefore most urgently invite revelation. As with gossip, so with narrative in general: it is hardly a wonder that stories of the rich and powerful hold a lasting fascination, or that the oldest written stories in the East Asian and European traditions—the Zhou hymns and the Homeric epics respectively—grew up around troves of extraordinary wealth, places where bronze was possessed in large quantities.

Both because of the way concentrations of wealth and power breed narrative and because monarchies the world around share certain basic features, it is not quite true, *pace* Tolstoy, that every unhappy family is unhappy in its own way or that only unique tales of unhappiness are worth the telling. The palace, with its enclosures and its mysteries, is a constant in kingdoms and in the stories about them, as is the problem of transferring power from one ruler to the next, usually along lines dictated by kinship, with all its attendant tensions. From these similar topographies of power and communication come similar narratives. Many royal families have been unhappy in roughly the same way, much to the narratival delight of their contemporaries and later audiences. In the Persia of Herodotus, the Rome of Suetonius and Tacitus, the China of Sima Qian 司馬遷 (ca. 145–ca. 86 BCE) and Ban Gu 班固 (32–92 CE), and in many another court, there is a sovereign who is overbearing or enfeebled, a wife

17

or mother who abuses her influence, a disputed succession, a secret murder, a perverse alliance, an unnatural hatred, revenge. And it is all worth recounting not because of its uniqueness—its novelty, the source of value Tolstoy may have assumed for the novel—but because it promises to reveal truths about how decisions were made in the hidden center of power. It might be the same old story, but it will claim to show how history was made. Attractively, too, it will discover, behind the vast impersonal moil of trend and accident that is history, intelligible human motives.

The history of the Western Han dynasty (202 BCE–8 CE), as represented even in the most relied-upon sources, *Shiji* 史記 (Records of the historian) and *Hanshu* 漢書 (History of the Han dynasty), is shot through with hearsay and gossip. Especially where these works tell their unhappy tales of the imperial family and its life in the palaces of Chang'an, one cannot for long escape the sense that the behind-closed-gates nature of the subject matter guarantees that much of what is reported as fact could not have been known as such. Accounts of how certain decisions were taken in the inner court—how an heir was replaced, for instance, or a court lady banished—may in some cases derive from eyewitness reports of events, but it is unlikely that they do so in all or even most cases. Instead, versions of inner court events offered in *Shiji* and *Hanshu* likely reflect accounts that were more or less widely accepted by members of contemporary elites, since too marked or frequent departures from common knowledge would have required a good deal more validation than the historians supply. Tales of the Western Han inner court no doubt capture the literal truth of many events, but they also preserve, as if in a narrative amber, the more communal and less literal truth of outsiders' gossipy speculations. Scandal-mongering makes for very durable stories; as Vergil observed in his grim personification of the rumor or *fama* surrounding Queen Dido's love of Aeneas, "there is no evil swifter; she thrives on movement and gathers force as she goes."

An examination of inner court accounts in *Shiji* and *Hanshu* suggests that the historians have accorded gossip-based narrative a crucial place in their histories. The authors of *Shiji* appear to have regarded it as their responsibility to include and respond to common opinion in their work, capturing public hearsay as itself an important component of historical knowledge. Ban Gu, in *Hanshu*, went even further, claiming for himself special familial access to some of the secrets of the inner court and structuring his work in such a way that these secrets become a kind of keystone supporting the whole edifice. In the end, the historians' mixing of dry facts and juicy unverifiables yields a form of narrative in which public judgment, even of the most scandalous court secrets, is made to confirm and perpetuate the unique charisma of the imperial family.

HEARSAY AND HISTORIOGRAPHY

Shiji, completed around 100 BCE, inherited from certain works of the preceding century and a half a model of the written text as a complete and internally coherent compendium of knowledge. Like the *Lüshi chunqiu* 呂氏春秋 (Annals of Lü Buwei) and the *Huainanzi* 淮南子, *Shiji* aspired to be, in Mark Edward Lewis's words, an "encyclopedic text."[2] In the architecture of knowledge it proposed and, of course, in its introduction of narrative forms such as the dynastic history, the family history, and the biography, *Shiji* differed a great deal from its predecessors. Still, it is important not to exaggerate differences in material. Both *Shiji* and *Lüshi chunqiu*—and *Huainanzi* only to a lesser extent—are built upon a foundation of anecdotal narrative. The most typical *pian* 篇 or "chapter" in either work collects a number of discrete anecdotes, linking these either by theme or, as in much of *Shiji*, in a coherent narrative. Such texts as the "Ten Errors" ("Shi guo" 十過) chapter of *Han Feizi* 韓非子 show that the construction of an essay as a series of principles with anecdotal illustrations was already an accepted mode of composition by the middle third century BCE, while the several "Stockpiled Explanations" ("Chushuo" 儲說) chapters of the same work strongly suggest that readers of *Han Feizi* looked to it as a source of anecdotal material they could use in their own argumentation. Against this background, *Lüshi chunqiu* stands out for the great consistency with which it pairs philosophical principle with narrative illustration, while *Shiji* departs from the model in most chapters by creating coherent narratives and downplaying principle. In any of these texts, right down to *Shiji* and beyond, the inclusion of anecdotes, especially where these were commonplaces often used by persuaders and writers, would tend to tie the claims of the speaker or writer closely to common knowledge and its sturdy truisms about the ways of the world.[3]

Given this context, it is not surprising that we often see the historians of *Shiji* testing popular opinion and discourse against their own observations and especially against privately transmitted accounts. Common knowledge is subject to evaluation, but it is also itself a standard for evaluation. Comments at the end of the biography of Su Qin 蘇秦 (fl. 4th cent. BCE), one of the most famous "crisscross persuaders" (*zongheng jia* 縱橫家) and a powerful proponent of the Warring States anti-Qin alliance, reflect the pressure of rumor around and within the narratives:

> When Su Qin died in the course of a counterplot, the whole world joined in laughing at him and spurned the study of his methods. Still, in what the world has to say about Su Qin there are many extraordinary accounts, and even events from different eras that somehow resemble his deeds have been attributed to him. That Su Qin could rise from among the hamlet lanes to join six states in the ties of the Vertical Alliance was because in certain respects his intelligence surpassed that of others. I have therefore lined up his deeds, putting them in their proper chronological order, so that he will not bear an ill reputation for them.
>
> 蘇秦被反間以死,天下共笑之,諱學其術。然世言蘇秦多異,異時事有類之者皆附之蘇秦。夫蘇秦起閭閻,連六國從親,此其智有過人者。吾故列其行事,次其時序,毋令獨蒙惡聲焉。[4]

The whole motive of the biography is to defend the true Su Qin, with his genuine accomplishments, against "what the world has to say" (*shiyan* 世言) and especially against its laughter. The historian, with his careful, chronological presentation of actual deeds (*xingshi* 行事), labors against the ceaseless, weed-like growth of legend. Because this chapter-ending comment, and to a certain extent every such comment in *Shiji*, becomes the designated place for the author's individual voice and judgment, it throws the preceding material into relief as common and widely accepted, the public's record.

Sometimes, with especially famous characters who acted in recognized moments of historical crisis, the world's readiness to spin legends will have produced absurdities, which the historian again steps forward to correct. Wild stories have proliferated, for example, around the doomed last ruler of the state of Yan 燕, Prince Dan 太子丹 (d. 226 BCE), and Jing Ke 荊軻 (d. 227 BCE), the man he sent to assassinate the future Qin Shihuang 秦始皇 (259–210 BCE):

> In what the world has to say [*shiyan*] about Jing Ke, reference is made to a command given to Prince Dan concerning "millet raining from the sky and horses growing horns." That goes much too far. It is also said that Jing Ke wounded the king of Qin. Both notions are false. Some time ago Gongsun Jigong and Master Dong visited with Xia Wuju and knew the details of the whole affair. They told it to me as I have told it here.
>
> 世言荊軻,其稱太子丹之命,「天雨粟,馬生角」也,太過。又言荊軻傷秦王,皆非也。始公孫季功、董生與夏無且游,具知其事,為余道之如是。[5]

Xia Wuju 夏無且 was the physician who defended the king of Qin with his medicine bag during Jing Ke's assassination attempt.[6] Legend held that Prince Dan had been told he would not go home until certain miracles occurred, such as horses growing horns and crows' heads turning white.[7] The supernatural absurdities about Prince Dan can be rejected out of hand, but only the historian's access to an eyewitness, through the two intermediaries he mentions, allow him to correct the rumor that Jing Ke succeeded in wounding the king.

One could cite many other examples of the way word of mouth has informed or motivated the narratives of *Shiji*. The historian as traveler, investigator, interrogator, and arbiter frequently weighs existing accounts of this or that episode, correcting it where necessary and adjudicating in an ongoing competition among differing narratives. It is important to recognize the process of differentiation that has taken place to allow this complex representation of competing voices. In earlier works, with few exceptions, the sources of historical information are neither mentioned nor questioned, contradictions among accounts are rarely advertised, and when something like word of mouth is cited, it is cited not as rumor, but as knowledge. Things "passed down and heard" (*chuanwen* 傳聞) or "heard from old" (*jiuwen* 舊聞) had once had all the credibility an authoritative tradition could give them. Now, however, the things the world says (*shiyan* 世言, *shiwei* 世謂, *shi suowei* 世所謂) or transmits (*shichuan* 世傳) are open to question. They are the stuff of "vulgar palaver" (*suyi* 俗議), the work of "busybodies" (*haoshi* 好事). Early Chinese language relating to gossip originates in this transition from a knowledge-system that appears to have valued the words of teachers to a much broader field of discourse, in which false reports threatened to smother true accounts. At one extreme, where no corrective is available, the historian is forced to present a version of what the world says, gathering accepted accounts and putting them in some order. At another extreme, as in the case of Xia Wuju's report, he is able to make a point of telling the truth while registering the existence of a whole field of discourse around it. In every case he captures existing voices, speaking to and channeling some public interest in the historical character under consideration.

Knowledge of the older kind might qualify as a sort of hearsay, generally speaking, but it does not quite meet the conditions of gossip. Gossip presumes an element of hiddenness: there must be a reason for hiding something, as well as specific people from whom one hides the gossip itself and the act of gossiping. And even though gossip generally has to do with contemporaries rather than figures from the past, and could therefore be checked with witnesses, it hardly requires corroboration to be effective among its hearers and users. The presence in the tale of something worth keeping secret makes efforts at verification irrelevant, and many scandalous stories are accepted as true, or true enough, precisely because of the scandal in them. Pseudo-knowledge of this kind has also found its way into *Shiji*. One example is to be found in a section added by the later writer Chu Shaosun 褚少孫 (104?–30? BCE) to the end of the chapter on the emperors' wives and their families:

> While residing at the Ganquan Palace, the emperor called for painters to depict the Duke of Zhou carrying King Cheng on his back. From this the courtiers around him knew that Emperor Wu wished to establish his young son as heir.[8] Several days later, the emperor found fault with Lady Gouyi. The lady removed her hairpins and ear jewels and bowed her head to the floor. The emperor said, "Drag her away and take her to Palace Discipline for judgment!"[9] When the lady turned to look back at him, the emperor said, "Hurry up and go. You won't come out of this alive." The lady died in the Yunyang Palace.[10] At the time a blast of wind made the dust fly, and the common people sorrowed for her. Men were sent by night to carry out her coffin and bury her. They marked the spot with a mound.
>
> 上居甘泉宮，召畫工圖畫周公負成王也。於是左右群臣知武帝意欲立少子也。後數日，帝譴責鉤弋夫人。夫人脫簪珥叩頭。帝曰：「引持去，送掖庭獄！」夫人還顧，帝曰：「趣行，女不得活！」夫人死雲陽宮。時暴風揚塵，百姓感傷。使者夜持棺往葬之，封識其處。

Despite efforts to hide the events, the news of them—if it is truly news and not mere fabrication—has somehow escaped the confines of court, perhaps by way of the courtiers who observed the events or the men who buried the lady and piled up a mound over her grave. Immediately and as if magically, the people mourn the innocent victim: one of gossip's functions is to call every one of its hearers into session as a knee-jerk court of justice.

> Some time later the emperor was sitting at his leisure and asked his attendants, "What are people saying?" His attendants answered, "People are saying: When he was going to set up the son, why did he get rid of the mother?" The emperor said, "Just so. This is not something that a mob of callow simpletons would understand. The reason that the states of olden times fell into chaos was that their rulers were young and their mothers in their prime. When a female ruler resides on her own in a position of arrogant elevation, giving free rein to excess and indulgence, there is no one who can stop her. Have you never heard of Empress Lü?"[11]
>
> Thus whenever anyone bore a child to Emperor Wu, whether it was a son or daughter, the mother in every case died after having been

accused of some misdemeanor.¹² Can this be considered anything but sagely wisdom? It is a perspicuous farsightedness that lays plans for future generations. To be sure, it is not the kind of thing that would be comprehensible to simple-minded classicist of shallow learning. It was not for nothing that he was given the posthumous name "Martial."

其後帝閒居, 問左右曰:「人言云何?」左右對曰:「人言且立其子, 何去其母乎?」帝曰:「然。是非兒曹愚人所知也。往古國家所以亂也, 由主少母壯也。女主獨居驕蹇, 淫亂自恣, 莫能禁也。女不聞呂后邪?」

故諸為武帝生子者, 無男女, 其母無不譴死, 豈可謂非賢聖哉! 昭然遠見, 為後世計慮, 固非淺聞愚儒之所及也。諡為「武」, 豈虛哉!¹³

In gossip, the public's pseudo-knowledge is sharply at odds with the self-knowledge of the subject, in this case the emperor, and the dynamics of rumor rarely allow any reconciliation. Of all people, the emperor should be the last to know how his treatment of Lady Gouyi 鉤弋夫人 is being judged. But with a prerogative and imperviousness that comes only with extraordinary power, he demands to hear the charges brought against him in the court of public opinion and to defend himself against them. Both he and the historian, in this case a scandal-mongering Chu Shaosun, get the chance to reconcile scandalized public knowledge with a higher and more exclusive insight into strategic savvy. This savvy appears to derive from the emperor's own calculations and, according to the narrator, far surpasses the heard tradition, the "shallow learning" (*qianwen* 淺聞) of the classicists.

As rumor, this final episode would have served both as the *pièce de résistance*—the murderer's inhuman and chilling rationalization of his crimes—and as an invitation to contemplate the unique exigencies of supreme power in the inner court. Gossip condemns the ruler and exonerates him, and in so doing justifies a certain crucial historical transition. In this respect, the tale of Lady Gouyi's death is an extreme example of a kind of squaring of accounts that historians carry out with much of the most corrosive gossip. Secret motivations imputed to the denizens of the inner court—and seized upon to explain historical shifts that would otherwise be incomprehensible—turn out to be both reprehensible and somehow necessary.

RUMOR IN THE CONSTRUCTION OF *HANSHU*

The final chapters of *Shiji*, before the summation of the grand scribe's postface, are a miscellany of collective biographies: swashbucklers, toadies, jesters, moneymakers, and fortune-tellers and diviners. Only with the postface's annotated table of contents do the work's shape and order begin to matter again, as the reader is taught to appreciate the architecture of the work and the significance of each of its chapters. This round of retrospection gives the text a seal and creates one of the first real endings for a Chinese work.[14] Ban Gu followed *Shiji*'s lead in this as in many other respects, but went considerably further in his effort to give his work an ending.

In the space following the chapters on peripheral regions or "barbarians" and preceding the postface, where *Shiji* has its grab bag of *hoi polloi* biographies, *Hanshu* substitutes a series of chapters that gradually narrow the focus of the historical narrative. Chapter 97, "Biographies of the In-laws" ("Waiqi zhuan" 外戚傳), brings together accounts of Western Han empresses and consorts preceding Empress Yuan 元后 (71–13 BCE), whose life is the subject of chapter 98, "Biography of Empress Yuan" ("Yuanhou zhuan" 元后傳). Chapter 99 is the life of Empress Yuan's nephew, the usurper Wang Mang 王莽 (ca. 45 BCE–23 CE). Finally, the postface ("Xu zhuan" 叙傳), chapter 100, includes both Ban Gu's own family history, with clear links to the imperial in-laws, as well as his autobiography and the annotated table of contents. Beyond the purely bookish closure that comes from the final list of chapters, Ban Gu offers something much more substantial, a reprise of his whole story of Western Han rise and fall, told this time from within the inner court, where successions and the final usurpation are determined, and where the Ban line's own history is a thread connecting the historian to the hidden sources of historical knowledge.

As suggested earlier, inner court gossip from diverse places and times appears to show certain common narrative habits and a corresponding epistemology. The stories gathered in the final chapters of *Hanshu* exemplify these habits of knowing and telling. Because institutions were relatively stable, restrictions on and opportunities for action were also stable, and events tended to repeat themselves, so that a handful of basic plot motifs account for a large proportion of the tales of inner court life. Gossip-historiography is marked by an emphasis on things people would have wanted to hide: unwelcome or unsanctioned desire, whether for sex or for power, and perfidious means of satisfying this desire. Poison works in these narratives the way it works in the body. Since it is made to be administered secretly, it is difficult to trace, and in theory almost any death at all can be explained as murder.[15] Witchcraft, likewise defined by its hidden methods, also features prominently in the efforts of inner court actors to achieve their ends.[16] In the anecdotes that make up this history, reported dialogue can serve as something of an index of gossip content: the point of an episode is sometimes a cutting or clever or pathetic remark that might have been overheard or invented but could not, by any stretch of the imagination, have been committed to writing by any contemporary official keeper of records.[17]

The episode of the death of Empress Xu 許后 (d. 71 BCE) illustrates the role of gossip in these sections of *Hanshu*. The villain of the piece, the wife of the powerful general Huo Guang 霍光 (d. 68 BCE), has a hidden desire and the slimmest of resources for realizing it: "Huo Guang's wife, Xian, hoped to win a noble place for her young daughter, but could find no path to this end" 霍光夫人顯欲貴其小女, 道無從.[18] From the outset, the problem is one of access. Xian 顯 is as ambitious for her daughter as many another parent in the "Waiqi" chapter. Her husband Huo Guang is at this moment the most powerful man in the empire: Emperor Wu had designated him as regent to the young Emperor Zhao 昭帝 (r. 86–74), son of the hapless Lady Gouyi; the general had also chosen to elevate Emperor Wu's great-grandson, the commoner Bingyi 病已, as Emperor Xuan 宣帝 (r. 74–49 BCE).[19] But Huo Guang does not seem to share his wife's hopes for their daughter, whose way into the palace is blocked by Empress Xu, wife of the emperor from his exile years.[20] There is really only one solution, if Xian is only determined enough to achieve it. According to the *Hanshu* account, she chooses not to bring her husband in on the scheme she hatches. Either as a matter of historical fact she feared her husband would veto the plan, or—we cannot know at this point—the whole supposed conspiracy grew up as a fiction in gossip's realm of secrecy and imputation.

A path opens when Xian's unspeakable ambition meets a more ordinary careerism:

> In the following year [71 BCE], Empress Xu was pregnant and feeling ill. The female doctor Chunyu Yan, who was well liked by the Huo family, was once going to enter the palace to treat the empress's illness. Chunyu Yan's husband, Shang, who was a door guard in the Palace Discipline Service, said to Yan, "You could go by and take your leave of Lady Huo before you go, and see if you can get me a position as director of the salt wells at An."
> 明年, 許皇后當娠, 病。女醫淳于衍者, 霍氏所愛, 嘗入宮侍皇后疾。衍夫賞為掖庭戶衛, 謂衍「可過辭霍夫人行, 為我求安池監。」[21]

The empress's illness may have been morning sickness or something more serious. That it forced the inner court authorities to seek beyond the palace walls for additional female doctors suggests that the illness was of the more threatening kind. What matters for the tale itself is that it opened the way for Chunyu Yan 淳于衍, already an associate of the

Huos, to enter the palace. This invitation is immediately recognized as a thing of value by Chunyu Yan's husband, who wants one of the lucrative appointments the salt monopoly has created.[22] He suggests that she cash it in with another who will recognize it, Lady Huo. His awareness that this access will be of value to Lady Huo suggests a deeper recognition of the latter's interests, perhaps even anticipation of the whole conspiracy to come.

Outside the normal and reputable ways of promoting court women and appointing salt-well directors, then, a byway now appears, cleared by a little commerce in private aims:

> Chunyu Yan reported to Xian just as her husband had said. This gave Xian an idea, and she sent her attendants out and addressed Yan by her personal name, Shaofu: "Now that you've done me the favor of telling me about your affair, may I too tell you about an affair of my own?" Chunyu Yan said, "Whatever you might say, could there be anything unacceptable in it?"
>
> 衍如言報顯。顯因生心, 辟左右, 字謂衍:「少夫幸報我以事, 我亦欲報少夫, 可乎?」衍曰:「夫人所言, 何等不可者!」

These words are interesting, implying already, as they do, that Xian might have something truly unacceptable to request and guaranteeing in advance that Chunyu Yan will accept the mission nevertheless. Only this acceptance signals Chunyu Yan's complicity and allows Xian to reveal her aim.

Chunyu Yan has either the naïveté or the wisdom to force Xian to make herself perfectly clear:

> Xian said, "The general has always loved his young daughter Chengjun and has hoped to win her a place of extraordinary nobility. I'd like to burden you with this, Shaofu."
>
> Chunyu Yan said, "Whatever can you mean?"
>
> Xian said, "It is a grave business for a woman to bear a child. For every one woman who lives, ten die. Now that the empress is about to deliver her child, you could take the opportunity [yin 因] to slip in some poison and do away with her, and then Chengjun would get to be empress. If the affair meets with success through your efforts, then we will share the wealth and status with you, Shaofu."
>
> 顯曰:「將軍素愛小女成君, 欲奇貴之, 願以累少夫。」衍曰:「何謂邪?」顯曰:「婦人免乳大故, 十死一生。今皇后當免身, 可因投毒藥去也, 成君即得為皇后矣。如蒙力事成, 富貴與少夫共之。」

No euphemistic statement of the plan is enough for Chunyu Yan. She must hear plainly of the deed itself and the *pro quo*. The dangers of childbirth, here exaggerated mercilessly by the survivor Xian, are to provide cover for the poisoning. It is assumed as a given that Chengjun—who is, we must remember, still outside the court—will step into the murdered woman's place. From a strategic point of view, Xian's savvy is to have discerned the *yin* 因, the secret extra route of influence and effect, that childbirth affords.

There are practical problems Chunyu Yan claims at first not to be able to solve:

> Chunyu Yan said, "We mix up our medicines together, and there's someone to taste them in advance. How is it possible?"
>
> Xian said, "It's only a matter of your doing it. With the general giving commands to the whole world, who would dare say anything? In times of ease and urgency we will protect each other. I'm only worried that you might not be interested."
>
> After a long while, Chunyu Yan said, "I'm willing to do my best."
>
> 衍曰:「藥雜治,當先嘗,安可?」顯曰:「在少夫為之耳。將軍領天下,誰敢言者?緩急相護,但恐少夫無意耳!」衍良久曰:「願盡力。」

Xian cannot or will not solve these problems for Chunyu Yan, who must use her own expertise to the extent of meeting these two challenges. She must own the plot. Only here, for the *fait accompli* and the protection the plotters will need, will Huo Guang's power be useful. As he will have no choice but to protect himself and his wife, he will be among the people deceived and plotted against, pulled into the conspiracy by the weight of his own position.

The practical problems turn out not to pose any sort of significant challenge. The process of mixing the medicine, which might have been intended to safeguard against poisoning by making sure that all doctors would share responsibility, instead provides cover for Chunyu Yan's solitary crime. And the matter of the medicine-tasting does not even bear mentioning:

> So she powdered some aconite and took it with her into the Changding Palace. Once the empress had delivered her child, Chunyu Yan took the aconite, mixed it with the senior physicians' great pill, and gave it to the empress to drink.
>
> After a time she said, "My head feels heavy. There wouldn't have been any poison in the medicine, would there have been?"
>
> Chunyu Yan replied, "No, there wasn't."
>
> She grew more incoherent and shallow of breath until she passed away.

即擣附子，齎入長定宮。皇后免身後，衍取附子并合大醫大丸以飲皇后。有頃曰：「我頭岑岑也，藥中得無有毒？」對曰：「無有。」遂加煩懣，崩。

The final exchange of dialogue suggests that Chunyu Yan and the empress were alone together near the end. The question and the lie would in that case introduce an element of pathos both on the victim's side and on the guilty murderer's side. If they were not alone, however, and if this took place in the presence of some other doctor or court attendant, the empress's question might be understood as the germ of gossip. This would be the first moment poison was mentioned beyond the supposed circle of conspirators. For any detective investigating the death, this would be the first hint of wrongdoing. The empress's question now becomes the point of access that leads back, by way of legal revelation or gossipy invention, to Xian's conspiracy.

The end of the story is all about blocking access and trying to prevent this blowback from the crime.

> When she left the palace, Chunyu Yan visited with Xian. They exchanged pleasantries, but Xian did not dare reward Yan with any great generosity.[23] Later, someone submitted a document reporting on the physicians in attendance on the empress during her illness who had not treated the case properly, and they were all arrested, tried, and found guilty of misconduct. Xian grew frantic in her fear and told her husband Huo Guang about the whole case, then said, "I made the wrong plan and carried it out. But don't let the officers come after me!" Shocked, Huo Guang sat silent and made no response. Later he memorialized the emperor and Yan was let off without a sentence.
>
> 衍出，過見顯，相勞問，亦未敢重謝衍。後人有上書告諸醫侍疾無狀者，皆收繫詔獄，劾不道。顯恐(事)急，即以狀具語光，因曰：「既失計為之，無令吏急衍！」光驚鄂，默然不應。其後奏上，署衍勿論。

The poisoner cannot profit from her crime because the reward itself will demonstrate that she has somehow, secretly, increased her value to Xian. It is unknown whether Chunyu Yan's husband ever got the post he originally wanted as director of the salt wells at An, but now that the success of the plot has seemingly undone all the terms of the original deal, it seems unlikely that he has won that promotion. Still, in this moment of danger Xian's plotting looks prescient. When the group of doctors is investigated for improprieties, and when it seems possible that Yan will be identified as the one who contributed poison to the collective "Great Pill," Xian is able to block all further discovery by invoking her most intimate connection with the most powerful man in the empire. Huo Guang's shocked silence becomes the official silence about the matter.

Since gossip's explanations of secret history may well arise from retrospection and speculation, it is not especially surprising that Xian's daughter did indeed become empress. Her little biography comes directly after Empress Xu's in the "Waiqi" chapter of *Hanshu*.[24] If the whole scandalous tale is true, then this is the climax of Xian's scheme. Things holds together for a time, supported by the power of Huo Guang and the silence imposed by his intervention. After Huo Guang's death, however, everything falls apart. Empress Xu's son is made heir—to be known to history as Emperor Yuan (r. 48–33 BCE)—and Xian and her daughter duly attempt to poison him, presumably in order to open the way for a son of Empress Huo 霍后 (d. 54 BCE). The talk starts up again. The new poisoning scheme fails, it turns out that the secret of the murder of Empress Xu has come out (literally, "leaked," *xie* 泄), and Xian plots revolt with members of her family. All are put to death except for Empress Huo, who is denounced and banished to an isolated palace. She ultimately commits suicide.

One might compare the relation of public knowledge and revealed backstory in this case to the relation of the *Chunqiu jing* 春秋經 (Spring and autumn annals) and *Zuozhuan* 左傳 (Zuo commentary). If the first version of the official story—death of empress in childbirth, banishment of successor, elevation of first empress's son as heir apparent—was too thin on detail to explain anything, the "Waiqi" version offers a plausible texture of motivation to connect the observed outcomes. Like the *Zuozhuan*, this expanded account brings its own preferred modes of explanation, in this case the imputations of murderous ambition that are so common in the tales of inner court life. Especially taken all together, the "Waiqi" tales bring into being a plausible world, if a scandalous one, where behind many official decisions lie private, base, and entirely selfish interests. This mode of narration amounts to a stark reduction of history and historical representation.

The trope of the true story is a powerful one. The gesture of revelation endows whatever has supposedly been hidden with far more truth-value than it could have without such framing. But as tempting as it might be simply to settle for the depiction of the Western Han inner court as a place of violent scheming—and as much general credibility as Ban Gu's reputation as a historian might add—it is important to recognize that the new story is just another story, and one that is remarkably weak on points of corroboration. Since gossip is defined largely by the veiled and unverifiable nature of its content, the revealed story comes full of blind spots, plot points where for gossips—and for historians—innocent coincidence and malicious intent will be indistinguishable.

Empress Xu is said to have been ill even before Xian is supposed to have begun her plotting, though the words Ban Gu uses make it difficult to say exactly how ill. Xian herself noted, albeit with some exaggeration, that women face a heightened risk of death in childbirth. According to the historian himself, the crucial conversation, in which Xian asked Chunyu Yan to poison the empress, took place after the only possible witnesses, Xian's household staff, had been sent out of the room. Chunyu Yan's colleagues are not said to have noticed any meddling on her part. The medicine-taster apparently noticed no irregularity in the dose given to the empress. No evidence is provided to show that Chunyu Yan or her husband profited from the supposed crime. Even in the investigation of medical malfeasance after the empress's death, the blame is general, and the narrative gives no indication that Chunyu Yan came under extraordinary suspicion.

In short, then, the evidence that the revealed story is the true story is far from conclusive. The account whose acceptance by contemporaries is signaled—and whose acceptance by later ages is guaranteed—by its inclusion in *Hanshu* might be a flimsy cover for something that is in its own way more scandalous: it may well be that there is no human, intentional meaning behind the chronicled events, or that the meaning is something as yet unrevealed. Empress Xu may have died in childbirth, without the help of poison. Empress Huo may have been set aside after the death of her father, quite without having involved herself in murder. Xian and Huo Guang's other survivors may have been caught up in one of the purges that predictably follow the fall of a court figure powerful beyond his position. In this construction, the story of Empress Xu's death by poison becomes one of the trumped up charges required for such purges. The scandal here would be that there was no scandal except the gossip itself and the backlash against Huo Guang's power that inspired it. In the place of individual intent and action we would have a set of meaningless accidents and sudden changes of political weather. But there is no better evidence for this banal "true" story than there is for Ban Gu's.

CONCLUSION: ACCESS AND THE TRUING OF HISTORICAL ACCOUNTS

What does it mean that the two founding works of the Chinese tradition of official historiography should accord such a prominent place to word of mouth, that is, to legendary material in the case of *Shiji*'s long retrospective on earlier eras, and to gossip and gossip-like material in the case of *Hanshu*'s accounts of inner court relations? What does it mean for the truth of these writers' historical representations that they must do justice simultaneously to narratives widely accepted by the public and to inside stories they may have learned by way of their privileged connections with court?

Both Sima Qian and Ban Gu, like the many scholars who would contribute to official histories in later centuries, enjoyed special access to court and to sources of information on court life. Sima Qian paid dearly for his place at court and—though the precise nature of his methods and sources remains obscure—appears to have benefited from his position, both during the writing of his work and afterward, when he laid the text by, putting it in an archive for future readers.²⁵ The Ban family's connections with the court extended deeper even than those of Sima *père et fils*, and on close reading offer an implicit validation of the *Hanshu*'s inner court tales. As we learn from the family history that Ban Gu has woven into the final chapters of *Hanshu*, Ban Gu's great grandfather Ban Kuang 班況 had been selected as Filial and Incorrupt (*xiaolian* 孝廉) and appointed Gentleman (*lang* 郎), ultimately rising to the position of Colonel, Picked Cavalry (*Yue ji xiaowei* 越騎校尉).²⁶ Ban Kuang's daughter, Ban Gu's great aunt, had been chosen as Lady of Handsome Fairness (*jieyu* 婕妤)—second among the ranks of concubines—to Emperor Cheng 成帝 (r. 32–7 BCE).²⁷ Ban Kuang's eldest son, Ban Bo 班伯, had been an intimate of the emperor and had offered him a firm warning against inappropriate drinking parties in the palace.²⁸

In this generation of Ban family history, familiarity with the emperor translates into access to some of the written sources of history. Of Ban Kuang's second son, Ban You 班斿, the *Hanshu* says, "the emperor regarded his ability as something of considerable use and bestowed upon him copies of restricted texts" 上器其能, 賜以祕書之副.²⁹ Ban Gu reminds us at this point that circulation of these texts—including *Shiji* and works of the masters (*zhuzi* 諸子), with their examples of oratory and strategy, and their concrete information on geography and terrain—was restricted, and copies had been denied to the king of Dongping, son of Emperor Xuan.³⁰ Ban You's son Ban Si 班嗣, who seems to have inherited the restricted texts, treasured them especially for the *Laozi* 老子 and *Zhuangzi* 莊子, imitating the style of these two works as he elegantly refused to lend the texts to Huan Tan 桓譚 (23–56). Ban Biao 班彪 (3–54), son of Ban Kuang's youngest son Ban Zhi 班稚, lived and studied with his cousin Ban Si and was able to use the restricted texts in Si's home.³¹

The *Hou Hanshu* 後漢書 biography of Ban Biao strongly suggests that *Hanshu* had its origins in the time Biao was able to spend with the restricted texts. Fan Ye 范曄 (398–445) writes, "Biao continued [*Shiji*] by selecting episodes left out in the earlier records, cross-referencing them with alternate versions that had been heard of. He composed an 'appended traditions' in several dozen chapters, using this opportunity to mull over the earlier records and to comment upon and correct the successes and failures in them" 彪乃繼採前史遺事，傍貫異聞，作後傳數十篇，因斟酌前史而譏正得失.[32] Biao's own essay on his work, incorporated in his biography, confirms that he composed annals of the emperors and biographies in an effort to improve upon *Shiji*.[33] Ban Gu, for his part, was well versed in all the masters' texts (that is, in the restricted works held by his extended family) by the time he was nine, and began his own historical work in a private effort to improve upon his father's beginnings.[34] Imprisoned on charges of "privately altering and composing a state history" 私改作國史, he was exonerated through the intercession of his brother, the general Ban Chao 班超, and given his first court appointment, as Clerk to the Director, Lantai Depository (*Lantai lingshi* 蘭臺令史), in which capacity he worked with the restricted texts.[35]

Access to restricted texts might have made for the composition of a historical work of a certain type, but this access alone could not have produced *Hanshu*. It is true that for four generations Ban men maintained and renewed a familiarity with the imperial court that kept the restricted texts before them both at home and in office. Still, at crucial moments Ban women and their reputation for virtue and learning proved indispensable to the project.[36] When Ban Zhi fell afoul of the rising Wang Mang during the reign of Emperor Ping (r. 1 BCE–5 CE), the Grand Empress Dowager, Wang Mang's aunt, recommended that Ban Zhi be treated leniently: "His is a worthy family of the rear palace and one that I would regard with pity" 後宮賢家，我所哀也. As the commentator reminds us, the empress dowager is remembering Ban *jieyu* (Lady of Handsome Fairness). This episode saved the Ban family from too close an involvement in Wang Mang's government and presumably preserved both their status and their ability to keep and work with the restricted texts.[37]

Ban women would have afforded more than just political protection for the family. They were no doubt conduits of information and court secrets that even the restricted texts could not have included. Ban *jieyu* enjoyed extraordinary favor for a time, distinguishing herself for her learning and her virtuous fastidiousness, before being accused of witchcraft in 18 BCE by her rival Zhao Feiyan 趙飛燕 (45–1 BCE) and withdrawing from life in the inner court. *Hanshu* preserves a plaintive *fu* 賦 ("poetic exposition" or "rhapsody") she composed in her retirement.[38] Herself the veteran of a vicious court battle and victim of one of the most common rumor-charges, that of sorcery, Ban *jieyu* would as a matter of course have heard talk of earlier inner court struggles, and might have passed this hearsay on to her brothers and her nephews. Ban Gu's sister, Ban Zhao 班昭, who was famous for her learning and for her role as a teacher and advisor to court women, would also have been privy to some inner court gossip.[39] Both before Ban Gu's death—itself the consequence of an entanglement with the general Dou Xian 竇憲 (d. 92), brother of powerful imperial ladies[40]—and afterward, when Ban Zhao completed *Hanshu* and interpreted parts of the difficult text for perplexed readers, her inside information may have found its way into the text, and she would have had the means to confirm that certain old accounts of scandal were still believed.[41]

Through his family's possession of restricted texts and through his work in the court archives, Ban Gu would have had access to the sorts of historical accounts that could for one reason or another have been written down. Through his female relations, he may well have learned tales of intrigue in the inner court that had not been committed to writing but were widely regarded, by those who had heard them, as the secret truths behind important power transitions. In short, Ban Gu would have faced the same problem Sima Qian faced, that of reconciling his specialized knowledge with the narratives widely and necessarily held to be plausible, but Ban Gu would have come to the challenge with the extra authority derived from his family's lasting access to the inner court. Perhaps uniquely in his era, Ban Gu would have been able to present claims about base motivations and brutal machinations in the inner court as crucial secrets, the inner truths of events, while fitting these claims within a broader narrative of political history. For readers, the scandalous inner court tales would have had a curious status. Shocking as they were, they would have confirmed the moralist's—and the gossiping public's—dire judgment that human nature is everywhere the same and that power corrupts. At the same time, by foregrounding the emperor's sexual choices and the force of ambition among the people around him, these tales would have tended to reinforce the power of the emperor, even to enshrine it. The cold calculations on imperial mothers and sons that Chu Shaosun attributed to Emperor Wu would set the tone for this aspect of the historian's representation: because the inner court is where desirous choices will have the very broadest repercussions, it is also where the ruler and others must reckon most powerfully and realistically with the consequences of desire, since without such *Realpolitik* the whole edifice will quickly crumble.

By mastering both sides—the inner scandals and the more widely known political narrative, the rumors and the mundane truths—the historian demonstrates an authority that derives from inside knowledge, but goes still further than that, revealing the raw fact and unique characteristics of imperial power in such a way as to subject this power to judgment while also ultimately protecting it from condemnation. The secrets of sorcery and murder that Ban Gu tells may or may not have been true. What mattered more, it would seem, is that they allowed him to claim for himself, and to offer to his readers, a "truing" of open and closed versions of Western Han history, a squaring of dry detail and juicy esoterica, of law and morality on the one hand and of deadly family drama on the other. With this truing of accounts in the final chapters of *Hanshu*, Ban Gu accommodates both common and specialized knowledge, creating a representation that marries the court to the world surrounding it.

NOTES

1. Mary Douglas, attributing this definition of dirt to Lord Chesterfield, follows out the implications in her analysis of pollution as a cultural phenomenon: "Dirt is a kind of compendium category for all events which blur, smudge, contradict, or otherwise confuse accepted classifications." See Douglas, "Pollution," in *Implicit Meanings: Essays in Anthropology* (London: Routledge & Kegan Paul, 1975), 51. From the perspective of Douglas's larger analysis, gossip demands to be told and retold because the tellers in this way deal with a perceived transgression of some stable system of classifications.

2. Mark Edward Lewis, *Writing and Authority in Early China* (Albany: State University of New York Press, 1999), 313–17.

3. These ideas are explored in greater depth in my "Chinese History and Philosophy," in *The Oxford History of Historical Writing, Volume I: Beginnings to AD 600*, ed. Andrew Feldherr and Grant Hardy (Oxford: Oxford University Press, 2011), 394–414.

4. Sima Qian, *Shiji* (Beijing: Zhonghua shuju, 1959), 69.2277. The comments at the end of the biography of Zhang Yi 張儀 (d. 310 BCE), a great rival of Su Qin, suggest that the latter's reputation was destroyed in part by the slanders of his enemies; see *Shiji*, 70.2304.

5. Ibid., 86.2538.

6. Ibid., 86.2535.

7. The *Suoyin* 索隱 commentary of Sima Zhen 司馬貞 (fl. early 8th cent.)

cites the early romance *Yan Danzi* 燕丹子 (Prince Dan of Yan) and other texts as sources of these legends; see *Shiji*, 86.2538.

8. Because the painting depicts the regency of the Duke of Zhou 周公 during the minority of his nephew King Cheng of Zhou 周成王 (r. 1042/35–1006 BCE), observers understand that Emperor Wu will choose an heir young enough to need an older guide.

9. For the Palace Discipline Service (*yiting* 掖庭), see Charles O. Hucker, *A Dictionary of Official Titles in Imperial China* (Stanford: Stanford University Press, 1985), 269–70.

10. According to the commentary of Takigawa Kametarō 瀧川龜太郎, the Yunyang Palace was at the site of the Qin emperor's Ganquan Palace, some three hundred *li* from Chang'an; see *Shiki kaichū kōshō* 史記會注考證 (Taipei: Yiwen yinshuguan, 1976), 49.31–32/780–81. Yan Shigu 顏師古 (581–645), commenting on the death of Lady Gouyi in *Hanshu*, adds that Yunyang was known popularly as "the tombs of the ladies" (*nüling* 女陵); see Ban Gu, *Hanshu* (Beijing: Zhonghua shuju, 1962), 97A.3957.

11. Empress Lü 呂后 (241–180 BCE), married to Liu Bang 劉邦 (247–195 BCE) long before his rise to power as Han Gaozu 漢高祖 (r. 202–195 BCE), survived him by fifteen years and dominated court life and policy in her capacity as empress dowager.

12. This assertion is false. As Takigawa points out (*Shiki kaichū kōshō*, 49.31–32/780–81), only Lady Gouyi died after this sort of accusation. Others died young, apparently of natural causes, or were implicated in charges of sorcery.

13. *Shiji*, 49.1985–86.

14. The single work earlier than *Shiji* that clearly has an ending is *Huainanzi*, where the final chapter, "Yaolüe" 要略 ("An overview of the essentials"), gives a table of contents and overview of the work's aims. The "Xuyi" 序意 ("Postface") chapter of *Lüshi chunqiu* furnishes a kind of ending, but only for the first part of the work, the twelve "almanacs" (*ji* 紀). The final chapter of *Zhuangzi* 莊子, if that work actually did predate the *Shiji*, offers a philosophical conspectus but no reflection on the chapters that precede it.

15. Besides the murder of Empress Xu and the attempted murder of her son, discussed later (*Hanshu*, 97A.3966, 3968), see the cases of Emperor Cheng's deposed Empress Xu (*Hanshu*, 97B.3983) and of Emperor Zhao's Lady of Bright Deportment Feng 馮昭儀 (*Hanshu*, 97B.4006–7).

16. See *Hanshu*, 97A.3948, 3950, 3961; 97B.3982, 3984–85, 4002, 4006–7.

17. See, for example, Empress Lü's remark to Lady Qi 戚夫人 (d. 194 BCE), who would end her life as "the human pig" (*renzhi* 人彘), just before she had Lady Qi's son, the king of Zhao 趙王, put to death: "So you want to lean on your son, do you?" 乃欲倚女子邪. In *Hanshu*, 97A.3983.

18. The account of Xian's plot translated in this chapter is to be found at *Hanshu*, 97A.3966. Another, shorter account of this episode is to be found in the biography of Huo Guang; see *Hanshu*, 68.2952–53.

19. See *Hanshu*, 8.238, 97A.3957.

20. *Hanshu* 97A.3964 tells of Empress Xu's background, including the Sima Qian–like decision by her father Xu Guanghan 許廣 to accept castration in place of execution and to live on as a court eunuch.

21. According to Shen Qinhan 沈欽韓 (1775–1832), An was near present-day Yuncheng 運城, Shanxi province, about 100 miles northeast of Chang'an; see Wang Xianqian 王先謙, ed., *Hanshu buzhu* 漢書補注 (Taipei: Yiwen yinshuguan, 1955), 97A.22b/1655.

22. On the salt monopoly under Sang Hongyang 桑弘羊 (152–80 BCE) and its continuation under Sang's rival Huo Guang, see Xu Fuguan 徐復觀, "*Yantielun* zhong di zhengzhi shehui wenhua wenti" 《鹽鐵論》中的政治社會文化問題, in *Liang Han sixiangshi* 兩漢思想史, 3 vols. (Shanghai: Huadong shifan daxue chubanshe, 2001), 3:73–131, especially 75–77.

23. The anecdote collection *Xijing zaji* 西京雜記 (Diverse notes on the Western Capital) reports by contrast that Xian lavished gifts of cloth, jewels, and money upon Chunyu Yan, who was resentful nonetheless; see *Hanshu buzhu*, 97A.23a/1656.

24. *Hanshu*, 97A.3968–69.

25. *Shiji*, 130.3320.

26. *Hanshu*, 100A.4198; cf. Michael Loewe, *A Biographical Dictionary of the Qin, Former Han and Xin Periods (221 BC–AD 24)* (Leiden: Brill, 2000), 7.

27. Ibid., 67B.3983–88, 100A.4198.

28. Ibid., 100A.4200–201; Loewe, *A Biographical Dictionary*, 5.

29. Ibid., 100A.4203.

30. Ibid., 100A.4203. For the full story of the king of Dongping's request, see *Hanshu*, 80.3324–25; Loewe, *A Biographical Dictionary*, 401.

31. Ibid., 100A.4205. That Ban Si guarded access to the texts is clear from his refusal to lend them to Huan Tan; see *Hanshu*, 100A.4206.

32. Fan Ye, *Hou Hanshu* (Beijing: Zhonghua shuju, 1984), 30A.1324.

33. Ibid., 30A.1325–27.

34. Ibid., 30A. 1330, 1335.

35. Ibid., 30A.1325–26; cf. Loewe, *A Biographical Dictionary*, 6. On the general Ban Chao, see Nancy Lee Swann, *Pan Chao: Foremost Woman Scholar of China* (New York: Century Co., 1932), 28–32. The *Hanshu* version of Ban Gu's biography includes few of these details and first mentions his contact with restricted texts after his appointment as Gentleman; see *Hanshu* 70A.4225. Ban Gu's account of the composition of *Hanshu* (100B.4235) does prefigure the language Fan Ye would use regarding Ban Biao's first efforts (*Hou Hanshu*, 30A.1324).

36. Anthony E. Clark has argued that Ban Gu's presentation of Ban family history, with its emphasis on Ban ancestors' virtuous interventions with the emperors, was designed in part "to persuade the reader that there are other reasons for the family's rise to prominence than Ban *jieyu*'s privileged position." See "Inscribing the Family: A History of the Ban Clan," in *Ban Gu's History of Early China* (Amherst, N.Y.: Cambria Press, 2008), especially 74.

37. *Hanshu*, 100A.4204. See Loewe, *A Biographical Dictionary*, 8.
38. Ibid., 97B.3983–88.
39. *Hou Hanshu*, 84.2784–92; cf. Swann, *Pan Chao*, 40–58.
40. *Hou Hanshu*, 40B.1386; cf. Clark, *Ban Gu's History of Early China*, 130–31.
41. For Ban Zhao's work on *Hanshu*, see *Hou Hanshu*, 40B.2784–85.

2 Tales from Borderland
Anecdotes in Early Medieval China
Xiaofei Tian

Anecdotes are small stories that, without necessarily being real, give the illusion of the real. Complete in themselves and yet often seemingly random or accidental, they disrupt the flow of grand historical narratives and seem to expose the real day-to-day life "behind" such narratives. New historicists have made much of the anecdote as a form that resists totalizing comprehensive histories, but anecdote itself must also be treated as a historical phenomenon that acquires different meanings in different social, cultural, and historical contexts. In this essay, I will examine the uses of anecdote in various types of material ranging from dynastic history and anecdotal collection to poetic expositions (*fu* 賦) and travel accounts in early medieval China. Anecdotes were, on the one hand, regarded as unpredictable forces that must be harnessed to serve multifarious functions; on the other hand, they also became the key in the birth of a personal narrative that stood at the far origin of the modern novel.

ANECDOTE AND DYNASTIC HISTORY

The biography of the famous fourth-century painter Gu Kaizhi 顧愷之 (ca. 349–ca. 410) in *Jinshu* 晉書 (History of the Jin dynasty) contains the following anecdote:

> Gu Kaizhi once painted a portrait of Pei Kai. He then added three hairs to Pei Kai's cheek [after he finished]. Viewers felt that the portrait possessed a superior spirit [compared to the time before the three hairs were applied].
>
> 嘗圖裴楷象，頰上加三毛，觀者覺神明殊勝。[1]

To modern mainstream historians, anecdotes may be, to quote Catherine Gallagher, "no-account items: tolerable, as rhetorical embellishments, illustrations, or moments of relief from analytical generalizations, but methodologically nugatory."² In dynastic histories of imperial China that adopt biographies as the basic format, anecdotes are, however, important trivia and central marginalia. Gu Kaizhi's biography has minimal narration of important events in his life; instead, it sketches out his character—"Kaizhi loved joking"; "[Kaizhi] was particularly skillful with painting"; and "Kaizhi was boastful and tended to blow the truth out of all proportion"—and illustrates each of these personality traits with a string of anecdotes like the one cited above. These anecdotes are used to illustrate the character of Gu Kaizhi in the same way as the three hairs on Pei Kai's cheek: that is, if the portrait presents the visual likeness of a person, the three hairs, as an addition and an after-thought, are supposed to bring out the invisible essence of the person and make him come to life.

As an anecdote is by nature brief, sketchy, and indeed "anecdotal," it can interrupt the flow of the grand historical narrative just as easily as it can serve such a narrative. The simplest way of managing an anecdote is for the historian to exercise the right of inclusion and exclusion of an anecdote in dynastic history biographies. In the fourth century, a young man named Pei Qi 裴啟 collected a number of anecdotes into a volume entitled *Yulin* 語林 (Forest of words). In it, we find a story about the second emperor of the Eastern Jin, Emperor Ming 明帝 (299–325/r. 323–25), as a precocious child:

> When Emperor Ming was a child, he once sat in Emperor Yuan's lap. It happened that an emissary came from Chang'an. Emperor Yuan asked him about Luoyang and shed tears. Emperor Ming asked him: "Why do you cry?" Emperor Yuan told him all about why he had crossed the Yangtze River to the South. He then asked Emperor Ming: "Which do you think is farther: the sun or Chang'an?" Emperor Ming replied: "The sun is farther. I have never heard anyone coming from the sun, so one can clearly tell." Emperor Yuan was impressed.
>
> The next day at a banquet Emperor Yuan told his staff members about it and then put the same question to Emperor Ming. He answered: "The sun is closer." Emperor Yuan changed countenance, saying: "Why did you change your words?" Emperor Ming said, "Raising our eyes we can see the sun, but we cannot see Chang'an."
>
> 晉明帝數歲，坐元帝膝上。有人從長安來，元帝問洛下消息，潸然流涕。明帝問：「何以致泣？」具以東渡意告之。因問明帝：「汝意謂長安何如日遠？」答曰：「日遠。不聞人從日邊來，居然可知。」元帝異之。明日，集群

臣宴會，告以此意，更重問之。乃答曰：「日近。」元帝失色，曰：「爾何故異昨日之言邪？」答曰：「舉目見日，不見長安。」³

The *Jinshu*, compiled in early seventh century, includes this anecdote with the opening statement: "[Emperor Ming] was bright and clever as a child; Emperor Yuan doted on him" 幼而聰哲，為元帝所寵異. The passage is more or less the same as in the *Yulin*, except for a remark added at the end: "From then on Emperor Yuan marveled at him even more" 由是益奇之.⁴ The anecdote is framed by these two statements to demonstrate Emperor Ming's precocity and Emperor Yuan's approval of his son.

The *Yulin* also records another story about a grown-up Emperor Ming:

Emperor Ming was quite an extraordinary young man. He often went out of the palace and wandered in disguise. Once, Emperor Yuan summoned him and sent someone to bring to him the proper clothes and cap. But Emperor Ming crossed a stream and his clothes and cap were all soaked. At the time he had already lost Emperor Yuan's esteem; so when this happened, he thought he would surely be deposed as heir. He went in, his cap tilting to the side; seeing that, Emperor Yuan himself adjusted it. Upon this Emperor Ming was overjoyed.

晉明帝年少不倫，常微行。詔喚人以衣幘迎之。涉水過，衣幘悉濕。元帝已不重明帝，忽複有此，以為無不廢理。既入，幘不正，元帝自為正之，明帝大喜。⁵

This second anecdote from the *Yulin* shows an intriguing continuity with the first anecdote in terms of sustained paternal affection, once again manifested physically: Emperor Yuan adjusts Emperor Ming's cap with his own hands, just as he once planted the child on his knee. The larger context of the second anecdote is the birth of Emperor Ming's young half-brother, Emperor Jianwen 簡文帝 (320–72/r. 371–72), who became Emperor Yuan's favorite son in his last years. Emperor Ming nearly lost his right to the throne, yet there is no trace of such a development in his extremely complimentary *Jinshu* biography. In line with the simple, straightforward portrayal of the unproblematized father-son relationship, the *Jinshu* biography does not include this second anecdote, even though there is a good chance that the anecdote is true, judging from Emperor Ming's well-known habit of "wandering in disguise" and his recklessness.

Not all anecdotes can be seamlessly subsumed into a larger piece of historical narrative such as a biography in dynastic history. Some anecdotes simply do not "fit," like the second anecdote about Emperor Ming. It is an aperture through which we catch a glimpse of the dark and troubled side of the father-son relationship. The image presented by the first anecdote—a static tableau of the perfect harmony between a loving father and an adorable son—is undermined by the second, which brings in the factors of change and time, the stuff life is made of. Such anecdotes are messy; they defy control; they are "the touch of the real."

ANECDOTAL COLLECTIONS

In the fourth and fifth century there appeared a number of anecdotal collections, Pei Qi's *Yulin* being one of them. Such collections record not only anecdotes—short tales with character, action, and plot—but also witty remarks stripped bare of their settings. The *Yulin* was particularly popular among the younger generation: "When it first came out, it was transmitted far and near; the young people of the day all had it reproduced and everyone possessed a copy" 始出，大為遠近所傳。時流年少，無不傳寫，各有一通。[6] The second anecdote about Emperor Ming cited earlier, though found unfit for his official biography, does find a place in *Yulin*, which in turn became one of the sources for the even more famous anecdotal collection, *Shishuo xinyu* 世說新語 (*A New Account of the Tales of the World*), compiled by Liu Yiqing 劉義慶 (403–44).[7] The anecdotes and *bons mots* in these collections not only provided material for gossip and idle chat but also for emulation: these are works of "know-how" designed less for those of the inner elite circle acting out the anecdotes and uttering the witty remarks than for those who yearned to join the inner elite circle, textbooks of "cool behavior" for would-be "famous gentlemen."[8] The practice of rarely using a proper name but instead always using an official title, courtesy name, nickname, or even baby name to refer to a personage, and of using different appellations to refer to the same person, so annoying to a modern reader because of the difficulty of identifying the person in question, shows off an intimate knowledge of elite society and invites the reader to participate in such intimate knowledge; it demonstrates that a work like *Shishuo xinyu* was designed for a particular audience: an audience either already in the know or wanting to be in the know.

Unlike the *Yulin*, which is no longer extant except as fragments preserved in commentaries and encyclopedias, the *Shishuo xinyu* has survived more or less intact; this enables us to make better observations on its editorial arrangement, which I argue is another way of managing the unruly force of anecdotes.

We no longer have the original version of the *Shishuo xinyu*; the current version is generally divided into thirty-six thematic categories, and every anecdote is listed under a thematic category.[9] These categories are sometimes construed by scholars as corresponding to "personality types" used in character evaluation and official appointment in early medieval China.[10] This claim may well be true, although it also needs to be pointed out that some of the categories, such as "Shangshi" 傷逝 ("Grieving for the Departed") or "Chumian" 黜免 ("Dismissed from Office"), do not exactly correspond to any personality trait. More important, we should note that the categories form a set of interpretive frameworks. In other words, a category under which an anecdote is listed implies the compiler's value judgment and conveys the "lesson" of the anecdote.

Sometimes an anecdote could easily appear under a different category but does not, in which case the implied editorial perspective on the anecdote is particularly illuminated. For instance, one of the anecdotes in *Shishuo xinyu* relates how Wang Xiuling 王修齡 (d. ca. 364), a member of the elite Wang clan from Langye, was suffering from financial difficulties and was offered a boatload of rice by Tao Fan 陶範 (fl. ca. 376), who was the local magistrate. Wang declined, saying, "If Wang Xiuling is hungry, he will beg for food from Xie Renzu. He does not need Tao Hunu's rice" 王脩齡若飢, 自當就謝仁祖索食, 不須陶胡奴米.[11] Renzu 仁祖 was the courtesy name of Xie Shang 謝尚 (308–57), a member of the Xie clan from Chenjun 陳郡 that also belonged to the top echelon of the society like the Wangs from Langye; Hunu 胡奴 was the baby name of Tao Fan, who was the son of Tao Kan 陶侃 (259–334), the great Eastern Jin general from a humble native Southern family. Wang's rejection of Tao's gift was clearly not based on affluence ("If Wang Xiuling is hungry . . .") but a mark of social snobbery, and referring to Tao Fan by his baby name demonstrated extreme contempt. However, instead of classifying this anecdote under "Qingdi" 輕詆 ("Contempt and Insults"), *Shishuo xinyu* categorizes it under "Fangzheng" 方正 ("The Square and Proper"), which shows the fifth-century compiler's approval of Wang's rude behavior as an appropriate response—indeed "square and proper"—to Tao Fan's gesture of generosity.

Sometimes the same anecdote may appear under different categories; in this case the narrative emphasis changes from one category to another. In 328, when Su Jun's Rebellion (*Su Jun zhi luan* 蘇峻之亂) was quelled, the general Tao Kan was so angry with the Yu 庾 family, whom he saw as the main culprits for the rebellion, that he swore to execute the Yu brothers upon arriving at the capital. Yu Liang 庾亮 (289–340), one of the Yu brothers, went to see Tao Kan and apologized for his part in the incident. It is said that Yu's manner and bearing were so gracious that Tao Kan changed his view the moment he saw Yu. In *Shishuo xinyu*, this anecdote is included in "Rongzhi" 容止 ("Appearance and Behavior"), and the narrative attention is clearly focused on Yu Liang, who is presented more or less in a positive light, at least in terms of his demeanor.[12] Essentially the same anecdote appears in "Jiajue" 假譎 ("Guile and Chicanery") in different wording and with changes in narration; in this case the narrative emphasis falls not on Yu Liang's elegant manner, but on his exaggerated humility before Tao Kan, which is described as instrumental in winning Tao Kan's admiration.[13] The editorial judgment on Yu Liang is, however, clearly not so positive, as the Northern aristocrat Yu Liang's deep humility in front of a military man of a lowly native Southern background is exposed as "guile and chicanery."

The famous encounter between Yu Liang and Tao Kan after Su Jun's Rebellion is presented yet again in an anecdote under the category of "Jianse" 儉嗇 ("Frugality and Stinginess"):

> After Su Jun's Rebellion, Yu Liang fled south to see Tao Kan. Tao Kan appreciated him deeply. Tao by nature was frugal and stingy. At mealtime they were eating wild garlic and Yu kept the white bulbs.[14] Tao asked, "What do you keep those for?" Yu said, "But of course they can be planted." Thereupon Tao greatly admired Yu for not only being such an elegant gentleman, but also possessing the substance for governing.
>
> 蘇峻之亂, 庾太尉南奔見陶公。陶公雅相賞重。陶性儉吝, 及食, 噉薤, 庾因留白。陶問:「用此何為?」庾云:「故可種。」於是大歎庾非唯風流, 兼有治實。[15]

By categorizing the anecdote under "Frugality and Stinginess," the compiler places the spotlight on Tao Kan, not Yu Liang. It is noteworthy that Yu Liang is the one who practices "frugality and stinginess" in this anecdote and yet Tao Kan is the one who is characterized as *"by nature frugal and stingy"* (*xing jianlin* 性儉吝). Yu Liang's frugality is thus no more than an act, which is designed to appeal to Tao Kan's "nature." If the anecdote appeared under "Guile and Chicanery," it would have been another criticism of Yu Liang, but the compiler in this case bypasses any judgment of Yu Liang's behavior and chooses to leave it ambiguous.

One may argue that the first two anecdotes concerning Tao Kan and Yu Liang's encounter, with Yu Liang as the protagonist, placed under different categories, one positive and one negative, could be taken as an indication of the multiple editorial hands in the compilation of *Shishuo xinyu*.¹⁶ But this at best remains a speculation because of the complicated textual history of this work. What stands out is the fact that all three anecdotes in one way or another position Tao Kan at a disadvantage: he was a Southerner of a modest social background who was easily charmed or duped by a sophisticated, smooth-talking member of the Northern aristocracy. Precisely because the anecdote as a form is not responsible for larger historical narratives, none of the anecdotes takes into consideration the fact that Tao Kan might very well have kept Yu Liang alive for a purely political purpose. A good story is a good story; when the immediate political situation became, so to speak, "history," the fifth-century compiler of the anecdotal collection cared only about the still immensely resonant issue of the sociopolitical *and* cultural competition between the Northern immigrant elite and the prominent native Southern families, and made sure that the "meaning" of the anecdotes was conveyed by the thematic categories.

ANECDOTE, NARRATIVE SUBJECTIVITY, AND THE PROBLEM OF GENRE

In an anecdotal collection like *Shishuo xinyu*, anecdotes that must have been circulated orally at the beginning are organized in an orderly fashion, neatly labeled, and filed away. Later on, the *Jinshu* historians selected from a vast number of anecdotes at their disposal to illustrate a point or the character of the subject of a biography. The messiness of the real is somehow contained in both cases. In this section we will examine the use of the anecdote in several different types of travel writings at the turn of the fifth century. In these writings the anecdote becomes crucial in the formation of a personal narrative.

The first kind of such travel writings is a subgenre of poetic exposition (*fu* 賦) styled "*fu* recounting travel" (*jixing fu* 紀行賦). This subgenre already had a long tradition by the time of the fourth and fifth centuries, with one of the earliest famous example being Ban Biao's 班彪 (3–54) "A Poetic Exposition on a Northward Journey" ("Beizheng fu" 北征賦).¹⁷ This work exemplifies a pattern of subsequent "*fu* recounting travel" in that it relates all the famous historical sites the author sees along the way.¹⁸ In such writings the poet presents a cultural itinerary on a cultural map, and the significance of geography is superseded by that of history. One notable example from the early fifth century is "*Fu* Relating My Journey" ("Zhuanzheng fu" 撰征賦) by the aristocratic poet Xie Lingyun 謝靈運 (385–433).¹⁹ In the winter of 416, Xie Lingyun was sent by the imperial court to visit the general Liu Yu 劉裕 (363–422), who stationed his army at Pengcheng (in modern Jiangsu) and was about to undertake a military campaign against the North; upon his return to the capital in the following spring, he completed this poetic exposition recounting his journey. In this *fu*, although the account itself follows a linear progress, Xie Lingyun constantly moves back and forth between the history of the Han, the Jin, and the Three Kingdoms, as his itinerary takes him through various historical sites. In such a case, time is organized along the continuum on the axis of space; in other words, historical narrative is not structured chronologically but is manipulated by the author's spatial movement. It is, moreover, a grand historical time, as opposed to Xie Lingyun's experienced time. Even Xie Lingyun's experienced time, represented in terms of his progress from place A to place B, is less personal than generic, because, except for the part where he praises his ancestors' accomplishments at relevant locales, he represents more of a general traveler than a particularized historical person known as Xie Lingyun. A typical passage reads:

爾乃	Thereupon
經雉門,	I passed through the Pheasant Gate,
啟浮梁;	and had the Pontoon Bridge opened up;
眺鍾嚴,	I gazed far at Bell Mountain,
越查塘。	as I sailed over the Zha Pond.
覽永嘉之紊維,	I examined the tangled fabric of the Yongjia era,
尋建武之緝綱。	and traced the restored laws of the Jianwu years.[20]
......	
次石頭之雙岸,	I moored at the banks of the Stone Fortress,
究孫氏之初基。	investigating into the foundation of the house of Sun.
......	
疾魯荒之誣辭;	I loathe the lies of Duke Huang of Lu;[21]
惡京陵之譖言。	I detest the slandering of Jingling.[22]
責當朝之憚貶;	I disapprove of these powerful men's fear of taking responsibility;
對囊籍而興歎。	facing the records of the past, I heave sighs.[23]

The poet does give voice to his homesickness and his weariness of traveling in the course of the long piece, but sentiments about past events when he comes upon a historical site are predominant. As we can see, poetic exposition is conducive to the expression of feelings and thoughts about history and life in general, but does not leave much room for the trivially personal—in other words, it does not leave room for anecdotes.

We have to wait for prose records to do that. A member of Liu Yu's staff, Dai Zuo 戴祚, also known as Dai Yanzhi 戴延之, followed the general Liu Yu on this military campaign against the Northern dynasty. He wrote an account of the campaign, known as the *Xizheng ji* 西征記 (Record of the westward campaign). *Xizheng ji* is now extant only as fragments in encyclopedias and commentaries. While it is impossible to piece together a complete picture, we can nevertheless tell that it follows more or less the pattern of recording the places the author passes through and relating the historical lore of a place. And yet, in the midst of the account, Dai frequently notes personal details: "I saw pigeons for the first time in my life only after I got to Yongqiu. Their size is about that of a pheasant, and the color is like that of a parrot. They play around in pairs" 祚至雍丘始見鴿，大小如鳩，色似鸚鵡，戲時兩兩相對。[24]

At another point Dai and a colleague were commanded by the general to navigate up the Luo River and see where and how far the watercourse could lead him. They reached a place called Sanle 三樂. According to Dai, "The men and women, old and young, of Sanle have never seen a boat before. Hearing that the Jin emissaries were sailing on the river, they all came out and gathered like ants on the riverbank, looking at us and doubling over with laughter" 三樂男女老幼未嘗見舡，既聞晉使溯流，皆相引蟻聚川側，俯仰顧笑。[25]

If by its generic nature a *fu* on travel has no room for such personal anecdotes, a prose record of travel certainly does. Anecdotes like these break up the impersonal long list of places with events unfolding in time. The author's experienced time is superimposed upon grand historical time. The appearance of such details in travel accounts is crucial because it turns the author from an abstract entity into a real historical person with a subjectivity, and also because, as Mary B. Campbell has put it, "reverence for the minutiae of time is essential to the concerns of the novel."[26] We are, of course, still a long way off from the modern novel, but at the turn of the fifth century we begin to see the emergence of narrative unified by a subject.

THE ANECDOTE ABOUT A FAN: ONE MAN'S STORY

At about the same time as Xie Lingyun and Dai Yanzhi wrote their travel accounts, a Buddhist monk, Faxian 法顯 (ca. 340–421), wrote another. He was the first Chinese traveler to write down his travel experiences in Central Asia, India, and Sri Lanka, and his account is commonly known as the *Foguo ji* 佛國記 (*A Record of Buddhistic Kingdoms*).[27] Faxian's account replicates the basic structure of the military campaign records by recording important sites of notable past events; the difference is that

Faxian substitutes a religious framework for the framework of dynastic history. In other words, Faxian is interested in topography primarily in the sense of seeing holy sites where an event of scriptural significance, such as the Buddha's birth, has occurred. He does not concern himself with secular political time.

The other thing that separates Faxian's travel account from military campaign record is that unlike an author such as Dai Yanzhi, who followed Liu Yu on a military campaign, Faxian had a personal objective for his journey: to seek the Vinaya Piṭaka, which comprised Buddhist works on monastic discipline. His account is structured around this quest. A major rhetorical paradigm underlying Faxian's quest narrative is a journey through demonic terrains to the land of bliss, through hell to heaven. During the first part of Faxian's travel, the landscape is often depicted as demonic. A typical passage reads:

> In the River of Sands there are many evil demons and hot winds. Travelers who encounter them will all perish, without a single survivor. Above there is no bird flying and down below there is no running beast. One looks around as far as one can for a path through, but one knows not which direction to go; all one has for landmarks are the bones and skeletons of dead people.
> 沙河中多有惡鬼熱風，遇則皆死，無一全者。上無飛鳥，下無走獸，遍望極目，欲求度處，則莫知所擬，唯以死人枯骨爲標幟耳。[28]

Faxian's arrival in Central India marks a watershed in his journey. In his account he clearly states: "Central India is called the Central Kingdom" 中天竺所謂中國.[29] It is very likely that Faxian is translating directly from the Sanskrit term *Madhyadeśa* (in Pāli, *Majjhima-desa*), which means "the Middle Country." Both Pāli and Sanskrit Buddhist texts tend to divide India into five regions, and Madhyadeśa is the center. As Debarchana Sarkar says, "The reason behind the supreme importance attached by the Buddhists to this division lies in the fact that Gotama attained enlightenment or Bodhi and became the Buddha in an eastern district of this division and 'the drama of his whole life was staged on the plains of the Middle Country.'"[30] The Chinese rendering of Madhyadeśa as *Zhongguo* 中國 uses the same phrase that has always been reserved for the Central Plain (i.e., the Chinese heartland to the north of the Yangtze River) and indeed for China itself. In the Buddhist geography, however, China becomes a periphery. In India, Faxian was constantly referred to as having come from the "borderland" (*biandi* 邊地); he and his fellow travelers themselves also accepted this as a fact.[31] Faxian's depiction of

Central India is highly complimentary; his account mentions a few uninhabited places, but there are no descriptions of danger or hardship once he sets foot in the Central Kingdom. It is as if the traveler has left hell behind and entered paradise:[32]

> All south from this point on is called the Central Kingdom. In the Central Kingdom the climate is temperate and there is no frost or snow. People are numerous and happy. There are no household registrars, no official codes of law; only those who plow the king's land pay tax on it. If they want to leave, they can leave; if they want to stay, they can stay. The king rules without capital punishment or other forms of corporal punishment. Those who commit a crime are only fined according to the seriousness of the crime. Even for those who commit the gravest crimes the punishment is no heavier than cutting off the right hand. The royal guards and attendants all enjoy salaries. Throughout the kingdom the people do not kill any living creature, do not drink alcohol, and do not eat scallion or garlic, except for the caṇḍālas. The caṇḍālas are wicked men who live apart from the others. When they come to a city or a marketplace, they beat on a piece of wood to distinguish themselves, so that the others know who they are and avoid them and do not come into contact with them. In the Central Kingdom the people do not keep pigs and chickens, nor do they sell livestock. There is no butcher shop or taverns that sell wine in the marketplace. They use cowries in buying and selling. Only the caṇḍālas are fishermen and hunters who sell meat.
>
> 從是以南，名爲中國。中國寒暑調和，無霜雪。人民殷樂，無戶籍官法，唯耕王地者乃輸地利。欲去便去，欲住便住。王治不用刑斬，有罪者但罰其錢，隨事輕重。雖復謀爲惡逆，不過截右手而已。王之侍衛左右皆有供祿。舉國人民悉不殺生，不飲酒，不食葱蒜，唯旃荼羅。旃荼羅名爲惡人，與人別居。若入城市，則擊木以自異，人則識而避之，不相搪突。國中不養猪鷄，不賣生口，市無屠估及沽酒者。貿易則用貝齒。唯旃荼羅漁獵師賣肉耳。[33]

The portrayal provided here is that of a Buddhist paradise, and in many ways it constitutes, just like Marco Polo's account of the wonders of the East, a reversed mirror image of the regimes in China.[34] The lesson is that one must first go through hell, as Dante does in his *Divine Comedy*, to get to heaven. The ultimate question is: what happens when one finally does gain paradise?

One can certainly stay—like Daozheng 道整, Faxian's only remaining traveling companion from the initial group of ten people—and that would be the end of the story. Faxian, however, chooses to go back to the "borderland" where he has come from. He has a noble purpose: "My original aim was to seek the Vinaya Piṭaka and have it circulated in the land of

Han, so I went on the return journey alone."³⁵ But there is a hidden narrative in the account that places Faxian in a unique position. Thanks to this hidden narrative, Faxian is no longer just the depersonalized bearer of an itinerary or the faceless recorder of a catalogue of exotic places nobody had visited before; his travel account becomes a first-person narrative, imbued with an unmistakable subjectivity.

While in Sri Lanka, Faxian visits a Buddhist monastery. The statue of the Buddha arouses awe and admiration in Faxian, and yet, what *touches* him is not the image of the Buddha; rather, it is the secular image of a fan made of white silk from his native land:

> In the monastery there is a hall decorated with gold and silver and finished with various precious stones. Inside there is a statue of the Buddha in green jade, which is about thirty feet tall, and shines forth with the glow of the Seven Jewels. Its majestic form is so solemn and dignified that words cannot describe it. In the right palm of the statue there is a priceless precious pearl.
>
> I, Faxian, had left the land of the Han for many years by that time. All the people I associated with were foreigners; my eyes had not seen the mountains, rivers, trees, and plants of old for a long time. My traveling companions had all become separated: some stayed behind, and some had died. I looked and saw myself alone with my shadow, and my heart was constantly filled with melancholy. All of a sudden I saw a fan made of white silk from the land of the Jin, left by some merchant in front of the jade statue as an offering to the Buddha. At that moment I could not help but feel deeply moved; tears of sorrow welled up in my eyes and fell.
>
> 起一佛殿，金銀刻鏤，悉以眾寶。中有一青玉像，高三丈許，通身七寶焰光，威相嚴顯，非言所載，右掌中有一無價寶珠。
>
> 法顯去漢地積年，所與交接，悉異域人。山川草木，舉目無舊。又同行分披，或留或亡。顧影唯己，心常懷悲。忽于此玉像邊見商人以一白絹扇供養，不覺淒然，泪下滿目。³⁶

The contrast between the opulent splendor of the precious jewels and the plain white silk fan is at once striking and poignant. If the first part of the passage evokes an impersonal catalogue of exotica commonly seen in an account of a foreign country or a faraway place, then the second part of the passage embodies an intensely personal and indeed intensely lyrical moment. This is due not the least to the fact that the white silk fan is one of the quintessentially poetic images in early Chinese classical poetry, and in particular the subject of a popular Southern song set in the fourth and fifth centuries; as such it would have especially resonated with

Faxian's Southern audience.[37] In an account that is largely characterized by a detached style and is often given to long narration of the Buddhist lore associated with a place, Faxian's reaction to the fan is remarkable in its emotive self-representation. It is not even the kind of personal information as revealed by Dai Yanzhi—"I have never seen a pigeon before!"—but something deeply emotional and revealing a subjectivity rarely seen in a travel account from this period.

This detail is an intensely personal anecdote. It is from Sri Lanka that Faxian finally embarks on his homecoming voyage. In some ways his seeing of the fan serves, if not as a catalyst for his decision to go home, then as a narrative preparation for that decision. It is certainly not a very Buddhist response—desire, longing, and homesickness are all emotions and forms of attachment that a Buddhist priest should learn to purge in the process of self-cultivation—but it apparently plays a key role in Faxian's life as a traveler. This one moment is deemed significant enough to be recorded in the account of his fourteen-year-long journey during which the traveler has presumably seen so many things worthy of attention that to see something or not see something becomes a deliberate choice instead of a random act, even more so when experience is being reconstructed in what is basically a personal memoir.

Faxian's experience with the image of the fan is structured as a powerful emotional response to a visual stimulus followed by the ensuing action. Such a narrative structure would have proved familiar to his audience in South China, as there are a number of contemporary stories that are structured along a similar continuum. The best known is perhaps the story about Liu Chen 劉晨 and Ruan Zhao 阮肇 (both fl. 1st century CE), which appears in *Youming lu* 幽明錄 (Records of worlds of darkness and light), a work attributed to the *Shishuo xinyu* compiler Liu Yiqing.[38] The element in these stories that I want to call attention to is not the journey to the earthly paradise itself, but rather the moment of "longing for return" (*sigui* 思歸). The important thing to remember about "paradise lost" is the element of free will. The renunciation of paradise is always voluntary, and it almost always is the consequence of a longing to return to the mortal world. Longing for return, either on the part of a soldier on a military campaign or on the part of an official going on the king's business, is a familiar source of pathos in classical poetry; but to be already in paradise (as opposed to being on the road as in the famous early poem *Lisao* 離騷) and to long for the mortal world becomes a recurring theme only in narratives in the fourth and fifth centuries.

Faxian's *Foguo ji* is not like the travel *fu* that records, in an emotionally even tempo, the progress from one site of history to another; nor is it a catalogue of exotic customs and products that serve the political, economic, and military interests of the empire. Faxian's singular feat, memorable in classical literary tradition, is his success in turning his travel account into a personal epic, even though no premodern reader would consider his work as part of literature. He does this by incorporating a cultural narrative of paradise gained and lost—which is familiar enough to early medieval Chinese readers—that is couched in a new framework, namely that of a first-person travel account. As opposed to prose records of military campaigns, which do not have any inherent "narrative" despite the many personal observations and encounters dotting such accounts, what we have is an autobiographical story, with a beginning, an end, and a dramatic turning point in between. This turning point is marked by an anecdote, a punctured hole in the largely faceless narration of Buddhist holy sites; it opens a window into history as it was lived by real people. Faxian's stated reason for coming back to China is to spread the Vinaya, but the anecdote exposes a hidden narrative in which the person Faxian, not the monk Faxian, longs for his homeland.

The apparent randomness of anecdotes creates the impression of a messy reality that threatens to disrupt the flow of grand historical narratives but also gives the illusion of the real. In this chapter, I have examined the various ways in which the potentially unruly power of anecdotes is brought under control in early medieval China: biographies in dynastic histories try to subsume anecdotes under a neat account of a life by selecting "appropriate" anecdotes and editing them in such a way so as to shed light on personalities and political events, while anecdotal collections such as *Shishuo xinyu*, which emerged for the first time during this period, impose meaning and order on anecdotes by grouping and classifying them. Travel writings from this period, meanwhile, make use of anecdotes in an inventive way: in contrast with "*fu* recounting travel"—the traditional form of travel writing imbued with grand sentiments but devoid of colorful details—prose accounts of military campaigns from the fourth and fifth centuries seem to be strewn with intimate anecdotes of a personal nature. This sort of narrative, stamped with the mark of a historical individual, culminates in Faxian's *Foguo ji*, which, by its use of anecdotes, turns a religious journey and a travel account into a personal journey and an autobiographical story of human interest.

NOTES

1. Fang Xuanling 房玄齡 (578–648) et al., comps., *Jinshu* (Beijing: Zhonghua shuju, 1974), 92.2405.
2. Catherine Gallagher and Stephen Greenblatt, *Practicing New Historicism* (Chicago: University of Chicago Press, 2000), 49.
3. Zhou Lengjia 周楞伽, ed., *Pei Qi yulin* 裴啟語林 (Beijing: Wenhua yishu chubanshe, 1988), 5.50.
4. *Jinshu*, 6.158.
5. *Pei Qi yulin*, 5.51.
6. See Yu Jiaxi 余嘉錫, ed., *Shishuo xinyu jianshu* 世說新語箋疏 (Shanghai: Shanghai guji chubanshe, 1993), 4.269.
7. For a discussion of this collection, see chapter 3 of this volume.
8. Lu Xun 魯迅 defines *Shishuo xinyu* as "a textbook for famous gentlemen" 名士底教科書 in the "arcane discourse" (*xuantan* 玄談). In fact, *Shishuo xinyu* records many occasions of arcane discourse but hardly contains any lengthy description of the content of the arcane discourse itself, and the kind of witty reply in the *bon mot* style cited by Lu Xun at best constitutes one small part of the arcane discourse. See his "Zhongguo de xiaoshuo de lishi de bianqian" 中國的小說的歷史的變遷, in *Lu Xun quanji* 魯迅全集 (Beijing: Renmin wenxue chubanshe, 1957), 8:322.
9. The original work may have had different numbers of categories, such as thirty-seven, thirty-eight, thirty-nine, and forty-five. It is impossible to decide which best represents the original, but we can be reasonably certain about the division into thematic categories itself. For the various numbers of categories, see Wang Nengxian 王能憲, *Shishuo xinyu yanjiu* 世說新語研究 (Nanjing: Jiangsu guji chubanshe, 2000), 35–36.
10. See, for instance, Wang, *Shishuo xinyu yanjiu*, 40–41; and Fan Ziye 范子燁, *Shishuo xinyu yanjiu* 世說新語研究 (Harbin: Heilongjiang jiaoyu chubanshe, 1998), 28–35.
11. *Shishuo xinyu jianshu*, 5.327. Translation from Richard B. Mather, trans., *A New Account of Tales of the World by Liu I-Ch'ing with Commentary by Liu Chün*, 2nd ed. (Ann Arbor: Center for Chinese Studies, University of Michigan, 1976), 184.
12. *Shishuo xinyu jianshu*, 14.615; Mather, trans., *A New Account*, 335.
13. *Shishuo xinyu jianshu*, 27.856; Mather, trans., *A New Account*, 479–80.
14. This is *xie* 薤, *Allium chinense*, commonly known as "Chinese onion" or "Chinese scallion," which grows in southern China.
15. *Shishuo xinyu jianshu*, 29.875; Mather, trans., *A New Account*, 492. The translation here is mine.
16. It has been long hypothesized that *Shishuo xinyu* was collectively compiled by Liu Yiqing's staff members under the prince's auspices. For a summary of this view, see Wang, *Shishuo xinyu yanjiu*, 3–4.
17. For an English translation, see David R. Knechtges, ed. and trans., *Wen xuan or Selections of Refined Literature* (Princeton: Princeton University Press, 1987), 2:165–171.

18. For a detailed discussion of Ban Biao's *fu* and "*fu* recounting travel" in the Han, see David R. Knechtges, "Poetic Travelogue in the Han Fu," in *Zhongyang yanjiuyuan di 2 jie guoji Hanxue huiyi lunwenji*, ed. Zhongyang yanjiuyuan (Taipei: Academia Sinica, 1989), 127–52.

19. For an English translation, see Xiaofei Tian, *Visionary Journeys: Travel Writings from Early Medieval and Nineteenth-Century China* (Cambridge, Mass.: Harvard University Asia Center, 2011), 287–340.

20. The Western Jin collapsed during the Yongjia era 永嘉 (307–13); Jianwu 建武 (317–18) was the reign title of Emperor Yuan of the Jin 晉元帝, who reestablished the Jin rule in South China.

21. Duke Huang of Lu was Jia Chong 賈充 (217–82), Emperor Wu of the Jin's favorite minister. He was made the commander-in-chief of the Jin army in the campaign against Wu. Fearing a negative outcome, he repeatedly wrote the emperor arguing the impossibility of the mission, even calling for the execution of Zhang Hua 張華 (232–300), the pro-war minister, in one letter, right up until the Kingdom of Wu surrendered. After Jia Chong's death, the officials in charge planned to give him the derogatory posthumous title *huang* 荒 (neglectful of duty and indulgent in sensual pleasures), but met with the emperor's disapproval. They thus changed his posthumous title to *wu* (meaning "martial"). Here, Xie chooses to use the posthumous title that was never adopted to pass his own judgment on Jia Chong. See Jia Chong's biography in *Jinshu*, 40.1165–71.

22. Jingling refers to the general Wang Hun 王渾 (223–97), the Duke of Jingling. He and Wang Jun 王濬 (206–86) were both instrumental in the conquest of Wu. Wang Hun was jealous of Wang Jun's achievements and slandered him in many letters to the emperor; this caused him no small loss of reputation at the time. See *Jinshu*, 42.1202.

23. Gu Shaobo 顧紹柏, *Xie Lingyun ji jiaozhu* 謝靈運集校注 (Henan: Zhongzhou guji chubanshe, 1987), 252–53.

24. Li Fang 李昉 (925–96) et al., *Taiping yulan* 太平御覽 (Beijing: Zhonghua shuju, 1960), 923.4228a.

25. Ibid., 770.3544a.

26. Mary B. Campbell, *The Witness and the Other World: Exotic European Travel Writing, 400–1600* (Ithaca: Cornell University Press, 1988), 135.

27. Like many early medieval works, Faxian's account has several variant titles: *Foguo ji* and *Faxian zhuan* 法顯傳 (Account of Faxian) are the most commonly used. The history of its textual transmission is complicated. In writing this paper I have consulted a number of editions, most notably Adachi Kiroku 足立喜六, *Faxian zhuan kaozheng* 法顯傳考證, trans. He Jianmin 何健民 and Zhang Xiaoliu 張小柳 (Shanghai: Shangwu yinshuguan, 1937); Zhang Xun 章巽, ed., *Faxian zhuan jiaozhu* 法顯傳校注 (Shanghai: Shanghai guji chubanshe, 1985); and Yang Weizhong 楊維中, trans., *Xinyi Foguo ji* 新譯佛國記 (Taipei: Sanmin shuju, 2004). For English translations, one may refer to Samuel Beal, trans., *Si-yu Ki: Buddhist Records of the Western World* (London: Trübner & Co., 1884), and James Legge, trans., *A Record of Buddhistic*

Kingdoms; Being an Account by the Chinese Monk Fâ-Hien of His Travels in India and Ceylon (A.D. 399–414) in Search of the Buddhist Books of Discipline (London: Clarendon Press, 1886). The page numbers of the quotations in this paper refer to Adachi Kiroku's collated edition.

28. Adachi, *Faxian zhuan kaozheng*, 34.

29. Ibid., 79.

30. Debarchana Sarkar, *Geography of Ancient India in Buddhist Literature* (Calcutta: Sanskrit Pustak Bhandar, 2003), 65.

31. See Adachi, *Faxian zhuan kaozheng*, 112, 137, 245–46.

32. The description of perils reappears only during the return journey, the ocean voyage undertaken from Sri Lanka to the Chinese mainland. Thus, Faxian elevates Central India as a heavenly kingdom surrounded by perilous terrain, treacherous seas, and nearly impassable barriers.

33. Adachi, *Faxian zhuan kaozheng*, 117.

34. Corporal punishment was, for instance, an important part of punitive law; even officials could not be entirely exempt from it. Household registers were another important issue because registered households are the taxpayers on whom the state relies for income and corvée labor. People tried to evade being registered either by moving to another place or by attaching themselves to landholding elite families and thus becoming exempt from taxation and corvée duty; in both cases the households became "hidden" or "shaded" from the imperial supervision and surveillance. The state had to constantly fight against such a practice, and the freedom of going or staying at will in a place, as related in Faxian's account of Central India, was quite unimaginable.

35. Adachi, *Faxian zhuan kaozheng*, 246.

36. Ibid., 255.

37. The origin of the song set, "Lover of a Round Fan" ("Tuanshan lang" 團扇郎歌), is attributed to the mistress of the Eastern Jin minister Wang Min 王珉 (361–88).

38. *Youming lu* 幽明錄, in *Han Wei Liuchao biji xiaoshuo daguan* 漢魏六朝筆記小說大觀 (Shanghai: Shanghai guji chubanshe, 1999), 697–98.

3   Knowing Men and Being Known

Gossip and Social Networks in the Shishuo xinyu

Jack W. Chen

The relationship between personal fame and the constitution of fame is a central concern of the *Shishuo xinyu* 世說新語 (*A New Account of Tales of the World*), a fifth-century anecdotal collection compiled by (or in the name of) Liu Yiqing 劉義慶 (403–44). The more than six hundred figures mentioned in the *Shishuo xinyu* represent a complex, though rather circumscribed, network of social and political elites who lived between the end of the Eastern Han (25–220) and the end of the Jin (265–420). However, the work's treatment of these figures is not primarily a function of their political or social status, but rather, one that arises from a fascination with individual reputations, both good and bad, within communities that often seem to gossip about little else. Indeed, the historical figures of the *Shishuo xinyu* are included because they are "famous" (*zhiming* 知名), making them members of a shifting and contested grouping referred to as *mingshi* 名士, or "gentlemen of repute."[1] In this chapter, I will examine the way in which the circulation of reputation figures in the gossipy anecdotes of the *Shishuo xinyu*, contextualizing this discursive economy both in terms of longstanding political concerns with the recognition of talent and virtue, and also in terms of what the interest in reputation might say about changing ideas of personhood in the period following the Han dynasty.

"KNOWING MEN" AND POLITICAL EPISTEMOLOGY

In many ways, the discourse on personal reputation in the *Shishuo xinyu* arose from an earlier problem in Chinese political thought, one of "knowing men" (*zhiren* 知人). By this was meant the capacity for a ruler or official to recognize talent and to discern the true nature of the men who served in government, so that the best men could be placed in appropriate offices. Within the received textual tradition, the question of *zhiren* is represented as first emerging within discussions of sovereignty during the age of the sage-kings. The following is from a conversation between the sage-king Yu 禹 and his minister Gaoyao 皋陶 in the *Shangshu* 尚書 (Esteemed documents):

> Gaoyao said, "Yea—it resides in 'knowing men'; it resides in bringing peace to the people." Yu said, "Oh, if it is to be both of these, then even the [former] thearchs would consider it difficult.[2] To 'know men' is to be wise, and so to be able to place men in [appropriate] offices. To bring security to the people is to be benevolent, and so the commoners will keep him in their thoughts. Why would he need to worry about a Huan Dou? Why would he have to displace the Youmiao? what would he have to fear from one of cunning words, beguiling looks, and unfaithful character?"[3]
>
> 皋陶曰：「都，在知人，在安民。」禹曰：「吁，咸若時，惟帝其難之。知人則哲，能官人。安民則惠，黎民懷之。能哲而惠，何憂乎驩兜？何遷乎有苗？何畏乎巧言令色孔壬？」[4]

The first part of the question of "knowing men" for Yu is concerned with the understanding of how to match talented men with positions appropriate to their talents—being able to place them in office (*neng guan zhi* 能官之). Inextricable from this discourse is the question of bringing security (*an* 安) to the people, since a properly functioning government will create conditions of peace throughout the kingdom. The second part of the passage then turns to the problem of seeing through the surfaces of words and appearances so that potent threats to the polity can be avoided or removed. The capacity to know men is thus not only the recognition of talent, but also the ability to recognize those without talent and to reject them before they can do harm.

This trope of knowing men would, toward the end of the Warring States Period (479–221 BCE), become one of the crucial concerns of the sovereign, who had to delegate power in order to rule successfully over larger territories. Thus, in the "Dalüe" 大略 ("Great Summation") chapter of the *Xunzi* 荀子, we find the following passage:

> The way of the ruler is to know men; the way of the subordinate is to know affairs. Thus when Shun governed the world, though it was not through his own tasks or commands, the myriad things were nevertheless brought to completion.
>
> 主道知人，臣道知事。故舜之治天下，不以事詔而萬物成。[5]

Faced with the growing complexity of political rulership, the knowledge of the ruler would have to be defined in a different manner than that of his subordinates. If the subordinate would know how to handle a particular thing or matter—what one might call technical knowledge—the ruler would have to know how to manage these particular "knowers," and in this way, possess a kind of metaknowledge, one that would not be technical in nature. After all, the example of Shun is one of disengagement from direct action and from the entangling world of things—that is, a model of *wuwei* 無為, or "nonpurposive action." This disengagement, however comes at the price of a reliance on other men, which, to be sure, takes place in a nontragic, nonalienated manner (unlike what one finds in Hegel's master-slave dialectic). Nevertheless, in order to act upon the world, other men must mediate the ruler's experience of the world and its exigencies, and only in this way does he remain undisturbed, in a state of sagely tranquility.⁶

This last point is significant for the sovereign's ability to know men, since there must be not only a remove between the knower of men and the world, but also a state of equilibrium. If the ruler is involved in the world, then his judgments will be affected by the multifarious claims of the world. This problem would be discussed in the *Lüshi chunqiu* 呂氏春秋 (Annals of Lü Buwei), a third-century BCE encyclopedic work of philosophy. In the chapter "Lun ren" 論人 ("Evaluating Men"), the *Lüshi chunqiu* begins with the injunction that the ruler who seeks to make use of others must first "reflect upon the self" 反諸己 and then "attune the senses and restrain desires" 適耳目, 節嗜欲. The result of this discipline will finally allow the ruler's thoughts to roam freely in "the dwelling-place of the unbounded" 無窮之次 and attain "the path of naturalness" 自然之塗.⁷ The ruler enters into a meditative state that allows him to see clearly how each man should be employed.

Following this, the text proceeds to strike a much more practical note, stating that:

> Generally speaking, one evaluates men as follows: (1) when they are successful, examine those toward whom they are deferential; (2) when they are eminent, examine those whom they promote; (3) when they are wealthy, examine those whom they nurture; (4) when they take advice, examine how they carry it out; (5) when they have leisure, examine that in which they delight; (6) when they are familiar with a subject, examine how they speak of it; (7) when they suffer poverty, examine that which they will not accept; and (8) when they are in humble straits, examine that which they will not do; and (a) make them pleased in order to test their self-composure; (b) make them happy in order to test their weaknesses; (c) make them angry in

order to test their self-restraint; (d) make them fearful in order to test their self-reliance; (e) make them sad in order to test their empathy; and (f) make them suffer in order to test their determination. These are the "eight examinations" and the "six tests," and these are the means by which the wise ruler evaluates men.

The one who evaluates men also must avail himself of the "six familial relationships" and the "four personal relationships." What are the "six familial relationships"? They are father and mother, elder brother and younger brother, and wife and child. What are the "four personal relationships"? They are friends, former acquaintances, people from one's hometown, and one's fellow officials. In domestic matters, use the "six familial" and "four personal relationships"; in nondomestic matters, use the "eight examinations" and "six tests." Then there will be no errors concerning whether a person is sincere or false, greedy or honest, good or bad. Compare this to running in the rain—one who can avoid getting soaked is unheard of. This is the means by which the sage-kings know men.

凡論人,通則觀其所禮,貴則觀其所進,富則觀其所養,聽則觀其所行,止則觀其所好,習則觀其所言,窮則觀其所不受,賤則觀其所不為,喜之以驗其守,樂之以驗其僻,怒之以驗其節,懼之以驗其特,哀之以驗其人,苦之以驗其志,八觀六驗,此賢主之所以論人也。

論人者,又必以六戚四隱。何謂六戚?父母兄弟妻子。何謂四隱?交友故舊邑里門郭。內則用六戚四隱,外則用八觀六驗,人之情偽貪鄙美惡無所失矣,譬之若逃雨,汙無之而非是。此聖王之所以知人也。 [8]

Despite the mystical overtones of the opening passage of the *Lüshi chunqiu* chapter, the possibility of knowing men is grounded in an empirical examination of human behavior under certain situations and a knowledge of the subject's situation within local networks. A person's true nature may be hidden beneath layers of deception; however, the text possesses an epistemological confidence in careful observation that allows one to go beyond the surface obfuscations and grasp a person as he actually is.

It is this logic that also underlies what is perhaps the most famous disquisition of all on the epistemology and evaluation of human nature—the *Renwu zhi* 人物志 (*The Study of Human Abilities*) of the third-century figure Liu Shao 劉劭.[9] In his preface to the work, Liu Shao writes,

> As for that which is excellent in sages and worthies, nothing is more excellent than acuity of perception; and as for that which is to be valued in intelligence, nothing is more valuable than the knowledge of men. If one indeed is wise in the knowledge of men, then the numerous kinds of abilities would attain their proper order, and the various undertakings would flourish and succeed.

夫聖賢之所美，莫美乎聰明；聰明之所貴，莫貴乎知人。知人誠智，則眾材得其序，而庶績之業興矣。[10]

As one can see from this, insight into individual talents is critical to the enterprise of imperial government, since a bureaucracy, no matter how ingeniously designed, can function only when it is properly staffed. Only the ruler, however, is capable of knowing how to staff the government, since it is only the ruler that has the ability to discriminate among the various kinds of human talents and capacities. Subordinates may have knowledge of things, but the sovereign has knowledge of persons—and this knowledge, in effect, places the subjects of the ruler into a special class of thinghood. Sovereign knowledge is both a knowledge of men and a form of metaknowledge—both a mastery of a particular skill (administration) and a knowledge of how to regulate all the other forms of knowledge for the purposes of the imperial enterprise.

"KNOWING MEN" AS SOCIAL DISCERNMENT

The epistemic grounds upon which one may stake the claim to "know men" is clear by the end of the Han dynasty, and it is inherited by texts such as the *Shishuo xinyu*, which place a premium on knowledge of men and character evaluation.[11] However, within the *Shishuo xinyu*, we also begin to see how the understanding of the phrase "knowing men" is changing, both in terms of what is meant by "knowing" and what is meant by "men." Let me turn here to an example from the *Shishuo xinyu* chapter "On Discerning and Understanding" ("Shijian" 識鑒):

> When Generalissimo Wang Dun began his descent [into the Jiankang capital region], Yang Lang strenuously remonstrated against this course, but his advice was not heeded. After this, Yang exerted all his energies on behalf of Wang. He rode in the "Resounding Cloud-Dew Chariot" and crossing directly before the generalissimo, said, "When you hear the sound of your subordinate's drum, the moment you advance, you'll be victorious." Wang, at that time, clasped Yang's hand and said, "If this endeavor is won, then I will give you charge of Jingzhou." When the venture was concluded, Wang forgot about his promise and gave Yang charge of Nan Commandery. After Wang was defeated, Jin Mingdi captured Yang Lang and intended to kill him. The emperor, however, passed away soon after, and Yang gained a reprieve. Later, Yang simultaneously held the positions of the Three Dukes, appointing scores of men to office. These men in this time certainly had no names to speak of, but afterward all were

accorded honor and respect. During this time, all praised Yang for his knowledge of men.

王大將軍始下，楊朗苦諫不從，遂為王致力，乘'中鳴雲露車'逕前曰：「聽下官鼓音，一進而捷。」王先把其手曰：「事克，當相用為荊州。」既而忘之，以為南郡。王敗後，明帝收朗，欲殺之。帝尋崩，得免。後兼三公，署數十人為官屬。此諸人當時並無名，後皆被知遇，于時稱其知人。[12]

Wang Dun 王敦 (266–324) was son-in-law of the Western Jin emperor Wu (r. 265–90). After the Eastern Jin was established, he became governor of the upper Yangtze region, rebelling and moving against the capital at Jiankang twice, in 322 and 324. As Richard B. Mather has pointed out, this account of Yang Lang's 楊郎 (fl. early 4th cent.) rise to the offices of the Three Dukes is contradicted by the historical sources, which show Yang as never having risen above the post of provincial governor.[13] Nevertheless, the (fictional) anecdotal detail given for Yang's power and influence is essential to his representation as a knower of men. It is not enough to have political and military insight; one must also command a position that allows this insight to be recognized as such. Thus, the generalissimo Wang Dun initially dismisses Yang's remonstrance not to move against the capital, and even after he follows Yang's tactical advice during battle, forgets to grant Yang the promised governorship of Jingzhou. Once, however, Yang's talents are universally recognized, he is able to appoint men who, without fail, all turn out to be praiseworthy officials, converting his own public recognition into the successful recognition of others.

The Yang Lang anecdote, like the earlier usages of *zhiren*, is focused upon success in the political arena. Knowledge, once recognized, becomes sociopolitical influence, and this influence in turn allows the knower to form a social network that will propagate and reinforce the power of the one who knows men. When the phrase is used in other anecdotes from the *Shishuo xinyu*, however, what appears to be at stake is not only knowing how to classify potential worthies and officials for the sake of government, but the way in which this knowing is expressed—which is to say, the performance and manner of the one who knows. The question of performance is central to this anecdote from the "Gradations of Excellence" ("Pinzao" 品藻) chapter of the *Shishuo xinyu*:

> Gu Shao once spent the night talking with Pang Tong [style-name Shiyuan], and asked, "I have heard that you have fame in knowing men. Between myself and you, honored sir, who is the superior?" Pang said, "In molding and smelting the customs of the world and in floating along with the currents of the age, I do not compare to you. In discussing the surviving plans of kings and hegemons and in

inspecting the critical points of fortune and misfortune, I would seem to be a day older."¹⁴ Shao was content with these words.

顧劭嘗與龐士元宿語, 問曰:「聞子名知人, 吾與足下孰愈?」曰:「陶冶世俗, 與時浮沉, 吾不如子。論王霸之餘策, 覽倚伏之要害, 吾似有一日之長。」劭亦安其言。¹⁵

Pang Tong 龐統 (177–214) known also by his nickname, the "Phoenix Hatchling" (Fengchu 鳳雛), served as military strategist and commander under Liu Bei 劉備 (162–223). As this anecdote shows, Pang's talents extend beyond his grasp of battlefield tactics to the recognition of other men's talents. When Gu Shao 顧劭 (fl. 3rd cent.) asks him to compare the two of them, Pang declares that Gu is the superior in guiding the customs of the present age, while he himself is superior in understanding how the rulers of the past would have acted.

Unlike the first example concerning Yang Lang, the focus of this anecdote is not on the way in which the ability to know men leads to advancement and the propagation of social influence, but rather, on the virtuosity with which Pang renders his judgment. Much of the *Shishuo xinyu* is concerned with such displays of verbal skill and wit. While it is possible to read such performances in terms of what Li Wai-yee has defined as "aesthetic self-consciousness," one must also bear in mind how verbal exchanges reveal an underlying agonistics.¹⁶ In this case, though Gu Shao and Pang Tong seem to be ensconced in a friendly, nightlong chat, Gu brings to the surface the actual underlying subtext of the conversation the moment that he asks, "Between myself and you, honored sir, who is the superior?" The ranking and evaluation of others is one of the prominent concerns in the *Shishuo xinyu*, and there can be much anxiety over one's standing in relation to one's friends and acquaintances. There is social capital at stake, and this is particularly pronounced in the relatively closed network of cultural and political elites represented in the *Shishuo xinyu*. On this point, Pang's response reveals his mastery not only of the elegant language of cultural discourse, but also of social discourse. Even though Pang is actually asserting that Gu's abilities reach only to the task of shaping contemporary morality, while he himself is one who possesses transcendent insight into the workings of rulership, he allows Gu to save face by casting the evaluation in seemingly equivalent terms.

Pang's evaluation of Gu does not reflect the *Shangshu*'s conception of *zhiren*, or even the way in which that term is described in the Yang Lang anecdote. Pang is neither evaluating Gu for a political office nor primarily interested in the way that Gu's abilities can be translated into service. Rather, his pronouncement addresses the persons of Pang and Gu in terms of what each of them is truly like, describing something that goes beyond the utilitarian considerations of talent. Here one is reminded of how scholars such as Donald Holzman and Yü Ying-shih have cast the period following the collapse of the Han dynasty as one marking the emergence of freely expressed individualism.[17] Indeed, it is the *Shishuo xinyu*, with its anecdotes of recluses and eccentrics, that is often taken as illustrative of this new emphasis on the individual. However, I would argue that the collection is less interested in the representation of the individual than in the representation of a kind of "public sphere." By invoking this phrase, I do not mean the kind of broadly construed space of public debate that functions as a counter to political authority, which would certainly be anachronistic for this period.[18] Rather, I intend a more modest space of discursive exchange governed by counter-conventional behavior, evaluations of personal character, and displays of wit. Here, status becomes defined not only by political position, economic basis, or family lineage, but also—and in some ways, more significantly—by one's personal reputation.

It is this aspect of personhood, shaped in the community of public opinion and talk, that becomes the paramount concern within the world of the *Shishuo xinyu*, since one must constantly assert and maintain one's place within the network of one's peers. Hence, one finds anecdotes such as the following:

> When the age evaluated Wen Qiao, he was ranked the highest of the second grade of men who crossed the Yangtze. When the famous fellows of the time came together to talk about personalities and were just about to finish with the first grade, Wen would always turn pale.
> 世論溫太真，是過江第二流之高者。時名輩共說人物，第一將盡之閒，溫常失色。[19]

Wen Qiao 溫嶠 (288–329) was a noted military commander and a prominent political figure in the Eastern Jin. Though he held high official position and rank during his time, the anecdote points to the anxiety and fear that could be generated through the kinds of evaluations that determined the true social rankings among the "famous fellows" (*mingbei* 名輩) of the age. These arbiters of personal reputation were the *mingshi* 名士 ("gentlemen of repute"), and in many ways, they came to represent a new societal locus of power, one that overlapped with already-existing political hierarchies but was not entirely defined by political influence.

Thus, when these famous gentlemen discuss and count down the men of first rank, Wen Qiao hopes to hear his own name spoken, but as the list comes to its end, he turns pale—and this is something that the gathered worthies notice—as he realizes that once again he will only be first on the list of the *second* rank.

FROM "KNOWING MEN" TO "BEING KNOWN"

From these anecdotes, it should be clear that speech and conversation are crucial both to the act of "knowing men" and to the production of personal fame. In the latter part of this chapter, I would like to focus on one figure in the *Shishuo xinyu* who is represented as being famous for his ability to "know men." This is Chu Pou 褚裒 (303–49), a person who is renowned for his laconic nature:

> Meng Jia of Wuchang served on the provincial staff of Grand Defender Yu Liang, and at that time was already famous.[20] Grand Tutor Chu Pou had clarity of mind in knowing men.[21] After Chu quit his post in Yuzhang and returned to the capital, he passed by Wuchang, where he asked Yu, saying, "I have heard that Meng has excellent qualities. Is he present or not?" Yu said, "You should find him by yourself." Chu cast his eyes back and forth for a good long while, then pointed to Jia, saying, "This gentlemen is slightly different from the others—did I get him or not?" Yu laughed loudly and said, "You're right!" At this time, not only did he sigh over how Chu possessed silent discernment, but was also pleased that Jia had been recognized and appreciated.
>
> 武昌孟嘉作庾太尉州從事，已知名。褚太傅有知人鑒，罷豫章還，過武昌，問庾曰：「聞孟從事佳，今在此不?」庾云：「卿自求之。」褚眄睞良久，指嘉曰：「此君小異，得無是乎?」庾大笑曰：「然!」于時既歎褚之默識，又欣嘉之見賞。[22]

Of the three figures mentioned in the anecdote, only two—Chu Pou and Yu Liang—are fully in the frame of the narrative. Meng Jia 孟嘉 (296–349), who is the ostensible subject of the conversation, is himself silent. If it were not for the indexical gesture of Chu Pou, who points to him, Meng Jia would almost seem invisible in the anecdotal scene. In fact, Meng Jia's near-invisibility is felt in the official historical record as well, where his brief *Jinshu* 晉書 (History of the Jin dynasty) biography consists of a retelling of the *Shishuo xinyu* anecdote and several other anecdotes (one about a feast during which Meng Jia's hat gets blown away without his noticing; the other about a prolonged bathroom break by

Meng Jia that is noticed by everyone at the feast). What is foregrounded is thus Chu Pou's performance of "knowing men," rather than the object singled out in the act of knowing.

One of the striking aspects of Chu Pou's performance is that it takes place by means of a visual examination of Yu Liang's subordinates and staff. The only reason that Chu gives for his identification of Meng Jia is that Meng seems "slightly different" (*xiao yi* 小異) from the others present. While the visual inspection might suggest a phrenological approach, there is nothing in the anecdote to suggest that Chu has seized upon extraordinary or abnormal physical features. Rather, that to which the anecdote is drawing our attention is the absence of an expected *verbal* exchange, one that would have demonstrated Meng's talents in the public medium of speech. This is underlined when Yu Liang praises Chu for his "silent discernment" (*moshi* 默識), to Chu Pou's celebrated abstention from speech—a quality that recalled Confucius, who both encouraged humility in scholarship and was suspicious of rhetorical facileness. Indeed, Chu Pou's silence resonates in complex ways with the silence of Confucius. By demonstrating his knowledge without recourse to speech, there can be heard a conscious echo of a passage from the *Analects*, where Confucius is recorded as saying, "To be silent and yet know it, to study and yet not be satisfied, to instruct others yet not tire of it—which of these can be said of me?" 默而識之, 學而不厭, 誨人不倦, 何有於我哉.²³

Moreover, Chu is first introduced in the *Shishuo xinyu* in the following passage: "Xie Taifu utterly esteemed Master Chu and always said, 'Though Chu Jiye does not speak, the airs of the four seasons nonetheless are complete'" 謝太傅絕重褚公, 常稱「褚季野雖不言, 而四時之氣亦備。」²⁴ This statement of praise by Xie An 謝安 (320–85) is meant to allude to another passage in the *Analects*, which reads:

> The Master said, "I would desire not to speak." Zigong said, "If the Master did not speak, then what would your disciples transmit?"
> The Master said, "In what way does Heaven speak? The four seasons pass in turn, and the hundred things arise. In what way does Heaven speak?"
> 子曰:「予欲無言。」子貢曰:「子如不言, 則小子何述焉?」子曰:「天何言哉? 四時行焉, 百物生焉。天何言哉?」²⁵

Spoken words, like a person's life, may be ephemeral, but the act of memorizing and recording them guarantees that the example of Confucius will live on in the teachings of his disciples. The Master's comment here cuts against the very nature of the *Lunyu*—a text whose purpose is to transmit (*shu* 述) a record of speech (*yu* 語) by an exemplary figure. Of course, by saying that he does not want to speak, Confucius apophatically creates an occasion for speech, one that claims to deny that which it simultaneously seems to solicit. He may seek to be like Heaven, which does not speak but nonetheless acts to bring all into completion, but his remarking of not wanting to speak is itself the instigation for speech. While Chu Pou does not talk about not wanting to talk, his silence is nevertheless only remembered because it is remarked upon by others: in the first anecdote, by Yu Liang, and in the second, by Xie An. In the end, language becomes the means by which Chu is made known, in a record of speech—the *Shishuo xinyu*—not unlike that of Confucius and his disciples.

The tension between language and silence for Chu Pou may be the reason why he—the one who "knows men"—is himself not recognized in two anecdotes in the collection. The first of these examples is from the chapter entitled "On Elegant Dignity" ("Yaliang" 雅量):

> When His Honor Chu Pou was transferred from the post of Zhang'an District Magistrate to Secretarial Aide on the staff of the Grand Defender [Yu Liang], his name was already illustrious, though his position slight. Other people for the most part did not recognize him. When Chu left for the east, he took a trader's boat and was seen off by a handful of his former colleagues. When they reached Qiantang Prefecture, they lodged for the night at an inn. At that time in Wuxing, Shen Chong was Prefectural Magistrate and was engaged in seeing off a guest across the Zhe River. When they showed up, the innkeeper bustled Chu off, moving him into the ox shed.
>
> When the tidal bore came in, Magistrate Shen stood up and paced back and forth. He asked, "Who is that person in the ox shed?" The innkeeper said, "Yesterday there was a Northern oaf who came to stay at the inn. Because I had you esteemed and honored guests, I temporarily moved him." The magistrate was a little drunk, and so he called out from a distance, "Northern oaf, want to eat some biscuits? What's your surname? We can talk together." Chu then raised his hand and responded, saying, "I am Chu Jiye from Henan." From far and wide, all had long venerated His Honor's name. Because of this, the magistrate was greatly panicked, and not daring [again] to move His Honor, accordingly went to the ox shed and presented his calling card. Moreover, he had the ox slaughtered as an accompanying dish for the wine, and had the innkeeper whipped before His Honor, wanting by this to express his deep embarrassment. His Honor drank and feasted with him, showing no alteration in either word or demeanor, his behavior as if unaware of the circumstances. The magistrate saw His Honor off to the borders of the prefecture.

褚公於章安令遷太尉記室參軍,名字已顯而位微,人未多識。公東出,乘
估客船,送故吏數人,投錢唐亭住。爾時吳興沈充為縣令,當送客過浙
江,客出,亭吏驅公移牛屋下。
潮水至,沈令起彷徨,問:「牛屋下是何物人?」吏云:「昨有一傖父,來寄
亭中,有尊貴客,權移之。」令有酒色,因遙問:「傖父欲食餅不?姓何等?
可共語。」褚因舉手答曰:「河南,褚季野。」遠近久承公名,令於是大遽,
不敢移公,便於牛屋下修刺詣公。更宰殺為饌具,於公前鞭撻亭吏,欲以
謝慚。公與之酌宴,言色無異,狀如不覺。令送公至界。[26]

The placement of this anecdote in the "Elegant Dignity" chapter speaks to Chu's equanimity in face of the innkeeper's insulting treatment and misrecognition. It is, however, not only the lowly innkeeper who fails to recognize Chu Pou. The anecdote explicitly notes that while his name was already well known, people (that is to say, the social elites) "for the most part, did not recognize him." It is this set of circumstances that plays out in the exchange between Shen Chong 沈充 (d. 324) and Chu Pou. Shen Chong, whose own reputation would become intertwined with that of the rebellious Wang Dun, at first thinks Chu Pou is just a "Northern oaf" (*cangfu* 傖父). Once Shen Chong finds out who it is that had been kicked out of the inn to make room for him and his guest, however, he hurriedly strives to make amends. Naturally, throughout the belated toadying and horsewhipping, Chu Pou acts as if nothing is out of the ordinary.

The other anecdote about the nonrecognition of Chu Pou appears in the chapter entitled "On Condescension and Calumny" ("Qing di" 輕詆), and it can be taken as the ironic version of the prior anecdote. It reads:

> When Grand Tutor Chu first crossed the Yangtze, he once entered into the east [here, referring to Wu], arriving at Jingchang Pavilion. The grandees of Wuzhong were gathered at a feast in the pavilion. Though His Honor Chu heretofore had a weighty reputation [*ming*], at this time he was traveling in haste, and no one recognized him. Thus, the host ordered the servants to give him more tea-water and fewer servings of rice-dumplings. When he finished his tea, they would then pour more, not permitting him, in the end, to eat. When Chu finished drinking, he idly raised his hand and told all present, "I am Chu Jiye!" At this, all seated were thrown into shock and confusion, and not a single person did not feel distress.[27]

褚太傅初渡江,嘗入東,至金昌亭,吳中豪右燕集亭中。褚公雖素有重名,
于時造次不相識別,敕左右多與茗汁,少箸粽,汁盡輒益,使終不得食。
褚公飲訖,徐舉手共語云:「褚季野!」於是四坐驚散,無不狼狽。[28]

Unlike the previous anecdote, there is no initial opportunity for speech or conversation; the host is busy with his guests and takes no notice of the eminent traveler in their midst. Chu Pou is not given an opportunity to make himself known, and thus has to resort to announcing himself to the assembled banquet-goers. Thus, when Chu once again raises his hand and tells his name, this gesture no longer seems to stem from a natural exchange of names between two people meeting for the first time, but reads rather as a calculated effort to claim the respect that is owed to him. His name is, of course, known to the banquet-goers, and the resulting clamor, as the party realizes how they have insulted a gentleman of repute, is born from the failure of the social network to acknowledge one of its own.

In the case of Chu Pou, we see how the act of *zhiren* ("knowing men") becomes bound up with that of *zhiming* 知名 (both "knowing names" and "being known"). Shen Chong, a Southerner, recognizes Chu Pou's name and is thus able to perform the appropriate acts of penance, thereby earning a place within the commemorating anecdote. However, the innkeeper has no such place within the network. Like the ox, the innkeeper turns out to be a mere object, to be a thing upon which punishment is visited, and not a speaking subject who has a place within the discursive network. This relationship between knowing men and knowing names is already suggested in the earlier anecdote about Chu Pou's silent identification of Meng Jia. After all, Chu had heard of Meng, who "was already famous" 已知名. Unlike Yang Lang in the first anecdote, Chu does not pluck a talented man from obscurity, but rather demonstrates how he can identify a talented person, knowing that one is already present on the scene. I would suggest that the Yang Lang mode of knowing men speaks to the practice of *zhiren* as described in early imperial political thought, where the purpose is precisely to identify and make use of talent from the indistinct masses, whereas the mode represented in the Chu Pou anecdotes indicates a different interest, one focused on recognition within the defined network of social relationships that stands at the heart of the *Shishuo xinyu*. The *Shishuo* insists on illustrating the discursive nature of the social network, on how those knowledgeable of names within the network are able to create relationships with one another.

CONCLUSION: NAMES AND NETWORKS

Names and talk of names circulate throughout the space of a social community more easily than people do. It costs a flesh-and-blood person time and money to move through space, and the fact of the body limits circulation to a single point and a single duration within that space. Talk is, by contrast, cheap, or at least, less expensive, since it can occur simultaneously at multiple points within a defined space.²⁹ I would here like to suggest that the circulation of gossip along the network points of a community is precisely that which constitutes the network. Further, I would like to supplement this with the observation that a person's name can be circulated in the same way as an anecdote or a piece of gossip, since both forms of knowledge define the discursive network. Thus, not only does the innkeeper not recognize Chu Pou physically, he would never have heard Chu's name. By contrast, while Magistrate Shen Chong may not have had the chance to meet Chu, he would certainly have heard his name. A knowledge of names is what allows a member of a community to map out the relationships that define the true workings of the community's networks. If one does not know any names, then there is no entrance point into the network. Names become the currency of the network's economy, the means by which one may enter into and negotiate the space of a social community. However, the space of the social community is not given in every moment, but is established and reestablished through the invocation of the community. Language is required to activate the network, even if that enunciation is merely the speaking of one's name.

Let me end here with one further quotation from Confucius, who said, "I am anxious not that other people do not know me, but rather that I do not know other people" 不患人之不己知, 患不知人也.³⁰ To be known is to have one's person recognized in the common sphere, in the shared space of a community. This is, for Confucius, a moral concern, one that would replace the self-interest underlying the archaic economy of mutual recognition, with a disinterested appreciation of other men's talents and capacities. Anxiety over the failure of recognition, however, pervades the statement, both in Confucius's uncertainty over whether he will succeed in "knowing men" and in the implied admission that he himself has not been recognized—which is perhaps the very reason why he might make such a statement in the first place. Yet while Confucius can claim not to care whether he is himself known, the question of personal fame (*zhiming*) is crucial to the personages of the *Shishuo xinyu*. These figures are defined as *mingshi*, gentlemen of repute, and the anecdotes of the collection serve both as occasional reflections of their contemporary fame and as the very means by which their fame is constituted.

NOTES

1. On the topic of *mingshi*, see Ning Jiayu 寧稼雨, *Wei Jin mingshi fengliu* 魏晉名士風流 (Beijing: Zhonghua shuju, 2007).

2. The "former thearchs" refer to Yao 堯 and Shun 舜.

3. Huan Dou 驩兜 was the untrustworthy minister of Yao who first recommended the arch-rebel Gong Gong 共工 to help quell flooding during Yao's reign. After Shun took the throne, Huan Dou was exiled to the south. The Youmiao 有苗 (or Sanmiao 三苗) were represented as historical enemies of the ancient Chinese. The last point refers to the arch-rebel Gong Gong. These are three of the "Four Villains" (Sixiong 四凶) of high antiquity, and they are all related to ancient flood narratives. See Mark Edward Lewis, *The Flood Myths of Early China* (Albany: State University of New York Press, 2006), 53–60.

4. See *Shangshu zhengyi* 尚書正義, 4.26b, in Ruan Yuan 阮元 (1764–1849), ed., *Shisanjing zhushu fu jiaokanji* 十三經注疏附校勘記 (Beijing: Zhonghua shuju, 1980), 138. This chapter belongs to the "Old Text" (*guwen* 古文) chapters of the *Shangshu*. As Edward L. Shaughnessy points out, this chapter is considered to date from the fourth century BCE at the earliest. See Shaughnessy, "Shang shu 尚書 (Shu ching 書經)," in *Early Chinese Texts: A Bibliographic Guide*, ed. Michael Loewe (Berkeley: Society for the Study of Early China and The Institute of East Asian Studies, University of California, Berkeley, 1993), 377–78.

5. See Wang Xianqian 王先謙, ed., *Xunzi jijie* 荀子集解 (Beijing: Zhonghua shuju, 1988), 19.27.504.

6. On the concept of *wuwei* in early Chinese thought, see Edward Slingerland, *Effortless Action: Wu-wei as Conceptual Metaphor and Spiritual Ideal in Early China* (New York: Oxford University Press, 2007).

7. Lü Buwei 呂不韋 (d. 235 BCE), *Lüshi chunqiu xinjiaoshi* 呂氏春秋新校釋, ed. Chen Qiyou 陳奇猷 (Shanghai: Shanghai guji chubanshe, 2002), 3.4.162.

8. *Lüshi chunqiu xinjiaoshi*, 3.4.162–63.

9. This is the translation of the title in J. K. Shryock, *The Study of Human Abilities: The Jen wu chih of Liu Shao* (New Haven: American Oriental Society, 1937). A more literal translation would be *A Treatise on Personalities*.

10. See Liu Shao, *Renwu zhi jiaojian* 人物志校箋, ed. Li Chongzhi 李崇智 (Chengdu: Ba Shu shushe, 2001), 1.

11. Also see the discussion of *Shishuo xinyu* in chapter 2 of this volume.

12. Liu Yiqing 劉義慶 (403–444), comp., *Shishuo xinyu jiaojian* 世說新語校箋, annot. Yang Yong 楊勇 (Beijing: Zhonghua shuju, 2006), 7.356.

13. This is noted in Richard B. Mather, trans., *Shih-shuo hsin-yü: A New Account of Tales of the World*, 2nd ed. (Ann Arbor: Center for Chinese Studies, University of Michigan, 2002), 215.

14. The phrase *yifu zhi yaohai* 倚伏之要害 refers to the following passage from the *Laozi Daodejing*: "Disaster is that upon which fortune relies; fortune is that in which disaster is concealed. Who can know the ultimate end of this?" 禍，福之所倚；福，禍之所伏。熟知其極？ See Zhu Qianzhi 朱謙之, ed., *Laozi jiaoshi* 老子校釋 (Beijing: Zhonghua shuju, 1984), 58.235.

15. *Shishuo xinyu jiaojian*, 9.447–48.

16. Li Wai-yee, "*Shishuo xinyu* and the Emergence of Aesthetic Self-Consciousness in the Chinese Tradition," in *Chinese Aesthetics: The Ordering*

of Literature, the Arts, and the Universe in the Six Dynasties, ed. Cai Zong-qi (Honolulu: University of Hawai'i Press, 2004), 237–76.

17. See Donald Holzman, "Les Septs Sages de Forêt des Bambous," *T'oung Pao* 44, nos. 4–5 (1956): 317–46; and Yü Ying-shih, "Individualism and the Neo-Taoist Movement in Wei-Chin China," in *Individualism and Holism: Studies in Confucian and Taoist Values*, ed. Donald J. Munro (Ann Arbor: Center for Chinese Studies, University of Michigan, 1985), 121–55.

18. On this, see Jürgen Habermas, *The Structural Transformation of the Public Sphere: An Inquiry into a Category of Bourgeois Society*, trans. Thomas Burger (Cambridge, Mass.: MIT Press, 1989); and Craig Calhoun, ed., *Habermas and the Public Sphere* (Cambridge, Mass.: MIT Press, 1992).

19. *Shishuo xinyu jiaojian*, 9.460–61.

20. For the biography of Meng Jia 孟嘉 (fl. 4th cent.), see Fang Xuanling 房玄齡 (579–648) et al., comps., *Jinshu* 晉書 (Beijing: Zhonghua shuju, 1974), 98.2580–81. Note that a good part of this is simply a retelling of the *Shishuo xinyu* anecdote. For the biography of Yu Liang 庾亮 (289–340), see *Jinshu*, 73.1915–24. Yu was brother-in-law of Jin Mingdi 晉明帝 (r. 323–25), and his clan dominated the court in the years following Mingdi's death. He is also discussed by Xiaofei Tian in chapter 2 of this volume.

21. For the biography of Chu Pou, see *Jinshu*, 93.2414–17. Chu was father-in-law of Jin Kangdi 晉康帝 (r. 343–44), and though he began by serving on Yu Liang's staff, he ended up (after Yu Liang's death) a member of the court faction opposed to the Yu clan.

22. *Shishuo xinyu jiaojian*, 7.359–60.

23. See *Lunyu* 論語 7.2, in Cheng Shude 程樹德, ed., *Lunyu jishi* 論語集釋 (Beijing: Zhonghua shuju, 1990), 13.436–39.

24. See *Shishuo xinyu jiaojian*, 1.33.

25. *Lunyu* 17.19, in *Lunyu jishi*, 35.1227.

26. *Shishuo xinyu jiaojian*, 6.326–27.

27. To "feel distress" here is *langbei* 狼狽, a phrase that literally refers to the wolf and its legendary cousin, the rather short forelegged *bei*, which must ride atop the wolf in order to travel.

28. *Shishuo xinyu jiaojian*, 26.743–44.

29. On the importance of conversation during this period, see Mou Runsun 牟潤孫, *Lun Wei Jin yilai zhi chongshang tanbian ji qi yingxiang* 論魏晉以來之崇尚談辯及其影響 (Hong Kong: Chinese University of Hong Kong Press, 1966).

30. *Lunyu* 1.16, in *Lunyu jishi*, 2.58.

4 Oral Sources and Written Accounts
Authority in Tang Tales
Sarah M. Allen

The world of eighth- and ninth-century classical tales is predominantly the world of the educated elite who were their recorders and audience. More consistently than in earlier eras, tales from this period focus on the adventures or misadventures of officeholders and aspirants, emperors and ministers. They record stories that members of this community—male, educated, and well-born—tell about their fellows and that travel well within the community. Many tales are about men who can still be identified today, and whom we may therefore presume were well known in their own time as well. For less recognizable figures, the opening found in numerous tales, with the protagonist identified by ancestral residence and his own status in officialdom as well as by name, allows readers to place him even if they do not know him personally or by reputation.[1] In short, these tales record gossip: allegedly true yet always slightly suspect stories that the gossiper tells about someone else within a community.[2]

The central question about any item of gossip is, of course, whether it is accurate. Despite the tales' claims to tell real stories about real people, the facts found in them are typically unverifiable. They deal with personal experience rather than matters of public record and are characterized most comprehensively by what Jack W. Chen has described as "the private and local perspective of the individual around whom the events unfold."[3] Where specific historical events are treated, it is through the lens of the individual's story. The consequence of this focus on the private perspective is that the information in the tales is necessarily private as well, impossible to authenticate beyond the eyewitness's claims. This is the case for tales about the court and capital as well as those about strange and inherently suspect material—ghosts, gods, animal spirits in human form, and other things whose modes of manifestation or very

71

existence were persistent matters of debate. Lies and exaggerations, not to speak of the evolution of a story over time, are all made easier when it is impossible to corroborate information through other sources.

The problem is vividly demonstrated by Chen Xuanyou's 陳玄祐 note at the end of his tale "The Severed Soul" ("Lihun ji" 離魂記), in which he recounts the circumstances under which he came to record the tale:

> [I,] Xuanyou, had often heard this story in my youth. There were many discrepancies, and some said it was fabricated. At the end of the Dali reign period [the late 770s], I met the District Magistrate of Laiwu,[4] Zhang Zhonggui, and he gave me a thorough account of the whole affair. [Zhang] Yi[5] was Zhonggui's uncle, and Zhonggui's [version of the] story was very complete and detailed, so I made a record of it.
>
> 玄祐少常聞此說, 而多異同, 或謂其虛。大曆末, 遇萊蕪縣令張仲規, 因備述其本末。鎰則仲規堂叔, 而說極備悉, 故記之。[6]

Chen Xuanyou's description evokes a practice of informal storytelling among friends that makes it easy to imagine how the details of such stories could evolve in the course of repeated tellings. His comments bring out two important problems in the evaluation of gossip, first among them the variation among multiple versions. In the absence of an authority that can compellingly claim access to the "real story," inconsistencies in different accounts leave the audience unable to determine which among the variations is correct. Such inconsistencies lead to the second problem, namely, suspicion that the story may be groundless. Instead of reading the repetition of the core story as evidence that it must possess some kernel of truth, the anonymous "some" (huo 或) referenced here suspect that all its permutations may be unsubstantiated. Their skepticism is understandable: "The Severed Soul" is about a woman (Zhang Yi's daughter) whose soul splits off from her body and lives independently of it for years, performing all the functions of the corporeal body down to bearing children (the ability to bring forth new life serving as proof that her approximated body truly functions as an ordinary one). Chen Xuanyou's answer to both of these problems is to assert that his own written version is derived from a credible source. Zhang Zhonggui both knows of the events in detail and, importantly, is the cousin of the woman in question. The implication is that he must have his facts right.

As Chen Xuanyou's remarks show, Tang writers and readers were keenly aware of the instability inherent in the circulation of information and texts in a medieval world where every act of reproduction, whether oral or written, held the potential for change. Christopher M. B. Nugent has recently demonstrated that composers of poetry and their audiences accepted a greater degree of fluidity in poetic transmission as a matter of course than is tolerated in our own print- and electronic information–centered world.[7] Concerns regarding changes introduced into tales in the course of transmission are somewhat different from those for poetry, since there is no evidence that word-for-word transmission was necessarily expected.[8] Rather the issue is discrepancies in the details and "facts" reported in different versions. Yet in texts purporting to convey information about past events—in which questions of truth and falsity play a different role from that which they play in poetry—the possibility of error was also potentially more troubling.

"The Severed Soul" deals with a private matter, a remarkable event that unfolds within the confines of one family and for which the recorder makes no broader claims; but in specifically illustrating the problems that conflicting information posed for a writer, it demonstrates both the uncertainties facing any writer trying to determine the worth of the gossip he has heard, and the importance to this particular recorder of getting the story right. In the remainder of this chapter I examine a set of three tales that, like "The Severed Soul," pointedly address the epistemological reliability of their content, but in which the stakes are higher because they deal with the much weightier matters of history and the evaluation of officials. Such tales are arguably the most gossipy within the tale corpus, because they bear on the subject's standing in the official world and also because they tend to involve the high and mighty, figures who are well known independent of whatever a tale might say about them. It is when the private story touches on the subject's public life and public evaluation that the problem of verification is especially pressing.

All three of the tales that are my focus here seek to establish the authority of their version of a set of events in the face of competing alternative accounts. And like "The Severed Soul," in all three the tale's recorder appeals to information, most often orally transmitted, from a reliable source close to the events to bolster his claims for a tale's superiority to other versions of the events. The tales use private information to refute public knowledge and the historical record, either implicitly or explicitly privileging the oral and proximate over written records, and suggesting that the commonly accepted version of events is corrupt.

"YAO HONG"

Because "The Severed Soul" deals with a private matter concerning one woman and her husband, the consequences of small alterations in the story are slight. Much more is at stake when a tale takes on the weight of recorded history. An entry from the ninth-century collection *Yishi* 逸史 (Uncollected histories) constructs an alternative to the orthodox version of history that has been handed down for centuries.[9] The tale "Yao Hong" 姚泓 recounts the experience of a monk during the reign of Tang Taizong, in the seventh century. The nameless monk receives an unexpected visit from a strange creature who walks like a man and has a face like a man's, but is covered in green feathers. The monk suspects he may be some species of owl, but the creature makes a claim that is possibly even more improbable: he says that he is Yao Hong, the last ruler of the short-lived Later Qin 後秦 in the early fifth century.[10] The conversation between the monk and Yao Hong continues:

> The monk said, "I've read the history of the Jin,[11] and it says that Yao Hong was arrested by Liu Yu,[12] who moved the Yao clan to Jiangnan and executed Hong in the Jiankang marketplace. According to what they record, then, Hong is dead. How can you go and claim you're Yao Hong today?"
>
> Hong said, "At that time, my state was indeed obliterated by [Liu] Yu, who took me to the Jiankang marketplace to proclaim [it] to the world. Who knew that before I got to the execution [grounds], I escaped and went into hiding? Yu hunted for me but didn't get me, so he took someone who looked like me and executed him, in order to establish his renown and show off to his descendants. I really am the true Yao Hong."
>
> The monk then invited [Yao Hong] to sit, saying to him, "How could it be that the account in the histories is groundless?" Hong laughed and said, "Monk, surely you've heard of Liu An, the Prince of Huainan, in the Han? In reality he rose to transcendence, yet Sima Qian and Ban Gu state that he was executed for treason. How could the untruths in the Han histories be greater than those in later histories? This is proof that historians tell lies."
>
> 僧曰：「吾覽晉史，言姚泓為劉裕所執，遷姚宗于江南，而斬泓於建康市。據其所記，泓則死矣。何至今日，子復稱為姚泓耶？」
>
> 泓曰：「當爾之時，我國實為裕所滅，送我於建康市，以徇天下。奈何未及肆刑，我乃脫身逃匿？裕既求我不得，遂假一人貌類我者，斬之，以立威聲，示其後耳。我則實泓之本身也。」
>
> 僧因留坐，語之曰：「史之說豈虛言哉！」泓笑曰：「和尚豈不聞漢有淮南

王劉安乎?其實昇仙,而遷、固狀以叛逆伏誅。漢史之妄,豈復逾於後史耶?斯則史氏妄言之證也。」[13]

"Yao Hong" revolves around the tension between the authority of the written text and that of the oral eyewitness account. The monk's naive assumption that what is written in the history books must be correct is laughed away by Yao Hong, who presents himself, in the flesh, as the true authority on the past by virtue of the fact that he lived through it—in this case literally, by surviving when the historians have pronounced him dead. The *Jinshu* 晉書 (History of the Jin dynasty), does indeed recount Yao Hong's death at Liu Yu's hands;[14] by Yao Hong's telling, the historians have fallen for the claims of the victor Liu Yu, whose attempt to "proclaim to the world" his defeat of Yao Hong is an uncontested success as the only version of history handed down to posterity. The monk's unquestioning belief in the words of recorded history only underscores how effective Liu Yu's manipulation of popular perceptions of what happened in the Jiankang marketplace was. The lesson Yao Hong imparts is reminiscent of Mencius's injunction that "it would be better to not have the [*Esteemed*] *Documents* than to believe the *Documents* completely" 盡信書則不如無書.[15] In another tale about a relict of an earlier dynasty, the interest might lie in the fact that someone had lived so long. But in "Yao Hong," the monk never marvels at Yao Hong's advanced age (though he does ask about the green feathers); rather what makes Yao Hong's assertion of his identity so shocking is that it goes against the written and widely believed account of what happened. If even Sima Qian's *Shiji* 史記 (Records of the historian) and Ban Gu's *Hanshu* 漢書 (History of the Han dynasty), the two foundational models for dynastic history writing, contain inaccuracies, how can readers hope that later (implicitly lesser) histories are completely accurate? Nor is Yao Hong's escape the only omission from the historical record:

> [Yao] then recounted the affairs of the Jin and Song for the monk, and it was as if he were pointing to them in the palm of his hand. There were other things that the historians had omitted and not written about, and Hong spoke of all of them in detail.
> 仍為僧陳晉宋歷代之事,如指諸掌。更有史氏闕而不書者,泓悉備言之。[16]

The tale's conceit is that a constructed historical account can never be as authoritative as the information of a Yao Hong, who saw the events for himself. Whether the historians themselves lie outright (as Yao Hong's use of *wangyan* 妄言 hints they might) or are simply victims of their incomplete or inaccurate sources, erroneous information spreads as a result. The limited viewpoint of personal observation is valued above the broader but indirect secondary knowledge derived from the historian's textual research.

"SHANGQING"

"Yao Hong" was likely written some five hundred years after the supposed execution of Yao Hong and two hundred years after the composition of the *Jin shu* account. That the historians might have misconstrued the truth is perhaps understandable given the gap between the events and the composition of their history. And since Yao Hong does not deny his defeat or suggest that the Later Qin lingered on past his supposed death, his continued existence contrary to his official biography is in a larger sense immaterial in the construction of the history of his period. At worst it makes Liu Yu look like a liar for having proclaimed Yao Hong's death, but otherwise it does not impact the interpretation of the past.

Other tales from the same period deal with events of the Tang itself, thus predating the completion of the final Tang histories, though not some of the court documents on which the histories would be based.[17] Liu Cheng's 柳珵 "Shangqing" 上清 takes place during the early 790s.[18] Like "Yao Hong," the tale highlights the ease with which powerful figures can mislead the public and obscure the truth, and again the truth is brought out through the oral testimony of an eyewitness. In this case, however, the contested point, the guilt or innocence of a former minister, would have been a much more gripping issue to a contemporary audience.[19] Shangqing is the intimate maid of Grand Councilor Dou Shen 竇參 (ca. 733–92), who, according to this tale, was framed by his rival Lu Zhi 陸贄 (754–805).[20] When Shangqing discovers an assassin (sent by Lu Zhi) hiding in a tree in the courtyard, Dou Shen foresees his own downfall, saying:

> Lu Zhi has wanted to snatch my powerful position for a long time. This person in the tree today—it means disaster is upon me. And whether or not I report this matter, I'll meet disaster. I'm sure to be driven into exile and die on the road. There aren't many like you among your kind. When I'm dead and my family destroyed, you are certain to become a palace maid. If the emperor inquires, explain this for me well.
> 陸贄久欲傾奪吾權位。今有人在庭樹上，即吾禍之將至矣。且此事將奏與不奏，皆受禍。必竄死於道路。汝於輩流中不可多得。吾身死家破，汝定為宮婢。聖居如顧問，善為我辭焉。[21]

Events unfold as Dou Shen predicted: when an Investigation Commissioner[22] sends up a memorial detailing complaints against him, Dou Shen is ordered to commit suicide and his property confiscated. Shangqing's opportunity to speak to the emperor comes four years later, when Emperor Dezong 德宗 (r. 780–804) asks her how she had come to be in the palace and she explains that she had been a slave in Dou Shen's household.

> Dezong said, "Dou Shen's crime wasn't just harboring assassins—he also took many bribes at the same time, and in the past his [purloined] tax grain and government silver was considerable." In tears, Shangqing said, "Ever since Dou Shen was Vice Censor-in-Chief and received the posts of Commissioner of the Ministry of Revenue, the Census Bureau, and the Salt Monopoly, up until he was Grand Councilor—six years altogether—each month he took in several hundred thousand, and the largesse he received at odd times throughout also knew no limits. The tax grain and silver sent in by Chenzhou that time had all been an imperial gift.[23] On the day the Ministry recorded it, I was in Chenzhou and I personally saw the prefectural and district officials cut [the markings] off completely, hoping for Lu Zhi's favor. They carved the titles and names of local officials on the silver that was presented, deceptively making it [seem to be] illicit goods. I beg you to send down [an order] to investigate this."
>
> Dezong then ordered that the silver confiscated from Dou Shen be brought. He turned [the silver] over and looked at where the characters were cut away, and it was all as Shangqing had said. At that time it was Zhenyuan 12 [796]. Dezong also asked about the matter of harboring assassins, and Shangqing said, "Originally in fact there were none; this was all Lu Zhi's trap—he had someone pretend to be an assassin." At this, Dezong was greatly enlightened [as to the truth about these matters] . . .
>
> 德宗曰：「竇參之罪，不止養俠刺，兼亦甚有贓污，前時納官銀器至多。」上清流涕而言曰：「竇參自御史中丞，歷度支戶部監鐵三使，至宰相，首尾六年，月入數十萬，前後非時賞賜，當亦不知紀極。迺者彬州送所納官銀器，皆是恩賜。當部錄日，妾在彬州，親見州縣希陸贄恩旨，盡刮去。所進銀器上刻藩鎮官銜姓名，誣為贓物。伏乞下驗之。」
>
> 於是宣索竇參沒官銀器。覆視其刮字處，皆如上清之言。時貞元十二年。德宗又問養俠刺事。上清曰：「本實無，此悉是陸贄陷害。使人為之。」德宗至是大悟 . . .[24]

The emperor exonerates Dou Shen and upbraids Lu Zhi, and the incident marks the beginning of Lu Zhi's own decline from favor.[25]

As in "Yao Hong," the information recounted in the tale provides a private perspective on public affairs, in this case the relationship between two prominent officials publically known to dislike each other. Dou Shen's perception of his own helplessness against Lu Zhi's machinations highlights the inadequacy of official information channels. He recognizes immediately that his only hope for exoneration lies in the possibility that Shangqing may in time be able to use a private interview with Dezong to explain the truth, which she knows through her own personal connection with Dou Shen. (Indeed, when Dou Shen himself attempts to explain that the crimes of which he seems guilty are "the doing of his enemies" 仇家所為耳, he is told to go home and wait for instructions, and is ultimately exiled.)[26] When that moment finally comes, Shangqing's account gains force from her declaration that she "personally saw" (*qinjian* 親見) the deceptions perpetrated against Dou Shen: her story is not secondhand rumor, but fact. Shangqing's oral testimony is set against the written memorial that led to Dou Shen's suicide order, which is not quoted in the tale but which the emperor presumably summarizes in the charges he cites in his conversation with Shangqing. If we turn to the surviving historical record, both *Han Yu's* 韓愈 (768–824) *Shunzong shilu* 順宗實錄 (Veritable record of Shunzong's reign), roughly contemporaneous to "Shangqing" itself, and *Jiu Tangshu* 舊唐書 (Old history of the Tang dynasty) do indeed reference a memorial presented by Dou Shen's enemy Li Xun 李巽, Surveillance Commissioner of Hunan 湖南觀察使, as leading to Dou's downfall.[27] Shangqing's information allows Dezong to reinterpret the evidence that had previously seemed to point to Dou Shen's guilt as proof that he was a victim. Her assertion that the assassins were part of a ploy by Lu Zhi then persuades the emperor fully.

The emperor is the pivotal figure whose knowledge and beliefs matter, and the use of "greatly enlightened" 大悟 to describe his reaction to Shangqing's words suggests a recognition of truth: he sees that it is her version of events that is real. Her evident inability to act until Dezong asks (four years after Shangqing sees the assassin in the tree) accentuates the difficulties of bringing the truth home to an emperor under the sway of biased advisors. Even after Dezong has learned the truth, Lu Zhi's influence is enough to keep the real story from reaching a wider public: the account ends with the comment that "since many of Lu Zhi's protégés were prominent in that era, [this information] couldn't be circulated at the time, and so no one knows of this matter" 世以陸贄門生名位多顯達者, 世不可傳說, 故此事絕無人知.[28] The tale stands as a corrective to the image of Dou Shen presented by Lu Zhi, a vehicle for a truth that political factionalizing has forced underground.[29]

Dou Shen and especially Lu Zhi were very prominent men in their time. It is likely that the enmity between the two would have been well known when "Shangqing" was written, just as it is highlighted in the two men's biographies in the *Jiu Tangshu*, *Xin Tangshu* 新唐書 (New history of the Tang dynasty), and in *Zizhi tongjian* 資治通鑑 (Comprehensive mirror for aid in governance). In all three of those histories the evaluation of Lu Zhi is positive, and Dou Shen's correspondingly negative, suggesting that the court documents that were the later historians' source material indicated similar opinions.[30] Although Dezong's alleged eventual change of heart regarding Dou Shen and the details of Dou's innocence related in "Shangqing" are not found anywhere other than in this tale, Han Yu's *Veritable Record* does note that "analysts often said Shen's death was caused by Zhi" 議者多言參死由贄焉.[31] But in the years and even decades immediately following Dou Shen's and Lu Zhi's deaths, their relative merits and faults may well have been less firmly fixed in popular evaluation than they became later, though "Shangqing" itself, by noting that "no one knew" that Lu Zhi had framed Dou Shen, implies that Lu Zhi may have had the better reputation. "Shangqing" draws on the authority of the oral eyewitness account to nudge readers in the direction of suspicions that Lu Zhi had a hand in Dou's death.

"THE ANCIENT INSCRIPTION FROM THE LIANG DATONG PERIOD"

Both "Yao Hong" and "Shangqing" rely entirely on private, eyewitness accounts to counter the authority of the written records they dispute. In the last tale I will discuss, the recorder's quest to confirm his story leads him to both oral and written sources. "The Ancient Inscription from the Liang Datong Period" ("Liang Datong guming ji" 梁大同古銘記) is a narrative of how oral hearsay is turned into a substantiated written record. More than either "Yao Hong" or "Shangqing," it is about a deliberate search for the truth and an effort to preserve information before it is lost forever. The dense tale recounts how the statesman Li Jifu 李吉甫 (758–814) reconstructed the details of the eighth-century scholar Zheng Qinyue's 鄭欽悅 decoding of a Han dynasty inscription that had been unearthed during the Liang and had mystified scholars ever since.[32] The tale, internally attributed to Li Jifu himself, is divided into three sections. First are two letters: one to Zheng Qinyue from Ren Shengzhi 任升之, whose ancestor discovered the inscription, asking for help deciphering it, and Zheng Qinyue's response, in which he interprets the inscription. The final section includes Li Jifu's "account" (*ji* 記) of how he learned about the events and his "discussion" (*lun* 論) of why he recorded them.

The "account" tells us that Li Jifu first heard of Zheng from his kinsman Xun 巽, who mentioned him in passing as a man whose story is already in danger of disappearing:

> Zheng Qinyue, former Right Reminder and Auxiliary Academician in the Academy of Scholarly Worthies, had a keen comprehension of prognostication, and his understanding penetrated abstruse mysteries. Why, the monk Yixing was no match for him.[33] Because of setbacks [in his career] at the time, you don't hear his name much.
>
> 故右補闕集賢殿直學士鄭欽悅, 於術數研精, 思通玄奧。蓋僧一行所不逮。以其天閼當世, 名不甚聞。

Li Jifu then traces his own process of investigation into Zheng's story, beginning by asking Xun "How can you prove that?" 凡何以覈諸.[34] Xun's "proof," the story of how Zheng deciphered the inscription, includes good detail but remains thirdhand information at best, not yet substantiated by an informant who is truly proximate to the events themselves or other evidence of its truth.

Li Jifu's opportunity to confirm the story comes some time later, when he finds himself serving with Zheng's son Kejun 克鈞: he tells us that he "repeatedly checked Xun's story with him [Zheng Kejun]" 數以巽之說質焉 and it "mostly matched what he said" 且符其言.[35] Yet unlike the tales discussed earlier, in which the events can be adequately represented by the (oral or written) narrative that recounts them, here the story is incomplete. Zheng Qinyue's deed cannot be proven or fully appreciated without Zheng's letter itself and the solution to the inscription's riddle, which Zheng Kejun has lost. This letter, which with Ren Shengzhi's letter appears first in "The Ancient Inscription," is the last piece of the puzzle Li Jifu obtains, discovering it in the private possession of a divination specialist in Mingzhou 明洲 (modern Ningbo 寧波). Only after finding the letter can Li Jifu truly appreciate Zheng's accomplishment and complete his account.

In this case the error in the record that Li Jifu sets out to correct is an omission rather than a lie. His discussion, which cites several examples of worthy men who did not achieve the status they deserved, sets out to redress two failures of justice: first, that Zheng was barred from the ranks of great ministers or imperial advisors because he was denied the opportunity to perform the services he would have been capable of within the government; and second, that in death he has been denied the reputation he deserved. The discussion concludes by elaborating on the "setbacks" mentioned by Xun and describing his own reasons for writing the tale down:

> From [the post of] Right Reminder Qinyue swiftly [rose to] assume the duties of Palace Censor. He was hated by then-minister Li Linfu, so he was cast out and did not become prominent. Thus I have related what I heard about him, and appended it after the two documents [i.e., Ren Shengzhi's and Zheng Qinyue's letters], to make clear the divine insight of divination, the perspicacity of intelligence, and the fatedness of marvelous coincidences, to present it to interested persons that later scholars may marvel at it. Recorded by Li Jifu of Zhao Commandery on the twenty-eighth day of the eleventh month of the ninth year of the Zhenyuan reign period [January 4, 794].
>
> 欽悅尋自右補闕歷殿中侍御史。為時宰李林甫所惡，斥擯於外，不顯其身。故余敘其所聞，係於二篇之後，以著蓍筮之神明，聰哲之懸解，奇偶之有數，貽諸好事，為後學之奇玩焉。 時貞元九年十一月二十八日趙郡李吉甫記。[36]

Again we have a case in which a prominent person has prevented knowledge from circulating. Zheng Qinyue is forced into obscurity and his qualities—perhaps most importantly, the learning and intelligence implied by his ability to crack the divination's code—remain uncelebrated and underutilized by the state. History proper has let Zheng Qinyue fall into obscurity, leaving his achievements unrecorded, and it is only the information obtained orally that can rectify that. Even though what the tale celebrates is Zheng Qinyue's trenchant powers of scholarly analysis and his skill at interpreting texts, written texts have ultimately failed him. Li Jifu writes his record to remedy that failure.[37]

Text and oral account work together here to provide the full story and final proof of Zheng Qinyue's erudition. Without the letter we only have a learned man whom few have heard of; without Xun's details we have no protagonist and no real story. Although Li Jifu resorts to a textual artifact as his final corroboration, it is the oral narratives he hears from Xun and from Qinyue's son that contextualize and give Zheng Qinyue's tale its interest, along with the hint of tragedy at the thought of the talented man blocked from success by the evil minister Li Linfu 李林甫 (d. 753).

CONCLUSION

In all of these tales we find an interest in bringing to light a truth that has remained hidden. These truths are discovered and authenticated through personal connections to events, which reveal information more reliable than a commonly believed alternative. The tales are thus predicated on an acknowledgement of the inherent instability of information, which a good—i.e., proximate—informant can correct. The problem is that when the informant is gone, so is the information. The privileged knowledge provided in these tales is almost always presented as having been conveyed orally, giving it immediacy but also impermanence: Yao Hong disappears, and Shangqing's knowledge and Zheng Qinyue's capabilities are suppressed. The recipient of the information therefore leaves behind a written record, in Li Jifu's words, to "relate what I heard . . . to present it to interested persons that later scholars may wonder at it" and to stake his claim to having the real story. But with each remove from the source comes a diminishing of the story's authenticity. Perhaps it is in an attempt to re-create in the reader the conviction that comes of hearing the oral recitation that Chen Xuanyou and Li Jifu either replicate or describe the experience of hearing the stories orally, in their earnest accounts of how they heard their stories from reliable sources with close connections to the events, or the long passages of quoted speech from the source him- or herself in "Shangqing" and "Yao Hong" (as well as "Ancient Inscription").

In none of these tales do we find the suggestion that the historian's research tools could excavate information that might elude or preempt the limited viewpoint of the individual observer. We can easily imagine the argument going the other way: that human memory is fickle, and the written source more reliable. But instead the citations of oral sources are used to bolster the immediacy, and hence accuracy, of the writer's sources rather than to acknowledge the possibility of distortion through shaky memories unaided by a written text.[38] Assessed through the formal historiographer's lens, the sort of material found in such tales was frequently found wanting, and we are accustomed to thinking of them as marginal, neither true history nor true literature.[39] Collections of anecdotal material were most often characterized either as supplements to official history (if their topic was chiefly the doings of human society) or as dealing with a different sort of material entirely (if they dealt significantly with events in which the supernatural played a role). But "Yao Hong," "Shangqing," "Ancient Inscription," and other tales like them ask us to read them as meaningful alternatives to orthodox history as it had been or was being formulated.[40] Collectively, such tales make an argument for the importance of gossip as information that would otherwise be forgotten or suppressed. Accepted public knowledge is wrong; gossip, recorded in these accounts, becomes a vehicle for truths that would not otherwise be remembered.

Whether or not we are persuaded, however, is another matter. We have no reason to doubt Li Jifu's account of Zheng Qinyue's erudition, but we may easily suspect Yao Hong's long life and sprouting of green feathers or (on different grounds) "Shangqing's" defense of Dou Shen. By setting themselves up against established truths, these tales simultaneously invite our skepticism. And as Stephen Owen points out in his postface to this volume, belief per se is not really the point. The tales would be less interesting if we unquestioningly accepted them at face value; their pleasure lies in entertaining the possibility that they may be true, even if ultimately we cannot believe them.

NOTES

1. For example, "Music from the Underworld" ("Mingyin ji" 冥音記) begins, "Li Kan, Commandant of Lujiang, was from Longxi" 廬江尉李侃者, 隴西人也. In Li Fang 李昉 (925–96), ed., *Taiping guangji* 太平廣記 (Beijing: Zhonghua shuju, 1961), 489.4021.

2. Although Tang tales (frequently classed under the rubric of *xiaoshuo* 小說 in bibliographies since the Song) have often been identified as the beginnings of Chinese "fiction" (*xiaoshuo* 小說, in modern Chinese) in scholarship of the last century, the evidence suggests that the prevailing assumption among writers and readers of tales in the Tang was that tales were supposed be read as "true stories"—though of course, as with any "true story" making the rounds, a given tale might simultaneously contain healthy doses of invention and distortion mixed in with the alleged facts.

3. Jack W. Chen, "Blank Spaces and Secret Histories: Questions of Historiographic Epistemology in Medieval China," *Journal of Asian Studies* 69, no. 4 (Nov. 2010): 38. Also see Andrew H. Plaks's discussion of historiography and fiction in the Chinese tradition in "Towards a Critical Theory of Chinese Narrative," in *Chinese Narrative: Critical and Theoretical Essays*, ed. Andrew H. Plaks, (Princeton: Princeton University Press, 1977), 318 and passim.

4. Laiwu 萊蕪 is in modern Shandong province.

5. Zhang Yi 張鎰 is the father of the tale's main female character.

6. See *Taiping guangji*, 358.2832, under the title "Wang Zhou" 王宙.

7. See Christopher M. B. Nugent, *Manifest in Words, Written on Paper: Producing and Circulating Poetry in Tang Dynasty China* (Cambridge, Mass.: Harvard University Asia Center, 2010).

8. A strong sense of authorship and concomitant integrity of detail and wording for stories appears to have developed only gradually, probably not beginning until the ninth century, and even then had only a limited sphere of applicability.

9. *Yishi* is attributed to Lu Zhao 盧肇 (ca. 821–ca. 879). For more on the history and contents of the collection, see Li Jianguo 李劍國, *Tang Wudai*

zhiguai chuanqi xulu 唐五代志怪傳奇敘錄 (Tianjin: Nankai daxue chubanshe, 1998), 2:670–92.

10. The Later Qin (384–417) was one of the Sixteen Kingdoms that ruled northern China in the fourth and fifth centuries, encompassing a shifting body of territory around Chang'an; Yao Hong reigned from 416 to 417.

11. The history of the Later Qin (which existed when the Eastern Jin ruled the south) is included in the *Jinshu* 晉書.

12. Liu Yu 劉裕 (356–422) was a military leader under the Eastern Jin who eventually rose up against the Jin and in 420 founded his own Song 宋 dynasty, which ruled southeast China for almost 60 years, ending in 479.

13. *Taiping guangji*, 29.189–190.

14. Fang Xuanling 房玄齡 (579–648) et al., comps., *Jinshu* (Beijing: Zhonghua shuju, 1974), 119.3017.

15. Jiao Xun 焦循, ed., *Mengzi zhengyi* 孟子正義 (Beijing: Zhonghua shuju, 1987), 28.959.

16. *Taiping guangji*, 29.190.

17. See Denis C. Twitchett, *The Writing of Official History Under the T'ang* (Cambridge: Cambridge University Press, 1992), 33–187, for a detailed description of the process by which official history was compiled during the Tang.

18. *Taiping guangji*, 275.2168–69, citing *Yiwen ji*. The tale is also preserved nearly verbatim in Sima Guang's 司馬光 (1019–86) *kaoyi* 考異 ("corrected discrepancies") to his *Zizhi tongjian* 資治通鑑 as "Liu Cheng's 'Account of Shangqing'" 柳珵上清傳 (Beijing: Zhonghua shuju, 1956), 234.7529–30. A slightly abridged but textually very similar version is found in Wang Dang 王讜 (fl. 1101–10), *Tang yulin jiaozheng* 唐語林校證, ed. Zhou Xunchu 周勛初 (Beijing: Zhonghua shuju), 1987, 6.542. For further discussion of the tale's authorship and the surviving texts, see Li Jianguo, *Xulu*, 1:421–23.

19. Li Jianguo dates "Shangqing" to the Yuanhe reign period (806–21), a decade or more after the events of the story, but soon after the story's villain, Lu Zhi, was rehabilitated by Shunzong following Dezong's death. See Li Jianguo, *Xulu*, 1:422.

20. Dou Shen was Grand Councilor under Emperor Dezong 德宗 (r. 779–805) from 789 to 792. Lu Zhi had a long and rich career at court. He entered the Hanlin Academy in 779 and quickly become a close personal advisor to Dezong, and was Grand Councilor (succeeding Dou Shen) from 792 until he fell from favor in early 795. See Liu Xu 劉昫 (887–946), comp., *Jiu Tangshu* 舊唐書 (Beijing: Zhonghua shuju, 1975), 136.3745–48 (Dou Shen); 139.3791–3819 (Lu Zhi); 139.3800–801, 3816–17 (for Lu's relations with Dou Shen); Ouyang Xiu 歐陽修 (1007–72) and Song Qi 宋祁 (998–1061), comps., *Xin Tangshu* 新唐書 (Beijing: Zhonghua shuju, 1975), 145.4730–32 (Dou Shen). Twitchett also discusses the ill-will between Lu Zhi and Dou Shen in his "Lu Chih (754–805): Imperial Adviser and Court Official," in Arthur F. Wright and Denis Twitchett, eds., *Confucian Personalities* (Stanford: Stanford University Press, 1962), 104–5, 119.

21. *Taiping guangji*, 275.2168. In the penultimate sentence in the previous quotation *Zizhi tongjian kaoyi* gives the easier reading *sheng jun* 聖君 instead of *Taiping guangji*'s *sheng ju* 聖居 (*Zizhi tongjian*, 234.7529).

22. As Hucker notes, Investigation Commissioner (*lianshi* 廉使) was an informal term for a Surveillance Commissioner (*guancha shi* 觀察使); see Charles O. Hucker, *A Dictionary of Official Titles in Imperial China* (Stanford: Stanford University Press, 1985), 312.

23. According to both Tang histories, the last position Dou Shen held was as Administrative Aide to Chenzhou 郴州別駕, a post he held only briefly before being further demoted to Huanzhou 驩州. The order to kill himself arrived before he had reached Huanzhou and taken up his position (*Jiu Tangshu*, 136.3747; *Xin Tangshu*, 145.4731). Shangqing is describing the confiscation of Dou Shen's Chenzhou possessions, which had (erroneously, according to Shangqing) evidently been reported to the throne as tax money wrongly appropriated by Dou Shen. The *Taiping guangji* text gives "Binzhou" 彬州 here instead of "Chenzhou" 郴州 (275.2169), but *Zizhi tongjian* has "Chenzhou," which should be correct (234.7530).

24. *Taiping guangji*, 275.2169.

25. "Shangqing" dates Lu Zhi's fall to 796 (Zhenyuan 12), though other evidence suggests that he was demoted in January of 795 (late Zhenyuan 10)—suggesting either misinformation on Liu Cheng's part or a transcription error at some point. See *Zizhi tongjian*, 235.7565.

26. *Taiping guangji*, 275.2168.

27. See *Jiu Tangshu*, 139.3817; and Han Yu, *Shunzong shilu*, in Ma Qichang 馬其昶, ed., *Han Changli wenji jiaozhu, waiji* 韓昌黎文集校注外集 (Shanghai: Shanghai guji chuban she, 1987), 2.713–14. The latter is translated in Bernard S. Solomon, *The Veritable Record of the T'ang Emperor Shun-tsung* (Cambridge, Mass.: Harvard University Press, 1955), 38–39. Han Yu's "veritable record" was presented in 815. Several versions of the *shilu* for Shunzong's reign are believed to have been compiled, and it is not clear which the extant version represents. See Twitchett, *Official History*, 145–51; and Solomon's introduction to his translation, xvi–xxiii.

28. *Taiping guangji*, 275.2169.

29. The distortion of the historical record due to politics was a very real danger in the mind of the Tang historiographer Liu Zhiji 劉知幾 (661–721), who in his *Shitong* 史通 (Generalities on history) complains about historians bending to pressure from the powerful. See, for example, "Direct Writing" ("Zhishu" 直書) and "At Odds with the Times" ("Wushi" 忤時), in *Shitong tongshi* 史通通釋, ed. Pu Qilong 浦起龍 (Taipei: Yiwen yinshuguan, 1978), 7.178–79, 20.542. The latter chapter is translated in Williams Hung, "A T'ang Historiographer's Letter of Resignation," *Harvard Journal of Asiatic Studies* 29 (1969): 5–52.

30. Sima Guang indignantly notes that "Lu Zhi was a worthy minister—how would he be willing to do this? And if he *had* wanted to trap Shen, his means were many indeed—why would he engage in such a puerile game? It

makes absolutely no sense" 陸贄賢相, 安肯為此! 就使欲陷參, 其術故多, 豈肯為此兒戲! 全不近人情 (*Zizhi tongjian*, 234.7530). More recently Li Jianguo has noted evidence that Liu Cheng was close to members of Dou Shen's faction, in his *Xulu*, 1:423.

31. *Han Changli wenji, waiji*, 2.714. *Jiu Tangshu* similarly records that "Opinion at the time said that . . . when Shen died, Zhi had a hand in it" 時議云 . . . 參之死, 贄有力焉 (139.3817).

32. This tale is found under the title "Zheng Qinyue" 鄭欽悅 in *Taiping guangji*, 391.3127–29. The longer title is found in the *Xin Tangshu* bibliography (60.1623), which also gives Li Jifu as the author. For more on the tale's history and Li Jifu, see Li Jianguo, *Xulu*, 1:274–76.

33. The historical Yixing (683–727) was a monk known for his erudition; the Yixing of legend is credited with thaumaturgical displays of many sorts at the court of Tang Xuanzong 唐玄宗 (r. 712–56). See, for example, *Taiping guangji*, 92.608–10, 136.974–75, 140.1009, 149.1072, 215.1647–48, 228.1749, and 396.3164. If Zheng was still more capable, he would have been a valuable person indeed.

34. *Taiping guangji*, 391.3128.

35. Ibid., 391.3128–29.

36. Ibid., 391.3129.

37. It is probably thanks to Li Jifu that Zheng Qinyue has a brief biography in *Xin Tangshu*. The biography consists chiefly of a summary account of Zheng's solving of the inscription riddle, with quotations from Ren Shengzhi's and Zheng Qinyue's letters as they appear in Li Jifu's account. See *Xin Tangshu*, 200.5704.

38. In fact one prominent example that does explicitly cite a written source is one in which we can see clearly the fallibility of memory. This is "Nun Miaoji" ("Ni Miaoji" 尼妙寂) by Li Fuyan 李復言 (fl. ca. 831), in *Taiping guangji*, 128.906–8. There Li Fuyan cites as his source Li Gongzuo's 李公佐 prior account of the same story in "Account of Xie Xiao'e" ("Xie Xiao'e zhuan" 謝小娥傳); see *Taiping guangji*, 491.4030–32. But while Li Fuyan's version preserves the gist of Li Gongzuo's story, many other details are altered (such as the names of all persons in the story except for Li Gongzuo himself).

39. See Chen, "Blank Spaces and Secret Histories," 17–21 for a discussion of premodern Chinese views of the role of anecdotal material within official historiography.

40. Another story germane to this point, but impossible to discuss at length here, is "Divine Pronouncement" ("Shengao lu" 神告錄), included in *Taiping guangji*, 297.2362–63 under the title "Master Danqiu" ("Danqiuzi" 丹丘子). The story, set about midway through the Sui dynasty at the turn of the seventh century, describes an interview between the first Tang emperor, Gaozu 高祖 (r. 618–26), and a mysterious man named "Master Danqiu" 丹丘先生, whom Gaozu has been told is his chief rival as the founder of the dynasty that will succeed the Sui. In the story Gaozu is ambitious, decisive, and eager to make his place as the emperor of a new dynasty. The "Basic

Annals" ("Benji" 本紀) of *Jiu Tangshu* (1.1–20, 2.21–38) and *Xin Tangshu* (1.1–21, 2.23–49), by contrast, all depict Gaozu's son Taizong 太宗 (r. 626–49), the second Tang emperor, as the real mastermind of the rebellion which led to the Sui's fall. These narratives, especially those of the two dynastic histories, derived ultimately from the veritable records of Gaozu's and Taizong's reigns. See Twitchett, *Official History*, especially 124 n. 13, 198–200, and 239. A private history written in the 620s, *Da Tang chuangye qiju zhu* 大唐創業起居注 (Court journal of the founding of the Great Tang) by Wen Daya 溫大雅 (ca. 572–629), however, also presents Gaozu as the true founder. "Divine Pronouncement" thus takes part in a contemporary debate regarding Gaozu's real place in the establishment of the Tang.

5 I Read They Said He Sang What He Wrote

Orality, Writing, and Gossip in Tang Poetry Anecdotes

Graham Sanders

If one believes even a part of what one reads in Tang dynasty collections of anecdotes as reflecting actual practice, then the notion of gossip was closely intertwined with the composition, performance, and appreciation of poetry among members of the Tang social elite in casual social settings. When the literati gathered over drinks and food in the entertainment quarters, in each other's homes and villas, during their travels, at inns and temples, on boats, the conversation often turned to details of who composed a certain poem, under what circumstances, for what audience, and what happened when it was received. Or new poems would be composed during these gatherings as a form of literary repartee, often with a satirical edge. Thus, the poems themselves were a vehicle for gossip, sometimes because a person was depicted in the poem, but more often because a certain type of poem was attributed to a person. Attribution is very important in these anecdotes, as what is said about a poem is really a statement about the kind of person who would compose it. Gossip could also focus on how a certain person appreciated or interpreted a poem, another marker of their character. Once an attribution is asserted and accepted, a poem is always construed as a reliable indicator of the character of the person behind it, making poetry a privileged form of truth-telling in a world full of hearsay and secondhand accounts. Poetry is also a powerful means of preserving memories in a form that is easily memorized, preserved, and transmitted to later ages through speech and writing.

The content of gossip is meant to affect the social status of the person or group of people being talked about, either to denigrate it or to enhance it. Gossiping is an entertaining pastime that also serves to strengthen the social bond among the friends who share the gossip. The gossiper seeks to elevate his or her own social status by citing a privileged "inside" source for his or her information, which is usually transmitted orally in its initial stages, and traces its origin back to someone with access to the person being targeted in the gossip. The link back to the target of the gossip is tenuous and, once broken, gossip can still circulate simply as something that "people say" and that one has "heard somewhere."

The natural vehicle for transmitting gossip in casual social gatherings is the oral recounting of anecdotes, which make an easy transition onto and off of the written page. Gossip can just be a bald statement of the "facts," but it usually takes the form of a narrative supporting the facts. (It is more satisfying to tell and hear the story of the affair than to simply state it happened.) The Greek root for the English word anecdote, *anekdota*, simply means "things unpublished," while the various Chinese terms that can be rendered as "anecdote" in English include a strong connotation of something heard from another person: *yiwen* 逸/軼聞 ("uncollected hearsay"); *yishi* 逸/軼事 ("uncollected matters"); *yiwen* 遺聞 ("remnant hearsay"); *wenji* 聞記 ("records of hearsay"); and *chuanwen* 傳聞 ("relayed hearsay"). The prevalence of the character *wen* 聞 in these examples denoting something "heard by the ear" suggests that the border between the written and the oral in Tang manuscript culture was extremely fluid.[1] The wider connotation of the word can cover things that are "known" through a combination of written and oral sources. The use of the specific words *shi* 事 ("event or affair") and *ji* 記 ("record") in these examples, however, suggests a more stable form of source, closer to the written end of the spectrum of knowledge transmission. But even these words can include oral sources that capture the "event" in question and "record" them in the memory. The compound *wenji* 聞記 (literally, "a record of something heard") neatly includes both the oral and written ends of the spectrum of anecdotes. The anecdote as a transmissible form of knowledge told through a story can easily shift from being told, to being written, and back to being told again. It is the context of a written anecdote—the source in which it appears and how that source is classified by later bibliographers—that dictates whether an anecdote is read as gossip or history.

However, the status of an anecdote as knowledge transmitted by word of mouth is so strong even in its written form that it often appears within a frame story, which depicts the conversation through which the anecdote is told and heard. Even in the absence of the framing device, the narrator of an anecdote might close by citing an oral source and appending his moral evaluation and/or emotional reaction to the story, thus casting himself as a proxy for the listener in the context of casual storytelling.

One interesting result of the easy conflation of written and oral sources in the transmission of anecdotes is that it allows them to cover a broad temporal range. Frame stories for anecdotes often depict them being told in a conversation that ranges across topics "ancient and contemporary" (*gujin* 古今). One is just as likely to hear gossip about a profligate emperor who lived centuries before as the latest juicy tidbits from the capital today. Gossip, then, relies not so much on a temporal immediacy as it does on proximity to privileged knowledge, whatever (and whenever) the source. Ambrose Bierce, in *The Devil's Dictionary*, famously defined a historian as a "broad-gauge gossip."[2] By that token, the literati of the Tang who gathered to tell stories and chant poems they had heard and read are fashioning a kind of oral history, one that is enriched by and enriches the whole range of historical writing. The poem holds a special place in this form of oral history for, as a purported first-person lyrical utterance, it promises to be as proximate as possible to its subject. If a poem is viewed as "articulating what is intently upon the mind" of the person who uttered it (*shi yan zhi* 詩言志),[3] then it is the ultimate stuff of gossip, for it is a privileged source of information granting immediate access to the interior of the person being discussed. Once a poem is completed by its author and enters the world of discourse circulating as gossip, however, it embarks on a long road of multiple iterations in oral and written form, subject to variation, misinterpretation, and misattribution.

Paul Ricoeur uses the term *distanciation* to describe the effect of a written text becoming more distant from its time, place, and context of production. As it moves out into the world, "writing tears itself free of the limits of face-to-face dialogue" and becomes "autonomous in relation to the speaker's intention, to its reception by its original audience, and to the economic, social and cultural circumstances of its production."[4] The appeal to eyewitness sources made so frequently in anecdotes is an attempt to arrest the effects of *distanciation* through the use of a narrative voice that claims to be in close proximity to the people and events being depicted. A written account, despite extreme *distanciation*, despite traveling across thousands of miles, over a thousand years, to a distant, unrelated culture, can still be read as a vivid anecdote because the moment of narration is close in space and time to the events and peopled described in it.

Yet, despite the claim to proximity maintained by anecdotes, they were routinely regarded with suspicion because of their status as a form of "unofficial history" (*yeshi* 野史), not only by later compilers who drew upon these materials, but also by the original compilers of anecdotal collections, who constantly apologize in their prefaces for spending time and energy gathering these sorts of "trivial matters" (*suoshi* 瑣事) and assure their readers that they have vetted these materials using the highest standards of veracity and morality. There is a tension between proximity and reliability; proximity holds out the promise of increased veracity, but only if we trust in the compiler as a judge of that veracity. There is a sense that for anecdotes to be converted into official history, they must be digested over a long span of time (often through multiple sources) and filtered through an editorial apparatus (often a state-sponsored one) to glean the reliable accounts from the fanciful or debased ones.[5]

Anecdote collections were compiled by individuals from all levels of Tang officialdom (some were outside of it altogether), working in a variety of capacities, including within the Historiography Institute (*shiguan* 史館) itself.[6] One Tang anecdote collection, *Yunxi youyi* 雲谿友議 (Friendly conversations at Cloudy Creek), was compiled by an obscure "recluse scholar" (*chushi* 處士) from the Suzhou region named Fan Shu 范攄 (fl. 877). Fan Shu lived at Auspicious Clouds Creek (Wuyunxi 五雲谿, an alternate name for Ruoyexi 若耶溪), and took the sobriquet Man of Auspicious Clouds Creek (Wuyunxiren 五雲谿人). He wandered among the mountains and rivers and never held an official post; the only evidence of when he lived is mentioned in the text of *Yunxi youyi* itself, and in a poem mourning his death by Li Xianyong 李咸用 (fl. 873).

The relative obscurity of Fan Shu might explain the ambivalence shown by the eighteenth-century editors of the *Siku quanshu zongmu tiyao* 四庫全書總目提要 (Annotated catalogue of the Imperial Library) toward *Yunxi youyi*, which they classify as "miscellaneous accounts" (*zashi* 雜事) under the "petty discourse" (*xiaoshuo* 小說) category. They grudgingly acknowledge the collection's value as a documentary source for Tang poetry and estimate that seventy to eighty percent of the sixty-five entries in the collection belong to the "remarks on poetry" (*shihua* 詩話) genre, characterizing the collection as:

> ... extraneous accounts of trivial matters, which are still somewhat worthy of transmission. Moreover, because these are Tang people speaking of Tang poetry and what was witnessed with their own eyes and ears, they are necessarily closer [to those events] than people who came afterward. Therefore, those investigating Tang poetry, such as Ji Yougong in his *Anecdotes of Tang Poetry* and other books of this sort, often rely on it as a source of evidence.

逸篇瑣事，頗賴以傳。又以唐人說唐詩，耳目所接，終較後人為近。 故考
唐詩者，如計有功《紀事》諸書，往往據之以為證焉。[7]

The *Siku* editors acknowledge that, even though they cannot vouch for the reliability of these anecdotes, their proximity to the Tang counts for something.

There are hundreds of anecdotes in Tang collections that depict poetry being chanted and/or written in the context of gossiping about someone. It is impossible to pick one representative piece, but there is a particularly rich example in *Yunxi youyi* that happens to be the very entry that gives us a clue as to where and when Fan Shu was active. Given the title "The Kindness of the River Traveler" ("Jiangke ren" 江客仁) in some editions, the anecdote first appears in *Yunxi youyi*, showing up later with slight variations in *Tangshi jishi* 唐詩紀事 (Anecdotes of Tang poetry), compiled by Ji Yougong 計有功 (*jinshi* 1121), and in *Tang caizi zhuan* 唐才子傳 (Biographies of talented Tang poets) by Xin Wenfang 辛文房 (fl. 1300).[8]

The account opens with Li She 李涉, who was appointed as an Erudite in the School for Sons of State during the Taihe reign of Emperor Wenzong (827–35), as he is paying a visit to his younger brother Li Bo 李渤 (773–831) at Mount Lu 廬山 in the Jiujiang region of modern-day Jiangxi province. As Li She is addressed by the title of Erudite at the time of the visit, he would be approximately sixty years old and have already established a reputation for his poetry. As young men the two brothers studied in reclusion at White Deer Cave (Bailudong 白鹿洞) on Mount Lu, so the visit is a homecoming of sorts.[9] Before taking his leave, Li She gives everything that he has with him—save for some rice, kindling, and books—to the hermits of Mount Lu, thus proving that he is a man of culture, who cares not for wealth, but only for physical and mental sustenance. On his journey home, outside of Huankou 浣口, he is accosted by a group of armed bandits, but the leader, upon finding out that his intended victim is Li She, says: "If this really is Erudite Li She, then my men and I need not plunder his gold and silks. Long have I heard of his reputation as a poet. I only hope for a single poem from him; next to that, gold and silk are worthless to me" 若是李涉博士，吾輩不須剝他金帛。自聞詩名日久，但希一篇，金帛非貴也. The bandit thus proves himself to be a "cultured bandit" (*yadao* 雅盜) who appreciates the value of literary over material capital. Note that the bandit claims he has "heard" (*wen* 聞) of Li She's "reputation as a poet" (*shiming* 詩名), suggesting that Li's fame is so great that word of it has spread even to the criminal elements of society. What the bandit is requesting, a poem from Li She's own hand, is much like a celebrity autograph: tangible proof that one has met a famous person face-to-face. Li She acquiesces and presents a poem to the bandit, who shows his appreciation by hosting a lavish banquet for him, giving Li She the chance to observe that the bandit is indeed a man of "extraordinary demeanor and impeccable principles" 神情復異, 而義氣備焉. In fact, Li She is so taken with him that he wants to recommend him for official service, in imitation of Lu Ji's 陸機 (261–303) promotion of the robber Dai Yuan 戴淵 (271–322) during the Eastern Jin dynasty.[10] He arranges to meet the robber at a temple in Yangzhou in order to normalize this "cultured bandit" and bring him into polite society. There is a form of compensation going on here as the bandit's appreciation of Li She's poetry (shipin 詩品) is repaid by Li's appreciation of the bandit's character (renpin 人品).

The narrative of the anecdote to this point provides an enjoyable, if somewhat fanciful, account of the intersection between the world of the elite official and the underworld of the lowly criminal. But the point of intersection, the very poem that the bandit demanded from Li as payment, is withheld by the narrator for the time being. Instead, the narrative follows Li to Yangzhou, where he searches in vain for the bandit in every temple, only to meet up with a woman named Song Tai 宋態, who was a concubine of one of Li She's old friends from years earlier, Liu Quanbai 劉全白 (fl. 791). As the bandit is nowhere to be found, Li ends up writing two poems for Song Tai 宋態 filled with reminiscences of her at his friend's banquets decades earlier. Li She presents these poems to Song Tai in the same way he gave a poem to the bandit in lieu of gold and silk. Unlike that poem, however, these are quoted immediately by the narrator, revealing themselves to be less about Song Tai herself and more about memories and the passage of time in Li She's own life:

當憶雲仙至小時,	I remember when the Cloud Fairy was so young,
芙蓉頭上綰青絲。	lotus blossoms wound in raven tresses atop her head.
當時驚覺高唐夢,	I suddenly wake from that dream of Gaotang,
唯有如今宋玉知。	all that is left now is what Song Yu knew.
陵陽夜燕使君筵,	Performing "Lingyang" at night banquets by your lord's mat:
解語花枝在眼前。	you were a speaking blossom before our very eyes.
自從明月西沉海,	Since then the bright moon has sunk westward into the sea,
不見姮娥二十年。	and I have not seen the Lady of the Moon for twenty years.

A poem is the vehicle by which past experience, or more precisely, the memory of past experience, can be made literary and thus be fixed in a form that bears performance, appreciation, and transmission. In figuring Song Tai as the Maiden of Wu Mountain who appeared to the King of Chu, or as Emperor Xuanzong's 玄宗 (r. 712–56) famed consort Yang Guifei 楊貴妃 (719–56), or as the Lady of the Moon, Li She treats her as a literary character in the story of his past, a story that is called to mind and configured as a past because of his chance encounter in the present with the aged woman in the flesh. The contrast between past and present is summed up poignantly in the closing couplet of the first poem, in which Li She juxtaposes a dream-like past with a present in which one can only recall the past through memory and storytelling. And just as the Lady of the Moon was transformed from a human being into an immortal, so too is Song Tai made immortal through these poems. Poetry allows timeless myth into the temporal space of the moment of poetic performance, permitting the time-ravaged body to be recast in eternal literary images. The poem itself is not timeless, but operates at the interface between the temporal and atemporal. The alchemy of poetry converts the mundane event of bumping into an old friend into something that is worthy of retelling, first as gossip perhaps, but later as a story worth recording in a written anecdote. The poems themselves were likely uttered aloud by Li She when he composed them, but he also would have kept a written copies of them that may very well have circulated on their own.[11]

Immediately after composing these poems, Li She is struck with melancholy at the fact that his old friend, Liu Quanbai, is no longer alive to share the poems with. He sighs heavily and says to himself, "I did not meet the bandit leader, but encountered Song Tai instead. I have achieved the happiness of a lifetime; my only regret is that I cannot speak of it with my old friend!" 不見豪首,而逢宋態。成終身之喜,恨無言於知舊歟. What good are poems if your friends are not around to hear them? The reader may begin to suspect that Li She, in his twilight years, wanted to reform the bandit as a last grand gesture of magnanimity. Instead, he ended up meeting a figure from his past who reminded him of friends no longer there.

At this point in the narrative, the single character *hou* 後 ("later") draws the first anecdote to a close with the sentence, "Later, when Provincial Graduate Li Huizheng of Fanyu was traveling in the south" 後番禺舉子李彙征、客遊於閩越, bringing the reader forward almost five decades to a time when Li She is no longer alive and has himself become a figure to be evoked in stories told by others. During his travels, the young examination candidate, Li Huizheng, encounters heavy rains, which force him to take shelter in the home of an octogenarian who leans on a cane and introduces himself as Rustic Wei Siming 野人韋思明. The stage is then set for trading gossip during casual conversation:

> [Wei] engaged in discussion with Scholar Li about matters literary and historical, keeping him there until evening. Huizheng was an excellent conversationalist, but he was unable to outdo the old man. Over wine they called forth topics ancient and contemporary until they eventually came to a discussion of poetry.
> 與李生談論，或文或史，淹留累夕，彙征善談而不能屈也。對酒徵古今及詩語.

The old rustic and the young sophisticated scholar start with a drinking game known as *jiuling* 酒令, in which the players chant extemporaneously composed couplets back and forth until someone fails to come up with one and must take a drink as forfeit. Wei Siming starts off the game in a somewhat refined manner, quoting lines from old *yuefu* 樂府 ("Music Bureau") poems to paint Li Huizheng as a decadent youth: "The young dandies of Chang'an / bridle their white horses with yellow gold" 長安輕薄兒，白馬黃金羈.[12] Both age and class figure in Wei's gentle jab, which contrasts the sophisticated lifestyle of a young metropolitan examination candidate with the humble circumstances of an old man in the Southlands. Li Huizheng retorts with: "Yesterday, you were a handsome youth, / but today, you've become old and ugly" 昨日美少年，今日成老醜. This couplet seems somewhat crude when read against Old Man Wei's more literary and allusive opening.[13] Even this brief exchange of poetry is enough to upset the reader's expectations: it turns out that the old man of the countryside is quite elegant in his manners, while the young scholar from the city is a bit of a boor. Wei Siming himself implies as much when he heaves a great sigh and says, "Ah, to be ugly in old age and sneered at by a young man" 老其醜矣，少壯所嗤, pointing out the arrogance of a youth who does not yet feel the weight of age upon him even though it will surely arrive in time.

It is then Li Huizheng's turn to start the round, but he does not give up his line of attack, chanting: "White hair has a before and after, / but the green mountains are timeless" 白髮有前後，青山無古今. Perhaps in response to Wei's remark that he was "sneering," Li raises the tone of his couplet to something that sounds more like poetry and less like mockery. Behind these lines contrasting the limited temporality of human experience with the eternity of nature, one can hear the famous opening couplet from "Spring View" 春望 by Du Fu 杜甫 (712–70) on the sacking of Chang'an during the An Lushan rebellion in 757: "A kingdom smashed, mountains and rivers remain / a city enters springtime, plants and trees grow deep 國破山河在, 城春草木深.[14] (Du Fu also mentions his white hair at the end of the poem.) The young Scholar Li is showing that he can rise to the occasion of forging a poetic couplet when he needs to, but the subtext is still implying that the old man is a relic of a bygone age, soon to pass from this world. Wei smiles at the irony of Li's couplet, as neither of them will outlast the mountains. He points out: "White hair is not far off for a young licentiate such as yourself. Why show such disdain for an old fellow like me" 白髮不遠於秀才, 何忽於老夫耶! He then retorts with a couplet of his own: "This old man's white hair is truly to be pitied, / alas for the ruddy-faced handsome youth he once was" 此翁頭白真可憐, 惜伊紅顏美少年. This couplet echoes Li Huizheng's first retort with its colloquial tone and its contrast between youth and age. Whereas the young man's couplet crudely contrasted the "handsome youth" that Wei was with the "ugly old man" he became, in this couplet Old Man Wei asks for a bond of sympathy with the young man seated before him. The language may be colloquial, but Wei skillfully deploys the imagery of color, comparing the corporeal marker of age in his white hair with that of youth's rosy complexion.

The game is really just a prelude, a warm-up, for a serious discussion of poetry in which the two men go through dozens of poets, until they end up citing poems by Li She, a poet for whom Old Man Wei seems to have a particular affinity. The two of them take turns chanting five of Li She's well-known verses, thus bringing his memory to life by introducing his lyrical first-person voice into their physical presence.

Li Huizheng starts by chanting the following poem:

遠別秦城萬里遊,	I left the capital far behind in my endless wanderings,
亂山高下出商州。	up and down a jumble of mountain paths, I emerge at Shangzhou.
關門不鎖寒溪水,	The gates of the pass do not lock out the cold mountain stream,
一夜潺湲送客愁。	all night, its murmuring brings a traveler woe.

The poem immediately evokes the description in the first anecdote of Li She's travels decades earlier, but it also serves to capture Li Huizheng's own situation, traveling in the Southlands far away from the capital. The voice of Li She is revivified and reapplied to a new situation through its evocation by Li Huizheng. The two anecdotes are bound together by the common presence of Li She, as a physical presence in the first and as a voice in the second. Repeating Li She's poems is a form of gossip that serves to form a bond, between Li Huizheng and Wei Siming through their mutual appreciation of Li She's poetry, which provides them with insider's knowledge of his state of mind at particular times in his life. Through the chanting of his poetry, Li She is present as a third member of their gathering, speaking simultaneously in his own voice and prefiguring the sentiments of the men who chant his poetry.

Li Huizheng follows up with another famous poem attributed to Li She:

華表千年一鶴歸，	Atop the pillar a crane returns after a thousand years,
丹砂為頂雪為衣。	with a cap of cinnabar and a cape of snow.
泠泠仙語人聽盡，	The clear words of the immortal are heard to the end,
卻向五雲翻翅飛。	to auspicious clouds it flaps its wings in flight.

This poem alludes to a famous story—recounted in *Soushen houji* 搜神後記 (Later record of searching for spirits), a collection of supernatural anecdotes traditionally (and erroneously) attributed to Tao Yuanming 陶淵明 (365–427)—of a Daoist adept named Ding Lingwei 丁令威 who returns to his native Liaodong after a thousand years of study, during which time he has learned to transform himself into a crane. When he arrives as a crane at the city gates of Liaodong and perches atop a pillar there, a young boy tries to shoot him down with his bow. Ding Lingwei flies over the crowds of people and chants a poem lamenting how the populace has changed since he left, then soars straight up into the "auspicious clouds."[15] Once again, the poem can be read as the plaint of a traveler who returns home to find unfamiliar faces about him. This poem is problematic, however, in that it is also appears under the title "Pacing the Void Lyrics" ("Buxu ci" 步虛詞) in the collected poems of Liu Yuxi 劉禹錫 (772–842), where the second line reads "with a cap of solid cinnabar and a cape of snow" 凝丹為頂雪為衣 and third line, "The scattered words of the immortal are heard to the end" 星星仙語人聽盡.[16] A natural result of a mode of textual transmission that slips easily between the oral and the written is that multiple attributions and variations are introduced as the poem wends its way through time and among places. (Even the Qing dynasty compilers of *Quan Tangshi* 全唐詩 (Complete Tang poems) were willing to give Li She the benefit of the doubt, appending the untitled piece on to the end of his poems as a possible attribution.) What matters to Li Huizheng and Wei Siming is that they do not question the authenticity of the poem as an articulation of Li She's thoughts. Whether it was composed by Li She or by Liu Yuxi (or by someone else altogether) is a matter for the literary historians to sort out.

Old Man Wei matches the young candidate by chanting two more poems by Li She that amplify the theme of return after a long absence. In citing these poems, both men are at once flaunting their knowledge of Li She's poetry and, at the same time, forming a bond with one another as fellow connoisseurs. As far as the young Li Huizheng is concerned, they are just trading the poems of another old poet who is dead and gone. But the tenor of the evening changes when the young man decides to chant a poem of Li She's referred to by the narrator as "Given to a Bandit" ("Zeng haoke shi" 贈豪客詩). The narrator describes Wei's reaction:

> Old Man Wei's countenance suddenly turned very serious and he said of himself, "This old fellow was unworthy when he was young, roaming about the lakes and rivers up to no good. I associated with criminals and committed unjust acts. But then I met Erudite Li She, received this poem from him and mended my ways. Master Li treated me well and had it in mind to recommend me for service after the manner of Lu Ji recommending Dai Yuan into the House of Jin. But I went into reclusion far away in Luofu Mountain,[17] spending twelve years there. Since Master Li passed away, I have never gone roaming as a bandit again in the regions of Qin and Chu." He brooded over his past and present regrets until he became tearful. Then he picked up a flagon of wine and poured out a libation [to the memory of Li She]. Wiping the tears from his face with his sleeve, he sang out: "The spring rain hisses softly over the riverside village, / even a bandit of Wuling knows my reputation this night. / What use was it to hide away back in those days, / when half the world now is already like you?"[18]

> 韋叟愀然變色曰:「老身弱齡不肖,遊浪江湖,交結奸徒,為不平之事。後遇李涉博士,蒙簡此詩,因而跧跡。李公待愚,擬陸士衡之薦戴若思,共主晉室,中心藏焉。遠隱羅浮山,經於一紀。李即云亡,不復再遊秦楚。」追惋今昔,因乃潸然。或持觴而酹,反袂而歌云:「春雨蕭蕭江上村,五陵豪客夜知聞。他時不用相回避,世上如今半是君。」

Suddenly, with the revelation that Wei Siming is indeed the bandit who received a poem from Li She in the first anecdote, the old man's proximity to Li She has reached a new level. The bandit himself is the persistent physical link between the two anecdotes, just as the poem is the persistent literary link. The narrator is very careful in choosing the point in the narrative at which the poem is actually cited. It is kept from us at the moment of composition in the first anecdote, when Li She presents it to the bandit. It is even kept from us decades later when Li Huizheng recites the verse as one of his favorite Li She poems. When Wei Siming hears it again after such a long time, his mind is cast back decades earlier in his life. He gives an account of his original encounter with Li She, one that explains why he never showed up to meet his would-be patron in Yangzhou: the bandit chose to give up a life of crime and of politics to become a recluse instead. Finally, with tears in his eyes, he raises a glass to his long lost friend and performs the poem for us to "hear." When Wei Siming pours out a libation on the ground for the ghost of his dead friend and then sings his poem aloud, he is giving voice to the ghost, to the memory of Li She, by breathing life back into the words that were first uttered by him so many years ago. This act is much deeper and more intimate than gossip. The narrator is careful to note the outward tears on the old man's face as a tangible sign of his inner state. Through literature there is an emotional connection across time and space, between the living and the dead, a connection that is more sincere and compassionate than that between the old and young man who are sitting face-to-face. The cocky young scholar before him is not the one who truly understands Old Man Wei (his *zhiyin* 知音); Li She is. But he has already passed, remaining only in the words and reputation that he has left behind.

And it is precisely this, a name (*ming* 名) or reputation, that is the topic of the poem that Li She presented to the bandit. On the surface, the poem is a tongue-in-cheek lament over the burdens of literary fame. ("How famous is Li She?" "So famous, that even robbers ask him for a poem!") The first line sets up the cliché of a dark, rainy night on the river as the typical setting for an encounter with a bandit, nicely prefiguring Li Huizheng's subsequent encounter with Old Man Wei on a rainy evening. But the second line puts a twist on the scenario as the bandit is not after Li She's material wealth so much as a piece of his cultural capital. Even the robber "knows the hearsay" (*zhiwen* 知聞) that has circulated about Li She's literary talents. One might expect that Li She would be happy to hand over a poem instead of gold and silk, but the second couplet shows that he would value even more highly the possibility of escaping his fame altogether. He and his younger brother, Li Bo, lived in reclusion on Mount Lu in their younger days before they were drawn into the machinations of official life, and Li She likely harbored hopes of returning there in his retirement to become a recluse once again, with nothing more on his mind than reading books and frolicking with the local fauna. His encounter with the bandit makes him realize the impossibility of this dream as "half the world these days is already like" the bandit in having heard of Li She. He will never be able to escape his reputation. This line also contains an implied critique of Li She's colleagues in officialdom: many of them are acting like bandits in their stealing from the people and the government through corruption. The bandit Wei Siming proved to be an extremely astute reader of Li She's poem, as he ended up rejecting his offer of recommendation into service and chose to become a recluse himself, giving up robbery and corruption altogether. Old Man Wei is Li She's *zhiyin*, the one who understands what is in his heart, and even carried out the dream of reclusion that the prominent official and poet was never able to realize.

Up to this point, the narrative has dealt almost exclusively with the realm of performed poetry. Li She presents the bandit with a manuscript copy of his poem, but he certainly chanted it at the time of composition or soon thereafter. Later, when Li She meets with Song Tai in Huaiyang, he presents her with two poems, which were just as likely chanted in her presence. Decades later, during their chat on a rainy evening, the young scholar, Li Huizheng, and Old Man Wei engage in an orally extemporized exchange of couplets, followed by recitations from the works of their favorite poets, and ending with two performances of Li She's poem from the previous anecdote: first chanted (*yong* 詠) by Li Huizheng, who knew it as just another poem, and then again sung (*ge* 歌) by the bandit, who received it personally from the author. The two types of performance—chanting and singing—mark different relationships with the text of the poem. The young Scholar Li recites it as he would any other text that he has committed to memory, but Old Man Wei is truly moved to perform it as a heartfelt offering to the memory of Li She, setting the stage with a libation, and wiping away his tears before he begins to sing.

That the poems cited in these anecdotes can be found in other sources with textual variations, or even attributions to different authors, is evidence of their oral transmission and occasional transcription at different times by different hands. This pair of anecdotes, along with the rest in *Yunxi youyi* and other Tang anecdote collections, suggest that poems were transmitted and enjoyed primarily through performance and listening. The written form of a poem in the Tang dynasty is really just a holding pattern awaiting subsequent performance.

This particular entry in *Yunxi youyi*, however, is framed by a coda in the voice of Fan Shu himself, in which he directly addresses the status of a poem as written artifact:

Master Cloudy Creek has considered Liu Xiang's claim that "hearing something secondhand is not as good as hearing it for yourself, and hearing it for yourself is not as good as seeing it for yourself." During the Qianfu era (874–79), I was traveling on Zha River when I met Scholar Li Huizheng, who related his story to me in detail.[19] When Huizheng was in Old Man Wei's home, he viewed the poem in Erudite Li She's own handwriting and hoped that I might introduce it into literati circles. As Wei Siming felt so grateful to be recognized [by Li She] and followed a good life thereafter, how could I excuse myself before these men of old?

雲溪子以劉向所謂「傳聞不如親聞，親聞不如親見」也，乾符己丑歲，客於霅川，值李生細述其事。彙征於韋叟之居，觀李博士手翰，冀余導於文林。且思明感知從善，豈謝古人乎？

In quoting Liu Xiang 劉向 (77–6 BCE)—the Han dynasty paragon of anecdote compilers, who edited collections such as *Xinxu* 新序 (New accounts) and *Shuoyuan* 說苑 (Garden of legends)—Fan Shu is appealing to a gold standard of fact-checking in anecdotes. By this standard, however, he has only really "heard for himself" (*qinwen* 親聞) the story told by Li Huizheng, which is the second anecdote. The first anecdote must already have passed through many tellers by the time it reached Fan Shu, who lived decades after Li She. Where does the first anecdote come from? It cannot be from the conversation that Wei Siming and Li Huizheng had, because it includes details that occurred before and after Wei Siming was involved in the story (he was present neither when Li She said farewell to his brother nor later, when he bumped into Song Tai in Yangzhou). The stories of Li She encountering a bandit and an old friend's concubine seem to be bits of gossip of unknown provenance that were circulating about Li She in order to contextualize some of the poems that he composed. We might imagine that stories were told to set up these poems when they were chanted at social gatherings of literati and that these stories then entered the large pool of gossip that was the common property of the literati class in Tang China. If a poem is to be heard (or read) as a faithful transcription of an emotional reaction to a certain situation, then it helps if that situation is described so that the skill and sincerity of the author can be better appreciated. The poems become talismans of truth in the gossip about their authors, evidence that the events really did happen because they generated a textual trace in the form of a poem. The actual content of the poem may vary through repeated transmissions (or even be taken from someone else entirely), but the stability of the text of the poem is not so much at stake as the fact that there was a poetic moment, a moment in which the author reacted to his surroundings and channeled that reaction into a special form of discourse, thus enhancing his reputation as someone skilled in poetry.

In this case, the actual written text of the poem in Li She's own hand survived for some fifty years after the moment of its composition in the care of its recipient, Wei Siming. As a concrete textual trace of the original encounter between Li She and the bandit, the poem requires the first anecdote to account for its existence. The second anecdote recreates the conditions under which the trace of that original encounter is reanimated in the conversation between the Li Huizheng and Wei Siming. By linking Wei Siming concretely to the point of origin, the written document serves as tangible proof that he is the ultimate insider when it comes to gossip about this poem. The young scholar realizes the importance of this text in Li She's own hand; it is almost as if he has discovered a significant fossil that has been hidden away in a private collection. When Li Huizheng encounters Fan Shu during his travels, they end up gossiping themselves. Li "relates his story in detail," telling of his discussion of the poem with Wei Siming, and asks that Fan Shu "introduce it into literati circles." He thus reinserts the poem and its story into the flow of gossip circulating among the literati.

One wonders why an examination candidate such as Li Huizheng, who must surely have been in the thick of literati, would look to a "recluse scholar" such as Fan Shu to introduce the text into literati circles. Although he never held an official position, Fan Shu did associate with officials and can be counted as a member of the literati. A friend by the name of Li Xianyong, who failed the examinations himself but still served as a judge (*tuiguan* 推官), composed the following poem, "Mourning the Recluse Scholar Fan Shu" ("Dao Fan Shu chushi" 悼范攄處士):

家在五雲溪畔住，	He made his home on the banks of Cloudy Creek,
身遊巫峽作閒人。	and roamed in the Wu Gorge as a man of leisure.
安車未至柴關外，	Official carriages never reached his barred bramble gate;
片玉已藏墳土新。	he is already a piece of fine jade newly concealed in his tomb.
雖有公卿聞姓字，	Although high ranking officials had heard of his name,
惜無知己脫風塵。	sadly he had no close friends, having cast off this dusty world.

| 到頭積善成何事，| In the end, what are all our good deeds for? |
| 天地茫茫秋又春。| Heaven and Earth are boundless as time marches on.[20] |

Fan Shu occupied, at least in this depiction by Li Xianyong, the enviable role of a scholar who held himself above the hurly-burly of official life, with all of its duties, social obligations, machinations, and compromises. And yet those officials had "heard" of him (again, *wen*) even if their carriages did not reach his bramble gate.

Fan Shu is being cast in the role of the cultured recluse, played so effectively by Tao Qian, among others. To judge by the contents of *Yunxi youyi*, however, Fan Shu had many visitors and stayed well connected with the gossip and stories that were circulating among the literati, paying close attention to the hearsay emanating from the mundane world of "wind and dust" (*fengchen* 風塵) from which he had escaped. One might imagine that Fan Shu was in the process of compiling *Yunxi youyi* when he met Li Huizheng on the River Zha, and that it was by means of this collection of anecdotes that Li hoped Fan Shu might introduce the story of his encounter with Wei Siming into literati circles. Fan Shu is operating much like a gossip columnist, collecting stories from a variety of sources and recording them for a wider readership. How wide that readership may have been in Fan Shu's lifetime is impossible to know. There may have been a few manuscript copies being passed around among his friends and their friends. It is likely that these friends then told these stories at social gatherings, where they were heard and repeated (and perhaps written down) by others. The entries of *Yunxi youyi* would have been a valuable currency in these social settings because most of them contain an interesting story plus a short poem to provide a satisfying, pithy closure to the anecdote. One can think of anecdote collections in the Tang as repositories in writing of the "state of gossip" to be found in oral and written sources during a given period of time. The collections were likely compiled over many months or years, then circulated, then added to and circulated again, perhaps by multiple hands. More mutable than a published book or a snapshot of a specific time, a collection of anecdotes resembles an ongoing conversation on paper that reflects and contributes to conversations happening among people meeting face to face.[21]

This complex entry in *Yunxi youyi* consists of a series of nested conversations spanning five decades and punctuated by poems: Fan Shu discusses with Li Huizheng the conversation that Li had with Wei Siming, a conversation that concerned Wei's conversation with Li She decades earlier. The record of the three conversations is a means to verify, preserve, and transmit the poem Li She presented to the bandit (along with its story and notice of the extant written text) into the literary world: the handwritten copy is the verification and Fan Shu's multiple nested anecdotes take care of the preservation and transmission. The problem is that Fan Shu was late to the game. The poem (with some version of its attendant narrative) was already circulating among literati if the young scholar, Li Huizheng, was able to chant the poem before the bandit told him about it. Fan Shu's only new piece of gossip was about the chance meeting between Li Huizheng and the aged bandit, who showed him the text of Li She's poem. Fan Shu's effort in preserving this chain of anecdotes is an attempt to replicate and thus foster a sense of community among his readers, a feeling of belonging to a diffuse, enduring group of literary men (*wenren* 文人) in a literary world (*wenlin* 文林). The particular appeal of this entry is that it reminds the members of this community that the story of Li She meeting a cultured bandit on the river actually happened many years ago on a rainy night and is not just a fanciful legend. The story increases the cultural (and even monetary) value of the handwritten poem treasured by Old Man Wei, which in turn is a testament to the truth of the encounter he had with its author. And Wei's performance of it in song so many years later is a testament to the truth of his own feelings of gratitude and regret provoked by hearing the poem again. These stories that are the stuff of gossip actually happened (or at least we like to think so); the connections made between these people were sincere and meaningful. The appeal of reading the anecdotes lies in knowing that the memories, words, and feelings of these people will not be lost to time. Fan Shu was part of that community and felt a responsibility towards its members—"how could I excuse myself before these men of old?" The anecdote collection he compiled is no longer a living form of gossip; nor would it be admitted into the annals of official Chinese history. Yet it persists as documentary evidence of a world of discourse—an admixture of poetry and gossip—that still has much to teach us about the depiction of poetry being composed, performed, preserved, transmitted, and received in its living context.

NOTES

1. See chapter 4 of the present volume.
2. Ambrose Bierce, *The Devil's Dictionary* (New York: Oxford University Press, 1999), *s.v.* "historian."

3. Stephen Owen, Readings in Chinese Literary Thought (Cambridge, Mass.: Council on East Asian Studies, Harvard University, 1992), 40.

4. Paul Ricouer, *From Text to Action: Essays in Hermeneutics, II*, trans. Kathleen Blamey and John B. Thompson (London: Athlone Press, 1991), 17.

5. See chapter 2 of this book, where Xiaofei Tian discusses the various editorial strategies used to tame unruly anecdotes as they are transmitted over time.

6. For a discussion of anecdotal collections in the Tang, the status of compilers, and their relationships with one another, see my *Words Well Put: Visions of Poetic Competence in the Chinese Tradition* (Cambridge, Mass.: Harvard University Asia Center, 2006), 160–64, 181–83.

7. Ji Yun 紀昀 (1724–1805), comp., *Siku quanshu zongmu tiyao* 四庫全書總目提要, rpt. Wang Yunwu 王雲五, ed., *Heyin Siku quanshu zongmu tiyao ji Siku weishou shumu: jinhui shumu* 合印四庫全書總目提要及四庫未收書目：禁燬書目, 5 vols. (Taipei: Taiwan shangwu yinshuguan, 1971), 3:2891–92.

8. For the text of the "Jiangke ren" see Fan Shu 范攄 (fl. 877), *Yunxi youyi* 雲谿友議 (Beijing: Zhonghua shuju, 1959), 3.61–63; and *Yingyin Wenyuange Siku quanshu* 影印文淵閣四庫全書, vol. 1035 (Taipei: Taiwan shangwu yinshuguan, 1983), 563–618.

9. In his youth, Li She's younger brother was known as Master White Deer (Bailu xiansheng 白鹿先生) because he had tamed one of the local deer and was often seen roaming about the forests of Mount Lu in its company.

10. The story of Dai Yuan's encounter with Lu Ji is recorded in Liu Yiqing 劉義慶 (403–444), comp., *Shishuo xinyu jiaojian* 世說新語校箋, ed. Yang Yong 楊勇, rev. ed. (Beijing: Zhonghua shuju, 2006), 15.573.

11. The unstable status of poems circulating both orally and via manuscripts in the Tang is discussed in Christopher M. B. Nugent, *Manifest in Words, Written on Paper: Producing and Circulating Poetry in Tang Dynasty China* (Cambridge, Mass.: Harvard University Asia Center, 2010).

12. Eastern Han *yuefu* include images of young men with golden bridles on their horses, but this line seems to allude to a Southern Dynasties *yuefu* by He Xun 何遜 (d. ca. 518) called "In Imitation of 'Frivolity'" ("Ni qibo pian" 擬輕薄篇): "The handsome youth east of the city / value themselves but think nothing of wealth. / They load their slings with gemstones / and bridle their white horses with yellow gold" 城東美少年，重身輕萬億。柘彈隨珠丸，白馬黃金飾. See Guo Maoqian 郭茂倩 (fl. 1264–69), comp., *Yuefu shiji* 樂府詩集 (Beijing: Zhonghua shuju, 1979), 67.964.

13. Li Huizheng's use of the term "handsome youth" (*mei shaonian* 美少年) echoes the original line in He Xun's *yuefu*.

14. Qiu Zhaoao 仇兆鰲 (1638–1717), *Dushi xiangzhu* 杜詩詳注 (Beijing: Zhonghua shuju, 1979), 4.320–21.

15. We might recall that the *Yunxi youyi* collection itself derives its name from the phrase "auspicious clouds," which is also found in the sobriquet of its compiler, Fan Shu.

16. See Qu Tuiyuan 瞿蛻園, ed., *Liu Yuxi ji jianzheng* 劉禹錫集箋證

(Shanghai: Shanghai guji chubanshe, 2005), 818. The poem is also attributed to Liu Yuxi in *Quan Tangshi* 全唐詩 (Beijing: Zhonghua shuju, 1985), 365.4111.

17. This is in modern-day Guangdong.

18. This poem is titled "Staying at Jinglansha, I Encountered a Traveler in the Night" ("Jinlansha su yu yeke" 井欄砂宿遇夜客), in *Quan Tangshi*, 477.5436, which also paraphrases the anecdote from *Yunxi youyi* by way of introduction. There, the poem reads as follows: "The evening rain hisses softly over the riverside village, / even a bandit in the green forest knows my reputation this night. / What use was it to escape fame in those days, / when half the world now is already like you?" 暮雨瀟瀟江上村, 綠林豪客夜知聞, 他時不用逃名姓, 世上如今半是君. The variants from the *Yunxi youyi* version are duly noted. The references to hiding away to escape fame recall Li She's youth, when he lived as a recluse with his brother on Mount Lu.

19. There is a discrepancy in the text regarding the date, which is given as *Qianfu jichou sui* 乾符己丑歲. There is no *jichou* year during the Qianfu era (874–79), so this may be a scribal error for *jihai* 己亥, which would make the year 879. Zha River is located in modern Zhejiang.

20. In *Quan Tang shi*, 646.7406.

21. For how multiple anecdotal collections during the Tang help to piece together a contemporary, polyvalent account of a given era, see chapter 6 of this volume.

6 Gossip, Anecdote, and Literary History

Representations of the Yuanhe Era in Tang Anecdote Collections

Anna M. Shields

Our understanding of Chinese culture in the eras before the Song is necessarily constrained by the nature of our sources: official historiography provides a top-down, political view of events and personalities, and primary texts give us first-person claims and self-representations, but we have limited material to mediate between these two perspectives. Where they exist, anecdotal texts can help fill the gap between historiography and individual collected works, offering us the perspective of "'this is what happened to someone' in between 'this is what happened' and 'this is what happened to me.'"[1] Tang anecdote collections that focus on politics, literature, and elite social interactions over supernatural or romantic tales can give us unexpected insights into literary and cultural history, since they stand as examples of increasingly diverse ninth-century prose forms and as personal historical records that predate the formal emergence of genres such as *biji* 筆記 ("brush jottings"). Men who had served as officials in Tang government for some years often took on the role of the amateur historian, and though they were happy to include gossip, stories, and accounts transmitted from other people in their collections, they also saw their work as both historical record and literary creation—a piece of their *wenzhang* 文章 ("literary works") on the basis of which their reputation would be assessed—and as a contribution to Tang historiography.

Anecdote collections such as the three I examine here—the *Guoshi bu* 國史補 (Supplement to the history of the state), also known as the *Tang guoshi bu* 唐國史補, by Li Zhao 李肇 (d. after 829); *Yinhua lu* 因話錄 (Records of hearsay) by Zhao Lin 趙璘 (803–after 868); and the influential *Zhiyan* 摭言 (Collected sayings), later known as the *Tang zhiyan* 唐摭言, by Wang Dingbao 王定保 (870–940)—provide us a view of

Tang culture from the vantage point of its literati chroniclers, men who lived in a world where writing, politics, and social status were inextricably entwined.[2] Unlike collections focused on narrow aspects of literary culture, or romantic or ghostly tales, these three collections situate themselves squarely in the social and political realms, either excluding or generally avoiding supernatural, erotic, and religious phenomena. Here we find some of the most memorable vignettes of Tang elite culture to survive; their survival happened not only through their original collections but, more significantly, through citation and reorganization in Song collections such as the *Taiping guangji* 太平廣記 (Extensive records of the Taiping reign), the *Tang yulin* 唐語林 (Tang forest of words), and the *Tangshi jishi* 唐詩記事 (Anecdotes of Tang poetry). These Tang works have strongly influenced readers' understanding of Tang culture for centuries, and they flesh out our view of Tang literary culture as it was experienced by its participants.

In this chapter, I consider representations of an especially dynamic, influential moment in Tang literary and cultural history, the Yuanhe 元和 reign period of Tang Xianzong 唐憲宗 (r. 805–20). The *Guoshi bu*, the *Yinhua lu*, and the *Zhiyan* were composed at very different moments in the ninth and tenth centuries—the 820s, the late 850s or early 860s, and the early 900s—and they provide us with shifting Tang perspectives on Yuanhe culture that were later obscured in Song works about the Tang. Eyewitness accounts of the Yuanhe era from contemporary poems, letters, and other prose texts converge to depict a scene of cultural cacophony and bitter struggle for success on the "literary battlefield" (*wenchang* 文場). The *Guoshi bu*, a product of the years immediately following the Yuanhe, confirms that impression strongly. But as the immediate concerns of the Yuanhe moment faded, the personal accounts of contemporary observers were replaced by the judgments of later Tang readers who compiled their collections with no stake in the earlier struggles; the passage of time gave them freedom to evaluate Yuanhe literary culture in new ways.[3] Thus, in the *Yinhua lu*, Zhao Lin was able to assess Yuanhe writers with greater attention to literary talent than to political success or failure; and fifty or sixty years later, in the *Zhiyan*, Wang Dingbao's nostalgic view of examination culture allowed him even more latitude to select his evidence according to his own intellectual and historical interests. In the Song, when Tang anecdotes were selected from these and other works and placed in new collectanea, the depiction of the Yuanhe itself splintered into conceptual categories that represented Song rather than Tang concerns. In the eleventh and twelfth centuries, Tang anecdotes were rationalized both according to biography (e.g., Han Yu 韓愈 [768–824]) stories were selected from different works and grouped together) and in terms of categories (*lei* 類) of experience or phenomena.[4] Although many of the Tang texts survived into the Song and later, the original ordering—and, in some cases, the agendas—of the Tang texts were lost in the Song consolidations. Rereading accounts of Yuanhe culture in the Tang originals therefore not only gives us snapshots of the period, but also reveals a significant shift toward a more historical and even more ideological assessment of Yuanhe literati and their achievements over the course of the late ninth and early tenth centuries.

The Yuanhe reign period of Tang Xianzong is especially ripe for this kind of analysis because it was a time of political renewal and literary flowering, a moment when the fundamental role and nature of literary writing were being debated by a wide range of figures. The Yuanhe writers whose work survived to the Song—particularly Han Yu and his fellow defenders of antiquity—influenced later intellectual and literary developments in ways that were unanticipated in the Tang. Thus, to a degree unlike the "good government" reputation of the Zhenguan 貞觀 reign (627–49) of Tang Taizong or the more ambivalent glory of Tang Xuanzong's Kaiyuan 開元 (713–42) era, the political meaning of "Yuanhe" remained stable over time, but the literary and cultural associations of the term shifted considerably from the Tang through the end of the Song. The era is known in political history as the sole reign period of the dynamic "restoration" emperor, Xianzong. Under Xianzong's rule, the bureaucracy gained a greater voice in court deliberations, the Hanlin Academy in particular became a training ground for informed debate, and examination graduates found greater celebrity.

From a literary perspective, the era was equally extraordinary, but almost impossible to characterize or capture neatly due to its diversity of styles and genres and the variety of literati who were actively writing, whether from the vantage point of capital or province. To many of the most vocal literati of the early ninth century, the Yuanhe reign seemed a perfect moment to be daring, ambitious, and hopeful about using *wenzhang*, literary writing, to transform public life; but they did not agree on how to achieve that goal.[5] To this stylistic and ideological diversity is added a chronological messiness, since many of the writers strongly associated with the Yuanhe, such as Han Yu 韓愈 (768–824), Bai Juyi 白居易 (772–846), and Yuan Zhen 元稹 (779–831), lived beyond its boundaries. Even the exiles of the Yuanhe, Liu Yuxi 劉禹錫 (772–842) and Liu Zongyuan 柳宗元 (773–819), were productive before and after the years of Xianzong's reign. As we will see, the reign period term endured through the end of the ninth century as an emblem of the dynasty's revival but, after the fall of the Tang, seemed inadequate to capture the period's cultural diversity.

If the Yuanhe had survived in standard historiography and in anecdotal texts only as a diverse period, its historical narrative might simply be a collage of different and perhaps irreconcilable viewpoints. However, one development in the story altered the Song understanding of the period forever: this was the ideological appropriation and redefinition of Han Yu by key Northern Song literati, beginning most prominently with Liu Kai 柳開 (947–1000).[6] The Northern Song elevation of Han Yu to the status of Confucian culture hero—the defender of *guwen* 古文 ("ancient-style prose") as an expression of the Dao—transformed him into someone who was both inside and outside his historical moment. Han Yu's failure to advance his ideas beyond a close circle of like-minded literati during the Zhenyuan 貞元 (785–804) and Yuanhe reign periods was seen as a loss for Tang government; yet what was seen as the enduring truth of his ideas, rediscovered and extended in the Song, was represented as a victory for the "greater culture" or *siwen* 斯文. Even Song literati who did not accord Han Yu such preeminence had to engage this new interest in his achievements as a writer and a thinker. Thus the Song representation of Yuanhe literati varied in texts with different aims, but the shadow of Han Yu's new stature fell across many of these representations.

What is true for all of Song texts about the Tang, however, is that whether in editions of Tang authors' collected works, philosophical discussions, *shihua* 詩話 ("remarks on poetry"), or collectanea, we find more and more specialized categories of analysis with which to read Tang texts. These categories sometimes overlapped, and sometimes conflicted in their portraits of Yuanhe figures, including Han Yu. More importantly, the evaluations of the Tang by Song literati were increasingly made on the basis of extant primary texts of Tang authors, despite the fact that the size and influence of those texts in the Song did not necessarily reflect the prominence of a particular Tang writer in his historical moment.[7] These Tang anecdotal texts, in short, "supplement" our understanding of literary culture from yet another perspective: they help us recreate a sense of the celebrity and influence of particular Yuanhe literati during and just after their lifetimes.

In the *Guoshi bu*, the *Yinhua lu*, and the *Zhiyan*, we find a narrow, even microscopic view of recent and current events, a concern for the details of locale, clan, office, and specific time period, as well as an assumed familiarity with the prominent officials of the day. The blend of poetry, letters, prefaces, official documents, and gossip incorporated in anecdotal texts also points to the access that those writers, many of whom held offices in the capital, had to a wide variety of sources.[8] As the texts move farther away from the events of the Yuanhe reign, we see a shift in perspective, from the participant-observer view of Li Zhao, an active player in Yuanhe politics, to the more respectful perspective of Zhao Lin in his *Yinhua lu*, to the far more ambitious approach to chronicling literati culture of Wang Dingbao, writing after the fall of the Tang in 907. The change that most clearly foreshadows Song reinterpretations of the Tang is Wang Dingbao's use, in *Zhiyan*, of primary text sources to tell his tale. In other words, once four generations had passed since the original events, Wang Dingbao relied less on gossip or personal stories about the period, and instead revived the Yuanhe literati voices that he found most important, allowing them to speak directly in his text. What we begin to see in Wang Dingbao's depiction of Yuanhe literati is the emergence of a portrait by collage as well as a new reliance on primary texts over hearsay with which to write history. Although he does not offer a systematic intellectual historical narrative, his selective representation of some of the most controversial Yuanhe positions creates a coherent portrait of the age, one that shaped later readers' views of the period considerably.

CONTEMPORARY VIEWS OF THE ERA: DEBATES OVER THE "YUANHE STYLE(S)" 元和體

Throughout the Yuanhe reign, writers sought to link themselves to the success and charisma of their emperor even as they battled one another over literary and cultural values. In primary texts from the late Zhenyuan of Tang Dezong 唐德宗 (r. 780–804) through the Yuanhe reign, we find no shortage of self-conscious, self-promoting, and critical discourse about the period and its styles, and no scarcity of terms floated to describe new interests.[9] Bai Juyi and Yuan Zhen claimed to be "new" (*xin* 新); Han Yu and Meng Jiao 孟郊 (751–814) portrayed themselves as "ancient" (*gu* 古) and "unusual" (*guai* 怪); Huangfu Shi 皇甫湜 (777–830) wrote eloquently of the importance of "the unconventional" (*qi* 奇) in literary writing; and many more chimed in.[10] Negative assessments of new trends were also easy to find, as in the letter from Pei Du 裴度 (765–839) to Li Ao 李翱 (774–836) about Han Yu's lack of seriousness, his "making a game out of writing" 以文為戲, or in Zhang Ji's letters to Han Yu on the same issue, or the critical remarks on their contemporaries made by both Bai Juyi and Yuan Zhen in their 815 exchange of letters on literature.[11] The debate over literary forms and styles was of course also a struggle for status, and in that context, opposing positions needed supporters. When promoting new styles or ideas, writers needed superiors whose approval and patronage could help, and there was of course no greater potential patron than Xianzong himself. Contemporary literati often expressed a strong connection to the Yuanhe ruler and portray him as an enlightened sage who would favor their own ambitions. Han Yu's long panegyric poem on Xianzong's accession to the throne, "On the Sagely Virtue of the Yuanhe [Emperor]" 元和聖德詩, is but one well-known example.[12]

Beyond commonplace praise of the emperor and his reign, certain literati such as Bai Juyi and Yuan Zhen also appropriated the reign period name for their own reputations. It is Yuan Zhen to whom we owe the first extant version of the very slippery label of *Yuanhe ti* 元和體, "the Yuanhe style." Yuan Zhen's earliest known use of the term as applied to poetry appears in a letter he wrote in 819 to accompany a small collection of verse presented to Linghu Chu 令狐楚 (766–837), a chief minister from whom he was seeking patronage. He claims that it was the less-talented provincial imitators of his and Bai Juyi's poetry who had produced the poorly constructed verses they claimed to be in the *Yuanhe shiti* 元和詩體, or the "Yuanhe poetic style."[13] In studies of the history of this term, most scholars have concluded that Yuan's reference is ambiguous: he seems to be both claiming and rejecting the period label, at the very least trying to narrow his role in popularizing it.[14]

But Yuan's statements show that that there was a term already in circulation, *Yuanhe shiti*, or perhaps simply *Yuanhe ti*, and that he was associated with the term in a troubling way. In later years, looking back at the Yuanhe from the 820s, Yuan Zhen makes a less precise claim about the term, and Bai Juyi also asserts Yuan's and his own importance in transforming the style of the period's poetry.[15] Although they complicate rather than clarify the meaning of the term during the period itself, these retrospective and nostalgic claims are good evidence of the staying power of the phrase *Yuanhe ti*. However, the Yuan Zhen text gives us important evidence that at least one set of writers was explicitly linked to the reign period and captured, at least for a while, in a fixed phrase. The post-Tang use of the phrase solely to describe the poetry of Yuan and Bai points to yet another issue: a Song perception of the inadequacy of "Yuanhe" as a term to fully encompass the many styles, forms, and writers found in the period itself.

A SKEPTICAL PARTICIPANT: LI ZHAO AND THE *GUOSHI BU*

Written in the mid-Changqing 長慶 reign (822–27), Li Zhao's *Guoshi bu* complicates and broadens this vision of a "Yuanhe style" in an influential, enduring way. Li Zhao prefaces the *Guoshi bu* with a brisk summary of the kinds of material he had collected or ignored, and he thereby makes clear his ambitions as a historian of contemporary culture:

> "[as for those accounts that] spoke of vengeance and retribution, or told of ghosts and spirits, or verified dreams and oracles, or approached the curtains [of the bedchamber], I completely expunged them. But if they recorded facts and events, investigated natural phenomena, distinguished the suspect and deluded, displayed good advice or warnings, collected local customs, or contributed to refined chat and pleasantry, then I wrote them down."
> 言報應, 敘鬼神, 徵夢卜, 近帷箔, 悉去之; 紀事實, 探物理, 辨疑惑, 示勸戒, 採風俗, 助談笑, 則書之。[16]

With no further defense of his methodology or credentials, Li Zhao launches into his three-chapter collection of brief anecdotes, most of which focus on prominent Tang figures "from the Kaiyuan up through the Changqing reign periods."[17] Li Zhao's anecdotes provide us brief glimpses of literati life in the Tang from the perspective of an official in the Yuanhe and Changqing reigns, vividly "supplementing" the approved biographies of the standard histories with his own and others' stories. Although Li Zhao's precise dates are unknown, he held a series of capital posts in the early Yuanhe, including the influential and visible post of Hanlin Scholar, which he acquired in the thirteenth year of Xianzong's reign (818).[18] He was demoted from capital office in the early Changqing reign period, the moment when he seems to have compiled this work.[19]

Li Zhao clearly intended his text to be historical and useful, and his interests range well beyond matters of politics.[20] He views life from the court status he had enjoyed during the reign, giving us remarks on state and cultural affairs, and concluding with comments on music, regional tastes, wine rules, gambling, even the weather.[21] Most of his stories are set in the Zhenyuan and Yuanhe reigns, or the period of his adult life, and several are explicitly aimed at praising the high moral character and abilities of Xianzong, under whom he had flourished. The famous passage of the *Guoshi bu* that summarizes the literary styles of the Yuanhe period reveals a sharp critical sense, whether this was Li Zhao's own or derived from someone else.

In the Yuanhe and after, prose writers emulated the unconventionality and weirdness of Han Yu, and emulated the bitterness and turgidity of Fan Zongshi. Those who wrote ballads emulated the fluid, carefree quality of Zhang Ji. Those who wrote *shi* [詩] poetry emulated the forceful vigor of Meng Jiao, the simple clarity of Bai Juyi, and the licentious richness of Yuan Zhen. All these were collectively called the Yuanhe style [元和體]. Generally speaking, the style of the Tianbao era valued straightforwardness, the style of the Dali era valued superficiality, the style of the Zhenyuan era valued a carefree quality, and the style of the Yuanhe valued being unusual [*guai* 怪].

元和已後，為文筆則學奇詭于韓愈，學苦澀于樊宗師；歌行則學流蕩于張籍；詩章則學矯激于孟郊，學淺切于白居易，學淫靡于元稹。俱名為元和體。大抵天寶之風尚黨，大曆之風尚浮，貞元之風尚蕩，元和之風尚怪也。22

The passage demonstrates the use of "Yuanhe" as a container for different writers, but it is by no means admiring of the period's diversity. It breaks down the period first by genres (prose, ballads or *gexing* 歌行, and poetry in *shi* form) and then by characteristic styles associated with particular men. But Yuanhe literati are not simply sorted into form and style groups—Li Zhao includes the extremes of each available *ti* and he defines the spirit of the age as the desire to be *guai* 怪, "unusual," implying that being "unusual" (which can of course be translated "strange" or "abnormal," the opposite of *zheng* 正, "orthodox") was the chief goal of these diverse writers. By including this passage, Li Zhao also confirms two critical premises of Yuan Zhen's 819 use of the term *Yuanhe shiti*: first, that a literary label associated with the Yuanhe was already in circulation, and second, that it described the work of imitators.

This literary assessment fits neatly with other passages and vignettes found in the third chapter of *Guoshi bu*, a chapter that includes stories about the increasing importance and fierce competitiveness of the *jinshi* examination, the literati struggle for advancement in the face of overwhelming odds, and the need to display one's literary talent at all costs. The passage represents "being unusual" as the practice of emulating the most extreme styles available at the time, a literati shortcut to notoriety, if not fame. But the quality of *qi* or unconventionality was not limited to literary work, as this anecdote of the hapless Tang Ju shows:

> Tang Ju was a client of Zhou Zheng who had some literary talent but grew old without having any success [in passing examinations or gaining office]. He was only good at wailing: every time he uttered a wail, its tone was mournful and keen, and all who heard it would shed tears. He often traveled to Taiyuan, where he once enjoyed himself in

the company of the military. As he began to feel his wine, he began to wail. The assembled guests were all unhappy, and the host made him quit the banquet.

唐懼,周鄭客也。有文學,老而不成。唯善哭,每一發聲,音調哀切,聞者泣下。常游太原,過享軍,酒酣乃哭,滿座不樂,主人為之罷宴。23

Li Zhao suggests that extreme behavior, as in Tang Ju's case, could be enough to make one famous but not to win real success. He also included stories that showed the desperate measures literati might pursue in order to support themselves, as in this anecdote:

> When Wang Zhongshu [762–823] was Director of the Bureau of Operations [after 810], he became friends with Ma Feng, and he always rebuked Feng, saying, "You are so unbearably poor, why don't you seek out stele inscriptions and funerary memorials to help you out?" Feng laughed and said, "If I chance upon someone riding a horse and calling for a doctor, should I stand around and wait?"
>
> 王仲舒為郎中,與馬逢有善,每責逢曰:「貧不可堪,何不求碑志見救?」逢笑曰:「適有人走馬呼醫,立可待否?」24

Yet another anecdote in this section of the text satirizes the fierce competition to earn money this way: when one high official was on the verge of death, his courtyard became like a marketplace full of shouting would-be composers of funerary texts, whose noise drowned out the mourners.25 In Li Zhao's view of Yuanhe literature, the valuing of *guai* above all else was yet another unfortunate outcome of the struggle of the literary field. Of Bai Juyi and Yuan Zhen, who claimed specific association with a Yuanhe style, there is little trace in the extant *Guoshi bu*. Yuan Zhen appears in a passage that tells the story (confirmed in many other texts) of his run-in with a high-ranking eunuch censor that led to Yuan's 810 exile. Brief passages about other literati known for poetry, such as Wang Wei 王維 (701–61), Li Yi 李益 (748–829), and Wei Yingwu 韋應物 (737–92), emphasize the relationship between their talent and their resulting fame. In the text we have today, Li Zhao seems less a connoisseur of literary writing than an official who was keenly aware of the utility of *wenzhang* for political success and critical of outlandish writing as a means to acquire celebrity.

Among its portraits of Yuanhe literati, the *Guoshi bu* includes three more anecdotes about Han Yu that flesh out Li Zhao's view of literary celebrity as an uneven blend of "being unusual," patronage, and literary talent. Two of the three anecdotes about Han Yu are very uncomplimentary; the one positive anecdote singles out Han's allegorical story, "The

Biography of Brush-hair" ("Maoying zhuan" 毛穎傳), as an example of the talent of a "good historian" (*liang shi* 良史). The fact that Li Zhao admired this story—a piece that was at the time regarded as quite unusual—surely reflects his own interest in writing history. The most pointed of the negative anecdotes reads much more like gossip, a swipe at Han Yu's well-known dramatic personality.

> Han Yu loved the unconventional, and with his fellow travelers he ascended Mount Hua's highest peak. But when he got there, he could not return. He thereupon wrote his final testament and became wild with bitter wailing. The Huayang magistrate, after trying dozens of ways, [finally] got him, and Han then descended.
> 韓愈好奇，與客登華山絕峰，度不可返，乃作遺書,發狂慟哭，華陽令百計取之，乃下。[26]

In this story, Han Yu's love of *qi* is not confined to the literary but even turns him into a buffoon. Based on the evidence of Han Yu's own poem written about his ascent of Mount Hua and other sources, it seems very unlikely that Han Yu had a fit of mountain-top hysteria of the kind Li Zhao describes—and yet this version makes for an excellent story.[27] The second negative anecdote is a barbed appraisal of Han as a patron:

> Those whom Han Yu recommended always succeeded, so among those seeking to pass the examinations, many sent him letters to ask for his help, and people of the time called them "the disciples at Han's gates." Once Han Yu rose to a high position, he no longer did this.
> 韓愈引致後進，為求科第，多有投書請益者，時人謂之「韓門弟子」。愈後官高，不復為也。[28]

Han Yu's success in recommending candidates was noted in a variety of sources, and his efforts to deal with the flood of students importuning him for help are revealed in the many letters he wrote in response.[29] Where the other anecdotes touched on Han's literary talent and his love of the strange, this anecdote clearly attacks Han Yu's political ambitions, which were well documented from the Zhenyuan reign on.

Li Zhao's view of the Yuanhe period and the role that Han Yu played in it may have been influenced by Li's brief tenure as a scholar in the Hanlin Academy, which during Xianzong's reign was active, prestigious, and dominated by Great Clan officials. Han Yu was never called to the Academy, and in fact never held a post that brought him into the inner circles of Xianzong's administration. In addition, the fact that Li Zhao held a post in Chang'an (though it seems no longer at the Hanlin) at the time of Han Yu's disastrous "Buddha bone" memorial may have skewed his opinion of Han Yu even further.[30] Beyond this specific perspective on Han Yu, however, it is clear that Li Zhao took a skeptical, even disapproving view of the combat for political position that was conducted through *wenzhang*. Li Zhao's *Guoshi bu* sketches of the Yuanhe era, when read across the whole collection, recreate a world in which literati competition for exams, posts, and celebrity too often led to outrageous behavior, extreme stances, and hypocrisy.

REASSESSING THE FIELD: ZHAO LIN'S *YINHUA LU*

Li Zhao's portrait of a divisive Yuanhe literary field is tempered by a more admiring and balanced version found in Zhao Lin's *Yinhua lu* a few decades later. We know much less about Zhao Lin; he was an 834 *jinshi* and occupied a series of capital posts, though as far as can be determined he never advanced beyond the sixth rank in any of these posts. He served in capital posts through 862, then was demoted to the office of prefect in two successive posts, at some point also serving as a secretary to the military governor Pei Tan 裴坦. Throughout the *Yinhua lu*, Zhao Lin pays close attention to details of the political and social status of his subjects, and his prominent mention of his own positions and famous ancestors (a maternal relative who was in Xuanzong's harem and also a Liu 柳 clan member; a great-uncle, Zhao Zongru 趙宗儒, who was a minister under Dezong) gives the work more than a touch of snobbery.[31] Although most of the stories of the six chapters of the *Yinhua lu* come from well after 820, there are several in each chapter from the Yuanhe, and a few that explicitly praise Xianzong's moral responsiveness.[32] The Yuanhe era seems to have personal meaning for Zhao Lin; as he explains in one anecdote, the period encompassed his own youth, and his sense of Xianzong as a noble ruler therefore overlays his own past.[33] More importantly, Zhao Lin's years of official service largely fell within the reign of the Dazhong 大中 reign (847–59) of Emperor Xuanzong 宣宗, the son of Xianzong, who was an obsessive admirer of his father's legacy, and who often sought out people to tell him stories about the Yuanhe reign.[34] The chapters are each titled with a musical note, and the first three chapters focus on the lives of the elite (emperors, then ministers, then other officials), in particular their use of skillful writing and remonstrance at court. Overall, the text contains many more lengthy narrative passages than does the *Guoshi bu*, including personal anecdotes from Zhao Lin's own years of official service and comments on the veracity of specific details in stories.[35] The resulting sense of Zhao Lin's authorial intervention and original composition of the anecdotes, rather than simple compilation of "hearsay," is quite strong.

In the opening to the third chapter, at the beginning of a series of stories on literary skills and the examinations, Zhao Lin attempts to sort out the literary groupings of the Yuanhe and early Changqing period. Like the *Guoshi bu* passage on Yuanhe style, this text from the *Yinhua lu* also reappears in the Song anecdotal text *Tang yulin*, where it appears in the "Literature" ("Wenxue" 文學) chapter.

> Han Wengong [Yu] and Meng Dongye [Jiao] were close friends. Han's prose compositions were of the highest quality, while Meng excelled in pentametric verse; they were called at the time "Meng the Poet and Han the [Prose] Brush." During the Yuanhe, younger writers modeled themselves on Han, and the styles of prose changed greatly. [At the same time,] there were also Liu Zongyuan of Liuzhou, Secretary Li Ao, Director Huangfu Shi, Head of Household Administration Feng Ding, Libationer Yang [Jingzhi 敬之], and my Chief Examiner Li [Han 李漢], all of whom were revered by students for their excellent prose.[36] But Han, Liu, Huangfu, and Li made it their aim to be emulated by those who came after. . . . Moreover, from the Yuanhe on, among others whose prose was unconventional, there were also Liu Zongyuan of Liuzhou, Minister Liu Yuxi and Yang. Liu and Yang, aside from their prose style, were also good at well-crafted poetic works. Moreover there was Director of Studies Zhang Ji, who was talented at ballads, and Li He, who composed "new" *yuefu*. If we speak of those who composed ballads at the time, these two were the most admired. Minister Li Cheng, Vice Director Wang Qi, Junior Mentor Bai Juyi and his younger brother [Bai Xingjian 白行簡], and Secretary Zhang Zhongsu were all the greatest rhapsodists in the literary field; among those regarded as models [for rhapsodies], these five were the most admired.
>
> 韓文公與孟東野友善。韓公文至高，孟長於五言，時號「孟詩韓筆」。元和中，後進師匠韓公，文體大變。又柳柳州宗元、李尚書翱、皇甫郎中湜、馮詹事定、祭酒楊公、余座主李公，皆以高文為諸生所宗，而韓、柳、皇甫、李公皆以引接後學為務。…又元和以來，詞翰兼奇者，有柳柳州宗元、劉尚書禹錫及楊公。劉、楊二人，詞翰之外，別精篇什。又張司業籍善歌行，李賀能為新樂府，當時言歌篇者，宗此二人。李相國程、王僕射起、白少傅居易兄弟、張舍人仲素為場中詞賦之最，言程式者，宗此五人。[37]

Rather than using the label *Yuanhe ti* pejoratively or positively, Zhao Lin acknowledges the diversity of Yuanhe literature and organizes it by styles, forms, and influential models. We might think of *Yuanhe ti* as the hidden term or subtext of the passage. Unlike Li Zhao, Zhao Lin is an admirer of Han Yu, or at the very least is willing to pass on stories of his superior reputation. Han Yu is portrayed here as a bellwether of Yuanhe literary change and even as emblematic of the period for several reasons: for the excellence of his prose, which was recognized by his contemporaries, for the fact that he was widely imitated and intended to have an influence on others, and for the way his model initiated literary change. If the "Chief Examiner Li" mentioned in the passage is Li Han, Han Yu's son-in-law and literary executor, then Zhao Lin had a personal connection to Han Yu that must have strongly affected his sense of literary models.[38] By highlighting the self-conscious efforts of Han Yu and others to become models, Zhao Lin suggests that the multivocal literary culture of the Yuanhe was extraordinary precisely because it produced so much excellence in so many different categories of writing and continued to be influential even through later imitations. The only real overlap with Li Zhao's account appears in crediting Han Yu as the most prominent prose author, Zhang Ji as a composer of songs or ballads, and Bai Juyi as a poet.

More noteworthy than Zhao's generous praise, however, are features of the text that reveal his greater distance from and respect for the writers and their period than we saw in the *Guoshi bu*. One is Zhao's consistent use of the highest official or posthumous honor titles for each man, beginning with Han Wengong 韓文公, or "Han, the Cultured Duke," an extension of Han's posthumous honor title of *wen*. This attention to political service, denoted in official titles, is consistent with the overall perspective of *Yinhua lu*, which is very much from the center, like the *Guoshi bu*. At the same time, Zhao's use of titles creates the false sense of a level playing field or a political world in which each of these literati played similarly important official roles. In this same vein, a more significant feature is the incorporation of the two famous literary exiles, Liu Zongyuan and Liu Yuxi, into the larger portrait of active, influential writers of the period. Zhao's decision to include the two exiles likely had to do with his family background: Zhao Zongru, Zhao Lin's grandfather, had been a supporter of Liu Zongyuan after his disgrace in the Shunzong era (805–6). Moreover, there appears to be a Liu family connection between Zhao Lin and Liu Zongyuan, which was likely responsible for Zhaos' inclusion of three anecdotes featuring Liu Zongyuan in a positive light. In one of these, Zhao reproduces a story about the two men that he most likely learned through his connection with the work of Han Yu. In his *muzhiming* 墓誌銘 ("funerary inscription") for Liu Zongyuan, Han Yu recorded the story of Liu Zongyuan's attempt to exchange posts with Liu Yuxi when they were both sent into a second exile in 815; according to Han Yu, Liu Zongyuan did so because Liu Yuxi's mother was still alive, and Liu Yuxi's new place of exile was too remote and uncivilized.[39] In Han Yu's hands, the story becomes a parable of the two men's friendship and integrity; Zhao Lin's version, however, stars Xianzong and his noble minister Pei Du (himself the subject of several flattering anecdotes in the *Yinhua lu*), with the two friends playing lesser roles.

> When Xianzong was still early in his reign, he summoned Liu Zongyuan and Liu Yuxi to come to the capital, and shortly thereafter he made Liu Zongyuan the prefect of Liuzhou and Liu Yuxi the prefect of Bozhou. But Liu [Zongyuan] felt that Liu [Yuxi] should serve his mother, and since Bozhou was the most vile location by far, he requested to exchange his post in Liuzhou with [Yuxi]. The emperor did not agree. His ministers said to him, "Yuxi has an aged mother." The emperor said, "But I wish to give him a vile prefecture; why should I worry that his mother is still alive?" Pei *Jingong* [Du] presented his opinion, saying, "His Majesty is himself serving the Empress Dowager, thus it is not fitting for him to utter these words." The emperor appeared ashamed. After a while, he said to his retainers, "Pei Du's love for me in the end is the keenest." And Liu Yuxi was then given Lianzhou.
>
> 憲宗初，征柳宗元，劉禹錫至京，厄爾以柳為柳州刺史，劉為播州刺史。柳以劉須侍親，播州最為惡處，請以柳州換。上不許。宰相對曰：「禹錫有老親。」上曰：「但要與惡郡，豈繫母在?」裴晉公進曰：「陛下方侍太后，不合發此言。」上有愧色。既而語左右曰，「裴度終愛我切。」劉遂改授連州。[40]

Despite his greater interest in showcasing the moral qualities of Xianzong and Pei Du, Zhao Lin's inclusion of this anecdote flattering the two Shunzong exiles signals an important shift in the portrayal of Yuanhe culture. It suggests not only that the stain of the Shunzong era had faded over the preceding decades (Liu Zongyuan died in 819, and Liu Yuxi in 842, at least a full generation before the composition of *Yinhua lu*), but also that their reputations and contributions to Yuanhe literature were being assessed as much through extant texts as through stories about their influence.

From his perspective as a descendent of its luminaries, either through kinship or intellectual affiliation, Zhao Lin paints the Yuanhe as a wide field of talent, one divided by models for discrete genres but also one that shone with brilliance throughout.[41] As the title of his text suggests, Zhao Lin pretends to be transmitting "what was said" about these writers at the time, yet he goes beyond that and attempts in a small-scale way to rationalize and expand the confusing literary field of the Yuanhe and to find value in multiplicity. The Yuanhe period term is still useful here as a container for diverse literati who flourished during the reign of a brilliant emperor, but the term no longer points to contestation or the struggle for career success that Li Zhao found so troubling in the period.

AFTER THE FALL: A VIEW FROM THE TENTH CENTURY

Zhao Lin composed his work in the wake of the most stable reign of the second half of the ninth century, Xuanzong's era. His work conveys respect for a Yuanhe literary scene more crowded with talent than his own more fragmented and undistinguished literary moment, but it does not seem overburdened with nostalgia. Decades later, after the fall of the dynasty, many literati began collecting, commenting on, and creating works that expressed their perspectives on Tang literary and cultural values, sometimes nostalgically but sometimes merely with the goal of preservation. The work that came to be known as the *Tang Zhiyan* was one such text. Framed by its author as an unofficial historical record, the *Zhiyan* has many direct links to Li Zhao's *Guoshi bu*, and it transmits a very particular vision of the Tang cultural and political past.[42] The *Zhiyan*'s many anecdotes center on the history and practices of the examination system in the Tang, but its contents range far beyond the repetition of clever stories. Its compiler, Wang Dingbao, is indebted to earlier Tang official and amateur historians: for example, he cites Li Zhao's work by name in the fifth passage of his work, and cites him another eleven times throughout the 15 extant *juan* and 480 passages of the *Zhiyan* (which in its present form is roughly four times the length of the *Guoshi bu*).[43] The text has a very loose thematic rather than chronological order; its passages are occasionally introduced with reign period names, but more frequently with the names of the main characters to be considered in each passage. We would assume that Wang Dingbao's focus on the topic of the examinations would slant his perspective on literary history toward the kinds of writers and texts that produced examination success or that resulted in spectacular failures. And indeed, Wang Dingbao's text lays out the ways in which the state's recruitment strategies shaped literary practice, but he rarely suggests that literature was warped by the examinations. Rather, his selection of stories and texts argues that the examinations proved the truest and most influential testing ground for literary and intellectual skills throughout the second half of the dynasty. In the case of his stories about Zhenyuan and Yuanhe literati, we find a preponderance of stories about talent: what constituted it, how to get it, who had it, and how it was all too often overlooked.

More importantly for our purposes, the *Zhiyan* is unique among Tang anecdotal texts for its unprecedented number of primary text citations, many of them running to hundreds of words. In the *Zhiyan*, in other words, we have a new version of the "anecdotal text," one that does not simply rely on hearsay, gossip, and clever stories, but a work that uses fragments of many different kinds of text to assemble a portrait of a complex cultural practice. Oliver Moore has noted hundreds of such citations from a wide variety of sources, including not only official documents such as memorials and edicts but also letters, poems, and funerary texts.[44] In the case of poetry, it appears that Wang's fondness for certain poems and couplets occasionally trumped his sense of their relevance to the examinations or to official service.[45] Wang's reliance on primary texts profoundly shapes the *Zhiyan* representation of Yuanhe literati culture, particularly his representation of Han Yu and the men in his circle. In the *Zhiyan*, as in no other extant anecdotal or historical text before the early tenth century, we see the emergence of Han Yu and his associates as intellectual soulmates—not simply good or strange prose stylists, but men with specific ideas and goals that derived from the texts of "the ancients." To give just a sample of the strong texts by Han and his circle that appear in the *Zhiyan*: we have Han Yu's eulogy for Ouyang Zhan 歐陽詹 (798–ca. 827) and his epitaph for the talented Li Guan 李觀 (766–94), both of whom were Han Yu's *tongnian* 同年 or "same-year" *jinshi* examination graduands, and both of whom died too young; citations from two of Li Ao's letters to potential patrons that praise Han Yu, Meng Jiao, Li Guan, and Zhang Ji not just as poets or prose writers but men of "antiquity"; and passages from Zhang Ji's letter to Han Yu rebuking him for a lack of seriousness, with a few sentences of Han Yu's letter in response.[46]

Wang Dingbao's esteem for this particular group of literati is conveyed by the repeated words of praise from different brushes that he cites in multiple places, as in this passage about Han Yu:

> Han Wengong's reputation spread all throughout the world; Li Ao and Zhang Ji both ascended to court. Ji had faced north and had taken [Han Yu] as his teacher, and that is why Yu wrote to Cui Lizhi saying, "Recently there have been Li Ao and Zhang Ji who are following me to study *wen*."[47] [Li] Ao wrote in his "Letter to Vice-minister Lu San," "Han Tuizhi's writing is not the *wen* of this generation but the *wen* of antiquity; as a person, he is not of this generation, but a person of antiquity." Thereafter, when Yu went from Chaozhou to Yichun prefecture, Huang Po of Yichun took Yu as a teacher for *wen*, and he [Huang] too gained great fame. . . . According to the [era not given] Veritable Record, "As for those with close connections to Yu, after

any of them passed away, Han Yu comforted and aided their orphans, and helped them make marriages; in the case of men such as Meng Dongye [Jiao] and Zhang Ji, it was like this."[48]

韓文公名播天下,李翱、張籍皆升朝,籍北面師之,故愈答崔立之書曰:「近有李翱、張籍者,從予學文。」翱《與陸傪員外》書亦曰:「韓退之之文,非茲世之文也,古之文也;其人非茲世之人,古之人也。」後愈自潮州量移宜春郡,郡人黃頗師愈為文,亦振大名⋯ 案《實錄》:「愈與人交,其有淪謝,皆能恤其孤,復為畢婚嫁,如孟東野、張籍之類是也。」[49]

Here, Wang Dingbao brings together lines from Han's primary texts, stories about Han, and praise of Han from a text by one of his disciples and friends, Li Ao, to create a portrait of Han Yu not only as a devoted teacher and mentor, but also as a sage like those of antiquity, someone whose stature was unequalled in his time. Whereas in the *Guoshi bu*, Li Zhao had attacked Han Yu for his love of the "unconventional" (*qi*), in the *Zhiyan*, Wang Dingbao defends the role of *qi* in Yuanhe culture by giving long citations from two letters in which Huangfu Shi responded to Li Ao's queries about successful *wenzhang* 文章 ("literary writings").[50] In those letters, Huangfu Shi defends *qi* as an essential component of powerful, individual writing. The *Zhiyan* chapters in which these passages appear are those that explore the use of writing to create strong social connections in the early years of a career, as in the teacher-student relationship (Zhang Ji writing to criticize Han Yu), the patron-client relationship (Li Ao writing of the death of his patron Liang Su),[51] or simply the relationship between a poet and an interested reader (Han Yu's appreciation and support of Li He).[52] Countering Zhao Lin's broader vision of literati who were influential models during the Yuanhe, Wang Dingbao nowhere mentions Liu Zongyuan or Liu Yuxi.

In his exploration of the examinations, Wang Dingbao uses his passages to demonstrate the ways Tang literati supported one another through letters of recommendation, critical appraisal, and other forms of praise, and he portrays the Han Yu circle, at least, as a network of training for the examinations and for becoming known in the world.[53] But by citing lengthy excerpts from the authors' primary texts rather than recounting clever stories about them, Wang Dingbao allows these literati to speak for themselves. In contrast to earlier accounts of the literary celebrity of Bai Juyi and Yuan Zhen, however, the two men are oddly peripheral to Wang's story, although they do appear in a handful of anecdotes that cite well-crafted lines of verse.[54] This may reflect the nature of the texts Wang had at hand, since in their collected works, both men proclaimed their examination successes, from the *jinshi* for

Bai to the *mingjing* 明經 ("explicating the classics") for Yuan Zhen and two further examinations, the *shupan bacui* 書判拔萃 ("selecting talent through written case verdicts") and a special decree examination (*zhiju* 制舉), that they passed together in 806. And yet of the four anecdotes that include Bai or Yuan, three contain at least one error or questionable attribution, suggesting that Wang was relying on thirdhand stories and oral accounts for those authors. One anecdote tells the story of Bai Juyi failing the *boxue hongci* 博學宏辭 ("comprehensive knowledge and vast words") examination, which he never attempted.[55] There is a marked difference in the way these different Yuanhe literati are represented, as well: except in one instance, Bai Juyi is consistently referred to in the text as "Bai Letian" 白樂天, whereas Han Yu is either "Han Yu" or, more frequently, "Han *Wengong*." Bai and Yuan both held a series of prominent posts at various points in their careers, Bai as an outspoken Hanlin Scholar for a brief period during the Yuanhe and Yuan as prime minister for a brief, unpopular spell in the Changqing era, and yet in the *Zhiyan* they are reduced to mere poets. Despite Wang Dingbao's reliance on the *Guoshi bu*, of the three *Guoshi bu* stories that were critical of the *Yuanhe ti* and of Han Yu in particular, none appears in the *Zhiyan*. The term *Yuanhe ti* is also not used in the text.

 Wang Dingbao's concern for reconstructing a particular history allows him to read past the chronological periods of Tang dynastic history, giving the words and actions of individuals much greater weight than their political status or context, and thereby creating a version of early ninth-century culture not seen in earlier texts. His work also represents a new, more ambitious version of the kind of history that could be compiled with "collected sayings," *zhiyan* 摭言, from the past. Although Han Yu, Bai Juyi, Meng Jiao, and others are frequently situated in Zhenyuan and Yuanhe time frames, they are not linked directly to Xianzong or to events of the period; instead, they are portrayed in the company of their literati colleagues. Wang Dingbao's motives for creating his collection are only implied at various moments throughout the text, and they do not seem to be self-consciously ideological in the manner of Song literati readings of Han Yu and his circle. However, his focus on the relationship between literary talent and the support of patrons and colleagues leads him to include extensive citations from texts exchanged in Han Yu's network. The result is an intellectually coherent portrait of literati who shared a commitment to a Confucian past and its values. In this respect, and in the text's diminution of Bai Juyi and Yuan Zhen, the *Zhiyan* anticipates moves made by other readers and compilers of anecdote collections in the Song. Wang Dingbao's preference for a cultural and official-centered view over a political, emperor-centered view of Tang history marks an important shift that Song readers must have absorbed. His relegation of Bai and Yuan to the realm of mere poets also hints at the emergence of a post-Tang distinction between the literary and intellectual realms of culture.

In all three of the anecdotal texts examined in this chapter, the authors speak from the viewpoint of current or former officials in Tang government, men with a vested interest in defending the contributions of the officiate to the state and Tang culture. An obvious next step in understanding different Tang perspectives on the Yuanhe would be to reintegrate these texts with other accounts of the ninth century that look back at the period, such as prefaces to individual collections, anthologies, and letters—other texts that function as broad cultural commentary, if not formal history. It would be equally important to juxtapose these views with the historiographical perspectives of the *Jiu Tangshu* 舊唐書 (Old history of the Tang dynasty), some of which preserve ninth-century views from contemporary sources. Although it is a small point, the shift from the chronological order of the *Jiu Tangshu* biographies, where the Yuanhe literati appear in temporal sequence according to their examination dates and time of official service, to the grouped hierarchies of the *Xin Tangshu* 新唐書 (New history of the Tang dynasty) biographies itself echoes the same shift we see in anecdotal texts, from a political to an ideological framing of the Tang past.[56]

As these Tang anecdotal texts were divided up and incorporated into Song histories and collectanea, their individual voices were muted, and yet the sting of some of their contingent and local assessments lingered on. In time, of course, these views become irrelevant, overly fine divisions of the "Tang" that do not conform to the generic histories and hierarchies of later dynasties. It is clear that anecdotal texts can, with careful contextualization, give us a finer-grained picture of Tang cultural activity. They do not provide us a more accurate sense of a literatus or his moment, a more reliable biography, but instead expose clearly the many stakeholders in Tang culture, and the perennial issues—such as the meaning of "success" or "fame" in the public realm—that were vigorously debated throughout the dynasty. The Tang authors of anecdotal texts claim to be competent observers, and they demonstrate little anxiety about the limits of their knowledge; this epistemological confidence is itself a reminder of the medieval sensibility of Tang literati that was overwritten in Song reordering and rationalization. However, we see even more clearly in these three texts from the ninth and tenth centuries a slow transformation in literati self-representation. As we move from Li Zhao's aristocratic and privileged view of the Yuanhe moment, when strivers like Han Yu and Bai Juyi were barely tolerated as writers of unusual texts, to the richer portrait of examination candidates and rituals found in Wang Dingbao's retrospective portrait, a portrait in which Han, Bai, and other Yuanhe figures are heard speaking in their own words, we move from a view of literati as participants in Tang culture to literati as makers of Tang culture. This is a significant transition, and it is one that Song readers, who also saw themselves at the center of their culture, found plausible and worth passing on.

NOTES

1. Rania Huntington, "Chaos, Memory, and Genre: Anecdotal Recollections of the Taiping Rebellion," *Chinese Literature: Essays, Articles, Reviews* 27 (Dec. 2005): 59.

2. The basic information for the works and their authors is taken from Zhou Xunchu 周勛初, *Tangdai biji xiaoshuo xulu* 唐代筆記小說敘錄 (Nanjing: Fenghuang chubanshe, 2008). Zhou's work, in turn, relies on his own and others' extensive research on Tang and Five Dynasties collections produced during the past few decades, including the work of Ding Ruming 丁如明 et al., eds., *Tang Wudai biji xiaoshuo daguan* 唐五代筆記小說大觀 (Shanghai: Shanghai guji chubanshe, 2000).

3. Although this chapter focuses on anecdotal texts, the issue of greater critical freedom in the late Tang also applies to compilers of poetry collections. On this issue, see Stephen Owen, "A Tang Version of Du Fu: The *Tang shi lei xuan,*" *T'ang Studies* 25 (2007): 57–90; and Shields, *Crafting a Collection: The Cultural Contexts and Poetic Practice of the* Huajian ji *(Collection from Among the Flowers)* (Cambridge, Mass.: Harvard University Asia Center, 2006), 119–48.

4. This reorganization of material occurred in different ways in different kinds of texts—for example, we see the same Tang anecdotes sorted into both the *lei* of the tenth-century *Taiping guangji* and the biographical entries of the early twelfth-century *Tangshi jishi*.

5. On this point, see David L. McMullen, *State and Scholars in T'ang China* (Cambridge: Cambridge University Press, 1988), 234–35, 244–49; and Peter K. Bol, *'This Culture of Ours': Intellectual Transitions in T'ang and Sung China* (Stanford: Stanford University Press, 1992), 123–24.

6. For a summary of Liu's rereading of Han Yu and self-fashioning in Han Yu's model, see Bol, *'This Culture of Ours'*, 162–65. Han Yu's increasing prominence in the eyes of early Song literati can also be seen in his representation in *Tang wencui* 唐文粹 (Essence of Tang prose), compiled by Yao Xuan 姚鉉 (968–1020), an anthology tilted toward *guwen* writers and compositions.

7. The Yuanhe has many examples of discrepancies between a writer's importance in the Tang and his later influence; it is clear that much depended on the survival of individual collections and the connoisseurship of Song readers. For an illuminating discussion of the relationship between Bai's corpus and Song assessments of his work, see Stephen Owen, *The Late Tang: Chinese Poetry of the Mid-Ninth Century (827–860)* (Cambridge, Mass.: Harvard University Asia Center, 2009), 41–48.

8. On the significance of this feature in Tang anecdotal texts, see Graham Sanders, *Words Well Put: Visions of Poetic Competence in the Chinese Tradition* (Cambridge, Mass.: Harvard University Asia Center, 2006), 160–64.

9. Meng Erdong 孟二束 provides a good introduction to the mid-Tang and the Yuanhe era in his *Zhong Tang shige zhi kaituo yu xinbian* 中唐詩歌之開拓與新變 (Beijing: Beijing daxue chubanshe, 1998), 25–35.

10. For Bai Juyi's remarks on the "newness" of his approach to *yuefu*, see Zhu Jincheng 朱金城, ed., *Bai Juyi ji jianjiao* 白居易集箋校 (Shanghai: Shanghai guji chubanshe, 1988), 3.136; for Yuan's remarks on the same, see the preface to his "new-style yuefu" 新題樂府, in *Yuan Zhen ji biannian jiaozhu* 元稹集編年校注, ed. Yang Jun 楊軍 (Xi'an: San Qin chubanshe, 2002), 106; and also Dong Gao 董誥 (1740–1818), comp., *Quan Tang wen* 全唐文 (Beijing: Zhonghua shuju, 1983), 653.3a–4b. For Huangfu Shi's discussions of *qi*, see his letters to Li, *Quan Tang wen* 685.22a–27a.

11. For Pei Du's letter, see *Quan Tang wen*, 538.3b–4a; Zhang Ji's letters are found most usefully alongside Han Yu's responses in Qu Shouyuan 屈守元 and Chang Sichun 常思春, eds., *Han Yu quanji jiaozhu* 韓愈全集校注 (Chengdu: Sichuan daxue chubanshe, 1996), 1326–41; for Bai's 815 letter, see *Bai Juyi ji jianjiao*, 45.2789–96; for Yuan's 815 letter, see Ji Qin 冀勤, ed., *Yuan Zhen ji* 元稹集 (Beijing: Zhonghua shuju, 1982), 30.352.

12. Qu and Chang, *Han Yu quanji jiaozhu*, 408–20. See also Charles Hartman, *Han Yu and the T'ang Search for Unity* (Princeton: Princeton University Press, 1986), 71–72.

13. *Quan Tang wen*, 653.18a–b.

14. For some examples of the numerous articles and chapters on this issue, see Zhou Guifeng 周桂峰, "Lun Yuanhe ti" 論元和體, *Huaiyin shifan xueyuan bao* 21, no. 5 (1999): 101–5; Jin Yizeng 靳義增, "Lun 'Yuanhe ti' de wenxue sixiang" 論元和體的文學思想, *Jiangxi shehue kexue* 6 (2003): 47–49; Qi Wei 綦維, "'Yuanhe ti' kaobian" 元和體考辯, *Sichuan daxue xuebao (zhexue shehui kexue ban)* 134, no. 5 (2004): 135–39.

15. The primary texts from after 819 are Bai Juyi's couplet in an 823 poem sent to Yuan Zhen, which reads, "From the Changqing [reign] forward, the language of decrees became elevated and ancient / as for poetry in the Yuanhe, its style became fresh and new" 制從長慶辭高古，詩到元和體變新 (Zhu, *Bai Juyi ji jianjiao*, 23.1532); and Yuan Zhen's statements in the preface to Bai Juyi's collected works of 824, in *Quan Tang wen*, 743.23a–24b.

16. In Li Zhao, comp., *Tang Guoshi bu*; Zhao Lin, comp., *Yinhua lu* (Shanghai: Shanghai guji chubanshe, 1979), 1.1.

17. The extant version contains 308 anecdotes, each of which is prefaced by a pithy five-word summary phrase that may date back to the work's inception or may be a Song addition. All but one Song bibliographic record for this work give it as having three *juan*, as it contains today; however, later collections cite passages that are no longer extant, suggesting that the original version contained more anecdotes. See Oliver Moore, *Rituals of Recruitment: Reading an Annual Programme in the* Collected Statements *by Wang Dingbao (870–940)* (Leiden: Brill, 2004), 42–43.

18. Cen Zhongmian 岑仲勉, in his notes on the *Guoshi bu*'s influence on *Zhiyan*, has reconstructed Li Zhao's career path and argues that Li Zhao transferred from the Hanlin to be a Right Omissioner in 819. See "Ba Tang zhiyan" 拔唐摭言, *Guoli Zhongyang yanjiuyuan lishi yuyan yanjiusuo jikan* 9 (1947): 246.

19. Li Zhao was also the author of a text about the Hanlin Academy, the still-extant *Hanlin zhi* 翰林志 (Account of the Hanlin Academy). For a translation of this work, see F. A. Bischoff, *Le forêt des pinceaux* (Paris: Presses universitaires de France, 1963).

20. In the 820s, the most notable historical work of this title, and the one Li Zhao's work was intended to supplement, was the *Guoshi* compiled by Liu Fang 柳芳 in the 760s, in 130 *juan*. See Denis Twitchett's study of this work, its compilation, and later incorporation into the *Jiu Tangshu*, in *The Writing of Official History under the T'ang* (Cambridge: Cambridge University Press, 1992), 178–87.

21. The influence of the *Guoshi bu* on later compilations was extensive: many passages appear in later Tang anecdotal texts, such as *Zhiyan*, and many of the *Guoshi bu* passages cited in the *Zhiyan* subsequently appear in the *Taiping guangji*, the *Tang yulin*, and later texts such as the *Tangshi jishi* and the *Tang caizi zhuan*. For the relationship between the *Guoshi bu* and the *Zhiyan*, see Moore, *Rituals of Recruitment*, 40–42.

22. Li Zhao, *Tang guoshi bu*, 3.57.

23. Ibid., 2.38.

24. Ibid., 2.42.

25. Ibid., 2.38. For a discussion of these anecdotes in the context of writing for money, see Alexei Ditter, "Genre and the Transformation of Writing in Tang Dynasty China" (PhD diss., Princeton University, 2009), 268–70.

26. Li Zhao, *Tang guoshi bu*, 2.38.

27. Hartman argues that the incident was not apocryphal, pointing to a section in Han Yu's poem, "Answering Zhang Che," that describes his ascent. See his *Han Yü*, 49–50, and n84). However, nowhere in the poem does Han Yu portray himself in the deranged condition described in Li Zhao's anecdote. *Han Yu quanji jiaozhu* notes that at least one edition of the poem reads *wang* 往 for *kuang* 狂 in the relevant lines (317). Han Yu's distress in the poem seems to spring from his having been exiled rather than from vertigo.

28. Li Zhao, *Tang guoshi bu*, 3.57.

29. As an example of the impact of Song reordering of Tang anecdotes,

both of these negative anecdotes about Han Yu reappear in *Taiping guangji*, in better light: the "fondness for *qi*" story appears grouped with other remarkable stories about the "Talented and Famous" (*caiming* 才名), and the "disciples of Han's court" story is placed alongside the account of Han Yu's defense of Li He, and thus becomes instead evidence of his ability as a mentor.

30. For two views on Han's relationship with Hanlin scholars, see Hartman, *Han Yü*, 139–40, and David L. McMullen, "Han Yü: An Alternative Picture," *Harvard Journal of Asiatic Studies* 49, no. 2 (Dec. 1989): 614–15.

31. Zhao Lin identifies himself as a Right Omissioner in the text. His claims to be a descendent of the Zhenyuan-era minister Zhao Zongru 趙宗儒 and also a descendent of a branch of the Hedong Liu 柳 clan are verified by Cao Zhongfu 曹中孚 in his annotations to *Yinhua lu*, collected in *Tang Wudai biji xiaoshuo daguan*, 831–32. Zhao Zongru's biography is found in *Jiu Tangshu*, 167.4361 and *Xin Tangshu*, 151.4856.

32. One such anecdote recounts the story of Pei Du's intercession on Liu Yuxi's behalf in 815, intended to move Liu to a place of exile that would not be as dangerous. The *Yinhua lu* anecdote portrays Xianzong as having been "shamed" by Pei's critique, thus the emphasis is on the talent of the wise minister to bring the emperor to a moral choice, a theme repeated elsewhere in the text.

33. *Yinhua lu*, in *Tang Guoshi bu*; *Yinhua lu*, 6.117; and *Tang Wudai biji xiaoshuo daguan*, 873.

34. Xuanzong also hired sons of high officials of the Yuanhe era for his staff and for positions in the government. See Denis Twitchett, ed., *The Cambridge History of China*, vol. 3, pt. 1, *Sui and T'ang China, 589–906* (Cambridge: Cambridge University Press, 1979), 670. Zhao's *Yinhua lu* would have appealed to Xuanzong for both reasons and may have helped Zhao win or advance in office.

35. The *Yinhua lu* is structured by both chronology and rank: the first chapter contains anecdotes about successive emperors from Xuanzong 玄宗 down to the seventh year of Xuanzong's Dazhong 大中 reign. Some of the anecdotes are clearly based on word of mouth, as the title suggests. This may be part of what led later bibliographers to consistently categorize it as *xiaoshuo*. See the preface in Zhou Xunchu 周勛初, ed., *Tang yulin jiaozheng* 唐語林校證 (Beijing: Zhonghua shuju, 1987), 4–5.

36. A few of these identifications are uncertain; I follow Zhou Xunchu's notes to *Tang yulin*, which are also cited by Cao Zhongfu in the *Tang Wudai biji xiaoshuo daguan* edition of *Yinhua lu*.

37. *Yinhua lu*, 3.82; *Tang Wudai biji xiaoshuo daguan*, 846.

38. That the note regarding the identity of his chief examiner is Zhao Lin's own is confirmed by Zhou Xunchu through the Qing dynasty *Dengkeji kao* 登科記考 (Verified record of successful examination candidates) and noted in *Tang yulin jiaozheng*, 2.146–47.

39. *Han Yu quanji jiaozhu*, 2391–93.

40. Zhao Lin, *Yinhua lu*, 1.72.

41. A detailed anecdote found in the Song-era text *Tang yulin* extends the *Yuanhe ti* problem further to the Kaicheng era (833–37) in an anecdote in which the minister Li Jue (李珏, fl. 840) chides emperor Wenzong 文宗 (r. 827–40) for wishing to establish Scholars of Poetry in the Hanlin and dismisses the "Kaicheng style" for frivolity. This story is translated and discussed in Owen, *The Late Tang*, 25–26. There is no extant Tang source for this text and no version of this story in Li Jue's *Xin Tangshu* biography (182.5359–62). I suspect that it may be a very late Tang or even a Song invention, a case of back-formation based on stories of the *Yuanhe ti*. Nonetheless, the anecdote confirms the persistence of the phrase *Yuanhe ti* into the Song.

42. Unlike the *Guoshi bu*, the *Zhiyan* was categorized as *xiaoshuo* in Song bibliographies. See Moore, *Rituals of Recruitment*, 46.

43. Moore notes that later citations of the *Zhiyan* point to texts that have been lost from the extant edition, though the figure of fifteen *juan* is cited consistently in the Song. See *Rituals of Recruitment*, 45–46, 58–59.

44. Moore examines the diverse composition of this large body of texts, noting that "294 documents are attributable to individual authors and compilers as well as to government drafting agencies" (51).

45. Moore points out that almost all the *Zhiyan* material on poetry was absorbed into the *Tangshi jishi* (63).

46. See Wang Dingbao, *Tang Zhiyan jiaozhu* 唐摭言校注, ed. Jiang Hanchun 姜漢椿 (Shanghai: Shanghai shehui kexueyuan chubanshe, 2003), 4.90 and 13.273 (for Li Guan), 5.107–8 and 6.131–32 (Li Ao's letters), 4.99 and 5.105 (Zhang Ji's criticism).

47. As Moore notes, this is a misattribution. The quoted passage instead likely derives from Han's letter to Feng Su (303).

48. As the funerary documents for Meng and Han recount, Han Yu and the others assisted Meng Jiao's family after Meng's death in 814; Zhang Ji, Li Ao, and others did the same for Han Yu's family after Han's death in 824.

49. Wang Dingbao, *Tang zhiyan jiaozhu*, 4.99.

50. Ibid., 5.109–112.

51. Ibid., 7.143.

52. Ibid., 5.115. Wang also cites and corrects a memorial by Wei Zhuang 韋莊 (*jinshi* 894) to posthumously honor those who had not passed the *jinshi* exam, a list that mistakenly included Meng Jiao (10.216).

53. Aside from the praise implied by the inclusion of texts from the Han Yu circle, Wang's closing encomium to the "teachers-as-friends" (*shiyou* 師友) section explicitly praises their reliance on others in adversity. See Moore, *Rituals of Recruitment*, 102. Moore also notes that subtitles like "teachers-as-friends" are likely late additions, but they provide evidence as to how these passages were read (44).

54. Wang Dingbao, *Tang zhiyan jiaozhu*, 3.81, 7.152, 10.194, 15.297. Although Yuan is referred to once as "Minister Yuan," that reference appears in the context of a critical anecdote about Yuan's revelry (12.262–63). Wang

also mentions the two together as "Yuan-Bai" in a later anecdote on Jia Dao (11.223).

55. Ibid., 10.194–95. For the possible confusion about which exam this anecdote was meant to refer to, see Moore, *Rituals of Recruitment*, 242. Other errors or problematic attributions are found in 12.143 and 13.149, discussed by Moore (341–42, 346).

56. To give just one example, we might consider the historian's evaluation that concludes Bai Juyi's *Jiu Tangshu* biography, in which he and Yuan Zhen both are praised for the excellence of their official compositions, in particular for their decrees, policy papers, and other prose writing (*Jiu Tangshu*, 116.4359–60). The *Xin Tangshu* evaluation, in contrast, explicitly rejects Bai's prose writing and praises only his poetry. In Yuan Zhen's biography, the *Yuanhe ti* phrase (not *Yuanhe shiti*) is given solely as a definition of the two men's *yuefu* (*Xin Tangshu*, 174.5228).

7 Shen Kuo Chats with Ink Stone and Writing Brush

Ronald Egan

Mengxi bitan 夢溪筆談 (Chatting with my writing brush at Dreams Creek) by Shen Kuo 沈括 (1031–95) is one of the premiere titles among Song dynasty *biji* 筆記 ("brush jottings"). Well known for its attention to the natural world and to many fields of technical knowledge, *Chatting with My Writing Brush* has been hailed as the apogee of scientific inquiry of its era, a rare foray into the sciences from a member of the classically educated and humanistically oriented official class. Studies of the work understandably focus on the technical and scientific entries it contains.[1] One of my goals here is to put the science entries back into the context of Shen Kuo's work as a whole, and to try to identify the distinctive features of Shen Kuo's interests in *Chatting with My Writing Brush*, considered in the entirety of their impressive range and in relation to other Song period anecdotal literature. It is clear, as Shen Kuo himself tells us in his preface, that much of the material he included in *Chatting with My Writing Brush* came from hearsay and informal chats he had over the years, which he reenacts as he "chats" with his ink stone and brush in writing the work. This paper concludes with reflections on the connections between such hearsay, informal conversation, and anecdote and the special traits of Shen Kuo's miscellany.

First we will briefly consider the organization and topical divisions of Shen Kuo's *Chatting with My Writing Brush* and the implications these have for the scope and distinctive features of the work. The transmitted version of *Chatting with My Writing Brush* has seventeen topical categories, which are presented in twenty-six chapters (*juan*). The distribution of topical categories and chapters is as follows:

CHAPTER HEADING	CHAPTER NUMBER(S)
Precedents 故事	1–2
Corrections and Verifications 辯證	3–4
Music 樂律	5–6
Astronomical Phenomena 象數	7–8
Human Affairs 人事	9–10
Governance 官政	11–12
Expedient Wisdom 權智	13
Literary Arts 文藝	14–16
Calligraphy and Painting 書畫	17
Technical Skills 技藝	18
Artifacts and Implements 器用	19
Divine and Supernatural 神奇	20
Strange Events 異事	21
Misunderstandings 謬誤	22
Jests and Jokes 譏謔	23
Miscellaneous Records 雜誌	24–25
Medicine 藥議	26

It was not expected that a *biji* would present itself in categories, yet the few that did so before Shen Kuo's took on a rather different look. (I am assuming that the present categories and structure of the work are Shen Kuo's own rather than some later editor's, because the categories fit the material so well and are rather idiosyncratic.) There were basically two earlier schemes. The first, exemplified by the Five Dynasties or early Northern Song work *Qingyi lu* 清異錄 (Records of the pure and unusual), sometimes attributed to Tao Gu 陶穀 (903–70), basically mimics the standard categories of comprehensive *leishu* 類書 ("encyclopedia"), opening with "The Heavens" and "The Earth," then proceeding through several human categories ("Rulers," "Officials," "Commoners," "Women," "Buddhists," etc.), next to botanical categories and animal categories, then to various types of inanimate objects ("Buildings," "Clothes," "Tools," "Weapons"), then to food groupings, and ending with "Ghosts," "Spirits," and "Demons." Such a scheme attempts to have entries on everything ordinarily thought of as the "ten thousand things" (*wanwu* 萬物).

A narrower scheme essentially focuses on the human world, dividing it up both by social classes and by personality types, so that we have not only emperors, distinguished ministers, and officials, but also persons of outstanding principle, the loyal and filial, the talented, the lofty and aloof, literary figures, and so on. Such an arrangement is found in Wang Pizhi's 王闢之 (b. 1032) *Shengshui yantan lu* 澠水燕談錄 (Record of banquet chats by Sheng River), completed just a few years after Shen Kuo's work.[2] Although not "encyclopedic" like the earlier scheme, this division too derives from a long tradition of categorizing persons by social role and personality.

Shen Kuo's categories are more selective. He makes no attempt at comprehensive coverage, either of the *leishu* kind or even of the narrower human personalities type. The first impression conveyed by his categories is that he has chosen topics that interest him, not caring about the obvious omissions, and that his interests are rather idiosyncratic. Several of his categories are specialized fields, such as music, calligraphy and painting, and medicine. There are some highly original categories, such as expedient wisdom and technical skills. Another distinctive feature is that disparate categories are included within the scheme; for example, the literary and artistic lie side by side with the practical and technical. Finally, the scheme as a whole gives remarkably little attention to the imperial government or, one might say, to a way of thinking about state and society in which the official bureaucracy is central and essential. *Chatting with My Writing Brush* does not begin with rulers and then move on to lower officials. Now, it is true that the opening chapters on precedents are mostly concerned with rites and protocols at the court. In this chapter we glimpse a vestige of the tradition of beginning written works of various kinds with the imperial court, giving it precedence. But actually the bulk of the entries in "Precedents" deal with rather trivial issues of ritual and protocol at the court, for example, which officials are allowed to ride horses into the imperial city, and how the prescribed rituals differ for receiving candidates for the different imperial degrees. He may begin with the court, but it is niceties of protocol that Shen Kuo tells us about rather than acts of wielding political clout. Even the chapter devoted to governance is consistent with this avoidance of the center of power. For what we find therein, contrary to expectation, are entries about particularly ingenious or effective acts by local government officials rather than about court policy or initiatives by high ministers. It is tempting to find a similar significance even in the decision to present the chapter on human affairs *before* that on governance. The normal order would be the reverse, the acts and lives of officials conventionally given precedence over those of non-officials.

The short preface that Shen Kuo wrote to *Chatting with My Writing Brush* is relevant to this discussion:

> Having retired and taken up residence in the woods, I live in deep seclusion and accept no visitors. Recalling discussions I used to have with guests, from time to time I record a single one of them with my brush. It seems, then, that I am engaged in pleasant conversation and this allows me to pass the day contentedly. My ink stone and brush are the only ones I chat with nowadays, and so I call my work "chatting with my brush." I have not presumed privately to make a record of anything concerning our sagely emperor's policies and imperial governance, or matters associated with the imperial palace and court departments. As for affairs connected with the praise or condemnation of gentlemen and officials of recent times, it is not simply that I do not want to talk about what is vile in men; I do not care even to write about what is admirable in them. What I have recorded is restricted to unrestrained chatting and laughter of the hills and woodlands, which bring no advantage or injury to people, on down to words transmitted in the back lanes and alleys—there is nothing I have not included here. Much of what I have recorded came to me by hearsay, and consequently it surely contains errors and omissions. Those who find that what I have said herein is very lowly are free to conclude that I have no desire to say anything at all.
>
> 予退處林下，深居絕過從，思平日與客言者，時紀一事於筆，則若有所晤言，蕭然移日。所與談者，唯筆硯而已，謂之《筆談》。聖謨國政，及事近宮省，皆不敢私紀。至於繫當日士大夫毀譽者，雖善亦不欲書，非止不言人惡而已。所錄唯山間木蔭，率意談噱，不繫人之利害者，下至閭巷之言，靡所不有。亦有得於傳聞者，其間不能無缺謬。以之為言則甚卑，以予為無意於言可也。³

There is much that is conventional rhetoric here, yet there are points of real interest too. In certain ways Shen Kuo's characterization of the contents of his work is very misleading. *Chatting with My Writing Brush* is, after all, known for containing some of the most perceptive observations about nature (including astronomy, botany, optics, magnetism, etc.), mathematics, music, and various crafts in all premodern Chinese writings. The work is hardly limited to "chatting and laughter done in the hills and woodlands." At the same time, Shen Kuo's insistence that he has deliberately avoided writing about the emperor and court, and has likewise refrained from saying anything, favorable or unfavorable, about eminent men of his time is worthy of our attention. First, it is largely true. It is striking how few of his entries broach imperial politics and the persons involved in them. When we recall how eminent Shen Kuo himself was for long periods of his career this silence is particularly noteworthy. It is easy enough to think of a reason for his refusal to write about this aspect of contemporary life that he knew so well. It may be that the court in Chinese history was always beset by factional rivalries and political strife, yet the New Policies period that Shen had lived through was marked by especially divisive and vicious factional conflict. Shen Kuo certainly knew about the trouble Su Shi 蘇軾 (1037–1101) got into for writing unguardedly about factional politics (according to one account, Shen Kuo was partly responsible for Su Shi's arrest).[4] Now that the reformers had fallen out of favor, he was not going to be so reckless as to write, even positively, about figures caught up in the political vortex of the day.

Even more significant than what he refuses to address is what that refusal directs him toward as an alternative. Having turned his back on officialdom, Shen Kuo finds himself facing a very different range of subjects: that which lies outside of the high circles of power, "on down to words transmitted in the back lanes and alleys—there is nothing I have not included here." Again, this may sound formulaic, but when we turn to the entries of *Chatting with My Writing Brush* themselves, this claim will be seen to have special resonance.

CRAFTSMEN AND LABORERS

We begin with the socially low material found in *Chatting with My Writing Brush*. Shen Kuo has an appreciation of the knowledge and expertise of such persons as craftsmen (e.g., builders, printers) and even laborers. He admires them for their know-how and insights into a particular craft or field of knowledge. Often these are the kinds of insights that only the laborer or craftsman could have—gained not from books but from years of toil in a particular line of work. Such admiration is not unprecedented in Song period *biji*, but in Shen Kuo's work it is unusually prominent.

In an entry on repairing a well that had been dug for collecting salt in Sichuan we glimpse Shen's respect for this know-how and creativity. A long wooden shaft had been put into the well, standing on the bottom and rising all the way up to ground level. Buckets were lowered by pulley along this shaft to the bottom, some five hundred feet down, where they filled with brine, and were then hoisted up. As the years passed, the bottom of the shaft gradually rotted and a new section needed to be spliced in. But whenever laborers were sent down to begin the work they were overcome by noxious gases at the bottom of the well and died. Eventually it was noticed that after a rain the air at the bottom of the well was less noxious. So workers improvised a large wooden container at the top of the well. Multiple tiny holes were drilled in this device so that when it was filled with water, droplets fell constantly into the well, simulating rain. Once this "rain bowl" (*yupan* 雨盤) was put to into operation, workers could be lowered to the bottom to complete the shaft replacement. This was obviously an ad hoc solution, created to resolve a particular problem and inspired by careful observation on the part of the well laborers. The entry describing it stands at the head of Shen Kuo's chapter on "Expedient Wisdom" 權智.[5] Later entries in that chapter feature ingenious actions by local officials, generals, spies, and swordsmen. But the well-diggers take their place beside the more celebrated types, and are even allowed to open the chapter. The very idea that the word "wisdom" (*zhi* 智) could be applied to well-diggers might have seemed strange to many in our author's social class.

Shen Kuo takes particular interest in builders. In one entry he provides a description of a builders' manual, now lost, entitled *Mujing* 木經 (The lumber classic), usually said to have been written either by the master carpenter Yu Hao 喻皓, who lived at the end of the Five Dynasties period and into the Northern Song, or by his daughter.[6] Shen Kuo provides a description of the manual, which is divided into three parts corresponding to the three levels of a building: the upper section on roofs, the middle section on main enclosures, and the lower section on steps and foundations. But the most interesting thing Shen Kuo has to say about the manual comes at the end of his entry:

> In recent years builders [literally "craftsmen in earthworks and wood"] have become more precise and skillful. Few of them consult the old *Lumber Classic* any more, and no one has yet produced an updated version. This would be a worthwhile task for some talented craftsman.
>
> 近歲土木之工益為嚴善,舊《木經》多不用,未有人重為之,亦良工之一業也。[7]

It is interesting to see that Shen Kuo clearly believes that the builders' know-how exceeds anything that can be found in written form. Shen Kuo wrote this around 1088. Within just a few years, the new work that Shen Kuo envisioned was completed by imperial commission under the direction of Li Jie 李誡 (d. 1110), who surely consulted directly or indirectly with numerous "talented craftsmen." Li's work, *Yingzao fashi* 營造法式 (Architectural methods), became the real "classic" of Chinese architecture for the next several centuries, supplanting the *Lumber Classic*, just as Shen Kuo hoped would happen, and caused it to go out of circulation.

Shen Kuo's most memorable entry on builders is an incident involving Guo Jin 郭進, an early Northern Song official known primarily for his military victories against the Khitan in the Taiyuan region during Song Taizong's 宋太宗 reign (977–97). When Guo was serving as governor of Xingzhou (modern Xingtai city, Hebei), he rebuilt the city wall there and also had a private residence constructed for himself in the city. When the residence was finished, he invited friends and relatives to a banquet there to celebrate the opening of the building. He even extended his invitation to the workers who had constructed it. He seated his family in a wing to the west of the main table and the workmen in a wing to the east of the main table, east being the place of higher honor in ceremonial protocol. One of his guests was disturbed by this and asked Guo how he could so honor the workmen. Guo pointed to the workmen and said, "Those are the men who built this residence" 此造宅者. He pointed to his relatives and said, "And those are the ones who will sell it. It is right that they be seated below the workmen" 此賣宅者，固宜坐造宅者下也. Before long Guo died, and the house was indeed sold to someone outside the family.[8] Shen Kuo's inclusion of the story shows unmistakably that he considered Guo Jin's reasoning to have a certain validity.

One of Shen Kuo's best-known entries concerns Bi Sheng 畢昇 (d. 1051) and his invention of movable type.[9] Shen describes at considerable length the procedure that Bi Sheng had developed for using individual, preformed characters, how they are set into a frame lined with pine resin, the frame then heated from below and the characters pressed down, so that they are perfectly aligned and held fast as the resin cools. The process is reversed once the page has been printed, freeing up the characters to be used again on a new page. Two points about Shen Kuo's account are of special interest. The first is that Shen tells us that Bi Sheng was a commoner (*buyi* 布衣), that is, a member of a class that was generally beneath the notice of men like Shen Kuo. It is worth emphasizing that Shen Kuo's is the only reference to Bi Sheng found in the Song textual record.[10] If it were not for Shen Kuo's entry, in other words, we would have no knowledge of Bi Sheng and the Northern Song invention of book printing by movable type. Shen's entry serves to remind us that below the official and literati classes was a social class of merchants, journeymen, and craftsmen who, like Bi Sheng, made their own contributions to the economic prosperity and technological innovations of Song history, though these are rarely taken account of in sources composed by the educated elite.

Second, there was an interesting personal connection between Shen Kuo and Bi Sheng's invention. At the end of his entry, Shen Kuo tells us that after Bi Sheng died, his set of movable type was obtained by Shen's own "followers" (*quncong* 群從) and was kept by him.[11] The language implies that Shen Kuo had a group of apprentices or helpmates whom we otherwise know nothing about. Now, Shen says nothing about *using* Bi Sheng's movable type for printing projects of his own. (Shen had already made it clear in his entry that Bi Sheng's invention only makes sense to use for large print runs.) Instead, his wording suggests that he stored it away, much as a collector interested in inventions and curios might keep something not to use but simply for its inherent interest as an invention. Clearly, Shen Kuo appreciated the ingenuity of the innovation Bi Sheng had made in the technology of printing, and he decided to do what he could to ensure that the invention would not disappear with the inventor.

THE OBSERVATION OF NATURE

It is Shen Kuo's curiosity about the natural world and his meticulous observation and study of it for which he is best known. This interest of his is amply attested to in *Chatting with My Writing Brush*. Yet *Chatting with My Writing Brush* was not the primary form in which he recorded his insights about nature. It was his sustained treatises on astronomy (including separate works on the calendar, eclipses, and the measurement of time) and on music and harmonics, his atlas of the entire Song state, as well as his works on medicine, that must have contained his most systematic and thorough explorations of the natural world. Unfortunately, these works were all lost, save for a portion of his writings on medicine.[12] Nathan Sivin, who has written the most detailed account of Shen Kuo's life and scientific thought, faults the entries on the natural world in *Chatting with My Writing Brush* for having an ad hoc quality and lacking sustained attention and depth: "The works of his final leisure, however valuable, were all superficial in form. Was this the result of habit, of distance necessitated by disillusion, or of a style appropriate for chatting with one's brush and ink slab in a silent garden? Of all three no doubt."[13] It seems somewhat unfair, given the conventions of the *biji* form, to which *Chatting with My Writing Brush* clearly belongs, not to mention Shen's authorship of extended treatises apart from what he included in *Chatting with My Writing Brush*. Shen Kuo should not be blamed for the loss of those more specialized and systematic studies.

Even within the limitations of the *biji* form, however, certain traits of Shen Kuo's treatment of nature are apparent. Consider the account of his investigation of the displacement of the pole star from true north. It had long been known that what was taken as the "pole star" did not exactly correspond to true north. In the fifth century the mathematician Zu Xuan 祖暅 suggested that the displacement was just over one degree. Shen Kuo was not satisfied with this and set out to make a more precise calculation. His method, described in a single *Chatting with My Writing Brush* entry, was to train a sighting tube on the star and observe how it moved in the field of vision through the duration of the night.[14] He began with a small diameter sighting tube and found that the star soon strayed outside the field of vision. He then switched to a larger diameter sighting tube and observed to see if the star still circulated outside what he could see. By thus experimenting with many different diameter tubes, larger and smaller, and observing at different stages of the night, he finally arrived at a sighting tube that was just large enough to contain the movement of the star around the perimeter of the circular field of vision, without ever moving outside of it. It took him three months to arrive at the right size sighting tube. The midpoint of the circle described by the rotating star was true north, and Shen determined that the star itself was somewhat more than three degrees removed from it. In the course of this investigation, Shen Kuo also produced over two hundred star maps that plotted the patterns of heavenly bodies lying close by the pole star. The entire experiment was described, presumably in greater detail, in his *Xining fengyuan li* 熙寧奉元曆 (Xining memorial calendar), one of his writings that does not survive.

There is great industriousness in Shen Kuo's investigations. We are reminded of the waterclock he built, which he spent over ten years redesigning and refining until he was satisfied with the accuracy of its measurement of time.[15] Beyond effort, however, there are also remarkable powers of observation evident in his inquiry into the natural world, coupled with an open-mindedness that gave him the ability to "see" things that he could not understand. He was honest about what he observed being contrary to widely accepted principles about the world or common sense. His entry on the house of a palace eunuch that was struck by lightning exemplifies this turn of mind. He describes how a steel knife inside a wooden cabinet was melted, while the cabinet itself was unharmed, then reflects how contrary this is to common sense, which holds that fire will burn wood before it can melt metal. These observations lead to these concluding reflections:

> People can only hope to understand phenomena of the human realm. Beyond the human realm, there must be infinite other phenomena. With our paltry human understanding we try to plumb the depths of the ultimate principles of the universe, but is it not impossible to do? 人但知人境中事耳, 人境之外, 事有何限。欲以區區世智情識, 窮測至理, 不其難哉?[16]

In many of the most celebrated passages in *Chatting with My Writing Brush* concerning the natural world we find evidence of Shen Kuo's talent for "seeing" phenomena that others might not notice, and for then reflecting on what those phenomena mean for, or how they challenge, commonplace understandings of the world. Such passages as his discussions of the fossils of ocean creatures in the mountains of Shanxi, petroleum seeps, magnetism, eclipses, the tides, rainbows, meteorites, fertilization of soil with silt, and so on, all manifest these habits of mind.

ECCENTRICS AND SOCIAL MISFITS

It was not only natural phenomena he could not understand that fascinated Shen Kuo. He was likewise intrigued by persons who behaved in unconventional or aberrant ways. The pages of *Chatting with My Writing Brush* are replete with entries concerning such eccentrics. They may be considered the human counterpart of the inexplicable natural events that intrigued Shen Kuo. *Chatting with My Writing Brush* has relatively few entries about persons who exemplify conventional virtues or conduct. But it is full of entries about peculiar people of a wide range of types. The persons may conveniently be divided into two groups. There is first a group of persons who belong to Shen Kuo's station in life—the educated official or literatus—but who exhibit odd traits or conduct. Then there is the type of person who stands distinctly outside Shen Kuo's social circle and usually beneath it.

Here is a translation of an entry concerning a wizard, a member of the second group:

> When Jia Weigong [Jia Changchao 賈昌朝, 998–1065] was grand councilor, there was a certain master of occult arts whose surname was Xu. The man never used his given name in referring to himself in front of anybody. No matter how eminent or lowly the person he spoke with was, he invariably referred to himself as "me." And so

people of the time called him "Xu Me." His conversation contained many observations that warranted notice, yet he was arrogant and treated even high ministers as not worthy of notice. Councilor Jia wished to meet him and sent messengers to invite him several times, but he would not come. Finally, Jia sent one of his own trusted retainers to earnestly entreat him, and only then did he agree. Xu, riding on a donkey, made as if to go straight through to the grand councilor's office. The gatekeeper tried to stop him, but he would not listen. The gatekeeper said, "This is the grand councilor's gate. Even vice ministers must dismount." Xu replied, "I seek nothing from the grand councilor. It was the grand councilor who summoned me. If it must be like this, I will be forced to go back." He turned around and left, without ever getting off his donkey. The gatekeeper chased after him but could not get him to come back, and so he informed the grand councilor. Councilor Jia then dispatched someone to apologize to him and invite him back, but he never returned. Jia sighed with admiration and said, "Xu is but a commoner of the marketplace. Yet because he seeks nothing from others, power and prestige cannot intimidate him. How much less could anyone be intimidated who commits himself to the Way and morality?"

賈魏公為相日，有方士姓許，對人未嘗稱名，無貴賤皆稱我，時人謂之「許我」。言談頗有可採，然傲誕，視公卿蔑如也。公欲見，使人邀召數四，卒不至。又使門人苦邀致之，許騎驢徑欲造丞相廳事，門吏止之不可。吏曰：「此丞相廳門，雖丞郎亦須下。」許曰：「我無所求于丞相，丞相召我來，若如此，但須我去耳。」不下驢而去。門吏急追之不還，以白丞相。魏公又使人謝而召之，終不至。公嘆曰：「許市井人耳，惟其無所求於人，尚不可以勢屈，況其以道義自任者乎。」[17]

Reading the end of this entry, one naturally wonders if there is not some disparity between the lesson that Grand Councilor Jia draws from Xu's behavior and Shen Kuo's interest in the same. The grand councilor is interested in morality as a compass to be used against unprincipled self-interest. Shen Kuo seldom writes about morality in that sense, and in this passage seems more interested in Xu's arrogance and obliviousness of social and political eminence. Councilor Jia wants us to think that if Xu were of higher standing than a mere man "of the marketplace" and embraced conventional Confucian morality, he would be even more uncompromising and impressive. But Shen Kuo already seems to find Xu impressive just the way he is, refusing to let anyone know his given name, resisting the grand councilor's invitation, and intent upon riding his donkey right into the ministerial compound. Shen Kuo opens his chapter on "Craftsmen and Artisans" with this entry. So we know that Shen must be thinking of Xu's identity as a "master of occult arts" (*fangshi* 方士). It is safe to assume that Shen discerns some connection between that identity and the character of the man that the anecdote focuses upon. Xu's disregard for conventional social distinctions is presumably linked, in our author's eyes, to his accomplishments in the occult arts. Such substitution of the prestige of specialized know-how, whether it be in Xu's field or in that of the master builder or well digger, for that of conventional social hierarchy, is the possibility that appears to intrigue Shen Kuo.

Certain individuals manifested economic anomalies in Song society, such as fabulously wealthy men who were completely ignorant of the ways of elite society. Shen Kuo is interested in in this type of oddity too, evidently for the challenge it poses to the assumption that wealth and elite culture go hand-in-hand. Shen writes about a peculiar neighbor Shi Yannian 石延年 (style-name Manqing 曼卿) had when he was living in the Caihe district of the capital (Kaifeng). The neighbor, named Li, was only twenty years old and lived by himself, but he was wealthy enough to keep "several tens" (*shu shi* 數十) of silk-clad concubines in his home. When Shi Yannian, whose curiosity was piqued by the sight of many servants coming and going from the man's gate, asked if he might meet Li, he was told that he had never received any "educated gentleman" (*shidafu* 士大夫). Yet Li had heard about Yannian's exceptional capacity for alcohol, and since he too liked to drink was willing to make an exception in Yannian's case. A date for a meeting was fixed, and when Yannian entered Li's home and was greeted by his host he noticed that Li was not wearing the customary robe and cap of the elite class, nor did he have any idea how to bow or greet him properly as host. They passed the evening eating and drinking together, entertained by music the concubines played. When Yannian took his leave, again his host did not know how to bow in farewell. As Yannian walked out, he marveled that such a boorish fellow, "who could not distinguish beans from wheat, would nevertheless enjoy such a privileged way of life. It was extremely bizarre" 殆不分菽麥, 而奉養如此, 極可怪也.[18] Beautiful and talented concubines, together with delicious wine and rare delicacies to eat, should not be found in the dwelling of a man who was ignorant of gentlemanly decorum.[19] But the incongruity was manifested in this strange neighbor, and Shen Kuo describes him in considerable detail.

Perhaps the most remarkable entry about an unconventional man is one about the Sichuanese rebel Li Shun 李順.[20] In this account we clearly see Shen Kuo's own unconventionality, as he gives a strikingly sympathetic description of Li Shun's endeavor as rebel. Li Shun inherited leadership of the uprising from Wang Xiaobo 王小博, his older sister's husband, in 994. The rebellion grew rapidly in that year and within a few months had taken the city of Chengdu, where Li Shun proclaimed himself king of the Shu (Sichuan) region.[21] The territory under the rebels' control eventually expanded to include most of the modern province of Sichuan, and they began to attack northward, evidently intending to extend the rebellion toward the heartland of the empire. Imperial armies under the command of Wang Jien 王繼恩 were sent to counterattack. The suppression of the rebellion took several months, and when Wang Jien eventually recaptured Chengdu later in 994, the rebel army he defeated is said to have numbered over one hundred thousand.[22]

Shen Kuo's entry begins by correcting the standard version of Li Shun's death—the version still found in orthodox historiographical sources such as *Xu Zizhi tongjian changbian* 續資治通鑑長編 (Continuation of the long version of the comprehensive mirror for aid in governance) and the *Songshi* 宋史 (History of the Song dynasty). That version holds that Li Shun was captured and put to death when the rebels were defeated at Chengdu.[23] Shen Kuo tells us that actually the man who was taken to be Li Shun at that time was an imposter. It was not until the 1030s that a military inspector in distant Guangdong, Chen Wenlian 陳文璉, reported that the real Li Shun, now over seventy, was still alive and hiding in that southeastern region. He was apprehended and taken to the capital for execution. But inasmuch as the court had been duped for thirty years, and had already rewarded the man who captured the false Li Shun, it handled the affair quietly and never publicly acknowledged its mistake. Shen Kuo was a personal friend of Chen Wenlian and had access to the formal report he wrote about the incident, "Deposition on Li Shun" ("Li Shun ankuan" 李順案款). Having set the record straight, Shen Kuo's entry continues:

> Shun was the younger brother of the wife of Wang Xiaobo of Weijiang. When Wang rebelled in the Shu region he was unable to keep control of his followers, who then put Shun forward as their new leader. As soon as he was installed, Shun summoned all the wealthy persons of great clans in the countryside and had them provide an accounting of their riches and grain. Appropriating everything they had beyond what they required to sustain themselves, he then distributed it all to people who were impoverished and in need. He gave posts to men of talent and ability and protected and comforted those who were good and upstanding. His commands were stern and unequivocal, and wherever he went no one opposed him. At the time, the two regions of Shu were experiencing a great famine. Within a week or so, tens of thousands of persons flocked to Shun. Every pre-

fecture and county he approached opened its gates to welcome him in, and wherever his manifestos arrived all defensive fortifications were abandoned. After his defeat the people still cherished him. That is why he was able to escape and why it was more than thirty years before he was finally put to death.

順本味江王小博之妻弟。始王小博反于蜀中，不能撫其徒眾，乃共推順為主。順初起，悉召鄉里富人大姓，令具其家所有財粟，據其生齒足用之外，一切調發，大賑貧乏，錄用材能，存撫良善，號令嚴明，所至一無所犯。時兩蜀大饑，旬日之間，歸之者數萬人。所向州縣，開門延納，傳檄所至，無復完壘。及敗，人尚懷之，故順得脫去，三十餘年乃始就戮。[24]

This remarkable passage shows Shen Kuo's ability to see the rebel in a most unusual way. Indeed, much of the language Shen Kuo uses to characterize Li Shun's policies and the popular reaction to him is drawn directly from the tradition of extolling idealized officials or even dynastic founders.

THE UNPREDICTABLE, PARADOXICAL, AND MULTIVALENT: GETTING BEYOND CONVENTIONAL MORALITY

In the foregoing I have discussed Shen Kuo's appreciation of the knowledge of craftsmen and laborers, his scrutiny of the natural world, and his interest in eccentrics. I turn now to a topical cluster of entries that is somewhat more diffuse and challenging to characterize succinctly. The common thread that runs through this group is Shen Kuo's attention to human affairs (as opposed to natural phenomena) that are unexpected or personalities that are odd or exhibit contradictory traits. Many of these entries touch upon ethics or moral issues, and often the gist of an anecdote is to call into question conventional ideas about right and wrong or to challenge the notion that the world is essentially a moral place. In Shen Kuo's mind, the human world (like the natural world) is full of paradoxical realities: there are consequences that do not follow logically or ethically from their causes, persons who do not conduct themselves according to social norms, and values whose validity is contingent and contested. One senses that Shen Kuo glimpsed a kind of human world that was far more complex and multivalent than that commonly perceived through eyes conditioned by conventional Confucian and Buddhist values.

We begin with a seemingly inconsequential example. In Northern Song period anecdotal literature, Shi Yannian is known primarily for his drinking capacity (we have already seen reference to this), in addition to his skill as poet. There are many, many stories about his extraordinary tolerance for alcohol. When Shen Kuo tells a Shi Yannian story, however, he does so with a twist. The passage begins predictably enough, describing Yannian's drinking bouts with his buddy Liu Qian 劉潛. In this account what is featured is the various outlandish postures Yannian made it his habit to assume for his guests' amusement during the long hours of indulgence. There was the posture he called "prisoner drinking" (*qiuyin* 囚飲), in which he untied his hair, took off his shoes, and donned shackles; there was what he called "turtle drinking" (*guiyin* 鱉飲), in which he wrapped his upper body in wheat stalks then extended his head out each time he wanted a sip, then withdrew his head back inside again; and there was the one known as "bird's nest drinking" (*chaoyin* 巢飲), in which he consumed his liquor while perched in the bough of a tree. The real surprise comes at the entry's end. Emperor Renzong, Shen Kuo tells us, cherished Yannian's talents and once remarked to his ministers that he wished Yannian would stop drinking, to safeguard his health. Eventually, the emperor's wishes were conveyed to Yannian, who immediately gave up drinking altogether out of deference to his ruler. Soon thereafter, however, Yannian contracted an illness and died.[25] Of all the stories about Shi Yannian, Shen Kuo's is the only one that includes this detail about how he died. That the famous drinker fell ill and died from *not* drinking is an aspect of his life that no other author relates, and it matches perfectly Shen Kuo's interest in the bizarre and inexplicable.

There are likewise certain things that happen that run completely contrary to reason. Consider the case of Mei Zhi 梅摯 (994–1059) and the Crowfoot Stream 烏腳溪 in southern Fujian. This stream darkened the feet of anyone who stepped in it. Anyone who drank from it was said to contract malaria. On his official travels in the region, Mei Zhi once had to cross it. Mei Zhi had long suffered from various ailments, and he was particularly apprehensive about crossing this stream. He took elaborate precautions and arranged to have himself carried across on the shoulders of several men. He even covered his entire body with matting, so that not a drop of the water could touch him. In his nervousness, he urged the men to hurry through the water, and somehow they dropped him into it. He was completely submerged, momentarily, and when he got to the other side his entire body looked "as black as a Kunlun man, and he was sure he would die" 黑如崑崙, 自謂必死.[26] Strangely enough, however, after this incident, Mei's many ailments all left him, and he enjoyed better health the rest of his life than he had ever known previously.[27]

One of the most interesting entries concerns virtue, compassion, and the unpredictability of their rewards.

When Wang Yanzheng occupied Jianzhou [and proclaimed himself king of Yin, in 943], he put one of his primary generals, a certain Zhang, in charge of defending the Jianzhou city. Zhang once ordered one of his lieutenants to reconnoiter the situation beyond the fortifications, but he was late in reporting back and faced execution. Zhang valued the lieutenant for his talent and had not yet decided how to handle the case. Returning home, he mentioned his quandary to his wife. This woman, née Lian, was virtuous and wise. She secretly sent someone to tell the lieutenant, "According to military law you deserve to be put to death. If you quickly run away you may yet escape with your life." She gave him several dozen taels of silver, adding, "Leave right away, and don't think about your family." The lieutenant succeeded in escaping surreptitiously and went over to Li Jing of Jiangnan [i.e., the Southern Tang], where he joined the staff of general Zha Wenhui. When Wenhui attacked Wang Yanzheng, this lieutenant was put in command of the campaign. When the city was about to fall, he let it be known that if anyone inside the city could protect the Lian clan and save it from harm, that person would be handsomely rewarded. Woman Lian, hearing of this, sent a messenger to tell him, "The people of Jian have done no wrong. I hope that you, general, will graciously agree to spare them. It is my husband and I whose misdeeds deserve death, and we dare not hope to survive. If, however, you cannot bring yourself to spare the people of Jian, I wish to be the first to die. I swear that I shall not be the only one saved." Her words were filled with noble sentiments, borne of her absolute sincerity. Having no choice, the lieutenant called his troops back, stopping their attack, and went into the city with weapons sheathed. In this way, the entire city escaped harm. Even today, the Lian clan is an important clan of Jian'an, and one after another have risen to be ministers in the imperial court. They are all the descendants of Woman Lian.

There was likewise what happened when Li Jing [ruler of the Southern Tang] sent his general Hu Ze to defend Jiangzhou. When the Jiangnan state [Southern Tang] surrendered, Cao Han besieged Jiangzhou for three years. The city wall was so well fortified that it could not be breached. One day Hu Ze became angry with one of his soldier-cooks for preparing a dish of shad poorly, and he said he intended to put the man to death. His wife abruptly stopped him, saying, "Your officers and soldiers have been defending the city for several years. The bleached bones of those who have died cover the ground. How could you kill one of these men over a single meal?" With this, Hu Ze spared the man. That night the man lowered himself over the city wall on a rope and joined with Cao Han. He told Cao everything about the defenses of the city. In the southwest the city wall abutted high ground, and so it had been left unfortified at the point. The man led Cao Han's troops to attack at that point.

The city fell on the very day they launched this attack, the entire Hu clan was killed and not one member was left alive. These two wives manifested the same virtue and compassion. Why were the consequences they brought about so different?

王延政據建州，令大將章某守建州城，嘗遣部將刺事于軍前，後期，當斬，惜其才，未有以處。歸語其妻，其妻連氏有賢智，私使人謂部將曰：「汝法當死，急逃乃免。」與之銀數十兩曰：「徑行，無顧家也。」部將得以潛去，投江南李主，以隸查文徽麾下。文徽攻延政，部將適主是役，城將陷，先喻城中能全連氏一門者有重賞。連氏使人謂之曰：「建民無罪，將軍幸赦之，妾夫婦罪當死，不敢圖生。若將軍不釋建民，妾願同百姓死，誓不獨生也。」詞氣感慨，發于至誠。不得已為之戢兵而入，一城獲全。至今連氏為建安大族，官至卿相者接踵，皆連氏後也。

又李璟使大將胡則守江州，江南國下，曹翰以兵圍之三年，城堅不可破，一日，則怒一饔人鱠魚不精，欲殺之。其妻遽止之曰：「士卒守城累年矣，暴骨滿地，奈何以一食殺士卒耶。」則乃捨之。此卒夜縋城走投曹翰，具言城中虛實。先是，城西南依嶮素不設備，卒乃引王師自西南攻之，是夜城陷，胡則一門無遺類。二人者，其為德一也，何其報效之不同。[28]

Of the two incidents narrated in this entry, the first is a type routinely seen in *biji* writings. A virtuous act is performed and eventually recompense for it returns to the person who performed it. The demonstration of goodness is not just repaid in equal measure; it is abundantly, extravagantly repaid and redounds upon the woman's entire city and generations of her descendents. The world evoked in this type of anecdote is an inherently moral place where good deeds, even those performed in secret, earn their appropriate rewards. It is a comforting vision of a moral world order. The second incident, considerably less common in this kind of writing, evokes a very different sort of world. It is a distinctly amoral or even perverse order, in which compassionate impulses lead not only to no reward but actually bring disaster upon the virtuous person.

The most striking aspect of Shen Kuo's entry is its juxtaposition of these two starkly different visions of how the world works. Shen is careful not to take sides. There is no suggestion that one vision of the world is more accurate than the other. What is implied, actually, is that the two are equal in significance and frequency, equally "right." It is the joining of the two incidents that points to Shen Kuo's true intent. He does not endorse one or the other possibility. He suggests that both sorts of sequences happen, and there is no rhyme or reason to why one occurs now and its inverse later. He is neither an optimist nor a pessimist regarding the exercise of virtue and its rewards. He is ultimately most interested in the coexistence of contrary consequences—that is the real lesson of his entry.

HEARSAY AND ANECDOTE IN SHEN KUO'S MISCELLANY

Material that came to Shen Kuo orally, mostly in the course of informal conversations with friends, accounts for a large portion of the content of *Chatting with My Writing Brush*. Sometimes Shen specifically identifies conversation as his source. More often it is left to us to posit such an origin. That is relatively easy to do, since so few of his entries could be based on written sources.

If we say only that hearsay was a crucial source for Shen Kuo's miscellany, we have not said much, since the same could be said for any number of Song period *biji*. But hearsay has a special significance in *Chatting with My Writing Brush*. It makes available to Shen Kuo the vast amount of material concerning socially "low" persons and topics that are a distinctive feature of his work: the material on crafts, artisans, and laborers, as well as the material on those many eccentrics whose conduct, if not social origins, made it impossible for them to be considered educated gentlemen. It is Shen Kuo's insight into the value of artisan and even laborer knowledge concerning everything from dike repair to weather forecasting, well digging, and book printing that is one key to the special nature of his work.[29] If Shen had not had an ear attuned to reports of what these members of the merchant and lower classes were doing and discovering, *Chatting with My Writing Brush* would be greatly impoverished.

We may even discern a distinctive type of hearsay and use to which it is put in Shen Kuo's collection. In many of the essays in this volume, gossip and rumor are presented as phenomena counterposed to "official" versions of biography and historiography, which they compete with or serve to challenge and destabilize. Among Shen Kuo's anecdotes discussed here, only one of them conspicuously involves that kind of hearsay: the one about the rebel Li Shun, which starkly challenges the official version of his capture and execution. Generally, Shen Kuo is attracted by a different kind of oral report. It is one that tends to stand outside the juxtaposition of official versus insider narrative, one that raises a different type of question concerning received wisdom. Shen Kuo is intrigued by the inexplicable or the anomalous, both in the natural world and in the social world. Yet the objects of his fascination transcend conventional interest in secrets lurking within the halls of the politically powerful and in anomalies as brought about by the supernatural powers of ghosts, gods, and demons. He is interested in anomalies that are not readily understood as the result of the intercession by the "usual suspects" of supreme human or supernatural agency. When he hears the report of the eunuch's house struck by lightning, and the unexpected effects the bolt had upon different materials inside the house, he does not try to understand the event with reference to conventional supernatural beings. Similarly, the eccentrics he is interested in (e.g., Shi Yannian's wealthy but boorish neighbor), or the inexplicable and unpredictable sequences of events that befall people (e.g., the effect that submersion in Crowfoot Stream had upon Mei Zhi's health) lie outside the familiar opposition of empowered and unempowered persons or that between "official" and thus suspect historiography as contrasted with unofficial and thus more credible historiography. Yet while what attracts Shen Kuo's attention may differ from gossip and hearsay as we usually find them reflected in other sources, we should recognize that the origin of much of what he writes about in *Chatting with My Writing Brush* is, indeed, anecdotes and stories that circulated orally and came to his attention in oral form. It is the nature of a large percentage of his material, the material he adopted and made his own, that it did not initially lend itself to being recorded in writing because it fell outside the conventional boundaries of what historians and literati wrote about.

Another sense in which "talk" is important in Shen Kuo's work is suggested by his title. As his preface explains, the model for the "chatting" he is doing with his writing brush is informal conversation he had had with friends over the years, which was the source of many of his entries. It is significant that Shen Kuo thinks of his writing this way. It is not "serious" or scholarly writing. He expects that readers may be disappointed by the inclusion of so much material that is "very lowly" (*shenbei* 甚卑), and tries to disarm any criticism by first acknowledging that he has no intent of "saying anything at all." Shen's "chatting" with his writing brush, that is, his act of composing this work, mimics the chatting with friends he had done over the years that originally brought the bulk of his material to his attention (as he indicates in his preface). Moreover, the material stands outside the types of subjects a person of his learning and political eminence would be expected to address in writing. Of course Shen Kuo's is not the only Song period *biji* to include such material, but against the background of his previous official eminence, the abundance of that material in *Chatting with My Writing Brush*, and his self-consciousness about the unconventional nature of what he is doing in the work, stand out.

The anecdotal form of Shen Kuo's work is also inseparable from its special traits, if by "anecdote" we mean a short self-contained account of behavior or events, and understand that in a collection of such entries there will be no integral connection between consecutive passages, except that they fit loosely into the same topical heading given to each chapter. Despite what Nathan Sivin says about the shortcomings of this mode of exposition, it has its advantages as well. It allows the author to offer up fleeting observations and insights into a subject that need not be subsumed inside a larger scheme or argument. It is particularly advantageous when all the author intends to do is to make a preliminary observation about, say, some anomalous phenomena or something seldom if ever noticed previously that he cannot yet necessarily make sense of or fit into a larger scheme of understanding. Considerable interest in *Chatting with My Writing Brush* comes from Shen Kuo's exercise of this freedom. How else could he have presented his observations concerning, for example, ink made from petroleum soot, the geologic effects of silting and erosion, the shape of the moon, and sympathetic resonance between stringed instruments?[30] Such passages may be only rudimentary "science," but each played its part in the gradual accumulation of knowledge in a particular field, and in many cases Shen Kuo's observations on a subject are the first recorded in Chinese writings. As noted earlier, it is not as if Shen Kuo was incapable of producing extended studies of certain subjects.

The irony is that those extended studies did not survive, while *Chatting with My Writing Brush* did. Or is it ironic? Actually, several of Shen Kuo's scholarly works were studies of the Confucian classics, hardly an underdeveloped field. It seems likely that the other major works, on such subjects as astronomy and calendar reform, eclipses, water clocks and time measurement, city walls as defensive fortifications, and medicinal herbs were so specialized and technical in nature that the number of readers who would or could read them would have been very small. So perhaps it is not unexpected that the survival rate among these works was low. *Chatting with My Writing Brush*, by contrast, was widely and eagerly read. Completed in the late 1080s or early 1090s, it seems to have been printed right away. It is already quoted in Wang Pizhi's work of 1095, *Shengshui yantan lu*.[31] Even more revealing is the statement found in a postscript to an 1166 reprint of Shen's work, done in Yangzhou, that the prefectural treasury, having stocked copies of an earlier imprint of *Chat-*

ting with My Writing Brush, was in the habit of selling them on the open market whenever it was short of funds.³² This is not the sort of statement often made about *biji* in twelfth-century sources. If there was a special market for *Chatting with My Writing Brush,* it was presumably because readers found it to be of unusual interest and utility.

NOTES

1. The fullest discussion in English of *Chatting with My Writing Brush* and Shen Kuo's contributions to scientific thought is Nathan Sivin, "Shen Kua," in *Dictionary of Scientific Biography,* ed. Charles C. Gillispie (New York: Scribner, 1975), 12:369–93. (Shen's given name is variously read as "Kuo" and "Gua"; the latter becomes "Kua" in the Wade-Giles romanization that Nathan Sivin uses.) This article was reprinted as "Shen Kua: A Preliminary Assessment of his Scientific Thought and Achievements," *Sung Studies Newsletter* 13 (1977): 31–56. An earlier study in English, which gives more attention to the humanistic material in *Chatting with My Writing Brush,* is Donald Holzman, "Shen Kua and his *Meng-ch'i pi-t'an,*" *T'oung Pao* 46 (1958): 260–92.

2. Wang Pizhi, *Shengshui yantan lu,* in Zhu Yi'an 朱易安 et al., ed., *Quan Song biji* 全宋筆記, 2nd ser., 10 vols. (Zhengzhou: Daxiang chubanshe, 2006), 4:1–107.

3. See Shen Kuo, *Mengxi bitan,* in Zhu Yi'an, *Quan Song biji,* 2nd ser., 3:7. All references are to this edition unless otherwise specified.

4. See Chen Zhensun 陳振孫 (fl. 1211–49), *Zhizhai shulu jieti* 直齋書錄解題, ed. Xu Xiaoman 徐小蠻 and Gu Meihua 顧美華 (Shanghai: Shanghai guji chubanshe, 1987), 20.591.

5. Shen Kuo, *Mengxi bitan,* 13.103.

6. Ibid., 18.132–33.

7. Ibid., 18.133.

8. Ibid., 9.79.

9. Ibid., 18.137.

10. In 1990 a stele was discovered in Yingshan County 英山縣 in Hubei that marked the tomb of someone it refers to as "Bi Sheng shenzhu" 畢昇神主. Local officials and scholars of national repute have declared this to be the tomb of Shen Kuo's Bi Sheng, although one suspects that local pride has played a considerable part in the authentication process. There are local places not far from the tomb site named after the Bi family, suggesting the family was (at some point in history) of considerable prominence in the area.

11. Shen Kuo, *Mengxi bitan,* 18.137.

12. For a list of all known writings by Shen Kuo, which contains as many as forty titles (some of which are surely variants of each other), see Shen Kuo, *Mengxi bitan jiaozheng* 夢溪筆談校證, ed. Hu Daojing 胡道靜 (Shanghai: Shanghai guji chubanshe, 1987), 1151–56.

13. Nathan Sivin, "Shen Kua: A Preliminary Assessment," 30.

14. Shen Kuo, *Mengxi bitan,* 7.56–57.

15. Ibid., 7.57–58.
16. Ibid., 20.151–52.
17. Ibid., 18.132.
18. Ibid., 9.74–75.
19. On the related theme of courtesans, see Beverly Bossler's essay, chapter 8 of the present volume.
20. Shen Kuo, *Mengxi bitan*, 25.193–94.
21. Li Tao 李濤 (1115–84), *Xu Zizhi tongjian changbian* 續資治通鑑長編 (Beijing: Zhonghua shuju, 1957), 35.767.
22. Ibid., 36.784.
23. Ibid., 36.784; and Tuotuo (Toghto) 脫脫 (1313–55), ed., *Songshi* (Beijing: Zhonghua shuju, 1977), 466.13603, 13624.
24. Shen Kuo, *Mengxi bitan*, 25.193–94.
25. Ibid., 9.82.
26. *Kunlun* was a broad term used to designate dark-skinned foreigners, including Malays, Javanese, Southern Indians, and even East Africans. For a discussion of the range of applications of the term during the Tang dynasty, see Edward H. Schafer, *The Golden Peaches of Samarkand: A Study of T'ang Exotics* (Berkeley: University of California Press, 1963), 45–47.
27. Shen Kuo, *Mengxi bitan*, 24.184.
28. Ibid., 9.73–74.
29. For the passage on the technique a merchant taught a State University professor for forecasting high winds on Jiangnan rivers and lakes, see ibid., 25.190.
30. In ibid., 24.177, 179–80; 24.180–81; 7.58; and 6.49–50.
31. Wang Pizhi, *Shengshui yantan lu*, 8.88.
32. Tang Xiunian 湯脩年, "Ba" 跋, in *Mengxi bitan*, 206.

8 Men, Women, and Gossip in Song China

Beverly Bossler

The Song dynasty (960–1279) saw a spectacular proliferation of anecdotal sources, ranging from gossipy reports of court politics to the newly popular genre of "remarks on poetry" (*shihua* 詩話).[1] Song anecdotes, like those of other periods, are a rich source for the kind of literary analysis exemplified by other essays in this volume. But in this chapter I am concerned not (or not only) with the nature of the texts themselves, but rather with what they can tell us about aspects of Song social life.

As a historian, I am interested in understanding "what really happened," and for that purpose anecdotes might seem a dubious genre to investigate: as other authors have pointed out, part of what marks gossip as gossip is its unverifiable nature. Still, the persuasiveness of gossip *qua* gossip depends on its general plausibility, and therein lays its usefulness to the historian. Although we cannot be certain that any particular event described in a gossipy Song anecdote actually transpired, we can be fairly sure that the social situation that forms the background to the incident was realistic and plausible to Song readers. As long as our focus is not on the "truth" of any given incident, but on the social contexts in which those incidents unfolded, the otherwise historically suspect nature of anecdotes renders them more rather than less useful. This is especially the case when anecdotes and other records of gossip reveal aspects of social and cultural life that are otherwise ignored in more formal or self-consciously historical genres.

One topic that gossips loved to discuss, and that formal sources rarely addressed, was romantic relationships between men and women. Anecdotes accordingly provide an important window on gender relations and on the contexts and social rituals that shaped male-female interaction.

In the discussion here, I explore some of the types of information about gender relations that can be gleaned from anecdotal sources, but I also consider what cannot be known. We will see that in some respects the sources are very rich: we can learn a great deal about the cultural institutions that framed men's interactions with women, and something of male romantic ideals. At the same time, we will find that the sources are heavily constrained. In part those constraints are due to generic conventions, but also, I suggest, to the demands of social convention. By taking note of topics that could not be discussed even in genres meant to amuse and entertain, we gain some insight into Song social taboos.

THE CONTEXTS OF SONG ROMANCE

With respect to the study of gender, anecdotal sources are perhaps most useful in providing (almost inadvertently) information about the social contexts in which men and women formed romantic attachments. As recent scholarship on gender in China has pointed out, much of Chinese social life in the imperial period was "homosocial" in nature.[2] In other words, to a great extent, the social circles of elite men and women were strictly segregated: elite women were excluded from the examination system and official careers that were the focus of elite men's lives, and except in the context of family relations men were barred from the inner quarters where elite women spent their time. Formal sources from the Song dynasty certainly uphold this image. Elite men spent their days with other men, studying for the examinations or carrying out the emperor's business in government offices devoid of women. Anecdotal sources, however, provide an important qualification of this image, for they reveal that elite men spent a great deal of their time in the company of non-elite women, especially female entertainers.

Judging from anecdotal sources, Song men were constantly attending banquets, both in the course of their official duties and in their private social lives.[3] The importance of banqueting as a social and even political ritual is neatly conveyed in a story told by the scholar-official Su Che 蘇轍 (1039–1112) about the famed strategic abilities of an early Song official named Li Yunze 李允則 (953–1028):

> When Yunze left Xiong [where he was serving as prefect] for an audience with the emperor, he traveled through Wei prefecture. The Wei prefect was Kou, Lord of Lai [Kou Zhun 寇準, 961–1023]. He remarked to Yunze, "I've heard that in Xiong your banquets are

particularly luxurious: do you think you could throw a small party for an old man [like me]?" Yunze replied, "I'm about to report to the emperor, so I dare not tarry, but when I return I will undertake your order."

When Yunze returned, Lord Kou feasted him. The curtains and hangings, dishes, food and drink, courtesans and musicians—everything was sumptuous and extravagant, as his intent was to overwhelm him. When the banquet was over, he said to Yunze, "[Now] you agreed to throw a party for me—how would tomorrow be?" Yunze respectfully assented. Lord Kou looked around and directed his subordinates, "The courtesans and musicians can be as today—[let's] dispense with the variety show, and save the hangings and chairs for him to borrow." Yunze replied, "The courtesans, musicians, and variety show can all be like today; the rest you can take with you, I can supply them all."

The next day, they saw that the hangings were all embroidered brocades from Sichuan; the chairs and couches all lacquerware from Wu and Yue; and everything else was of similar quality. Lord Kou was already flabbergasted. Then, as the variety players entered, Yunze said, "I'm afraid that the miscellaneous artists are still outside," and had them called in. They turned out to be the most skilled performers of the capital; more than a hundred of them were there. Lord Kou regarded them with great astonishment. He sent someone secretly to investigate: it turned out that [Yunze] had disposed of the [previous day's] couches and chairs, [and had new ones] wrapped in felt and brought in great haste; the miscellaneous artists had changed their clothes and entered the city disguised as merchants.

The next day Lord Kou recommended [Yunze] to the court, greatly praising his talents. [But] the Xiong officials chided him, saying, "Lord Kou likes to win, why did you outdo him like this?" Yunze replied: "I wasn't just showing off: I was demonstrating the technique of having military troops appear and disappear."

允則自雄入奏過魏，魏守，寇萊公也，謂允則曰：「聞君在雄，筵會特盛，能為老夫作小會否？」允則曰：「方入奏，不敢留，還日當奉教。」

及還，萊公宴之，幃帘、器皿、飲食、妓樂，百物華侈，意將壓之。既罷，謂允則曰：「君許我作會，來日可乎？」允則唯唯。公顧謂左右：「妓樂如今日，毋設百戲，幃帘、床榻留以假之。」允則曰：「妓樂、百戲皆如今日，其他隨行，略可具也。」

明日，視其幃帘皆蜀錦綉，床榻皆吳、越漆作，百物稱是，公已愕然矣。及百戲入，允則曰：「恐外尚有雜伎。」使召之。則京師精伎，至者百數十人。公視之大驚，使人伺之，則床榻脫卸，氈裹馳載，雜伎變服為商賈以入。

明日薦之於朝，極稱其才。雄之僚史尤之曰：「萊公尚氣，奈何以此勝之？」允則曰：「吾非誇之，示之以行軍出沒之巧耳。」[4]

Although this tale is meant to display Li Yunze's logistical skills, it simultaneously reveals that banquets were a form of status display, requiring elaborate planning and expense. The anecdotalist shows clearly that Kou Zhun expected to intimidate Li Yunze with the elegance and sumptuousness of his banquet, only to end up awed instead. Yet, although he loses out in the competition to impress Li Yunze, Kou Zhun is astute enough to recognize Li's talents, and by recommending him for office demonstrates his own political worthiness.[5]

Other anecdotes suggest that if throwing a banquet was an opportunity for status display, proper behavior at banquets was also critical to establishing literati social credentials.[6] One anonymous author describes a party held at the official residence of the eminent writer and official Cai Xiang 蔡襄 (1012–67), attended by the literatus Li Gou 李覯 (1009–59) in the company of the commoner Chen Lie 陳烈. It was spring and the government courtesans were in the courtyard selling wine. They came forward to greet the banqueters, and Cai invited them to join the party. Chen Lie—a man known for his moral probity—began to be ill at ease. Then the wine began to circulate and the entertainers to sing. Chen suddenly overturned the wine on the table and, with a terrified look, jumped over the garden wall, climbing a tree to escape. Later, Li Gou entertained the company by composing a humorous poem at Chen's expense, ending with the line, "The mountain bird doesn't understand the pink-powder music / One beat of the clappers and it flies away in fright" 山鳥不知紅粉樂，一聲檀板便驚飛. Hearing of this, Chen Lie submitted a plaint, charging Li with conduct unbecoming a gentleman and even suggesting he should be executed. Cai Xiang responded to the plaint by laughingly instructing the messenger to tell Chen he would no longer hire courtesans; but thenceforth whenever he held a party he showed [Li's poem] to the company for a laugh.[7]

Here Chen Lie's inability to appreciate the pleasures of courtesan entertainment—though perhaps morally admirable—renders him the butt of mockery and derision from his more sophisticated peers. The importance of proper banquet etiquette to social status is similarly evident in Shen Kuo's description of the encounter between Shi Yannian 石延年 (994–1040) and his wealthy but déclassé neighbor, as described in Ronald Egan's chapter in this volume.[8] Still other anecdotes along these lines suggest that men who do not know how to behave at parties are lacking in "gentlemanly restraint" (*shijian* 士檢).[9] All of these anecdotes confirm the importance of banquets as a site of status negotiation. In other anecdotes, we see that entertainers at these banquets played a role as arbiters of male status. One account describes a visit by the commoner-poet Wei Ye 魏野 (960–1019) to the residence of the Chang'an courtesan Tiansu 添蘇. Prior to the visit, we are told, Wei Ye had written a poem comparing Tiansu to the famed historical beauty and poet Su Xiaoxiao 蘇小小 (d. ca. 501). Wei Ye's patron, also an admirer of Tiansu, had presented the poem to her. She was delighted, so much so that she had an accomplished calligrapher transcribe the poem on the wall of her residence. Sometime thereafter, Wei Ye came to Chang'an. Then,

> Some busybody secretly invited [Wei] Ye to visit Tiansu's home, but didn't mention his name. Seeing that Ye's appearance was simple and crude, Tiansu deliberately avoided him. When Ye suddenly raised his head and noticed the writing on the wall, she informed him, "That is a famous poem by scholar Wei." Without bothering to answer, Ye found a brush and wrote another quatrain next to the first. Finally realizing who he was, Tiansu began to treat him with great courtesy.

有好事者密召過添蘇家，不言姓氏。添蘇見野風貌魯質，固不前席。野忽舉頭見壁所題，添蘇曰：「魏處士見譽之作。」野殊不答，乃索筆於其側別紀一絕。添蘇始知是野，大加禮遇。[10]

The point of this anecdote is that poetic talent trumps an unsophisticated appearance, and it makes fun of Tiansu for failing to recognize Wei Ye. Here again we see the theme of "knowing men." Tiansu's failure to recognize the commoner-poet marks her as somewhat superficial and undiscerning. However, in suggesting that entertainers calibrated their actions to the perceived social standing of their guests, it demonstrates again the function of banquets as venues for status performance and highlights the importance of female entertainers as judges of that performance.

In addition to revealing the importance of banqueting in the social lives of Song men, anecdotal sources convey extremely useful information about Song entertainment culture. We have seen thus far that courtesans were central figures at Song banquets, but anecdotes also show us that such women belonged to several different categories of entertainer.[11] At parties held in government offices to honor the arrival or departure of dignitaries, or to celebrate imperial birthdays, entertainment was provided by government courtesans (variously called *guanji* 官妓, *guannu* 官奴, or *yingji* 營妓). Such women, at least in the early Song, were attached to the government offices at every prefecture, and by Southern Song the custom had spread down to the county level. As one late Northern Song anecdote describes them:

> Female entertainers are subordinate to prison officials at the regular and superior prefectures, in the manner of female prisoners. In recent eras they are selected for their looks and taught to sing and dance; they welcome and see off official guests and serve as drinking partners at banquets.
> 倡婦, 州郡隸獄官以伴女囚。近世擇姿容, 習歌舞, 迎送使客, 侍宴好。[12]

Government courtesans, then, served at the prefectures as a type of quasi-slave or indentured labor. Other anecdotes show that the names of government courtesans were recorded on official registers (*ji* 籍) and that the approval of the prefect was required for a woman to be released from those registers, a process called "becoming respectable" (*cong liang* 從良). Only after she had "become respectable" could a courtesan marry someone outside of the dishonorable (*jian* 賤) courtesan profession.

Song anecdotes suggest that in general, government courtesans were released upon reaching a certain age, but authors particularly loved to tell stories of women who were released from service under unusual circumstances—especially when those circumstances involved the composition of clever poetry. Thus the anecdotalist Zhao Lingzhi 趙令畤 (1051–1107), an imperial clansman and friend of many Northern Song literary luminaries, repeated a story originally recorded by Su Shi 蘇軾 (1037–1101) describing the release of the government courtesan Zhou Shao 周韶. The story first introduces Zhou, telling us that she served at the prefectural offices in Hangzhou, was a collector of fine teas, and was also known for her poetry. It then explains how, at a banquet given by the prefect Chen Xiang 陳襄 (1017–80) for the visiting official Su Song 蘇頌 (1020–1101), Zhou tearfully begged to be released from the registers. Su Song suggested that she compose a verse; she did so on the spot, and the company was so impressed with her poetic offering that Chen agreed to release her.[13] This *topos* of an entertainer earning her freedom by means of a clever poem, a favorite of Song anecdotalists, highlights the fact that courtesans were admired for their poetic skills; but it also reveals that prefects had the power to release government courtesans at their discretion.

That point is reiterated in another of Zhao Lingzhi's anecdotes, this one describing a set of "humorous judgments" (*huapan* 花判) that Su Shi wrote while serving temporarily as prefect of Qiantang 錢塘 (modern-day Hangzhou). Su's judgments came in response to the requests of two government courtesans to be released from service. The first request reportedly came from an entertainer who was so bewitching that she was known as "Nine-Tailed Wild Fox" (*jiuwei yehu* 九尾野狐). Su's judgment played both on her moniker and his own temporary status: "The five-day prefect can make judgments freely, / the nine-tailed wild fox may 'become respectable' and do as she pleases" 五日京兆判斷自由，九尾野狐從良任便. But when a second courtesan attempted to use this precedent to make a similar appeal, Su was less accommodating. His judgment read: "To respect the transformation of Southern Shao / Such an intention is indeed admirable, / [But] this would empty the stables of Northern Ji / Your request should not be approved" 敦召南之化，此意誠可佳，空冀北之羣，所請宜不允.[14] In the first judgment, the five-day prefect and nine-tailed fox are syntactically parallel, and the freedom of his judgments and her "suiting herself" are both semantically and syntactically parallel. The second judgment syntactically juxtaposes the "south" of Shaonan ("Shao's south") with the "north" of Jibei ("Northern Ji"). The "transformation of Shaonan" refers to a line from the preface to "Falling Plums" ("Piao you mei" 摽有梅), a poem in the "Shaonan" section of the *Shijing* 詩經 (Classic of poetry). The allusion refers to the salutary influence of King Wen, under which males and females of the region were able to marry at appropriate ages. Thus, here, releasing the courtesan would allow her to marry before she becomes too old. Both judgments make clever use of allusive language and parallel structures, and the narrator's goal is undoubtedly to highlight Su's effortless erudition and élan; but the anecdote reveals as well the significant power that prefects had over the entertainers in their government offices.

Still, other anecdotes show that not all female entertainers in the Song were attached to government offices. Many other women played music, danced, sang songs, and bantered with guests at teahouses and in other commercial venues. The services of government courtesans were theoretically limited to men who enjoyed official rank, but banquets with commercial courtesans could be arranged by anyone with sufficient means. In contrast to government courtesans, commercial courtesans do not seem to have been registered, although short stories suggest that they were sometimes asked (or pressured) to join the official registers. And it is clear that the most successful commercial courtesans enjoyed tremendous wealth and status. An early Southern Song raconteur reports:

> In the Zhenghe period [1111–17], the capital Bian [Kaifeng] flourished in peace and prosperity. The two courtesans Li Shishi and Cui Nianyue were famous throughout the era. Whenever [the poet] Chao Zhongzhi [fl. 1126] held a drinking party, he would invite them to facilitate the festivities. Some ten years later, when he returned to

the capital, the two were still there; their reputations spread over the whole region. The household of Ms. Li was especially lofty and unapproachable.... In the Jingkang period [1126–27, during which time the Jin invaded], Ms. Li, along with others like the imperially favored [courtesan] Zhao Yuannu and the ball-players and flautists Yuan Tao and Wu Zhen, all had their property confiscated [to help ransom the court]. Ms. Li drifted to the Zhe region. Gentlemen and officials still invited her so they could hear her songs, but she had become haggard and drawn and no longer had the panache of earlier days.

政和間，汴都平康之盛，而李師師、崔念月二妓，名著一時。晁冲之叔用每會飲，多召侑席。其後十許年，再來京師，二人尚在，而聲名溢於京國。李生者，門第尤峻....。靖康中，李生與同輩趙元奴及築毬吹笛袁陶，武震輩，例籍其家。李生流落來浙中，士大夫猶邀之以聽其歌，然憔悴無復向來之態矣。[15]

We see here that some late Northern Song entertainers were so wealthy and well known that, in the crisis of the Jin invasion, they were obvious targets for the court's desperate efforts to gather funds. And while the fall of the Northern Song put an end to the flourishing courtesan quarters of Kaifeng, other authors reveal that an equally flourishing entertainment center was soon established in the new Southern Song capital of Hangzhou.[16]

Finally, in addition to government and professional courtesans, another important type of entertainer was prominently featured in Song anecdotes. This was the household courtesan (*jiaji* 家妓 or 家姬), who entertained her master and his guests at private parties in his home. Song law frowned on intimacy between officials and government or commercial courtesans, but a household courtesan was construed as a type of concubine and was therefore not subject to the regulations that restricted intimacy with more public women. A late Northern Song author gives us a rare glimpse into the market for household courtesans, observing that the nobility of the capital were so anxious to find lovely and talented girls that over the course of the Northern Song the price of a beauty had risen from between 150 and 250 strings of cash to as high as 5,000 strings.[17]

Anecdotal sources also reveal that, in spite of government regulations, entertainers were in some cases able to move from professional to household-courtesan status. Wang Mingqing 王明清 (1127–ca. 1215) recounts that a public performer once admired by the Northern Song general Wang Yuan 王淵 (1077–1129) was first taken into the household of an imperial clansman and later ended up in the household of one of Wang Yuan's retainers, another military man. She eventually bore the retainer a son and, when he himself became a decorated general, ended up enfeoffed with a noble title.[18] Gossips also reported that the general Zhang Jun 張浚 (1097–1164) took a courtesan as a concubine and eventually even promoted her to the status of legal wife.[19] In this regard the rules for military men (or perhaps particularly for powerful generals!) were clearly less strict than those for civil officials, as we see in another of Wang Mingqing's tidbits:

> There was a prefectural courtesan named Yang Shu, whose looks and skills had been praised in the poetry of Huang Shangu [Huang Tingjian 黃廷堅, 1045–1105]. Duanshu [the retired official Li Zhiyi 李之儀, 1038–1117] had mourned his wife and was without issue, and being old with no one to depend on, he took Yang Shu into his home. Soon after she bore a son who, on the occasion of the suburban sacrifices, received official privilege.[20] When [the notorious] Cai Yuanzhang [Cai Jing 蔡京, 1046–1126] returned to the office of grand councilor, Gongfu [Guo Xiangzheng 郭祥正, 1035–1113] knew that Cai hated Duanshu, so he tricked a locally powerful man named Ji Sheng into bringing suit at court, charging that Li had fraudulently had his son receive privilege. An investigation was opened and Li was slandered; he was sentenced to be removed from the roster of officials. . . . Yang Shu was also convicted.
>
> 郡娼楊姝者，色藝見稱於黃山谷詩詞中。端叔喪偶無嗣，老益無憀，因遂畜楊於家。已而生子，遇郊禮受延賞。會蔡元長再相，功父知元長之惡端叔也。乃誘豪民吉生者訟於朝，謂冒以其子受蔭。置鞠受誣又坐削籍 . . . 楊姝者亦被決。[21]

Li Zhiyi's case shows that the penalties for an official taking a courtesan as a concubine could be severe. But it also reveals that some officials were undeterred by such penalties (possibly because the likelihood of prosecution was remote). That taking a courtesan as a concubine was not all that unusual is also suggested by Song short stories, which prominently featured the *topos* of courtesans leaving the profession to marry officials. The anecdotal literature also suggests that the reverse could be true: erstwhile household entertainers might become public courtesans. Thus we learn that a case involving the prosecution of a corrupt monk was complicated by the actions of the monk's lover, a teahouse entertainer. She had once been the concubine of a well-connected official, and only by cleverly preventing her former master from interfering in the proceedings were the prosecuting officials able to convict the monk.[22]

We have seen thus far that anecdotal sources have much to tell us about the social and institutional contexts that shaped romances between entertainers and literati. They also provide us with at least some clues about how Song men envisioned romantic partners.

THE COURTESAN IDEAL

If entertainers were the central focus of Song romantic relationships, what qualities did men seek in them? Song anecdotes suggest that courtesans were esteemed for both talent and beauty. For the most part, their talents were musical: the great majority seem to have been able to sing, dance, or play an instrument such as the pipa or flute. Yet we get surprisingly little description of the content of their performances, and where we do, the descriptions tend to be in the form of clichéd poetic images. For example, we are told that Chao Buzhi 晁補之 (1053–1110) once brought out a very young household courtesan to dance for the visiting literatus Chen Shidao 陳師道 (1053–1102). Chen thereupon composed a *ci* 詞 ("song-lyric") poem that read:

娉娉裊裊，	Graceful and elegant, twisting and sinuous,
芍藥梢頭紅樣小。	The bud of the peony flower is barely pink.
舞袖低垂，	Your dancing sleeves drape down,
心到郎邊客已知。	That your heart is at his side, this guest already knows.
金尊玉酒，	Jade wine in a gold goblet,
勸我花前千萬壽，	You urge me to drink to longevity among the flowers.
莫莫休休，	Don't, don't! Stop, stop!
白髮簪花我自羞。	I am too embarrassed to stick a flower in this white hair.[23]

Chen's poem shows clearly this young courtesan was a dancer, and it hints at a romantic attachment between the young girl and his host, but it tells us little else about her. Descriptions of courtesans are only slightly more susceptible to historical analysis when poetic conventions are upended—or, more accurately, deployed in an unconventional manner:

> Dongpo [Su Shi] was once drinking at the house of a powerful gentleman. The host brought out a dozen or so handmaidens, all beautiful and skilled. Among them was one named Mei'er, who was good at singing and dancing. Although her face and form were very beautiful, her body was quite big. The host was particularly fond of her and directed her to beg a poem from Dongpo. Dongpo playfully wrote four lines, saying, "The dancing sleeves swirl and whirl, / Shadows flicker for 1,000 feet—dragons and snakes writhe. / The singing throat bends and turns, / The sound shakes half the sky, the wind and rain are cold."
> 東坡嘗飲一豪士家，出侍姬十餘人，皆有姿伎。其間有一善歌舞者，名媚兒，容質雖麗而軀幹甚偉。豪特所鍾愛，命乞詩於公。公戲為四句云：舞袖蹁躚，影搖千尺龍蛇動。歌喉宛轉，聲撼半天風雨寒。[24]

The anecdote concludes that (in the face of this poetic suggestion that her dancing and singing were like the roar of a thunderstorm) the humiliated and unhappy performer beat a hasty retreat. This anecdote gives us no more concrete sense of the performer's looks than the last, but it does seem to provide textual corroboration of a shift that is visible in pictorial art, away from the Tang ideal of somewhat plump female beauty to a Song aesthetic that admired slenderness. We might even take Su's anecdote as evidence that the Song penchant for dancing entertainers was a factor in that shift.

In earlier examples we saw that courtesans were also often admired for their literary skills, and especially for the ability to compose clever or apropos poetry. Thus when Su Shi described how Zhou Shao's clever poem won her release from the courtesan registers, he also took the trouble to record poems that two of her courtesan "sisters" wrote to send her on her way.[25] Another anecdotalist poked fun at the much-despised Northern Song grand counselor Cai Jing by describing an encounter Cai had with a Suzhou government courtesan named Su Qiong 蘇瓊. We are told that Su Qiong was ranked ninth among the courtesans and had a reputation for being able to compose song lyrics. Attending a banquet convened by the prefect, Cai Jing ordered Su Qiong to compose an extempore poem. When she asked him to set the rhyme, he chose the word "nine," presumably to tease or even humiliate her. She responded with a poem that turned the tables on him, for her final couplet concluded:

記得南宮高選，	I remember at the lofty selection at the Southern Palace,
弟兄爭占鼇頭；	The young men competed to place at the top;
金爐玉殿瑞烟浮，	In the jade palace auspicious smoke wafted from golden censers:
高占甲科第九。	He was ranked in the first level, number nine.[26]

She thereby cleverly reminded Cai Jing that he, too, had been ranked ninth on the list of examination graduates.

Elsewhere we see that courtesans were esteemed for their mastery of the quintessential literati art of calligraphy. The eleventh-century government courtesan Wang Yingying 王英英 in Chuzhou 滁州 (in modern Anhui province) modeled her writing on that of the famous Tang calligrapher Yan Zhenqing 顏真卿 (709–85), but also received instruction from the eminent Cai Xiang. One gossip reports that the poet Mei Yaochen 梅堯臣 (1002–60) once wrote a humorous poem that simultaneously praised her skill at writing large characters while teasing her for not being much concerned with her appearance.²⁷ Another author reports that Su Shi was delighted with the beautiful and talented government courtesan Ma Pan 馬盼, who was skilled at imitating his calligraphy. Once when he was preparing a text to be carved on a stele, she surreptitiously wrote in four of the characters. When Su saw it, he laughed; he made a few minor adjustments but otherwise did not change her work, and the stele was carved with her characters.²⁸

We have every reason to believe that the women mentioned in these anecdotes were historical individuals: some of them appear in more than one source, and we know that courtesans were among the celebrities of their day. But (as these examples show, and as Paul Rouzer has also observed for the Tang), they appear in anecdotal literature largely as foils for the talents of the men who describe them. This is true even when they appear in the context of romantic relationships. Song anecdotalists readily discussed the existence of romantic relationships, but they reveal surprisingly little that could be called truly personal. Rather, their depictions of romance—like those of courtesans' talents—tend to be framed in terms of long-standing literary conventions.

For example, in Song China as elsewhere, women who were the object of romantic interest were routinely described as "beautiful" (*mei* 美) or "alluring" (*jiao* 嬌). But what constituted "beautiful" in this context? Our sources tend to be vague. The twelfth-century courtesan Qin Miaoguan 秦妙觀 was known for having "looks that crowned the capital" (*se guan duyi* 色冠都邑),²⁹ and the eleventh-century Zhuan Chunying 囀春鶯, the songstress-concubine of the painter and calligrapher Wang Shen 王詵 (1037–ca. 1093), was reputed to be a "beauty of the realm" (*guose* 國色), but these terms are unenlightening.³⁰ Where we do get more detailed descriptions, it is often in poetry, where historical specifics give way to literary imagination. Typical here is the set of poems that, according to Zhao Lingzhi, Zhang Lei 張耒 (1054–1114) wrote in parting for his lover, the government courtesan Liu Shunü 劉淑女:

可是相逢意便深，	Indeed, every time we meet, my feelings for you grow deeper.
為郎巧笑不須金，	For this lad your lovely smile did not require gold.³¹
門前一尺春風髻，	Before the door a towering spring-breeze coiffure,
窗外三更夜雨衾。	Outside the window at midnight, a coverlet of nighttime rain.

別燕從教燈見淚,	At the parting banquet the lamplight exposes your tears,
夜船惟有月知心,	In the nighttime boat, only the moon knows my heart.
東西芳草渾相似,	East and west, the fragrant grasses all resemble one another,
欲望高樓何處尋?	But when I want to see your lofty dwelling, where can I find it?
未說螬蟻如素領,	I needn't say the chrysalis is like your pure throat,
固應新月學蛾眉,	And certainly the new moon copies your moth eyebrows.
引成密約因言笑,	We extract secret promises and then talk and laugh,
認得真情是別離。	But we know that the reality will be separation.
尊酒且傾濃琥珀,	Just now the wine cup tips out its thick amber contents.
淚痕更著薄胭脂。	The tracks of tears again appear against your faint makeup.
北城月落烏啼後,	After the moon sets over the northern walls, and the crow's cries end,
便是孤舟腸斷時。	On a solitary boat, my heart again will break.[32]

Zhang highlights his lover's towering coiffure, the chrysalis-like translucence of her neck, her moth eyebrows curved like the new moon, and the way her tears leave tracks in her lightly-applied make-up. These are striking but utterly conventional images, and they give us only the most general sense of what Liu Shunü actually looked like. In like fashion, Chao Buzhi, watching the gorgeous courtesan Ms. Tian 田氏 at her toilette, was moved by the way she unwound her "conch-shaped coiffure" (*luoji* 螺髻); by her "jade fingers" (*yuzhi* 玉指) as she retrieved a fallen hairpin; by the white powder lightly dusting her face; by the green-black of her eyebrows, and by the way her eyes sparkled like "autumnal waters" (*qiushui* 秋水) when she met his glance in the mirror.[33] We do learn from these descriptions that clear features set off by white skin were prized and that the artfulness of the courtesan's appearance was appreciated (she was distinguished by her elaborate make up and intricate coiffure). Moreover, although in these clichéd images the courtesan's "beauty" is more evoked then described, we should also note the potential of literary conventions to shape lived experience. In other words, we might ask to what extent men came to understand and experience the features of beautiful women in terms of these literary tropes?[34]

Song anecdotes also suggest that the courtesan's allure was enhanced by her romantic and elegant surroundings. As in Zhang's poem, entertainers are typically seen at night, at luxurious banquets, under moonlit skies, or in their elegantly appointed boudoirs. Liu Chang's 劉敞 (1019–68) parting poem for the government courtesan Chajiao 茶嬌 is again typical:

玳筵銀燭徹宵明，	On tortoiseshell mats, the light of silver candles penetrates the night darkness,
白玉佳人唱渭城。	The white jade beauty sings "The City of Wei."[35]
更盡一杯須起舞，	Empty another cup, and in a moment we will rise to dance.
關河秋月不勝情。	Facing frontier streams under the autumn moon, I am overcome by emotion.[36]

Just as Zhang Lei's "coverlet of nighttime rain" had evoked the intimacy of the bedchamber, Liu Chang's "tortoise shell mats" and "silver candles" are meant to bespeak luxury. Although historical experience is obscured by a veil of literary tropes, we see that part of the appeal of courtesans is their association with opulence and elegance.

We might suspect that it was also poetic convention that helped create an image of romance with courtesans as beset by parting, separation, and loss. The poignance of taking leave from a courtesan lover fit all too smoothly into long-standing traditions of poetry about separation, with their emphasis on loneliness and heartache. Admittedly, the aura of loss that suffuses so much of the discussion of romance with courtesans had some basis in reality: given the peripatetic nature of literati life, relationships with government and independent courtesans were almost inevitably temporary, cut short when the man was transferred to a new post. Legal strictures, and the social distance they were meant to enforce, likewise rendered long-term relationships between courtesans and literati problematic. Still, the highly stylized rhetoric that pervades writing about courtesans tempts us to see the relationships between Song men and their entertainer-lovers as little more than romantic (and/or literary) playacting. This is especially the case when we see that Song men quite clearly understood that the courtesan's job was to persuade her clients that she was in love with them: in a collection of humorous aphorisms, Su Shi characterized as "not to be taken seriously" 未得便信 "a courtesan who, on parting, cries bitterly that she no longer wants to live" 妓別慟哭不欲生.[37] But in any case, whether by dint of poetic convention, cruel realities, or both, Song depictions of romance with courtesans were typically characterized by heartbreak (*duanchang* 斷腸) rather than "happily ever after." Indeed, awareness of the ephemeral nature of these relationships seems to have been part and parcel of their romantic allure. But here, I think, we need to investigate what the anecdotal literature about courtesans does *not* say. What is obscured by this emphasis on courtesan romance as an intense but short-term phenomenon?

COURTESANS AS CONCUBINES

As we have seen, Song anecdotal literature treats men's relationships with public courtesans and household entertainers as essentially similar, and in many respects, they were. The same sorts of looks and talents were admired in both public courtesans and concubine-entertainers, and we have seen that there was even some movement between the two statuses. Still, as a resident of the master's household (and thus in a position of quasi-kinship to him), the courtesan-concubine had legal and social roles significantly different from that of a public courtesan.[38] I would like to suggest that the tendency of anecdotal literature to treat men's relationships with household courtesans as equivalent to their relationships with public women worked to obscure these important differences, and to mask their implications for Song social and family life.

One aspect of the household-courtesan's position that tends to be obscured in the romantic anecdotal literature is that a household courtesan was essentially a type of servant. A late Song anecdote suggests that the functions of women brought in as "pleasure companions" (*yushi* 娛侍) for literati could range from kitchen maid to seamstress to laundress.[39] In popular parlance (though significantly, rarely in anecdotes) all of these women were regarded as "concubines" (*qie* 妾), but not all necessarily had a sexual or romantic relationship with the master.[40] While entertainers seem to have been particularly likely to have been envisioned as potential romantic partners—often distinguished as "favored concubines" (*chongqie* 寵妾)—the distinction between entertainers and other kinds of female domestic laborers was seldom absolute. Thus the retired official Gao Wenhu 高文虎 (1134–1212) praised the concubine he acquired late in life for being able to sing, for managing his food and medicines, and for being sufficiently literate to help him with his reading and letter-writing.[41] Anecdotes that warn against the taking in of strange women divulge in passing that girls hired as kitchen help might also be taught to sing or dance.[42] The potential fluidity between entertainer and servant in the household context is likewise evident in an anecdote recorded by Wang Zhi 王銍 (fl. 12th cent.) about the much-excoriated former grand councilor Zhang Dun 章惇 (1035–1105). Gossips reported that Zhang had greatly favored a lovely concubine whom he suspected of having an affair with a monk: unable to stand the thought of beating her, he simply had her relegated to doing kitchen duty. The story continues that when Zhang eventually relented and tried to reinstate the concubine at his side, she swore she would rather die than serve him again and promptly expired.[43] In having duties that could go beyond her purely entertainment function, then, the household courtesan differed from courtesans in government offices or private teahouses. Anecdotes that focus on the romantic aspects of household courtesans obscure their domestic roles.

Anecdotal literature masks the tensions between the household courtesans' "public" and private roles in other ways as well. Authors tend to take as a given that, like courtesans (and decidedly unlike wives), a man's courtesan-concubines would perform in front of his friends and interact socially with them. Only occasionally do we see oblique acknowledgement that a household courtesan's availability to other men might be distinctly limited and that her relationship with her master was generally expected to be exclusive (at least while she was in his household). We see these limits implicitly recognized in an anecdote highlighting the remarkable equanimity with which the high official Wang Shao 王韶 (1030–81) handled the inexcusably boorish behavior of one of his guests. Per common practice, Wang had brought out his entertainer-concubines to perform at a party. However,

> As night drew on, the guest Zhang Ji grew drunk and attempted to pull the one of girls forward. When she resisted he suddenly tried to embrace her. The other guests blanched in dismay as she tearfully complained to her master. Wang slowly remarked, "I brought you girls out for the enjoyment of my guests, and now you have made them unhappy." He ordered that a large goblet be brought for her to drink as a forfeit. Thereafter his manner was unchanged, chatting and laughing as before. Everyone admired his equanimity.
>
> 入夜席，客張繢沉醉，挽家妓不前，遽將擁之。家妓泣訴於韶，坐客皆失色。韶徐曰：「此出爾曹以娛賓，而乃令賓客失歡。」命取大杯罰家妓，既而容色不動，談笑如故，人亦伏其量也。[44]

Here Wang is regarded as remarkable in not taking offense when a guest makes advances to one of "his" entertainers. Elsewhere—though rarely in anecdotes—the relatively exclusive nature of relationships with household courtesans is revealed in references to men restricting their entertainer-concubines to performing from behind a screen, especially when his guests were not close friends.[45]

The contradictions between the household courtesan's role as entertainer and her position as potential consort are also subtly evident in the kinds of poetry that anecdotalists circulated. We have seen that men wrote romantic and even erotic poetry for their paramours in the courtesan quarters, and that such poetry circulated publically. Likewise, some men wrote freely (and appreciatively) about the beauty and seductiveness of their friends' entertainers, and those writings, too, sometimes circulated for the amusement and titillation of wider literati circles. Yet anecdotalists conspicuously refrained from recording romantic poetry that men wrote for their own household courtesans. This is not to say that such poetry was not written. The literatus Ye Mengde 葉夢德 (1077–1148), for example, relates that when the grand councilor Han Zhen 韓縝 (1019–97) was sent on a mission to negotiate with the Jin, he was loathe to leave his beloved concubine. On the eve of his departure, Han and his beloved drank heavily through the night, and Han composed a parting lyric. By the next day, Ye tells us, the lyric had already reached the inner palace, and the emperor abruptly ordered the Metropolitan Infantry Command to dispatch soldiers to move Han's family (and note the assumption that the concubine would be part of his "family") to join him. In recording this incident, Ye Mengde emphasizes the extraordinary benevolence of the emperor in showing this type of concern for his underlings' personal affairs. He then relays a poem that the poet Liu Chang—an affinal relative of Han—composed to comment on the affair. The poem, which playfully compares Han Zhen and Emperor Shenzong 神宗 (r. 1067–85) to dedicated ministers and gracious sovereigns of old, is not at all romantic or suggestive. Ye concludes that because of Liu's poem, Han's own lyric became widely popular. But he does not transmit that lyric.[46]

If the poetry that men wrote for their household-courtesans is virtually absent from anecdotal accounts, the exception that proves the rule is a poem that Su Shi wrote for his household courtesan Wang Zhaoyun 王朝雲 ("Morning Cloud") (fl. 11th cent.), which was transmitted by the anecdotalist monk Huihong 惠洪 (1071–1128). But the context of this poem was that it commemorated Zhaoyun's wish to accompany Su to the malarial south, where he had been sent in exile. Su's poem does gesture to Zhaoyun's appearance and skills in dancing and singing, and in that sense it is reminiscent of poetry that men composed for courtesans. It might even be said to be romantic in tone, in that it suggests that they practice Daoist alchemy and become immortals together. But it is in no way erotic or sensual in the manner of poetry written for public courtesans.[47]

This difference in the poetic record, I believe, reflects the ambiguous social position of the household courtesan, and especially literati anxiety about that ambiguity. The household-courtesan could be a servant or a paramour, but she was also a potential life-partner and mother of sons. To be sure, she could not legally become a wife: Chinese law drew a strict and severe line distinguishing a man's wife—and he could have only one at any given time—from any other consorts he might have. Yet the Song fad for romance with household courtesans, and the emotional attachments it sometimes engendered, threatened to make a mockery of this neat legal hierarchy. We have seen a hint of this kind of situation already in the figure of the courtesan Yang Shu, who bore a son to the official Li Zhiyi. But where Yang had been a public courtesan (and any relationship she had with Li was thus illegal), there was no legal restriction preventing a man from maintaining a long-term—even permanent—relationship with a household courtesan. Although she could not legally become his wife in name, she could fulfill that role in most other respects.

Significantly, anecdotal sources tend to downplay the potential for household courtesans to become consorts or mothers of descendants, at least where literati are concerned. Although, as we have seen, anecdotalists were not shy about describing the long-term relationships of entertainers with military men, they portray the great majority of literati relationships with household courtesans (like those with government courtesans) as temporary. They stress, for example, that many wives were intolerant of infatuations with entertainers and put pressure on their husbands to get rid of them. The eminent Yan Shu 晏殊 (991–1055) expelled a songstress concubine for this reason, only to change his mind and retrieve her when a friend's poem convinced him that life was too short to deprive himself.[48] The minor official Xu Ganchen 徐幹臣 (fl. 1111–17), on the other hand, waited until after his wife's death to retrieve the concubine she had pressured him to expel.[49] Note that the emphasis in these anecdotes is on the heartbreak of separation and the lengths to which men might go to retrieve a lost paramour: nothing is said of what happens thereafter.

Other anecdotes stress that men could easily become disenchanted with favored concubines. Thus we read:

> The wife of Academician Wang Kui (991–1072), née so-and-so, was constantly being humiliated by his concubine. She complained to Kui but he was unresponsive, so she let it go. When someone asked her about it, she remarked, "That girl will be leaving soon anyway,

there is no point in making a fuss." Before long, Kui grew angry and expelled her.

王學士逵妻某氏, 妾常辱之, 愬于逵不受, 亦不校也。或問之曰:「彼將去矣, 不必校也。」已而逵怒逐之。[50]

The point of the anecdote is to demonstrate the uncanny accuracy of predictions made by Kui's wife. In like fashion, we are told that after the death of his wife, the middle-aged statesman Han Qi 韓琦 (1008–1075) sent his twenty-some household entertainers away with generous gifts. When asked why he did not keep some around to bring enjoyment to his declining years, he replied, "How much enjoyment would there be? On the contrary, they constantly cause aggravation: how could that compare to enjoying my peace and quiet?" 所樂能幾何? 而常令人心勞, 孰若吾簡靜而樂也。[51] Here household courtesans are imagined as contentious and disruptive.

Still other anecdotes suggested that household entertainers were likely to be shallow and disloyal, abandoning their masters when the latter fell into political or economic trouble. When Wang Shen was sent into exile, his beautiful songstress concubine was acquired by another man. Upon his return to the capital Wang was able eventually to determine her whereabouts, but since she was already in another man's household, he could only compose a poem lamenting that she'd been stolen away.[52] An oft-cited story describes Su Shi breaking into tears on encountering at a banquet an entertainer who had been the adored favorite of a recently deceased friend. In contrast to Su's display of sadness, the young woman reacted to Su's distress by callously laughing with her companions. The anecdotalist concludes by noting that Su mentioned this incident often as a warning against keeping concubines.[53] Even Su himself, when writing of Wang Zhaoyun's decision to follow him into exile, made a point of contrasting her behavior with that of several other concubines he had had, who "in the space of four or five years successively took their leave."[54] The impression we get is that household courtesans, like their professional sisters, were understood to be objects of short-term romance.

We cannot know, of course, how often household courtesans actually became long-term consorts of their masters. It may indeed have been the case, as much of the evidence presented here suggests, that the majority of relationships with household entertainers were temporary. And even when an entertainer stayed with her master until his death, she was not necessarily regarded as a permanent family member. Rather, the understanding—or at least the understanding conveyed by anecdotal literature—was that such women (like the favorite of Su Shi's friend) would move on to the household of another man.

Yet outside of anecdotal sources evidence abounds that courtesan-concubines could and did sometimes become long-term partners of their masters. Wang Zhaoyun spent decades with Su Shi and bore him a son: at her early death he dignified their relationship by commemorating her in a funerary inscription.[55] A poem by Huang Tingjian teasingly refers to the graying hair of his friend's musician concubine, suggesting that she was growing old in his household.[56] References to the "birth mothers" (*suosheng mu* 所生母) of literati men reveal that at least some of those mothers remained with their fathers throughout their lives.[57] Finally, that men's relationships with entertainers could be deep and enduring is seen in the fact that, over the course of the Song, not one but two female entertainers succeeded in becoming empresses of the realm.[58]

The potential for household courtesans to become more than the focus of temporary romance made their role in Song families problematic. Romances that turned into long-term relationships had a tendency to undercut family hierarchies and undermine conjugal harmony, as the expanding discourse on wifely jealousy in this period suggests. Concubine parentage, though not unusual and not formally stigmatized, was often fraught, and generally not a topic for polite conversation.[59] Not surprisingly, then, when Song anecdotalists depicted literati relationships with household-courtesans, they tended to limit their focus to romantic vignettes.

In sum, Song anecdotes convey much information about the roles of female entertainers in the lives of elite men, but the view they present is hardly transparent or neutral. We learn about how men thought romance should be portrayed and about stereotyped ideals of feminine looks and behavior, but little about individuals or the tenor of emotional relationships. More importantly, the tendency of the anecdotal literature to blur distinctions between different types of entertainers serves to obscure significant social implications of those distinctions. In highlighting the role of household entertainers as objects of romance, Song authors conveniently elided the awkward social fact that such women were sometimes the mothers of their peers.

NOTES

1. Authors of *shihua* evaluated and transmitted prized verses or explained the purported origins of this or that famous couplet. On the Northern Song development of the genre see chapter 2 in Ronald Egan, *The Problem of Beauty: Aesthetic Thought and Pursuits in Northern Song Dynasty China*

(Cambridge, Mass.: Harvard University Asia Center, 2006), 60–108. The spread of printing in this period undoubtedly also contributed to the survival of a larger percentage of sources from the Song as compared with earlier eras.

2. Susan Mann, "The Male Bond in Chinese History and Culture," *American Historical Review* 105, no. 5 (2000): 1606.

3. Cf. Beverly Bossler, "Shifting Identities: Courtesans and Literati in Song China," *Harvard Journal of Asiatic Studies* 62, no. 1 (Jun. 2002): 8–28.

4. Su Che, *Longchuan biezhi* 龍川別志, 2.95–96; rpt. in *Longchuan lüezhi* 龍川略志; *Longchuan biezhi*, ed. Yu Zongxian 俞宗憲 (Beijing: Zhonghua shuju, 1982). Su Che says that he heard of Li's exploits from an elder at the northern capital of Daming.

5. On the theme of "knowing men" and "being known," see Jack W. Chen in chapter 3 of this volume.

6. On Tang courtesan banquets as a site for literary competition and evaluation, see Paul F. Rouzer, *Articulated Ladies: Gender and the Male Community in Early Chinese Texts* (Cambridge, Mass.: Harvard University Asia Center, 2001), 249–84.

7. *Daoshan qinghua* 道山清話, in Zhu Yi'an 朱易安 et al., gen. eds., *Quan Song biji*, 2nd ser., 10 vols. (Zhengzhou: Daxiang chubanshe, 2006), 1:1.116–17. Chen was known for his moral behavior and had received Cai Xiang's sponsorship on numerous occasions. The last line of the anecdote does not specify whether Cai showed his guests Li's poem or Chen's indictment.

8. See chapter 7 of the present volume.

9. Wei Tai 魏泰 (fl. 11th–12th cents.), *Dongxuan bilu* 東軒筆錄, ed. Li Yumin 李裕民 (Beijing: Zhonghua shuju, 1997), 7.82–83.

10. In Wenying 文瑩 (fl. 11th cent.), *Xiangshan yelu, xulu* 湘山野錄, 續錄, 81; rpt. with *Xiangshan yelu* 湘山野錄; *Yuhu qinghua*; 玉壺清話, ed. Zheng Shigang 鄭世剛 and Yang Liyang 楊立揚 (Beijing: Zhonghua shuju, 1984).

11. On the historical evolution of the Chinese term *ji* 妓 and its cognates, see Beverly Bossler, "Vocabularies of Pleasure: Categorizing Female Entertainers in the Late Tang Dynasty," *Harvard Journal of Asiatic Studies* 72, no. 1 (Jun. 2012): 71–99. On the differing categories of entertainers in the Song, see chapter 1 of my book, *Courtesans, Concubines, and the Cult of Female Fidelity: Gender and Social Change in China, 1000–1400* (Cambridge, Mass.: Harvard University Asia Center, 2013). Much of this essay draws upon themes explored in greater detail in this book.

12. In Chen Shidao 陳師道 (1053–1102), *Houshan tancong* 後山談叢, 3.16; rpt. with Zhu Yu 朱彧 (fl. between 11th and 12th cents.), *Pingzhou ke tan* 萍州可談, ed. Li Weiguo 李偉國 (Beijing: Zhonghua shuju, 2007).

13. In Zhao Lingzhi, *Houqing lu* 侯鯖錄, 7.180–81; rpt. with Peng Cheng 彭乘 (fl. 1080) *Moke huixi* 墨客揮犀; *Xu moke huixi* 續墨客揮犀, ed. Kong Fanli 孔凡禮, (Beijing: Zhonghua shuju, 2002).

14. Ibid., 8.199. Jibei was the proverbial home of fast horses.

15. In Zhang Bangji 張邦基 (fl. 12th cent.), *Mozhuang manlu* 墨莊漫錄, 8.222–23; rpt. with Fan Gongcheng, *Guoting lu* 過庭錄; Zhang Zhifu, *Keshu* 可書, ed. Kong Fanli (Beijing: Zhonghua shuju, 2002).

16. See Zhou Mi 周密 (1232–1308), *Wulin jiushi* 武林舊事, 6.440–43; rpt. in Meng Yuanlao 孟元老 (fl. 1126–47) et al., *Dongjing menghua lu: Wai sizhong* 東京夢華錄: 外四種 (Beijing: Zhonghua shuju, 1962).

17. Zhu Yu 朱彧 (fl. between 11th and 12th cents.), *Pingzhou ke tan* 萍州可談, 1.127; rpt. with Chen Shidao, *Houshan tancong*, ed. Li Weiguo 李偉國 (Beijing: Zhonghua shuju, 2007). Presumably, inflation was also a factor here, but the author is explicit that prices have risen due to increased demand.

18. Wang Mingqing, *Huizhu lu* 揮麈錄 (Beijing: Zhonghua shuju, 1961), *disan lu* 第三錄, 2.250–51. In this anecdote, the retainer is identified only as "Han" 韓, but is likely to have been the famous general Han Shizhong 韓世忠 (1089–1151). Wang describes Han as taking in the Hangzhou courtesan Lü Xiaoxiao 呂小小 in his *Yuzhao xinzhi* 玉照新志, 3.56; rpt. with *Touxia lu* 投轄錄; ed. Wang Xinsen 汪新森 and Zhu Juru 朱菊如 (Shanghai: Shanghai guji chubanshe, 1991). Other sources also report that Han Shizhong's wife was originally a courtesan, but it is unclear whether these refer to either of the above women, as they tell a completely different story of how the two met. See Luo Dajing 羅大經 (1196–1242), *Helin yulu* 鶴林玉露, ed. Wang Ruilai 王瑞來 (Beijing: Zhonghua shuju, 1983), 3:2.266.

19. See Zhou Hui 周煇 (1127–after 1193), *Qingbo zazhi jiaozhu* 清波雜志校注, ed. Liu Yongxiang 劉永翔 (Beijing: Zhonghua shuju, 1994), 7.318–20. The promotion of a concubine to the status of wife was also strictly illegal.

20. Emperors commonly celebrated auspicious occasions by granting favors to members of the bureaucracy, such as bestowing office on their sons.

21. Wang Mingqing, *Huizhu lu, houlu* 後錄, 6.159.

22. Fan Gongcheng 范公偁 (fl. 12th cent.), *Guoting lu* 過庭錄, 354–55; rpt. with Zhang Bangji, *Mozhuang manlu*; Zhang Zhifu, *Keshu*.

23. Zhou Hui, *Qingbo zazhi jiaozhu*, 9.413. The girl is described as a *xiaohuan* 小鬟 (lit., "small chignon"), a term generally used for prepubescent and/or virginal entertainers.

24. Zhu Mu 祝穆 (fl. 13th cent.), *Gujin shiwen leiju* 古今事文類聚, *houji* 後集, in *Wenyuange Siku quanshu* 文淵閣四庫全書, vols. 925–29 (Taipei: Taiwan shangwu yinshuguan, 1983), 16.18b–19a. The images of writhing sea creatures are a conventional way of suggesting (among other things) bad thunderstorms.

25. Zhao Lingzhi, *Houqing lu*, 7.180–81.

26. Wu Zeng 吳曾 (fl. 1150), *Nenggaizhai manlu* 能改齋漫錄 (Shanghai: Shanghai guji chubanshe, 1979), 16.476–77.

27. Wei Tai, *Lin Han yinju shihua* 臨漢隱居詩話, in He Wenhuan 何文煥 (1732–1809), ed., *Lidai shihua* 歷代詩話 (Beijing: Zhonghua shuju, 1981), 332.

28. Zhang Bangji, *Mozhuang manlu*, 3.92.

29. Wang Mingqing, *Yuzhao xinzhi*, 2.24–25.

30. Wang Mingqing, *Yuzhao xinzhi*, 2.24–25; Xu Yi 許顗 (fl. 1130), *Yanzhou shihua* 彥周詩話, in *Lidai shihua*, 391.

31. That is, he did not have to pay for her affections, indicating that she must truly care for him.

32. Zhao Lingzhi, *Houqing lu*, 1.49.

33. Zhou Hui, *Qingbo zazhi jiaozhu*, 9.414–15.

34. Cf. Peter Hessler's account of late twentieth-century Chinese students asked to imagine the intended recipient of a Shakespeare love sonnet. They envisioned her with features akin to those just described, eg., "Her fingers are so slender that scallions can't compare with them." See Peter Hessler, *River Town: Two Years on the Yangtze* (New York: Harper Collins, 2001), 43.

35. The "City of Wei" was the name of a famous tune; the title refers to the ancient Qin capital of Xianyang (near the present day city of Xianyang in Shaanxi province), renamed Wei during the Han period. The tune appears to be associated with parting from old friends and heading to places where one will be a stranger.

36. Zhao Lingzhi, *Houqing lu*, 8.193.

37. Su Shi, *Zazuan erxu* 雜纂二續, in Li Yishan 李義山 [Li Shangyin 李商隱] (813–58), et al., *Zazuan qizhong* 雜纂七種, ed. Qu Yanbin 曲彥斌 (Shanghai: Shanghai guji chubanshe, 1988), 89.

38. On the complicated legal status of Song concubines, see Dai Jianguo 戴建国, "'Zhu pu ming fen' yu Songdai nubi de falü diwei—Tang Song bianqe shiqi jieji jiegou yanjiu zhi yi" '主仆名分' 與宋代奴婢的法律地位—唐宋变革時期階級結構研究之一, *Lishi yanjiu* 歷史研究 no. 4: (2004): 55–73.

39. See Liao Yingzhong 廖瑩中 (fl. 1260), *Jiang xing zalu* 江行雜錄, *Congshu jicheng xubian* 叢書集成續編 ed., vol. 87 (Taipei: Xinwenfeng, 1985), 256. Cf. Patricia Buckley Ebrey, *The Inner Quarters: Marriage and the Lives of Chinese Women in the Sung Period* (Berkeley: University of California Press, 1993), 220.

40. On the varied Song meanings of the term *qie*, see Ebrey, "Concubines in Sung China," *Journal of Family History* 11, no. 2 (1986): 1–20; Beverly Bossler (柏文莉), "Songdai de jiaji he qie," in *Jiatingshi yanjiu de xinshiye*, ed. Zhang Guogang 張國剛 (Beijing: Sanlian shudian, 2004), 206–17.

41. Zhou Mi, *Guixin zashi* 癸辛雜識, ed. Wu Qiming 吳企明 (Beijing: Zhonghua shuju, 1988), *bieji xia* 別集下, 272–74. See also Ebrey, *The Inner Quarters*, 226–27. Zhou Mi's anecdote refers to Gao Wenhu by his style name Bingru 炳如.

42. E.g., Hong Mai 洪邁 (1123–1202), *Yijian zhi* 夷堅志, ed. He Zhuo 何卓 (Beijing: Zhonghua shuju, 1981), *jiazhi* 甲志, 3.22.

43. Wang Zhi 王銍 (fl. 1110), *Moji* 默記, 3.47; rpt. with Wang Yong 王栐, *Yanyi yimou lu* 燕翼詒謀錄, ed. Zhu Jieren 朱杰人 (Beijing: Zhonghua shuju, 1981).

44. Wei Tai, *Dongxuan bilu*, 7.82–83.

45. E.g., see the preface to "Shuangxi xing" 雙溪行, in Chen Shunyu 陳舜俞 (d. 1072), *Duguan ji* 都官集, in *Wenyuange Siku quanshu*, vol. 1096, 12.20a–22a.

46. Ye Mengde, *Shilin shihua* 石林詩話, in *Lidai shihua*, 1.408. Liu Chang was admittedly the better-known poet, and Ye's circumspection might be attributed to simple literary taste; but I believe a sense of propriety was also

at issue here. Note that a Qing recension of Ye Mengde's anecdote attributes the poem that moved the emperor to Han's entertainer-concubine, rather than to Han himself, and includes both the lyric she supposedly wrote and an answering one by Han. See Shen Chenyuan 沈辰垣 (fl. 17th–18th cents.), Wang Yiqing 王奕清 (d. 1736?), and Zhu Yizun 朱彝尊 (1629–1709), *Yuxuan lidai shiyu* 御選歷代詩餘, in *Wenyuange Siku quanshu*, vols. 1491–93, 114.20a–20b.

47. Huihong 惠洪 (1072–1128), *Lengzhai yehua* 冷齋夜話, in Zhu, ed., *Quan Song biji*, 2nd ser., 9:1.31.
48. *Daoshan qinghua*, 100.
49. Wang Mingqing, "Yulu" 餘錄, *Huizhu lu*, 2.299–300.
50. Chen Shidao, *Houshan tancong*, 5.64–5.
51. Jiang Shaoyu 江少虞 (fl. 12th cent.), *Songchao shishi leiyuan* 宋朝事實類苑, 2 vols. (Shanghai: Shanghai guji chubanshe, 1981), 2:8.79.
52. Xu Yi, *Yanzhou shihua*, 391.
53. Wang Mingqing, *Huizhu lu*, houlu, 7.174–75. Cf. Ebrey, *The Inner Quarters*, 226.
54. As cited in Huihong, *Lengzhai yehua*, 1.31.
55. Zhaoyun died at age thirty-three, in exile in Huizhou with Su Shi; their son died before his second year. Another anecdotalist relates that Zhaoyun died from eating snake in Huizhou; whether or not that was the case, his account shows that Su Shi's relationship with Zhaoyun was widely known and discussed. See Zhu Yu, *Pingzhou ke tan*, 2.137.
56. See *Huang Tingjian quanji* 黃庭堅全集, ed. Liu Lin 劉琳, Li Yongxian 李勇先, and Wang Ronggui 王蓉貴 (Chengdu: Sichuan daxue chubanshe, 2001), 11.1136.
57. E.g., Han Qi, *Anyang ji biannian jianzhu* 安陽集編年箋注, ed. Li Zhiliang 李之亮 and Xu Zhengying 徐正英 (Chengdu: Ba Shu shushe, 2000), 49.1517–19.
58. On the musician origins of Empress Liu 劉后 (968–1033), consort of Song Zhenzong 宋真宗 (r. 997–1022), see Sima Guang 司馬光 (1019–86), *Sushui jiwen* 涑水紀聞, ed. Deng Guangming 鄧廣銘 and Zhang Xiqing 張希清 (Beijing: Zhonghua shuju, 1989), 5.100–101. On Empress Yang 楊后 (1162–1232) of Song Ningzong 宋寧宗 (r. 1194–1224), see Ye Shaoweng 葉紹翁 (fl. late 12th–early 13th cents.), *Sichao wenjian lu* 四朝聞見錄, ed. Shen Xilin 沈錫鄰 and Feng Huimin 馮惠民 (Beijing: Zhonghua shuju, 1989), 3.110–11. I have discussed both cases in my "Gender and Entertainment at the Song Court," in *Servants of the Dynasty: Palace Women in World History*, ed. Anne Walthall (Berkeley: University of California Press, 2008), passim.
59. Anecdotalists did occasionally remark on the concubine parentage of political enemies.

9   Glyphomantic Dream Anecdotes
Richard E. Strassberg

Within the large corpus of dream anecdotes, those that employ glyphomancy in various ways form a significant group worth exploring. Not only do they document a pervasive cultural practice, but they also transmit distinct beliefs about writing, reading, and human consciousness. "Glyphomancy" denotes a group of nonnormative procedures applied to the reading of Chinese graphs that purport to reveal hidden meanings.[1] These are often denoted by such terms as *chaizi* 拆字 ("disassembling graphs"), *cezi* 測字 ("prediction using graphs"), *pozi* 破字 ("breaking apart graphs"), or *xiangzi* 相字 ("interpreting the forms of graphs"). As a literary practice, it can be traced back at least to the Warring States Period (475–221 BCE), and it has since appeared in a wide variety of genres, ranging from canonical histories to dictionaries to occult texts. Concurrently, glyphomancy has also been employed in fortune-telling both privately among the educated elite and in public spaces such as temples, teahouses, and marketplaces, where it is still performed by professionals.[2] While a class-based distinction developed that contrasted its use by literati for higher political, intellectual, and artistic purposes, and the commercialized services offered by poorer, less educated professionals, the procedures themselves were not markedly different. Rather, regarded as a branch of *bowu* 博物 ("knowledge of things"), judgments about glyphomancy's legitimacy and efficacy were usually influenced by social context and the spiritual or intellectual abilities of the individual practitioner.[3] As an act of decoding surface meaning, glyphomancy can reflect the skepticism about ordinary consciousness and use of language expressed by such early philosophical schools as the writers of the *Zhuangzi* 莊子 and the Logicians. It is also a manifestation of mystified beliefs, perhaps rooted in ancient *wu* 巫 shamanism, about the magical power of writing and the Chinese graph's ability to represent the deeper recesses of the mind. Not surprisingly, glyphomancy was employed early on to interpret events in dreams.

Dream anecdotes can be traced back even earlier to the dawn of Chinese writing, if one accepts the brief statements in the Shang dynasty oracle bone inscriptions as deriving from oral narratives.[4] Certainly by the Warring States period, the recording of dreams had evolved into a generic form that was included in a wide range of books, including philosophical works and annalistic histories, and it was later incorporated into *zhiguai* 志怪 ("anomaly accounts"), *chuanqi* 傳奇 ("transmitted marvels"), and *biji* 筆記 ("brush jottings"). From the Tang dynasty on, these anecdotes were also collected in general encyclopedias as well as in compendia specifically devoted to dream narratives and theory. This culminated in Chen Shiyuan's 陳士元 (1516–97) *Mengzhan yizhi* 夢占逸旨 (Lofty principles of dream interpretation, published 1562), which contains the largest collection of nearly seven hundred examples with a separate chapter devoted to glyphomantic dreams.[5]

Leaving aside the abundant corpus of allegorical and fictional dreams, as well as a small number of autobiographical accounts, the generic dream anecdote in its written form purported to be a record of an actual experience and employed a common, historiographical linguistic style. Among its conventions were the use of a third-person narrator who is impersonal and omniscient as well as standard markers of a character's normative identity such as time, place, social status, gender, and ethnicity. The vast majority of examples conformed to a tripartite structure: (1) a description of an oneiric experience (*meng* 夢); (2) a scene of interpretation (*zhan* 占); and (3) a confirmation of the interpretation in events that subsequently occur in waking life (*yan* 驗 or *zheng* 徵). Such dreams are usually situated within a larger narrative chronotope, which is to say, the matrix frame of calendric time and geographical space. As strange events, they disrupt regular, observable cosmic patterns by revealing hidden threats that must be resolved before the conclusion of the story, when order is restored.

These narratives function as anecdotes in a double sense. Internally, they usually present a scene of iteration whereby the dreamer tells his dream to someone else in the form of a coherent narrative. Despite the medium of classical Chinese and the obvious editing into a terse account, these scenes trace the passage from private experience to public articulation, indicating various modes of oral transmission. They include the following situations: intimate confessions between husband and wife and between friends; consultations with shamans, monks, priests, fortunetellers, and famous interpreters; reports by crime victims to investigating judges; as well discussions between rulers and their officials, including *shi* 史, or "historian-astrologers." Sometimes, on this internal level, there is an awareness of a repertoire of literary dream anecdotes already circulating in the culture when characters sometimes refer to the recorded dreams of others.

Externally, literary dream anecdotes were transmitted in the same ways as other kinds of anecdotes that became components of longer texts and books. However, the circumstances behind their recording were rarely disclosed. Very few examples reveal the process by which a dream was transformed from an oral into a literary anecdote; and this obviously creates problems of veracity and historical authenticity. Certain dreams of rulers and palace women related to state affairs may well have originated as gossip within elite circles that was later preserved by scribes and compiled into official and unofficial histories. In a few instances, the dreamer or listener is said to have written the story down, or, more rarely, the transcriber revealed his own identity. In most cases, these anecdotes must have spread casually among indeterminate communities before later being written down by literati far removed from the original iteration.

Many anecdotes have been recycled through the centuries, usually with textual variations, and were easily incorporated into established genres such as *zhuan* 傳 ("biographical accounts"), which preserved many examples in a kind of literary amber. There has always been a strain of skepticism about the reality of dreams and their interpretability: the philosopher Zhuang Zhou's 莊周 (fl. 4th cent. BCE) widely known "Dream of a Butterfly" 蝴蝶夢 episode is emblematic of these doubts.[6] Chen Shiyuan and other theorists acknowledged that in actual life, most dreams cannot be interpreted. The dreamer may not fully remember his dream or cannot articulate it. The interpreter may be unskilled, insincere, or lack spiritual understanding. Or the content may be unworthy of being treated seriously. However, Chen argued that dreams are real because they have actual consequences in waking life and presented his collection as evidential cases that affirm their efficacy.[7] Although an anecdote may include mistaken interpretations on the part of various characters, it ultimately demonstrates a closed hermeneutic, for only one reading of the dream finally emerges. This is then validated by the confirmation, which is often prefaced by the term *guo* 果 ("indeed" or "as expected"). There is the intriguing possibility suggested in one account that the consequences of a dream may be suspended as long as the dreamer refrains from telling it to someone else, as well as instances where predicted events can be altered for better or worse based on the dreamer's subsequent knowledge and behavior. But neither the reliability of the outer, tripartite structure nor the accuracy of the dreamer's own account is typically problematical. While the generic dream anecdote narrates extraordinary cases, most are not presented as opaque. Rather, they demonstrate the triumph of interpretation over uncertainty by revealing personal destiny and the mechanism of social and cosmic order—at least to the reader.

Of the various techniques employed in the interpretation section of dream anecdotes, the use of glyphomancy can be regarded as the most quintessentially Chinese, for the obvious reason that it focuses on decoding meanings concealed within the forms of Chinese graphs. As with attitudes toward glyphomancy in general, dream anecdotes often blur the distinction between the techniques used by literati and professional fortune-tellers. In fortune-telling, the client usually presents his or her own graph for analysis, or the client may select one from a group provided by the fortune-teller. In some cases, the fortune-teller can also provide a character for analysis. In dream interpretation, though, the graph arises from an oneiric experience that has occurred in the past and is narrated by the dreamer based on memory. Moreover, the graph itself may be either clearly manifest in the dream or is identified by the interpreter from imagery or a situation in the dreamer's account. Thus, the origin of a graph in dreams is not only involuntary, but also shrouded in the mystery of a hidden state of consciousness. As a technique of dream interpretation, glyphomancy represents a far higher level of literary and spiritual competency than the use of *mengshu* 夢書 ("dream manuals"), which provide glossaries of stereotypical imagery.[8] Thus, the subgenre of glyphomantic dream anecdotes also paralleled, and sometimes was included within, a subgenre of biographies that celebrated famous dream interpreters as well as outstanding professionals.[9]

An early example of a glyphomantic dream anecdote appeared in the third-century work, *Diwang shiji* 帝王世紀 (Annals of the thearchs and kings) by Huangfu Mi 黃甫謐 (215–82):

> The Yellow Emperor dreamt that a great wind blew away all the dust in the world. He also dreamt that someone picked up a crossbow weighing about four thousand pounds and drove a herd of several tens of thousands of sheep. After he awoke, the emperor sighed and said, "The wind [*feng* 風] stands for a command and is a sign for holding the reins of government. When one removes the element for

'earth' [*tu* 土] from the written graph for 'dust' [*gou* 垢], what remains is the graph *hou* 后. Where can there be someone in the world named 'Feng Hou' [風后]? A four thousand pound crossbow requires unusual 'power' [*li* 力]. Anyone who can drive a herd of several tens of thousands of sheep is capable of 'shepherding' [*mu* 牧] people toward goodness. Where can there be someone in the world named 'Li Mu' [力牧]?" The Yellow Emperor searched for them based on these two interpretations of his dream, and he found Feng Hou at the edge of the sea and raised him to the position of minister, and he found Li Mu in the great marshlands and promoted him to the position of general. Based on this experience, he wrote *The Book of Dream Interpretation* in eleven chapters.

黃帝夢大風吹天下之塵垢皆去，又夢人執千鈞之弩驅羊數萬群。帝寤而歎曰：「風為號令執政者也，垢去土后在也。天下豈有姓風名后者哉？夫千鈞之弩，異力能遠者也。驅羊數萬群，是能牧民為善者也。天下豈有姓力名牧者哉？」於是依二夢之占而求之，得風后於海隅，登以為相；得力牧於大澤，進以為將。黃帝因著占夢經十一卷。[10]

This interpretation combines two techniques of glyphomancy: the graphs for *feng*, *gou*, *li*, and *mu* are derived from a process of associative reasoning based on imagery similar to that used to solve riddles and rebuses while the graph for *hou* results from a subtraction of strokes (*jianbi cefa* 減筆測法). In the *Cezi midie* 測字密牒 (Secret writings on glyphomancy) by the early Qing practitioner and theorist Cheng Xing 程省 (fl. mid-17th–early 18th cents.), the latter technique is identified as the seventh among his "Ten Methods of Glyphomancy" ("Cezi shifa" 測字十法).[11] This particular anecdote was also included in a fifth-century commentary added to the chapter "Basic Annals of the Five Thearchs" ("Wudi benji" 五帝本紀) in the *Shiji* 史記 (Records of the historian).[12] That a glyphomantic dream was connected with the divine figure of the Yellow Emperor and shown to be useful in conducting state affairs suggests that this method of interpretation was accepted by the Northern and Southern Dynasties period, if not earlier, as a legitimate practice by the educated elite.

Narrowly defined, glyphomancy is often assumed to only involve readings based on alterations to the visible form of graphs. A simple demonstration of Cheng's fifth method, "breaking apart and analyzing graphs" (*pojie zi* 破解字), can be seen in the following anecdote in which the dreamer, like the Yellow Emperor, serves as his own interpreter:

Earlier, when Ding Gu [丁固 (fl. mid-3rd cent.)] was serving as an imperial secretary, he dreamt that a pine tree grew forth from his stomach. He told someone, "The graph for 'pine' [松] is composed of the graphs for 'eighteen' [十八] and 'duke' [公]. Eighteen years from now, perhaps I will become a duke!" In the end, it turned out just as he had dreamed.

初,固為尚書,夢松樹生其腹上,謂人曰:「松字十八公也。後十八歲,吾其為公乎!」卒如夢焉。[13]

This follows a simple procedure: the graph is dismantled into three components that are read as individual graphs in a sequence that follows the stroke order of the original graph.

A more complex procedure involves rearranging the components of graphs to form another sequence whose reading manifests a more mysterious, paranormal process of reasoning. The Western Jin scholar and official Zou Zhan 郗湛 (246–99), in an anecdote included in his biography in the *Jinshu* 晉書 (History of the Jin dynasty), demonstrated his superior spiritual and literary understanding by interpreting his dream thus:

> Zou Zhan dreamt of a man who gave his name as Zhen Shuzhong [甄舒仲] but then said nothing more. This occurred on more than one occasion. After a while, Zou understood and said, "West of my house is a mound of earth and broken tiles—there must be a dead man buried there. 'Zhen Shuzhong' means a 'man' [亻] 'in' [中] the 'earth' [土] and 'broken tiles' [瓦] 'west' [西] of 'my' [予] 'house' [舍]." He investigated and found it to be so. Zou collected the remains and generously reburied them. Afterward he dreamt that the man came and thanked him.
>
> 初,湛嘗夢見一人,自稱甄舒仲,餘無所言,如此非一。久之乃悟曰:「吾宅西有積土敗瓦,其中必有死人。甄舒仲者,予舍西土瓦中人也。」檢之,果然。厚加斂葬,葬畢,遂夢此人來謝。[14]

Here, the graphs of the name "Zhen Shuzhong" conceal a reality literally hidden underground.[15] If this anecdote is detached from its biographical context and read separately as a didactic *zhiguai* account, one can identify such generic themes as the transgression of the boundary between the *yin* 陰 world of the dead and the *yang* 陽 world of the living, the conflicting demands over space, as well as the grievance of a ghost because of his improper burial. The moral resolution that restores normalcy involves an act of charity by Zou that the ghost repays with his thanks.

Among Cheng Xing's "Ten Methods" are other procedures involving adding strokes, selecting a single component of a graph for analysis, and finding opposite meanings in a single graph or component. Homonyms and other phonological manipulations, correlations with various cosmological systems, and reference to contextual factors are also among the methods identified in his treatise. Cheng Xing called another group of techniques "Six Methods Based on Mental Response and the *Classic of Changes*" ("Xinyi liufa" 心易六法).[16] The famous dream interpreter Suo Dan 索紞 (fl. early 4th cent.) had eclectically employed several techniques from these groups as recorded in his biography in the *Jinshu*:

> Zhang Zhai, an assistant magistrate of a commandery, dreamt that he rode a horse up a mountain and circled a house three times. All he could see were pines and junipers, and he was unable to locate the door. Suo Dan interpreted it, saying, "'Horse' is associated with the trigram *Li* [離, 'Clinging']. *Li* is correlated with the agent 'fire' [*huo* 火], which has the same sound as 'disaster' [*huo* 禍]. When the graph for 'man' [*ren* 人] climbs up that for 'mountain' [*shan* 山], it becomes the graph 'unlucky' [*xiong* 凶]. Seeing only pines and cypresses symbolizes the gate to a tomb. Not to be able to find the door indicates that there is no door. 'Circling three times around' symbolizes three years. In three years, a great disaster will befall you." Indeed, Zhang plotted a rebellion and was executed.
>
> 郡主簿張宅夢走馬上山，環繞舍三周，但見松柏，不知門處。紞曰：「馬屬離，離為火，火禍也。人上山，為凶字。但見松柏，墓門象也。不知門處，為無門也。三周，三歲也。後三年必有大禍。」宅果以謀反伏誅。[17]

In this case, Suo correlated dream imagery with trigrams in the *Yijing* 易經 (*Classic of Changes*). This reflects another method of glyphomancy where the trigrams and hexagrams are read as primordial graphs. The interpreter can also produce more complex readings based on the *yin* or *yang* character of individual lines and the transformation of one trigram or hexagram into another. The association of fire with disaster on the basis of their common pronunciation is "phonetic borrowing" (*xiesheng* 諧聲), the fourth of Cheng Xing's "Six Methods." The additional stroke that transforms the graph "mountain" into "unlucky," meanwhile, is number six of his "Ten Methods," or "glyphomancy by adding strokes" (*tianbi cefa* 添筆測法).

Hidden aspects of sounds as well as visual forms can be employed in glyphomancy as recorded in in the Tang dynasty miscellany *Youyang zazu* 酉陽雜俎 (*Miscellaneous morsels from Youyang*), which was completed around 850. It makes use of "phonetic recombination" (*fanyu* 反語), whereby the initial and final sounds of graphs are switched:

> Junior Commander of the Awe-Inspiring Army for Distant Regions Mei Bocheng was skilled at interpreting dreams. Nearby, an entertainer, Li Bolian, was traveling through Jingzhou seeking money and obtained one hundred *hu* in rice. When he was going to return home, he ordered his younger brother to collect the rice, but the time passed

when they were to meet up, and the brother had still not arrived. During daytime, Li dreamt about washing a white horse. He paid a call on Mei Bocheng and asked him to interpret this. Mei thought deeply about it and said, "Generally, people are fond of phonetic recombinations, but 'washing a white horse' [*xi baima* 洗白馬] means 'flowing away of white rice' [*xie baimi* 瀉白米]. You will have cause to worry due to wind and water!" Several days later, the brother arrived. Indeed, he said that the boat carrying the rice had capsized in the Wei River leaving not even a single grain.

威遠軍小將梅伯成以善占夢。近有優人李伯憐遊涇州乞錢，得米百斛。及歸令弟取之，過期不至。晝夢洗白馬，訪伯成占之. 伯成佇思曰：「凡人好反語，洗白馬，瀉白米也。君所憂或有風水之虞乎！」數日弟至，果言渭河中覆舟，一粒無餘。[18]

While most procedures involve some kind of deconstructive analysis, the opposite can also occur. The graphs of the written language can constitute a private landscape where the dreamer, like a lyric poet, selects and combines elements into an image revealing an aspect of personal destiny normally inaccessible to consciousness.

The wife of Zeng Chongfan had agreed to marry several different men, but in each case the groom suddenly died.[19] One night, she had a dream where someone told her, "The one with deer horns on the head of a field [*tian* 田] and a brilliant sun [*ri* 日] as the field's tail will be your husband." She realized what this meant when she later married Mr. Zeng [曾].

曾崇范之妻許聘數人，其夫輒死。一夕夢人謂曰：「田頭有鹿迹，田尾有日炙，乃汝夫也。」後嫁崇范方悟。[20]

Interestingly, glyphomancy occurs in this case within the dream itself. It also indicates that gender is not an obstacle to glyphomantic experience despite the different rates of literacy among men and women. Later, this anecdote was preserved in the *Quan Tangshi* 全唐詩 (Complete Tang poems), under the title "Words in a Dream" 夢中語 and with Zeng's wife as the author.[21] Generally, though, few women are shown as performing these procedures on their own. In one of the longest of such anecdotes, the widow Xie Xiao'e 謝小娥 (fl. ca. 813) dreams that her murdered father and husband appear to her in a dream and utter nonsensical statements that are only later decoded by the official and *chuanqi* writer Li Gongzuo 李公佐 (778–848). He tells her that the statements conceal the graphs of the names of the murderers, which enables her to take revenge.[22]

When glyphomantic interpretations are performed by others in dream anecdotes, they usually turn out to be true. But when someone interprets his own dream this way, it can result in a misreading that may indicate a defective moral character. Such stories offer an opportunity for political criticism of arrogant officials as well as other kinds of ridicule:

> Meng Dechong [fl. mid-10th cent.], Vice Minister of the Court of the Imperial Clan during the Latter Shu dynasty, was the son of Yiye, Prince of Yan. He relied on his aristocratic family and was unrestrained, haughty, and boastful. Meng even used to bring along courtesans when carrying out his duties in the Imperial Ancestral Temple. One night, he dreamt that an old man berated him. Furthermore, the man took a brush from a table and suddenly ordered Meng to open the palm of his hand. On it he wrote "ninety" in large graphs before Meng awakened. The next day, Meng discussed this incident with his retainers saying, "When this old man berated me, he was actually expressing his compassion for me. When he wrote 'ninety,' it meant that he was granting me a long life of ninety years." One of his retainers, Feng Lian, joked about this by saying, "The graphs for 'nine' [九] and 'ten' [十] make up the cursive form of the graph for 'death' [卒]. You, Vice Minister, will surely die." And, in less than ten days, Meng did indeed die.
>
> 蜀宗正少卿孟德崇, 燕王貽鄴之子也。自恃貴族, 脫略傲誕, 嘗太廟行香, 攜妓而往。一夕, 夢一老人責之。且取案上筆, 叱令開手, 大書九十字而覺。翌日, 與賓客話及此事, 自言:「老人責我, 是惜我也。書九十字, 賜我壽至九十也。」客有封璉戲之曰:「九十字, 迺是行書卒字, 亞卿其非吉徵乎!」不旬日, 果卒。23

While historical dream anecdotes rarely question the cultural assumptions underlying glyphomancy, these were explored fictionally in the eighteenth-century novel *Honglou meng* 紅樓夢 (*A Dream of Red Mansions*).24 In chapter 94, the incompetence of the fortune-teller Liu Tiezui 劉鐵嘴 (Iron Mouth Liu) is exposed when he provides the wrong interpretation of a graph selected in order to solve the mystery of the disappearance of the hero Jia Baoyu's 賈寶玉 jade. His error is compounded by the credulity of those who then attempt to follow his instructions. Only after the jade is later recovered does Baoyu's cousin Xue Baochai 薛寶釵 realize that the graph did indeed contain other graphs that, had they been analyzed correctly, would have revealed the truth.

While this may reflect the disdain by some literati for professional practitioners, the novel makes serious use of the glyphomantic dream anecdote in chapter 5. Here, Baoyu's spirit travels back to his origins in the divine Land of Illusion (*Taixu huanjing* 太虛幻境). The goddess Disenchantment (Jinghuan xiangu 警幻仙姑), in a vain attempt to liberate him from emotional attachments, permits him to view images with captions in registers. These disclose the destinies of the women in his family if decoded glyphomantically. Baoyu's failure to comprehend or even remember them conveys one of the novel's central themes: the inherent limitation of the human condition to read the world correctly because of the interference of personal desire. Like Baoyu, the first-time reader is suspended in a similar state of ignorance as the events of the plot unfold, underscoring the author's initial challenge to guess the true meaning behind his writing.[25]

The abundance of dream anecdotes of all varieties testifies to the perennial human need to tell others of our innermost thoughts, including our desires and fears. Yet Chinese culture has also maintained an ambivalent attitude toward expression, as evidenced by the many admonitions regarding speech that were transmitted through the Confucian classics as well as in popular idioms. There is also the suggestion that refraining from articulating an oneiric experience may even circumvent predestined events and enable an individual to exercise some control over his fate. The following anecdote comes from the *Zuozhuan* 左傳 (Zuo commentary):

> Earl Sheng [d. 574 BCE] dreamt that he was crossing the Huan River. Someone gave him jade, which he ate. He then wept tears that turned to jade, which filled up his chest. He sang, "The Huan River gave me jade. I must return home, I must return home! My chest is filled up with jade!" He was frightened by this and dared not have the dream interpreted. He returned from the state of Zheng and on the day *renshen* in the eleventh lunar month, he arrived back in Lishen in Lu where he had the dream interpreted. He said, "I was afraid of dying, therefore, I dared not have it interpreted. But now, a multitude of supporters has been with me for three years, so no harm will come of it." After he spoke about it, when evening arrived, Earl Sheng died.
>
> 初, 聲伯夢涉洹, 或與己瓊瑰食之, 泣而為瓊瑰盈其懷, 從而歌之, 曰:「濟洹之水, 贈我以瓊瑰。歸乎歸乎! 瓊瑰盈吾懷乎!」懼不敢占也。還自鄭, 任申, 至于貍脤而占之, 曰:「余恐死, 故不敢占也。今眾繁而從余三年矣, 無傷也。」言之, 之莫而卒。[26]

Earl Sheng 聲伯 was an aristocrat and an official of Lu. His fear that his dream predicted death derived from the funerary practice of putting jade into the mouth of the deceased. It is implied that the earl might have succeeded in postponing his death as long as he did not narrate his experience. But perhaps this only proves that the urge to tell others is ultimately irresistible, both on the part of the earl as well as the transmitters of this anecdote.

The history of glyphomantic dream anecdotes does not quite follow a linear pattern of development: essential features appearing in early examples from the Six Dynasties continue to be seen in those from later periods. Certain changes can be noticed that reflect broader cultural evolutions. For example, as literary fame and the official examinations came to play greater roles in the careers of literati, there are more dreams about predicting success in these arenas. Stories set within the imperial court and those recorded in official histories seem to have reached a peak during the Tang and Song dynasties along with a fashion for glyphomancy among scholars. Yet, one of the most enduring characteristics of these anecdotes throughout the tradition is the transactional fluidity that occurs on several levels—social, linguistic, and textual. Despite the evident markers of class and gender and the boundaries delimiting public and private spaces, the events involving glyphomantic dreams trace multiple crossings. In the earlier examples, an itinerant actor is able to gain access to the residence of a substantial military official and solicit his expertise in interpretation. The literatus Li Gongzuo recorded that he heard of the dream of a merchant's widow from a monk while temporarily residing in a temple. In *Honglou meng*, the young hero journeys to a divine dimension in an erotic episode that occurs in a female relative's bedroom. We may read these interactions as constituting a map of some of the itineraries that these anecdotal materials followed in the process of their transformation from oral accounts to written form.

It is tempting for the modern and, especially, the Western reader to want to interrogate these anecdotes in terms of their status as truthful statements, if truth is simply regarded as either indicating personal integrity or emerging from a correspondence to observable facts.[27] With rare exceptions, however, traditional Chinese dream literature assumed a willing suspension of disbelief on the part of its readers, especially when oneiric experience was transmitted in authoritative genres. In the standard, tripartite form, the final events that confirm the interpretation are usually recorded as historical occurrences, which implicitly validate the accuracy of the dream as initially reported. Although it was recognized that in real life most dreams cannot or should not be interpreted, in the vast majority of dream anecdotes, the authenticity of the dream itself is not questioned.[28] That this issue was of little concern is revealed in two anecdotes about Zhou Xuan 周宣 (d. ca. 239 CE), regarded in China as the greatest dream interpreter of all time. Appointed as a palace attendant under the grand astrologer during the Wei dynasty, his official biography in the *Sanguo zhi* 三國志 (Record of the Three Kingdoms) states:

Emperor Wen consulted Xuan, saying, "I dreamt that two roof tiles from the palace fell to the ground and changed into a pair of mandarin ducks. What does this mean?" Xuan replied, "Someone in the rear palace will die violently." The emperor said, "I was just fooling you!" Xuan replied, "Dreams are nothing but intentions. If these are expressed in words, one can then interpret their fortunate or unfortunate consequences." He was not finished speaking when the director of eunuch attendants reported that a palace woman had been killed."

文帝曰：「吾夢殿屋兩瓦墮地，化為鴛鴦。此何謂也？」 宣曰：「後宮當有暴死者。」帝曰：「吾詐卿耳！」 宣曰：「夫夢者，意耳。苟以形言，便占吉凶。」 言未畢，而黃門令奏宮人相殺。

The second account relates how the grand astrologer consulted Zhou on three occasions, telling him each time that he had dreamt about straw dogs, which were objects used in religious sacrifices. Zhou interpreted each dream differently, and these were confirmed with increasingly unfortunate results for the grand astrologer. Finally, the astrologer admitted that he fabricated all three dreams in order to test Zhou's skills and asked Zhou how he arrived at such accurate predictions. Zhou replied, "You were moved to speak by a numinous spirit, and the result was no different from an actual dream."[29]

In Zhou Xuan's sophisticated method of interpretation, it clearly did not matter if the initial accounts of the dreams were true. That he did not focus on first determining their factuality suggests that cognitive priority was given to recognizing the "propensity" (shi 勢) of the broader context.[30] As he explained it, a pervasive, invisible energy or "numinous spirit" (shenling 神靈) could influence consciousness including individual "intentions" (yi 意), and he treated these as actual events with consequences for personal welfare. Zhou's process of reasoning reflects a basic disposition of Chinese culture toward perceiving multiple levels of reality unfolding through a complex interweaving of dynamic patterns of power and then adopting pragmatic responses. While both anecdotes also demonstrate that insincere intentions bring retribution, Zhou's interpretative procedure ignored the issue of truthfulness in favor of responding to articulated thoughts as valid manifestations of cosmic forces. The biography concluded by affirming that, "When Xuan discussed dreams, it was always in this way, and he hit the mark eight or nine times out of ten."[31] Chen Shiyuan maintained that dreams are real because they are recorded in the Confucian classics, but readers have always been free to believe this or not.

NOTES

1. On the term *glyphomancy*, see Joseph Needham, *Science and Civilisation in China*, vol. 2, *History of Scientific Thought* (Cambridge: Cambridge University Press, 1956), 364.

2. For Western studies of professional glyphomancy, see J. J. M. de Groot, "On Chinese Divination by Dissecting Written Characters," *T'oung Pao* 1 (1890): 239–47; Wolfgang Bauer, "Chinese Glyphomancy (*ch'ai-tzu*) and Its Uses in Present-day Taiwan," in *Legend, Lore, and Religion in China: Essays in Honor of Wolfram Eberhard on His Seventieth Birthday*, ed. Sarah Allan and Alvin P. Cohen (San Francisco: Chinese Materials Center, 1979), 71–96; Lindy Li Mark, "Orthography Riddles, Divination, and Word Magic: An Exploration in Folklore and Culture," in *Legend, Lore, and Religion in China*, ed. Allan and Cohen, 43–69. Among recent popular treatments of glyphomancy in Chinese, a useful survey can be found in Song Chuanyin 松傳銀 and Yang Chang 楊昶, *Shenmi de cizi* 神秘的測字 (Nanning: Guangxi renmin chubanshe, 2004). A comprehensive anthology of gyphomantic anecdotes including dream anecdotes was compiled in 1667 by the Qing bibliophile Zhou Lianggong 周亮工 (1612–1701) in *Zichu* 字觸, rpt. in Zhan Xuzuo 詹緒佐 and Zhu Liangzhi 朱良志, eds., *Zhongguo gudai cezishu* 中國古代測字術 (Chengdu: Sichuan daxue chubanshe, 1993), 1–199.

3. The intellectual classification of glyphomancy as a technical art within *bowu* can be found in the section entitled "Chaizibu" 拆字部 (*juan* 747–48), in the Qing dynasty encyclopedia *Qinding gujin tushu jicheng* 欽定古今圖書集成, comp. Chen Menglei 陳夢雷 et al., vol. 482 (Shanghai: Zhonghua shuju, 1934).

4. These have been studied in Hu Houxuan 胡厚宣, "Yinren zhanmeng kao" 殷人占夢考, in Hu, *Jiaguxue Shangshi luncong chuji* 甲骨學商史論叢初集 (Hong Kong: Wenyoutang shudian, 1970), 1:1a–10b; also see Song Zhenhao 宋鎮豪, "Jiaguwen zhong de meng yu zhanmeng" 甲骨文中的夢與占夢考, *Wenwu* 文物 600 (Jun. 2006): 61–71.

5. Chen Shiyuan, *Mengzhan yizhi*, in *Congshu jicheng chubian* 叢書集成初編, vol. 727 (Shanghai: Shangwu yinshuguan, 1937). This work has been translated in Richard E. Strassberg, *Wandering Spirits: Chen Shiyuan's Encyclopedia of Dreams* (Berkeley: University of California Press, 2008). In regard to the topic of this essay, see especially chapter 10 of *Wandering Spirits*, "Written Graphs" 字畫, 169–76.

6. For a study of ambivalent attitudes toward dreams during the Warring States period, see Wai-yee Li, "Dreams of Interpretation in Early Chinese Historical and Philosophical Writings," in *Dream Cultures: Towards a Comparative History of Dreaming*, ed. David Shulman and Guy Stroumsa (Oxford: Oxford University Press, 1999), 17–42.

7. See Chen, *Mengzhan yizhi*, 15–16; Strassberg, *Wandering Spirits*, 98–99.

8. For examples, see Zheng Binglin 鄭炳麟 and Yang Ping 羊萍, eds., *Dunhuangben mengshu* 敦煌本夢書 (Lanzhou: Gansu wenhua chubanshe,

1995); also Liu Wenying 劉文英, *Zhongguo gudai de mengshu* 中國古代的夢書 (Beijing: Zhonghua shuju, 1990). These texts have been studied in Jean-Pierre Drège, "Notes d'Onirologie Chinoise," *Bulletin de l'École française d'Extrême-Orient* 70 (1981): 271–89 and his "Clefs des Songes de Touen-houang," in *Nouvelles contributions aux études de Touen-houang*, ed. Michel Soymié (Geneva: Librairie Droz, 1981), 205–49.

9. For modern versions of biographies of famous practitioners, see Song and Yang, *Shenmi de cizi*, 93–123.

10. Huangfu Mi, *Diwang shiji* 帝王世紀, in Yan Yiping 嚴一萍, ed., *Baibu congshu jicheng* 百部叢書集成, vol. 54 (Taipei: Yiwen yinshuguan, 1967), 1.7b–8a.

11. See Cheng Xing 程省, *Cezi midie* 測字密牒 (Secret writings on glyphomancy), rpt. in Yang Chang and Song Yinchuan, eds., *Gudai cezishu shuping* 古代測字術注評 (Guilin: Guangxi shifan daxue chubanshe, 1992), 209–10.

12. In Pei Yin 裴駰 (fl. 5th cent.), *Shiji zhengyi* 史記正義, quoted in Sima Tan 司馬談 (d. ca. 110 BCE) and Sima Qian (ca. 145–ca. 86 BCE), *Shiji* (Beijing: Zhonghua shuju, 1959), 1.8.

13. This is Ding Gu, who served as an imperial secretary under Sun Hao 孫皓 (r. 264–80), the last ruler of the Kingdom of Wu. This story was originally recorded in Wei Zhao 韋昭 (204–73), *Wushu* 吳書 (History of Wu) and is preserved in Pei Songzhi's 裴松之 (372–451) commentary, in Chen Shou 陳壽 (233–97), comp., *Sanguozhi* 三國志 (Beijing: Zhonghua shuju, 1959), 5.1167. It later became a well-known anecdote and poetic allusion. Also recorded in Chen, *Mengzhan yizhi*, 27; and Strassberg, *Wandering Spirits*, 132–33. Chen Shiyuan, however, identifies the source as another lost work of the period, *Wulu* 吳錄 (Record of Wu, completed ca. 265–89) by Zhang Bo 張勃 (fl. third cent.)

14. Fang Xuanling 房玄齡 (579–648), et al. eds., *Jinshu* 晉書 (Beijing: Zhonghua shuju, 1974), 8.2380; also see Chen, *Mengzhan yizhi*, 41; and Strassberg, *Wandering Spirits*, 175.

15. The glyphomantic reading is as follows: 甄 = 西 瓦 土; 舒 = 舍 予; 仲 = 亻[人] 中.

16. Yang and Song, *Gudai cezishu zhuping*, 214–18. As these modern editors point out, Cheng's "Xinyi liufa" are actually categorized according to the *liushu* 六書 ("six forms of graphs") of traditional Chinese etymology, which Cheng credited to Paoxi 庖義 (also known as Fuxi 伏羲), the mythical creator of the trigrams in the *Yijing*. In other texts, the term *xinyi* 心易 usually denotes interpretive methods attributed to the Northern Song philosopher Shao Yong 邵雍 (1011–77) that combine individual cognition with the imagery and mathematics of the *Yijing*.

17. *Jinshu*, 8.2494; also Chen, *Mengzhan yizhi*, 40; and Strassberg, *Wandering Spirits*, 171.

18. Duan Chengshi 段成式 (d. 863), *Youyang zazu*, in *Baibu congshu jicheng*, vol. 46 (Taipei: Yiwen yinshuguan, 1965), 8.11a–b. Phonetic recombinations are similar to the *fanqie* 反切 method, which was employed in tra-

ditional dictionaries to indicate the pronunciation of a graph by combining the initial sound of one character with the final sound of a second character. Here, the initials and finals of the three graphs pronounced in modern Mandarin *xi baima* ("washing a white horse") are recombined to produce *xie baimi*, which, in Tang pronunciation, could be interpreted as concealing the graphs meaning "flowing away of white rice."

19. Zeng Chongfan 曾崇范 (fl. mid-10th cent.) was an official and bibliophile during the Latter Zhou dynasty.

20. Preserved in Xie Weixin 謝維新 (*jinshi* 1202), comp., *Gujin hebi shilei beiyao: chubian* 古今合璧事類備要: 初編 (Taipei: Xinxing shuju, 1969), 61.463. The original source is only identified as a *yeshi* 野史 ("unofficial history"). Chen Shiyuan, however, gives the source as *Xijing zaji* 西京雜記 (Diverse notes on the Western Capital); this is not the same book traditionally attributed to Liu Xin 劉歆 (ca. 50 BCE–23 CE) or Ge Hong 葛洪 (ca. 283–363). See Chen, *Mengzhan yizhi*, 41; and Strassberg, *Wandering Spirits*, 174.

21. See *Quan Tangshi* 全唐詩 (Beijing: Zhonghua shuju, 1985), 868.9840.

22. This anecdote originated as a *chuanqi* story by Li Gongzuo 李公佐 (ca. 778–848), "Biography of Xie Xiao'e" ("Xie Xiao'e zhuan" 謝小娥傳), and is a rare example in which the writer discloses the process of recording a dream anecdote. It was abridged to serve as Xie's official historical biography in the "Righteous Women" ("Lienü" 列女) biographical section of Ouyang Xiu 歐陽修 and Song Qi 宋祁, comps., *Xin Tangshu* 新唐書 (Beijing: Zhonghua shuju, 1975), 18:5827–28. It was also retold in a number of other genres. See Wang Pijiang 王辟疆, ed., *Tangren xiaoshuo* 唐人小說 (Shanghai: Shanghai guji chubanshe, 1978), 93–97. See also Chen, *Mengzhan yizhi*, 41; and Strassberg, *Wandering Spirits*, 173.

23. Li Fang 李昉 et al., comps., *Taiping guangji* 太平廣記 (Beijing: Zhonghua shuju, 1961), 279.2225–26. The source is given as *Yeren xianhua* 野人閒話, a 965 miscellany by a writer known either as Geng Huan 耿煥 or Jing Huan 景煥 (fl. 965–84).

24. On the topic of gossip in *Honglou meng*, see chapter 10 of the present volume.

25. See Cao Xueqin 曹雪芹 and Gao E 高鶚, *Honglou meng* 紅樓夢, 4 vols. (Beijing: Renmin wenxue chubanshe, 1972), 5.51–66, 94.1217–18. The glyphomantic interpretations of the images in the registers is discussed in Cao Xueqin, *The Story of the Stone*, vol. 1, *The Golden Days*, trans. David Hawkes (Harmondsworth: Penguin Books, 1973), 527–34. In chapter 116, as the novel draws to a close, Baoyu's spirit revisits the scene of his earlier dream, but even then he is only barely able to comprehend the meanings in the registers.

26. In Yang Bojun 楊伯峻, ed., *Chunqiu Zuozhuan zhu* 春秋左傳注, rev. ed. (Beijing: Zhonghua shuju, 1990), 899. Also see Chen, *Mengzhan yizhi*, 5; and Strassberg, *Wandering Spirits*, 71.

27. For a comparison of the Western philosophical concept of truth and Chinese thought, see David L. Hall and Roger T. Ames, *Thinking from the*

Han: Self, Truth, and Transcendence in Chinese and Western Culture (Albany: State University of New York Press, 1998), 103–80.

28. For a rare example transmitted through unofficial literature that problematizes the conventional dream account, see the Daoist allegory (*yuyan* 寓言) in the *Liezi* 列子 about a woodcutter and the carcass of a deer that he has killed. It begins by asserting an actual event and then proceeds to trace the confusion caused by mistaken dreams about it and competing interpretations. Finally, when the ownership of the carcass becomes a legal case, a judge abandons any hope of discovering the facts. See Yang Bojun 楊伯峻, ed., *Liezi jishi* 列子集釋 (Beijing: Zhonghua shuju, 1979), 3.107–8. Translated in A. C. Graham, *The Book of Lieh-tzǔ* (London: John Murray, 1960), 69–70.

29. *Sanguo zhi*, 1.810–11. Zhou Xuan was subsequently mythologized in popular culture. As "Mr. Zhou" (Zhougong 周公), he was credited with the authorship of innumerable dream books that are still included in almanacs today. However, this biography indicates that his actual methods were regarded by official historians as far superior to such mechanical interpretations. For a complete translation of the biography, see Kenneth J. Dewoskin, trans., *Doctors, Diviners, and Magicians of Ancient China: Biographies of Fang-shih* (New York: Columbia University Press, 1983), 138–40.

30. For a discussion of *shi* as a foundation of Chinese thought, see François Julien, *The Propensity of Things: Towards a History of Efficacy in China*, trans. by Janet Lloyd (New York: Zone Books, 1995).

31. *Sanguozhi*, 1.811.

10 The Retributory Power of Gossip in *The Story of the Stone*
Dore J. Levy

As *The Story of the Stone* (*Shitou ji* 石頭記) is the great cultural compendium of the Qing dynasty (1644–1911), the presence, significance, and effects of gossip, loose talk, and innuendo in it should be emblematic of the perception of these social elements in the lives of the Chinese gentry of this period.[1] In the Jia 賈 household, where imagination frequently substitutes for direct communication and there is chronic fear that the image presented to society outside its walls will crack, gossip is often the catalyst of major confrontations. Even in the sanctuary of the Garden of Total Vision (*Daguan yuan* 大觀園),[2] those characters with the least regard for outside appearances are susceptible to whiffs of rumor that chivvy their karmic destinies toward their inevitable ends.

If the phrase for "retributory illness" is *yuannie zhi zheng* 冤孽之症, the phrase for talk that has a retributory purpose might be *yuannie zhi hua* 冤孽之話, the point being that in *Story of the Stone*, all features of the narrative are aimed toward fulfilling the destinies of the characters—or at least, the fates of the hero, Jia Baoyu 賈寶玉, and the Twelve Beauties of Jinling 金陵十二釵, the women who play the most important role in his earthly career.[3] While much of the material we think of as gossip and innuendo may not seem to affect these characters directly, when we consider their influence as catalysts of events, it is apparent that these most mundane aspects of social exchange play as significant a role in fulfilling the cosmic imperatives of the text as more overtly supermundane events.

In *The Story of the Stone* there are two main arenas of gossip: outside the Jia enclave and within. Rumors have a significantly different impact and affect a different set of people within the extended family, depending on their source. Sociologist Ronald de Souza suggests that gossip is not intrinsically vicious, but has a vital life in a local community. He writes,

"Gossip is inherently democratic, concerned with private life rather than public issues, and 'idle' in the sense that it is not instrumental or goal-oriented. Yet it can serve to expand our understanding of life in ways other modes of inquiry cannot."[4] This reflects provocatively on the question of perspective in the reception of gossip, at least from the perspective of the characters in the author Cao Xueqin's 曹雪芹 (1715–63) narrative. On the social level, gossip does seem to have this democratizing quality. On the symbolic and cosmic levels, however, and especially from the perspective of the reader, gossip can definitely seem purposive, instrumental, and goal-oriented. Purveyors of snippets of inside information, eager recipients of tidbits, or aghast figures of rumor, all participants have roles in a society in which each member has a stake and shares responsibility. Furthermore, if we consider the possibility that gossip does play a role in the retributory patterns that underlie all human interactions in a society that gives credence to Buddhism, then idle chat is anything *but* idle. In this context, notions of scale of significance for any given experience are illusory, and the smallest events may be just as significant as great ones in pushing the characters of The Story of the Stone to the destinies laid out by the Stone, who is represented as the narrative's author in chapter 1.

Gossip generated outside the Jia mansion but concerning events within the Jia household tends to be speculative and hyperbolic, on a spectrum from plausible scenario to baseless fantasy. Within the household, gossip is a much subtler force, usually originating with the maids and other serving staff, and therefore as often as not focusing on the minute doings of the young mistresses and Baoyu. The fact that gossip tends to be generated, or at least transmitted, by individuals of lower class or financial status than the people they gossip about simultaneously pushes toward the democratic, "idle" notion of gossip, and an instrumental function; namely, to gain some kind of symbolic or psychological equality with the higher ranks by arrogating to themselves, through intimate information, some of the status of the masters.

Gossip from outside the mansion's walls is what worries the adults of the Jia family, or at least those who have responsibility for the family's external affairs and therefore for its reputation.[5] Those most concerned with the implications of outside gossip are Jia Zheng 賈政, father of the hero, Baoyu, and Wang Xifeng 王熙鳳, the strong-minded wife of Jia Zheng's nephew Jia Lian 賈璉, who has usurped the authority both of her own mother-in-law and of her aunt, Jia Zheng's wife, Lady Wang 王夫人, in her position as manager of the Rongguo House 榮國府. Technically speaking, Jia Zheng's older brother, Jia She 賈赦, should oversee the family's affairs and care for its social position. Unfortunately for the scrupulous younger brother, Jia She is a self-absorbed libertine, who takes interest in household affairs only as they concern his pleasures, leaving Jia Zheng to represent him and protect their social standing. Because with a living older brother he is not officially the head of household (*jiazhang* 家長), Jia Zheng symbolically defers to Jia She at every turn, undermining the little authority he has and making him a laughing stock to the outside world.[6] Wang Xifeng likens her position as de facto household manager to riding a tiger: "I daren't relax my grip for a single moment for fear of being eaten" 雖然看破些, 無奈一時也難寬放 (lit. "if you see it through part way, unfortunately it is hard to let go, even for a moment").[7] And she has much to hide: in order to protect her financial position and supplement the Jias' dwindling fortunes, she lends money at fabulous rates of interest and finesses awkward contracts for her "clients"—underhanded dealings that, when discovered, cause her to be disgraced universally.

At the beginning of the novel, for the reader's benefit, the author uses gossip as a rhetorical strategy to introduce the background and complexities of the family that will be the center of the Stone's life as a human boy. Our introduction to the Rongguo and Ningguo 寧國 households in chapter 2 comes from their distant kinsman from the south, Jia Yucun 賈雨村, whose name, appropriately enough for this context, is a pun on the phrase for "false discourse" (*jiayu cunyan* 假語存言). A consummate operator, his career depends on making the right social connections, connections best exploited through the use of topical knowledge, and in order to exploit these, there is nothing like a local informant. Over a few cups of wine, he and his old friend, the antique dealer Leng Zixing 冷子興, settle in for a detailed discussion of the background and affairs of the Jia family. The subject is raised when Yucun asks his friend for the news from the capital and Zixing replies, "I can't think of anything particularly deserving of mention . . . except, perhaps, for a very small but very unusual event that took place in your own clan there" 倒沒有甚麼新聞, 倒是老先生的貴同宗家出了一件小小的異事.[8] Leng Zixing's insider knowledge comes from his in-laws, who are senior servants of Lady Wang. When Jia Yucun shrugs off the connection with the Jias of the capital as too exalted for him, his friend obligingly gives him (and the reader) a complete background sketch of the family's history, from the first spectacular rise of the brothers who became the Dukes of Ningguo and Rongguo under the current dynasty. This is our most sustained introduction to the Jia family, couched in terms of gossip, but amazingly accurate and, as suggested by de Souza's observations, not even particularly mean-spirited. It is a masterful device to fill in the background narrative of the current generation, running over the rise and the impending decline of the family fortune and introducing all the important characters, down to their birth order or marriage alliances. Leng Zixing is the first to quote the proverb, "the beast with a hundred legs is a long time dying" 百足之蟲, 死而不僵,[9] in reference to the Jias' having fatally overextended their resources in order to conform to the imperatives of their social position.[10] Thanks to this *tête-à-tête*, the reader knows the reality of the Jias' financial position before a single member of the household is introduced, refining the irony of their denial to themselves as well as the outside world.

The wineshop talk rapidly settles on the strange case of Baoyu, the boy who was born with the jade, and whose name literally means "precious jade." Leng Zixing describes Baoyu's unique position in the family, his eccentricities, and the way they have negatively affected his relations with his father. Jia Yucun treats his friend to a long and pompous theoretical disquisition on the cosmic heredity of the child, which while it is nonsense on the mundane level, does reflect the boy's heritage as the incarnation of the very Stone encountered by the reader as "author" of *The Story of the Stone* in chapter 1—a matter of which these two gentlemen are completely ignorant, but the reader is not, and here discovers where the monk and the Taoist deposited the Stone they found at the base of Greensickness Peak in the first chapter. Leng Zixing has the pleasure of revealing to his learned friend that the mother of his current pupil, Lin Daiyu 林黛玉, was the daughter of the matriarch of the Rongguo household, a detail that prepares Yucun to make the most of his opportunity to meet them when he acts as Daiyu's escort to her grandmother's home in the capital. The two men wind up this productive chapter with: "There's nothing like good gossip about other people's affairs to make the wine go down!" 只顧酸別人家的賬 (lit. "just looking over other people's accounts").[11] This conversation lays out the three subjects of external gossip around which most of the Jia family's woes revolve: the sexual and financial shenanigans of the members of the household who are supposed to uphold its reputation and status, the family's (supposedly) fabulous wealth, and the endlessly fascinating origin and career of Baoyu. According to Paul Ropp, "the obsession with private life and with rich imagery and descriptive detail"—of which gossip is a very effective vehicle—"marks an important innovation in the history of Chinese fiction." He further nuances this narrative convention by suggesting that its penetration into private lives is a form of social criticism.[12] This suggests a literary complement to de Souza's notion of gossip, with this difference:

in literature, all materials being by definition the conscious production of the author, even in cases of grossly incompetent authors, gossip as represented in fiction will have instrumental function. Timing is everything. There are some cases in which the forces of external and internal gossip combine to cause emotional human combustion. The worst nightmare of the keepers of the family reputation is the specter of a family retainer let loose in the outside world to tell tales that would harm their image. In a burlesque on the proper deportment of a faithful family retainer, the venerable Big Jiao 焦大, from the Ningguo House, drunkenly bawls for all to hear:

> Who would ever have believed the Old Master could spawn this filthy lot of animals? . . . Up to their dirty little tricks every day. *I* know. Father-in-law pokes in the ashes. Auntie has it off with nevvy. Do you think I don't know what you're all up to? Oh, we "hide our broken arm in our sleeve"; but you don't fool me.
> 那裏承望到如今生下這些畜生來！每日偷狗戲雞，爬灰的爬灰，養小叔子的養小叔子，僣們胳膊折了往袖子裏藏！[13]

Big Jiao's tirade has at least some truth in it: "father-in-law pokes in the ashes" (lit. "those who poke in the ashes, poke in the ashes") is a pun for "father-in-law debauches daughter-in-law," referring to the incestuous affair that Jia Zhen 賈珍, head of the Ningguo House, is carrying on with his daughter-in-law, Qin Keqing 秦可卿.[14] There are already plenty of rumors about this beyond the walls, and with the prospect of a family intimate confirming them, Xifeng warns Jia Zhen's cuckolded son, Jia Rong 賈蓉, "It's positively dangerous to keep a man like this on the premises. If any of our acquaintance get to know that a family like ours can't keep even a semblance of discipline about the place, we shall become a laughing stock!" 還不早些打發了沒王法的東西！留在家裏，豈不是害？親友知道，豈不笑話僣這樣的人家聯個規矩都沒有！[15] There may be more to this than Jia Rong's reputation. The claim that "Auntie has it off with nevvy" (lit. "those who take care of their husband's younger brothers *really* take care of them") may refer to rumors about Xifeng's own conduct with this feckless cousin, whose flirtatious behavior puts her at risk.[16] Xifeng couches the matter in terms of authority and discipline, but the underlying fear is personal, as her personal authority and integrity, at least as regards financial if not sexual affairs, cannot bear the scrutiny of outsiders. External exposure of sexual misconduct would indeed be a dangerous threat to the family's public image and may reflect the fears of exposure among the author's family circle, especially given their precarious position as long-time bondservants of the Manchus.¹⁷

Parallel to Xifeng's case is Jia Zheng's situation in chapter 33. Jia Zheng's character is diametrically opposed to what he understands of Baoyu's, and this causes him to treat his son, on the few occasions they encounter one another, as a stranger. Because of his lack of insight into Baoyu's nature, Jia Zheng succumbs to malicious tittle-tattle and erupts in near-fatal violence toward him without coming near the truth. This is only one example of how unfounded gossip, implicitly believed, wreaks havoc in the family. Chapters 30 through 35 are a sustained fugue of rumor and innuendo, with near-fatal consequences for Baoyu. Lady Wang overreacts to her maid Qinchuaner's 金釧兒 flirtation with Baoyu, smacks her and throws her out, driving her to suicide. This is a public humiliation for the Jias, as a suicide must always be investigated by the authorities; because a suicide is assumed to be the result of unbearable injustice, such an investigation inevitably exposes a family's intimate affairs in a harsh light.¹⁸ Before he hears of this, however, Jia Zheng is humiliated to learn from the chamberlain of the Manchu Prince of Zhongshun 忠順親王 that Baoyu has not just been consorting with an actor, but has been consorting with an actor who is under the protection of this prince. He nearly boils when Baoyu compounds his *lèse-majesté* by lying about it to this high-ranking outsider's face.

Baoyu is in quite enough trouble, but unfortunately for him, his father encounters his youngest son by a concubine, Jia Huan 賈環, as he returns from seeing the prince's chamberlain out. Jia Huan's position in the household is ambiguous, not least because he remains under the care of his mother, the envious Aunt Zhao 趙姨娘, instead of being acknowledged by Lady Wang as a son and taking his proper place in the family hierarchy.¹⁹ The narrator underlines that he is an unreliable informant by remarking, "Jia Huan saw in his father's anger an opportunity of exercising his malice" 賈環見他父親甚怒，便乘機說道 (lit. "when Jia Huan saw his father so angry, he took the opportunity of increasing it by speaking").²⁰ Jia Huan tells Jia Zheng in lurid detail of Qinchuaner's drowning, declaring that her suicide was a result of an attempted rape by Baoyu. Jia Zheng responds with incredulous horror, mourning both the death and more generally the disappearance from the Jia tradition of benevolence toward their inferiors. He winds up with "What a terrible disgrace to our ancestors if this should get about!" 自祖宗以來，皆外人知道，祖宗顏面何在！ ²¹ In a frenzy of shame, Jia Zheng orders that Baoyu be beaten to death. Baoyu is saved by the interference of the womenfolk over whom Jia Zheng, as "head of household," is supposed to exercise supreme authority: first his own wife, Lady Wang, then his own mother, Grandmother Jia 賈母. Surprisingly, they do not attempt to appeal to his fear of how it would look to outsiders if he beat his son to death.[22] In Qing China, "family murder" was in a different legal category from "stranger murder," and the worst that could happen to a father who beat his son to death was to receive one hundred strokes with the heavy bamboo and a year of penal servitude—nasty enough, but easy for someone of Jia Zheng's status to avoid by paying bribes and fines.[23] No, Lady Wang appeals to his filial piety, and his mother torments him with the shame to his father's memory: "How did *your* father teach you?" 你夫親是怎麼教訓你來者?[24] She refers not just to physical discipline, but to the whole social complex of standards of conduct and personal deportment set by her late husband, standards she still represents in the household because of her second son's compromised status as family head. Jia Zheng's failure of control is his own failure and shames him in his father's memory.[25]

When Baoyu's chief maid, Xiren 襲人 tries to find out how such a disaster could have occurred, she gets equivocal information from Baoyu's page, Beiming 焙茗, who implicates Xue Pan 薛蟠, brother of Xue Baochai 薛寶釵, in the matter of the actor with the stage name Qi Guan'er 琪官兒 (in Hawkes's translation, "Bijou"): "Well, the Bijou business he probably knew about indirectly through Mr. Xue. . . . Mr. Xue had been feeling very jealous, and it looks as though he may have put someone up to telling the Master about it out of spite" 那琪官兒的事, 多半是薛大爺素昔吃醋, 沒法兒出氣, 不知在外頭挑唆了誰來在老爺跟前下的蛆 (lit., "As for that Bijou business, it's probably because Mr. Xue has been jealous for some time, without any means of venting his feelings; I don't know whether he stirred up trouble outside and someone came to the Master to sting his heel like a centipede").[26] This revelation in turn creates a tremendous row at the Xues, where Xue Pan is no match for his enraged mother and tearful sister. It does not seem unlikely that the chamberlain would have gotten his information about Baoyu's intimacy with Bijou from Xue Pan's vocal complaints about this favoritism, but the young man swears up and down that he did not intentionally start the rumor, and he is probably sincere. The problem is, his reputation for indulging his passions and shooting off his mouth is such that even his own mother and sister think the worst of him, when it comes to matters where discretion could save face.

Another example of sexual misconduct in the Jia clan is carried to Jia

Zheng by a time-honored method: the public bill-sticker. In chapter 93, Jia Zheng's blood pressure is once more put to the test as one of the servants shows him a poster bearing the pasquinade:

> Jia Qin's a lucky young sod—
> He's in charge of the family nunnery.
> All those girls for just one bod—
> Whoring, gambling, loads of funnery!
> Now that rakes are running the place,
> Rongguo House is a public disgrace!
>
> 西貝草斤年紀輕,
> 水月庵裏管尼僧。
> 一個男人多少女,
> 窩娼聚賭是陶情。
> 不肖子弟來辦事,
> 榮國府內好聲名!²⁷

Jia Qin 賈芹 is a cousin and hanger-on of the main clan, doing odd jobs and hoping for a sinecure. He is especially loyal to his childhood pal, Jia Lian, who agrees to cover for him when Jia Qin is brought before him in disgrace. Jia Qin has been in charge if the Temple of the Iron Threshold, where the pet nuns who attended the Visitation of the Imperial Concubine have lived since their service, and indeed, he has used the temple as his own pleasure preserve. Jia Lian shields him from Jia Zheng's wrath, as sexual misconduct is the older man's "particular abomination" (*zuinao* 最惱) and the nuns are dispersed. In spite of the Jias' good intentions to allow them to return to their homes, the rumors about the matter may prevent these good intentions from bearing fruit: "The news that the Jia household had dismissed twenty-four girl novices soon spread, and every young rake in town fancied the idea of getting hold of one of them for himself" 獨有那些無賴之徒, 聽得賈府發出二十四個女孩子來, 那個不想?²⁸ The reason for this interest is that all these young fellows assume that the Temple of the Iron Threshold was more of a brothel than a nunnery, and any attractive young lady under the care of the Jias must have considerable sexual experience to share.

This is not the only bit of doggerel quoted to the embarrassment of the senior Jias. When the family begins to prepare for the Imperial Concubine's Visitation in chapter 16, Xifeng reminisces with her husband Lian's Nannie Zhao 趙媽媽 about the many imperial progresses witnessed by her family during their glory days in the south. As a relic of their reputation for wealth and extravagance, Nannie Zhao quotes to Xifeng the rhyme: "The King of the Ocean / Goes along, / When he's short of gold beds, / To the Nanking Wang" 東海少了白玉床, 龍王來請江南王 (lit. "When the Eastern Sea lacks a few white jade beds, the Dragon King comes to ask the Wangs of Jiangnan [for some]").²⁹ This is basically taken as a compliment, although later references to the state of the family's resources are not so well received. Chapter 83 contains Xifeng's most sustained disquisition on gossip, as part of her disclaimer about the need for economy:

> Some people are under the illusion that it's all caused by bad management on my part. Some even have the nerve to suggest that I am lining the Wang nest at the Jia family's expense. But you know better, my dear Mrs. Zhou. You've seen far too much of what really goes on to pay any attention to such gossip.
> 不知道的, 還說我打算的不好。更有那一種嚼舌根的, 說我搬運到娘家去了。周嫂子, 你倒是那裏經手的人, 這個自然還知道些。

Mrs. Zhou 周嫂子 (Xifeng's primary factotum for affairs outside the mansion) reassures her mistress that she, as an insider, knows her true worth, although she laughs to relate: "Mind you, Mrs. Lian, the things people *will* say!" 奶奶還沒聽見呢, 外頭的人還更糊塗呢。[30] There follows a long description of popular notions of the family's wealth, of rooms filled with silver and gold, imperial treasures smuggled back from the Imperial Concubine's private store, and the clothing of even the maids. And then she almost trips herself with another bit of uncomplimentary verse:

There's even a song about us:	還有歌兒呢, 說是:
Moneybags Nong	寧國府,
And Rolling Rong	容國府,
Treat their cash	金銀財寶
Like piles of dung.	如糞土。
It seems so fine,	吃不窮,
But please beware!	穿不窮,
If you look too . . .	算來 . . .

Mrs. Zhou stops herself at this point, but not quite soon enough for Xifeng to be unaware of the end of the poem : "If you look too close, / The cupboard's bare!" 算來, 總是一場空 (lit. "when the reckoning comes, it will be one empty space").[31] Xifeng is clear-headed about the implications of the unspoken finale of Mrs. Zhou's ditty. The worrying thing is the slender threads of true events within the household that have been blown out of all proportion by rumor outside. While the only thing to do is laugh, Xifeng points out the fatality of it: "The trouble is that behind our magnificent façade things are going from bad to worse . . . and our fame has been won under false pretenses anyway. Sometimes I worry a great deal about where all this will lead to" 偺們一日難似一日, 外頭還是這麼講究…況且又是個虛名兒。終久還不知怎麼樣呢! To which Mrs. Zhou gives the ultimate philosophical response: "But talk like that has been going around for over a year, in the teahouses and wineshops, in every alleyway. It's too late to stop it all now, isn't it?" 只是滿城裏茶坊酒舖兒以及各衙衙兒,那是這樣說,況且不是一年了。那裏握的住眾人的嘴?[32] But what could have been done to stop it in the first place? While none of the matters Mrs. Zhou details are strictly true, they are lies with a thread of truth. The Jias' lives have been far from blameless, and there will be consequences, as Xifeng has prophetically observed. The question is how long it will be before their mistakes, the extent of the Jia family's moral Ponzi scheme, are laid bare to the public.

The long-suffering Jia Zheng receives the news of his worst humiliation from within the Rongguo house in chapter 95, when he is the last member of the family to hear the news that Baoyu has lost his jade. Grandmother Jia kept it from him, leaving him to hear of the loss from a conversation in the street as he is on his way home:

> If you want to get rich, I know of an easy way ... at the Rongguo House one of the young nobs has lost a jade, and they've posted a notice of reward, with all the details—shape, size, color, etc. Ten thousand they're offering to anyone who hands it in, and five thousand for information!
>
> 人要發財,也容易的很!今日聽見榮府裏丟了什麼哥兒的玉子,貼著招帖兒,上頭寫著玉的大小式樣顏色,說:有人檢了送去,就給一萬兩銀子,送信的還給五千呢![33]

When Jia Zheng hears that it was by his mother's order that his son's affairs have been bared to the world, his alarm changes to despair. He is dismayed by what he regards as an obscene exposure, but because of the dysfunctional hierarchy in his house, there is nothing he can do about it:

> "We are doomed!" said Jia Zheng to himself with a bitter sigh. "This son of mine is the bane of our lives! When he was a child he was the talk of the neighborhood. It has taken the last ten years or more to stop their tongues, and now we go putting up a poster like this, announcing our troubles to the world!"
>
> 賈政便歎氣道:「家道該衰!偏生養這麼一個孽障!纔養他的時候,滿街的謠言,隔了十幾年,略好了些。這會子又大張曉諭的找玉,成何道理!」[34]

Jia Zheng's despair is not just about the renewal of Baoyu's notoriety. The boy has always been a favorite subject of wagging tongues—his social position, poetic talent, and personal beauty make him a fond object of anyone's social-climbing dreams. This "emblematization" of individuals as sounding boards for public morals is a universal commonplace. The public airing of opinion on local notables, "celebrities," if you will, can impact a community by allowing open discussion of moral issues of importance to the community while maintaining distance from the questionable actions that prompt the discussion. As James Farrar states, "Gossip is an effective and important means for negotiating local moral standards."[35] Gossip makes all its subjects emblematic, which allows the community to treat issues of concern at a remove that may yet have practical and positive results for the community.

Nor is Jia Zheng moaning because he loathes his son. He does take Baoyu's notoriety personally; he refers to him as *niezhang* 孽障—that is, a child born to be a vehicle of retribution for sins of the parents. In that sense, Jia Zheng's greater grief is part of this retribution: such an exposure is about the whole family, with Baoyu as its emblem. Baoyu, as the boy born with the jade, has been the public *and* private symbol of all the family's hopes for renewal. If the jade is gone, it may be seen as a sign that none of these hopes will be fulfilled, and Jia Zheng is crushed by this. Furthermore, the fact that Grandmother Jia has taken this rash public action, calling on the populace for help by appealing to its basest motives, exposes the disintegration of strong, traditional family solidarity to the most humiliating light, and the brunt of this disgrace, alas, falls squarely upon Jia Zheng's shoulders. He sees all his failures as a son, husband, and father revealed to the world.

While Jia Zheng bears the brunt of the family's vulnerability to outside scrutiny, his son Baoyu is the subject and object of most of its internal intrigues. To cut to the chase, the topic of most vital interest to everyone, it seems, is: Who will marry Baoyu? This is his cousin Lin Daiyu's 林黛玉 greatest concern, as she has carried into this world her love for him from their previous existence together as the Divine Luminescent Stone-in-Waiting 神瑛侍者 and the Crimson Pearl Flower 絳珠仙草. On a distinctly mundane level, the question is also of absorbing interest to the maids who attend the young couple in the Garden, and the maids are the ones who carry the tales, however confused, bogus, or just plain wrong. Baoyu seems oblivious to gossip in general, although when he is confronted with mistaken information and assumptions about the state of his heart, he vigorously refutes them. Unfortunately for Daiyu, she almost never asks Baoyu to confirm or deny rumors about him directly, and so deprives herself of the emotional solace his direct answers would give. On the level of the narrative, this can be explained by their peculiar personalities; on the cosmic level, it can be explained by their destinies from the Land of Illusion. For the reader, it can be downright agony. Our hero and heroine, whose ability to communicate with one another is blocked, inhibited, and vexed, will clutch at the straws of anything that seems to offer new insight into the beloved, even if its source is seriously compromised. The reader is aware of this, and aware, also, that Baoyu and especially Daiyu are both enablers of the "Debt of Tears" 還淚 (*huanlei*), the obligation that Daiyu, in her incarnation as the Crimson Pearl Flower, felt she owed the Stone for watering her with sweet dew and endowing her with consciousness: "the tears shed during the whole of a mortal lifetime" 一生所有的眼淚.³⁶ This is where the significance of gossip as "retributory talk" makes its power felt: for woe in their current existence, but ultimately for their spiritual liberation.³⁷

The most damage, paradoxically, is done through the maid who is closest to Daiyu and most solicitous of her welfare: Zijuan 紫鵑. In fact, her attachment to Daiyu is so strong that Li Wan 李紈, duenna of the Garden, remarks, "The truth is . . . that this maid and Miss Lin have an affinity from a past life" 當真的，林姑娘和這丫頭也是前世的緣法兒! ³⁸ Furthermore, if her mistress were to marry outside of the family, Zijuan would have to accompany her, perhaps far away from her own family in the capital. In chapter 49, when the Xue cousins Xue Ke 薛蚵 and Baoqin 寶琴 arrive, Grandmother Jia is so taken with Baoqin that she inquires about her betrothal status. This is part of what is in Zijuan's mind when she teases Baoyu about his attachment to her mistress. Talk about mixed signals! Zijuan is not sophisticated in her approach: on the one hand, she affects the pseudo-careless airs of her young lady; on the other hand, her own earnest nature makes her want to know the explicit truth, the truth that her mistress will never get. When she probes Baoyu's feelings for Daiyu by telling him that Daiyu plans to return to Suzhou, she gets more of a reaction than she could have expected: Baoyu immediately lapses into catatonic shock, and the family is, predictably, thrown into an uproar. When he starts to recover, the thoroughly penitent Zijuan explains her concern, and Baoyu reassures her:

> If only I could die this minute and my heart burst out of my body so that you could *see* how true it is! After that I shouldn't care if all of me—flesh, blood and bones—was burned to ashes, and the ashes turned to smoke, and the smoke blown by the winds to every corner of the earth!
>
> 我之願這會子立刻我死了，把心迸出來，你們瞧見了，然後連反帶骨，一概都化成一股灰，再化成一股煙，一陣大風，吹的四面八方都登時散了，這纔好! ³⁹

And as if that was not explicit enough, he adds, "Let me try to put it for you in a nutshell. In life we shall live together; in death we shall mingle our dust. How will that do?" 活著, 咱們一處活著; 不活著, 咱們一處化灰, 化煙如何? (lit. "While we live, we will live in one place; when we are no longer living, we will become ashes and smoke in one place—will that do?"[40]

Zijuan's failure simply to report Baoyu's statement word for word to Daiyu must relate to that "affinity from a past life" mentioned by Li Wan, as the maid's well-meaning ineffectiveness seems to further the payment of the Debt of Tears. Like so many of Baoyu's and Daiyu's failed attempts at communication, this is a missed opportunity for fulfillment in *this* life, exquisitely frustrating in spite of the fact that the ultimate purpose of their existence is liberation from that illusion. The news of the effect of Zijuan's tale on Baoyu causes her mistress nearly to choke to death, yet Zijuan cannot just correct the rumors, cannot just relate to Daiyu exactly what he really said, so as to allay (both of their) fears. She still refers to the matter obliquely, and Daiyu's insecurities are fanned into a blaze, blocking her access to true knowledge and leaving her prey to the next rumor that comes along.

Unfortunately, that next rumor is much of her own making. In chapter 82, alarmed by the fate of the Xue concubine Xiangling 香菱 at the hands of Xue Pan's shrewish wife, Xiren goes to visit Daiyu to probe her attitudes toward concubines in general and herself (if Daiyu should become Baoyu's bride) in particular. Daiyu is surprised to hear Xiren gossip: "She had never before gotten wind of Xiren's talking about people behind their backs" 從不聞襲人背地裏說人.[41] She then tries to ascertain Xiren's disposition in turn. While they chat, a garrulous old woman from the Xue household delivers some lychees in honey, praises Daiyu's beauty, and declares that her "Madam" (Aunt Xue, Baochai's mother) has stated that only Baoyu is fit for Daiyu, and vice versa. Typically, Daiyu refuses to eat this fruit (or to accept the sweet emotions the gift traditionally symbolizes) and, brooding on the old woman's "tactless gossiping" (*yifan hunhua* 一番混話), drifts off into a nightmare.[42] While the old woman has said exactly what Daiyu wants to hear, this gossip has a paradoxical effect, plunging her into a horrible anxiety dream. In her nightmare she runs from plausibility to plausibility: her father survives, has remarried and has been manipulated by his new wife into making a match for his daughter with a widowed relation; she is rebuffed by Grandmother Jia when she asks for help; then Baoyu reminds her that she was originally betrothed to him; and when she asks him whether she should stay, he cuts open his chest and shows her his heart, which "kills" him.[43] She wakes in a cold sweat, but even in the light of day she suspects the dream of revealing truth and becomes even more suspicious of everyone. It is as if ignoring the gossip she *wanted* to hear makes her easier prey to the innuendos of her own dream, illusion piled upon illusion.

Soon afterward, Daiyu's other maid, Xueyan 雪雁, tells Zijuan she has heard that Baoyu is engaged to be married to some prefect's daughter. This rumor is also bogus, but unfortunately she is overheard by Daiyu.[44] Daiyu is particularly susceptible because she has just had a visit from Baoyu in which he revealed that he had overheard her composition of poetry and music for the *qin* the evening before. Speaking about music, with its connotations of emotional intimacy, draws them very close, but this very closeness heightens her vulnerability. When she hears this totally unfounded rumor, Daiyu attempts to starve herself to death—and almost succeeds. She hears the counter-rumor just in the nick of time: "Her Old Ladyship has someone else in mind for Master Bao, someone here in the Garden" 老太太心裏早有了人了，就在偺們園子裏的 (lit. "The Old Lady earlier had someone in mind, from inside our own garden").[45] Daiyu recovers, although too late for the marriage sweeps. One of the reasons given by Grandmother Jia for her rejection is her health: "I'm afraid that with such a delicate constitution she is unlikely to live to any age" 況且林丫頭這樣虛弱，恐不是有壽的.[46]

While a word from Baoyu to his grandmother, even with her reasonable objections, would undoubtedly put paid to all the rumors and confirm Daiyu as his bride, Baoyu, after the loss of his jade in chapter 94, falls into imbecility and is in no condition to act for himself. This precipitates the tragedy of their love and the triumph of their release from the World of the Red Dust (*hongchenshi* 紅塵世, that is, the mundane world of mortal affairs)—but who wants to hear that? The senior ladies see marriage as a chance to change his current run of bad luck—and if he should not recover, a wife who is healthy, wealthy, and wise looks like a better bet than a sickly and neurotic one. Baochai is confirmed as the family's choice. Daiyu has assumed, on the basis of overhearing that Grandmother Jia selected someone for Baoyu from the Garden long ago, that she herself is Baoyu's betrothed and has therefore modestly kept away from him. By the time she learns the truth, even Baoyu cannot help.

The truth comes from the mouth of a mentally handicapped maid named Elder Sister Sha 傻大姐兒, or "Simple," in Hawkes's translation. The senior Jia ladies, who regard Simple as an idiot (her affect suggests a mild level of Down syndrome), have neither taken the precaution of concealing the marriage plot from her nor sworn her to secrecy. Daiyu happens upon the weeping maid, and when she asks her the source of her distress, Simple explains that she has been scolded for talking out of turn: "That's what I'd like to know! It was only to do with Master Bao marrying Miss Chai!" 就是為我們寶二爺娶寶姑娘的事情！⁴⁷ In order to hear her out, Daiyu leads Simple to the very spot where she and Baoyu first mourned the prospect of her death: the site where she buried the fallen spring flowers and, in their honor, composed the ballad that gave Baoyu his first intimation of mortality by likening her existence to the ephemeral spring season.⁴⁸ Dazed by the revelation, she visits Baoyu for the last time. The two lovers smile senselessly at each other, and Baoyu readily admits, "I'm sick because of Miss Lin" 我為林姑娘病了.⁴⁹ Sick because of his lovesickness for her? Or sick because his incapacity is necessary for his marriage to Baochai, which is necessary for the triumphant discharge of what catalyzed the plot in the first place, the Debt of Tears?

Perhaps it is an essential part of Daiyu's psychological makeup that, though she holds herself above most of the rest of humanity, she can be so emotionally self-destructive as to believe everything she hears. Alas, for Daiyu the mortal being, her delusion that she can beat the destiny of the Debt of Tears is the last impediment to her spiritual release. Daiyu's final, fatal bit of news comes from a mentally—though not morally—compromised source. Simple is the one person in the Garden who is constitutionally incapable of spreading malicious gossip with intent, or even of unconsciously slanting a story for her own ends. In allegorical terms, Simple's speech is explicitly retributory: it is the last push down for Daiyu to complete the karma of her Debt of Tears. In narrative terms, Daiyu's final decline is, ironically, the result of too much practical and not enough emotional truth, as she returns to her original home in the Paradise of Truth (*Zhenru huodi* 真如禍地), deluded to the very end as to the truth and fidelity of Baoyu's love.

Plenty of ink has been spilled resisting the end of the version of *The Story of the Stone* left to us by Cao Xueqin, his commentators, and Gao E 高鶚 (1740–1815?)—the author and editor who put Cao Xueqin's unfinished draft manuscript into its first published version in 1792—out of wishful confusion over the true end to which the hero and heroine are directed. Yet from the outright officious interference in their destinies by Mangmang daoshi 茫茫道士 and Miaomiao zhenren 渺渺真人 ("Mysterioso" and "Impervioso" in Hawkes's translation), the vagrant immortals who arranged for the Stone to experience a mortal lifetime in chapter 1, to the smallest actions and words of the oblivious, ordinary mortals who surround them, it is clear that the Stone and the Flower must leave their illusions behind and return to their former state. The second song

The Retributory Power of Gossip in The Story of the Stone / 209

in the musical suite called "Honglou meng" 紅樓夢 (rendered by Hawkes as "A Dream of Golden Days"),[50] which was performed in the palace of the Jinghuan xiangu 警幻仙姑 (in Hawkes, the "Fairy Disenchantment") in chapter 5, warned Baoyu (and the readers) that gossip was only a distraction, though in Daiyu's case a fatal one.[51] This poem details the tension between the two incarnations of the Stone/Baoyu and the Flower/Daiyu, emphasizing the protagonists' romantic frustration and appealing to the readers by asking a series of "why" questions. So, for example, given their "marvelous affinity" 奇緣 (qiyuan), why should they be brought together to share a mortal existence of emotional pain for nothing? The poem points directly to the futility of their intercourse, and the verbal medium of the text that inscribes it in line 6: "Why must their hearts' purpose come to an end as empty words?" 如何心事終虛話?[52]

Baoyu is finally pushed into explicit understanding. Many months after Daiyu's death, he has not ceased to mourn her, nor has he recovered his jade. His condition deteriorates, and just as his family has despaired of his recovery, Impervioso appears with the life-reviving stone. Baoyu's spirit rushes to follow its master, who leads him back to the Paradise of Truth he visited in chapter 5. He passes through a doorway over which the motto "Awaken from Love's Folly" (yinjue qingchi 引覺情癡) is inscribed, and reads for a second time the registers containing the fates of all the women he loves in his present existence. Even with this knowledge, however, Baoyu does not realize its implications until Impervioso exasperatedly exclaims, "You have seen the Registers again and you *still* don't understand? Predestined affinities of the world are all of them just so many obstacles to our vision!" 你見了冊子,還不解麼?世上的情緣,都是那些魔障![53] In a fictional world where all dice are cast by retributory causes, all words are empty while at the same time to the purpose, all actions futile though inevitable. There is no difference between the fiction of *The Story of the Stone* and the avowed truth of the Stone's story: the reader must follow their illusion to awaken to the truth of the illusion of existence.

This "true end" of *The Story of the Stone*, determined decades before Cao Xueqin's manuscript came into the hands of Gao E, is underlined by the Stone in chapter 1, who defends his text's integrity to the Daoist figure Kongkong daoren 空空道人 ("Vanitas" in Hawkes's translation). Cao Xueqin and his commentators never refer to *The Story of the Stone* as a "novel" (xiaoshuo 小說), but only as a "record" (ji 記 or zhuan 傳).[54] This emphasizes the veracity of the Stone's account. The term xiaoshuo, while now commonly used to refer to prose fiction in any form, was used by the Han historian, Ban Gu 班固 (32–92), to describe hearsay evidence of events. This was material that, as Kenneth J. DeWoskin has stated, he "regarded as unreliable or downright spurious, but that he was reluctant to let drop completely from existence." DeWoskin further notes that "the term *hsiao-shuo* [*xiaoshuo*] emerged with the rather weak and unappealing sense of defective history."[55] The term *xiaoshuo* is never used as part of a title in a Chinese work. The terms *ji* and *zhuan*, by contrast, are used as generic (in the sense of "genre") titles for works of narrative prose that move easily across the boundaries of historiography and fiction in their subject matter.[56] Vanitas, the first to be enlightened by reading the narrative, refers to the writing on the Stone as a "story" (*gushi* 故事), when he reads it before his awakening, and so does the Stone himself.[57] In their ensuing debate on the merit of various forms of narrative, the Stone deplores "historical romances" (*lilai yeshi* 歷來野史), "erotic novels" (*fengyue bimo* 風月筆墨), and "boudoir romances and other such works" (*jiaren caizi dengshu* 佳人才子等書) as indecent, immoral, and absurd. His tale is different: "All that my story narrates, the meetings and partings, the ups and downs of fortune, are recorded exactly as they happened. I have not dared add the tiniest bit of touching up, for fear of losing the true picture" 其間離合悲歡, 性衰際遇, 俱是按跡循蹤, 不敢稍加穿鑿, 至失其真.[58]

Perhaps Cao Xueqin's ambivalence as to the genre of his creation, manifested in his process of composition as well as the Stone's apologia, allowed him to pursue the cosmic imperative of his material with the ruthlessness required for the enlightenment of the hero and his audience. As stated in the previous quote, the Stone/narrator asserts that he omitted nothing, that everything was recorded exactly as it happened. Whatever the genre of his creation, his aim was truth, and if truth sacrificed his characters, it never compromised his art. It is the very appetite for life and experience of Cao Xueqin's characters that draws his readers into the illusion of the text: not for the sake of emotional fulfillment, but to *dis*-illusion them through the vanity of the fiction of their existence. Experience of that passion for the Stone's fictional world is what leads Vanitas to enlightenment and causes him to change his name from Vanitas to what Hawkes renders as "Brother Amor or 'the Passionate Monk'" (Qingseng 情僧).[59] The perfect rightness of his original name "Vanitas," however, is revealed in the final paragraph of the novel, when the Stone's amanuensis takes his manuscript into the world to look for a publisher. Jia Yucun directs him to consult Cao Xueqin in his Nostalgia Studio 悼紅軒, and perusing the text, the man chosen to transmit the Stone's story to the world teases the monk for acting as if such a true narrative needs his recommendation for publication? Vanitas finally understands the purpose of retributory talk in all its forms, the emptiness of which is an allegory for reputation, for fiction, and for life: "From the very beginning it was all careless verbiage! It doesn't matter that the writer didn't understand, the copyist didn't understand, even the critic didn't understand! It was nothing more than a game of pen and ink, in the spirit of diversion!" 原來是敷衍荒唐! 不但作著不知, 鈔著不知, 並閱著也不知。不過游戲筆墨, 陶情適性而已! [60]

More explicitly, the cosmic plan for the characters to whom we grow so attached is laid out by the Registers and the "Dream of Golden Days" pageant in chapter 5. At the request of Baoyu's great ancestors, the two Dukes of Ningguo and Rongguo, Disenchantment agrees to initiate Baoyu into the pleasures of the flesh, in the hope that understanding the ephemeral nature of those attachments would tear him away from his romantic view of life and allow him to focus on his duty to family and society. Both the Registers, which reveal the fates of the women in his life through rebuses and riddles, and the suite of song and dance "Dream of Golden Days," which is more explicit and reveals everything but the names of the women described in each poem, give Baoyu the information he needs to free himself from doubt, hope, and reliance on his own agency. *If* he could understand, *if* he could remember, *if* he could transmit the information from his dream, his path to liberation would be direct—and there would be no story. But Baoyu's sympathetic nature (and ours) causes him to focus on the characters around him, and willy-nilly, we follow him away from the short path to spiritual liberation. The journey from emptiness, through form and passion and finally back to emptiness followed by Vanitas/Brother Amor is truly ruthless, and most individuals cannot or will not follow the direct route. Because this is a retributory process, however, and therefore inexorable, Baoyu will finally come to the right place in his existence, and in his story, to recognize its truth. Whether the reader can follow him there is another matter.

NOTES

1. Also known as *Honglou meng* 紅樓夢, usually translated into English as *The Dream of the Red Chamber* or *A Dream of Red Mansions*. All citations in English translation are from *The Story of the Stone*, trans. David Hawkes and John Minford, 5 vols. (Harmondsworth: Penguin Books, 1973–86), unless otherwise noted. I have undertaken to provide more literal translations when necessary to address the theme of this chapter. The Chinese text I have

used is Cao Xueqin 曹雪芹 (ca. 1715–63), *Honglou meng*, ed. Zhao Cong 趙聰, 3 vols. (Hong Kong: Youlian chubanshe, 1960). Henceforth, *SS* and *HLM*, respectively.

2. Hawkes translates this as "Prospect Garden"; I adopt "Garden of Total Vision" from Andrew H. Plaks in his *Archetype and Allegory in* The Dream of the Red Chamber (Princeton: Princeton University Press, 1976), 178. I prefer Plaks's translation in this context, because it evokes the complex Buddhist allegory of the text.

3. For the notion of "retributory illness," see Dore J. Levy, *Ideal and Actual in* The Story of the Stone (New York: Columbia University Press, 1999), 69–70, 73–74. The term *yuannie zhi zheng* is first used in chapter 12 (*SS* I.12.251, *HLM* I.12.118), when the wandering Taoist Mysterioso (Mangmang dashi 茫茫大士) offers to cure a man whose lovesickness has put him beyond the reach of medicine. Retributory illnesses are difficult to treat clinically, because they have their aetiology in the deeds of a previous existence.

4. Ronald de Souza, "In Praise of Gossip: Indiscretion as a Saintly Virtue," in *Good Gossip*, ed. Robert B. Goodman and Aaron Ben Ze'ed (Lawrence: University Press of Kansas, 1994), 25.

5. For discussions of representations of the difficulties walking the tightrope of external reputation and internal authority, see Martin W. Huang, *Literati and Self-Re/Presentation: Autobiographical Sensibility in the Eighteenth Century Novel* (Stanford: Stanford University Press, 1995), 75–108; and Susan Naquin and Evelyn S. Rawski, *Chinese Society in the Eighteenth Century* (New Haven: Yale University Press, 1987), 33–54.

6. For the traditional role of "head of family" in Chinese gentry society see Marion J. Levy Jr., *The Family Revolution in Modern China* (Cambridge, Mass.: Harvard University Press, 1947), 66–71.

7. *SS* III.55.62, *HLM* II.55.589.

8. *SS* I.2.72, *HLM* I.2.15.

9. *SS* I.2.73, *HLM* I.2.16.

10. For a discussion of the subversion of Confucian orthodoxy implicit in Leng Zixing's gossip, see Maram Epstein, *Competing Discourses: Orthodoxy, Authenticity and Engendered Meanings in Late Imperial Chinese Fiction* (Cambridge, Mass.: Harvard University Asia Center, 2001), 165–67. Proverbs and other aphorisms represent a form of poetic reference that almost always has a sociocritical purpose in this text. See Dore J. Levy, "Embedded Texts: How to Read Poetry in *The Story of the Stone*," *Tamkang Review* 36, nos. 1–2 (Spring 2006): 210–17.

11. *SS* I.2.83, *HLM* I.2.20.

12. Paul Ropp, *Dissent in Early Modern China* (Ann Arbor: University of Michigan Press, 1981), 243–45.

13. *SS* I.7.183, *HLM* I.7.75.

14. For a discussion of this pun and the textual evidence for this family-shattering affair, see Levy, *Ideal and Actual*, 30, 45.

15. *SS* I.7.183, *HLM* I.7.75.

16. Like the comment about "poking in the ashes," this expression relies on repetition for emphasis.

17. On this issue, see Martin Huang, *Literati and Self-Re/Presentation*, 84–85.

18. See Andrew C. K. Hsieh and Jonathan Spence, "Suicide and the Family in Pre-Modern Chinese Society," in *Normal and Abnormal Behavior in Chinese Culture*, ed. Arthur Kleinman and Tsung-yi Li (Dordrecht: D. Reidel Publishing, 1981), 29–47.

19. For the peculiar position of Jia Huan in the household, see Levy, *Ideal and Actual*, 36–37, 164–65. For the power dynamics of the inner chambers in late imperial China, see Francesca Bray, *Technology and Gender: Fabrics of Power in Late Imperial China* (Berkeley: University of California Press, 1997), 335–68. For a meticulous and evocative study of similar issues in the Song dynasty, see Patricia Buckley Ebrey, *The Inner Quarters: Marriage and the Lives of Women in the Sung Period* (Berkeley: University of California Press, 1993), 217–34.

20. *SS* II.33.145, *HLM* I.33.331.

21. Ibid.

22. Robert E. Hegel and Katherine Carlitz, eds., *Writing and Law in Late Imperial China: Crime, Conflict, and Judgment* (Seattle: University of Washington Press, 2007).

23. See Ann Waltner, "Breaking the Law: Family Violence, Gender and Hierarchy in the Legal Code of the Ming Dynasty," *Ming Studies* 36 (1996): 30–31; and Geoffrey MacCormack, *The Spirit of Traditional Chinese Law* (Athens: University of Georgia Press, 1996), 79.

24. *SS* II.33.151, *HLM* I.33.334.

25. Louise P. Edwards analyzes this scene in terms of the importance, especially for Lady Wang, of deflecting any possibility of criticism for the conduct of Baoyu onto herself. See *Men and Women in Qing China: Gender in the Red Chamber Dream* (Leiden: E. J. Brill, 1994), 121–22.

26. *SS* II.33.153, *HLM* I.33.335.

27. *SS* IV.93.271–2, *HLM* III.93.1027.

28. *SS* IV.94.283, *HLM* II.94.1032.

29. *SS* I.16.314, *HLM* I.16.147.

30. *SS* IV.83.81, *HLM* III.83.921.

31. *SS* IV.83.82–83, *HLM* III.83.925.

32. *SS* IV.83.83, *HLM* III.83.922.

33. *SS* IV.95.317–318, *HLM* III.95.1052.

34. *SS* IV.95.318, *HLM* III.95.1053.

35. In Farrar, "'Idle Talk': Neighborhood Gossip as a Medium of Social Communication in Reform Era Shanghai," in *Social Connections in China: Institutions, Culture and the Changing Nature of* Guanxi, ed. Thomas Gold, Doug Guthrie, and David Wank (Cambridge: Cambridge University Press, 2002), 200.

36. *SS* I.1.53, *HLM* I.1.4.

37. David L. Rolston introduces the notion of "auto-commentary" to describe the dynamic relations of authors of fiction and their critic/commentators and discusses the late Qing practice of authors including their own textual commentary in publication, as much to be spared accusations of political subversion as to make sure the public could understand their texts. See his *Traditional Chinese Fiction and Commentary: Reading and Writing Between the Lines* (Stanford: Stanford University Press, 1997), 6–11, 281–83. Daiyu's excruciating dissection of her exchanges with Baoyu and every scrap of news she hears about him are almost another level of authorial commentary, a warning about how to go wrong on the way to spiritual liberation.

38. *SS* IV.97.358, *HLM* III.97.1075.

39. *SS* III.57.100, *HLM* II.57.614.

40. *SS* III.57.101, *HLM* II.57.614.

41. *SS* IV.82.60, *HLM* III.82.906.

42. *SS* IV.61, *HLM* III.907.

43. That Baoyu presents their betrothal as a "fact" in the dream does indeed reflect the interpretation the outside world would put upon the Jias' receiving this orphaned cousin under their roof, and any change in that plan would have started the gossip mills going overtime. See Levy, *Ideal and Actual*, 53. Also see Eugene Cooper and Meng Zhang, "Patterns of Cousin Marriage in Rural Zhejiang and in *The Dream of the Red Chamber*," *Journal of Asian Studies* 52, no. 1 (Feb. 1993): 90–106.

44. *SS* IV.89.207, *HLM* III.89.989.

45. *SS* IV.90.213–214, *HLM* III.90.996.

46. *SS* IV.90.218, *HLM* III.90.998.

47. *SS* IV.96.335, *HLM* III.96.1061.

48. *SS* II.27.38–39, *HLM* I.27.270–271.

49. *SS* IV.96.338, *HLM* III.96.1062.

50. Hawkes explains his translation of *honglou meng* as follows: "One bit of imagery which *Stone*-enthusiasts will miss in my translation is the pervading *redness* of the novel. One of its Chinese titles is red . . . and red as a symbol—sometimes of spring, sometimes of good fortune and prosperity, recurs again and again throughout it. Unfortunately . . . redness has no such connotations in English and I have found that the Chinese reds have tended to turn into English golds and greens . . . I am aware that there is some sort of loss here, but have lacked the ingenuity to avert it" (*SS* I.45).

51. On the dream in chapter 5, see also Richard E. Strassberg's essay, which is chapter 9 of the present volume.

52. *HLM* I.5.50.

53. My translation, *HLM* III.116.1269.

54. Chen Qinghao 陳慶浩, ed., *Shitou ji Zhiyenzhai pingyu jijiao* 石頭記脂硯齋評語集校 (Taipei: Lianjing chuban shiye gongsi, 1985), 1–34 passim.

55. Kenneth J. DeWoskin, "The Six Dynasties *Chih-kuai* and the Birth of Fiction," in *Chinese Narrative: Critical and Theoretical Essays*, ed. Andrew H. Plaks (Princeton: Princeton University Press, 1977), 45.

56. See Plaks, "Towards a Critical Theory of Chinese Narrative," in *Chinese Narrative*, 311–12.
57. *SS* I.1.49, *HLM* I.1.3.
58. *SS* I.1.50, *HLM* I.1.3.
59. *SS* I.1.51, *HLM* I.1.3.
60. My translation, *HLM* III.120.1324.

Postface

"Believe It or Not"

Stephen Owen

A seventeen-hundred-year span of essays on a given topic, organized chronologically, has the distinct flavor of Chinese Studies, which tends to look at continuities across millennia—or at least see a single continuum. I suspect our Europeanist colleagues would be far less likely to produce a volume on gossip from Suetonius to Addison and Steele, with essays fairly evenly distributed to suggest historical continuity. The "Introduction" to our volume, beginning with a silent-film actress's suicide note, referencing a poem from the seventh century BCE, lends a certain persuasive touch to such a venture. The actress sees her own case in terms of a voice from Chinese antiquity, while caught in distinctly modern scandal and a legal case pressed by her estranged husband; she elides radical historical change in favor of eternal pressures of gossip on a woman.

The "Introduction" has already suggested some of the issues that hold the topic and the chapters together. I would like to conclude with another continuity that has both echoes in the European tradition and differences from a classical European theory centrally engaged with the truth claims of literature. Anecdotes and gossip raise the question of truth—or, in a significant variation, credibility, as distinguished from verisimilitude.

I did a quick tally of the Chinese bibliographical categories represented in these essays; although works from every category are represented, it is hardly surprising that the "marginal" subcategories of the *zibu* 子部 (roughly translated as "books of knowledge") predominate. The bibliographical and generic site of an anecdote is central to its credibility: an anecdote included by Ban Gu 班固 (32–92) in the canonical *Hanshu* 漢書 (History of the Han dynasty) commands credibility (even if reflection tells us quite otherwise), while the same anecdote in lower status subcategories puts the truth in question—just as we read a story in the *New York Times* and one in the *National Enquirer* differently.

The truth or credibility of an account has been important in China, as it is in the European tradition. In the European tradition, however, decisive adjudication of historical truth or falsity (in the sense of "did it really happen?") has been a stronger force, with protocols of judgment closely related to legal decision. Thucydides famously took care to acknowledge that his speeches were fictional constructs based on the gist of what had been said or what the historical figure should have said. While written documents are cited exactly in the Chinese case, Chinese historians were rarely troubled by a distinction between direct and indirect discourse in speech. In adjudicating the veracity of narrative, the Chinese tradition in general has been more comfortable with degrees of probability, using bibliographical subcategories to situate the reader.

For the modern reader, whether culturally European or Chinese, the issue of truth-claims becomes essential here. While it has been persuasively argued that China did indeed have a notion of "fictionality" at least by the Qing dynasty, it was never a central theoretical concern in premodern China. And the presence of fictionality as a recognized possibility in certain accounts complicates the issue of truth claims. It foregrounds the autonomy of narrative per se from "what happened."

However much historians are actually bound to a received tradition of discursive habits, narrative finesse in Western historiography can suggest a "literariness" that calls historical credibility into question. The familiar techniques of verisimilitude can make veracity suspect. The historian's statements must be built upon sources, each of which is subject to critique of its credibility. I hope the legal model is clear. The representation of what a historical subject thought on a given occasion, of events and exchanges in private, and of direct discourse (before the age of the tape recorder) are all perilous. We are always on the lookout for narrative motive in the construction of accounts. The narrative historian who tells his story all too well is suspect.

This may go back to Aristotle's basic distinction in the *Poetics* between history and poetry/literature—the distinction between what actually happened and what should have happened. This distinction presumes that the two cannot correspond, and this often breaks down in the Chinese case. That is, if one works with a system of truth and degrees of probability of truth or untruth, "what should have happened" and "what should have been said" have an entirely different status than they do in a system of truth, falsehood, and fictionality.

If there are consequences to the absence of a developed and widespread theory of fictionality in Chinese, there are equal consequences in the Anglo-European intellectual repertoire to ignore veracity as relative credibility, and hence probability, especially on the margins of belief and disbelief. This has an interesting class history. There is an early modern European motif (found in China as well) that makes fun of rustics for taking dramatic representations as true; this blends seamlessly into taking reports of aliens in Kansas as true, with the same contempt for rustics. The problem occurs in the next stage, in our local drugstore, with *National Enquirer* headlines some years ago that Obama's marriage was falling apart because of his infidelities. This may not be true—we have generic reason to very seriously doubt it—but it might be true. We have no theoretical place for that "maybe" as a stable discursive condition; it is a claim on trial, awaiting juridical decision as true or false, demonstrated "beyond the shadow of a doubt," even while we know that such a demonstration will likely never occur. In practice, however, it is still as popular a discursive mode in this culture, as it was (and remains) in China.

In this spirit I would like to add to the standard critical distinction between "fictional"/"nonfictional" the enduring category of what I like to call "Bermuda Triangle discourse"; that is, something presented as true, which some believe, but many like to read without necessarily believing. The pleasure of "Bermuda Triangle discourse" is precisely its claim to truth—as films often say in the opening credits: "based on real events." We may not believe such discourse, but the claim that it is true rather than pure fiction is essential to its peculiar pleasure. Even if we do not believe, we enjoy the truth-claim and the way in which a text or film tries to authenticate it. The popularity of such representations should make us rethink our categories. This is, more properly, the "suspension of disbelief," rather than fiction, where belief is not an issue.

We may not believe "Bermuda Triangle" stories or urban legends, but do we believe in gossip? Gossip is the world of oral information in which we float. Let me suggest that, barring compelling evidence to the contrary, we like to entertain good gossip, especially shocking stories, so long as they are within our margins of belief. We have entirely left the realm of fiction and nonfiction and entered a realm in which the pleasure of belief exceeds the usual standards of evidence. Now we are closing in on the Chinese case.

Belief is the issue. We belong to a world with as much class solidarity in belief as among late imperial intellectuals in China. To truly believe in certain things places one in a community and outside other communities. If I told those around me that I was a devoted follower of Scientology or believed in aliens in Kansas or that close study of the Bible tells me that the word will end next Thursday, I would never be treated quite the same way by my dearest friends and students (many of whom enjoyed the fiction of the "Terminator" series, premised on questioning community standards of belief and disbelief). In that question of belief the medieval Chinese categories begin to fracture, dividing texts by communities of belief. One community's hagiography of successfully achieving immortality is another community's example of a "wild, fantastic" tale. It can still be read with pleasure, but not quite as "fiction."

In Li Shangyin's 李商隱 (ca. 813–58) "Short Biography of Li He" ("Li He xiaozhuan" 李賀小傳) we have an act of firsthand historical investigation that is rare in the Tang. After Li He's (790–816) works first appeared posthumously in the 830s with Du Mu's preface, the young Li Shangyin took the usual step of going to visit Li He's sister to find out about the poet's life. The account, with all its famous and unprecedented details of Li He's compositional practice, concludes with the poet's death, summoned with celestial music to heaven to write poems for the emperor in heaven. We say that this is like *chuanqi*, an account of the fantastic. But the young Li Shangyin had studied Daoism and may well have believed. If we notice a familiar plot-motif from Daoist hagiography, is that narrative convention or is that the way things happen repeatedly in the context of a certain belief about the order of the universe? What is the boundary, if any, between the patterns of discourse and the truth of the world? What if Aristotle was wrong, and there is no clear-cut division between the way things are and the way they should be?

Some communities of belief might have thought Li Shangyin's account of Li He's death was fantastic, not credible. There was, however, a "bottom line" of belief, shared by most communities in the middle period and late imperial China, in sanctioned texts that represented history. The exemplary historical anecdote about a person "should have happened," and therefore "must have happened." Some might not believe stories of immortals; others might not believe retribution in reincarnation stories; but everyone could believe the *authorized* historical anecdote. Anecdotes about historical figures in lower status genres, both from the *zibu* and *shibu* 史部 (the "history" category), were subject to criticism for factual error (for example, a poet encounters an emperor who, in fact, ruled after the poet's death). But the elite historians who prepared the records that went into the "official" histories were generally very careful to avoid such factual error and anachronisms, the standard of veracity that made the plausible acceptable as the historically true. Their procedures guaranteed a social credibility that was not unlike the social credibility of the *New*

York Times, guaranteed by different, but no less strenuous procedures of verification.

We return to bibliographical categories, and the telling alternative to these "official" histories: this is *yeshi* 野史, best translated as "unofficial history." This single category contains everything from what we would call historical romances, to dubious anecdotes about famous figures, to eyewitness accounts, to works by very serious historians who were not part of the state history establishment (and thus lacked access to state-controlled documentation when writing on recent and contemporary history). In the "official" histories we have fact; in the "unofficial" histories we have a spectrum of probable credibility.

Gossip is not-yet-verified information in a regime that admits only truth or falsity, but not fictionality. If I tell something I know to be a fiction as gossip, I am transgressing the discursive rules of the genre. Furthermore, gossip can neither be easily known, general information, nor can it cross the boundaries of credulity of the community in which it circulates. If I go into our department office and inform the staff that it's raining outside and that the department chair has been abducted by aliens and replaced by an alien of identical appearance, neither statement satisfies our sense of "gossip." There are some, perhaps, in which the putative misfortunes of our department chair might indeed be "gossip," but the fact that it's raining (or that it rained yesterday) is too easily verified to ever be gossip.

The question, then, turns on communities with shared beliefs and social hierarchies of belief and the pleasure of playing on the margins of belief, whether one is finally disposed to believe or not believe. The interest in astrology seems to work this way for many. The notion that a person's nature is determined by birth under a certain zodiac sign—or in the Chinese case, the animal sign of a birth-year—pleases as a conditional or "entertained" belief that is very different than the faith we have in science (despite the fact that in many areas the consensus of scientific evidence seems to reverse itself every few decades).

The dark side of gossip is actual belief in the unverified, and entertaining belief can easily slip into actual belief and action. At several points in the Western Han, reports of witchcraft in the palace became a serious matter, for which a great many died. European history is filled with similar cases in which gossip became the general belief of the community, with ugly consequences. Later, in the Western Han case, those who did not believe in witchcraft attributed the events to palace intrigue—on no greater evidence than plausibility due to putative motive. What separates a story about witchcraft in a community that believes in witchcraft from a historian's story about court intrigue that charges rivals with witchcraft, circulating in a community that was more inclined to believe in false charges from an upstart harem faction than in witchcraft?

Like Europe, China was a society of laws, which struggled, as we still struggle, to find mechanisms to practically distinguish opinion from fact. But the Chinese were less inclined to interrogate the grounds of veracity of a good and harmless story. Few question the historical truth of anecdotes in Shishuo xinyu 世說新語 (*A New Account of Tales of the World*), and, at the same time, few try to adduce evidence that they actually happened. By contrast, once a generation of history teachers learned that George Washington did not, as a boy, cut down the cherry tree, it can no longer be taught as part of history—except, perhaps, as nineteenth-century construction of moral education using national heroes.

When I think of my own practice and that of my colleagues in premodern Chinese studies, there is an interesting moment when we decide whether to formulate an explanatory reference: "X did Y" or "X was supposed to have done Y." The boundaries seem to be those of our own belief. Great Yu 大禹 "was supposed to have" cut the channels for China's rivers; Ruan Ji 阮籍 (210–63) showed the white of his eyes to express contempt for someone. Our criterion is not historical knowledge but relative credibility. We mark Great Yu's deed as myth (while to many they were—and to some, still are—historical fact). At the same time we willingly treat stories of Ruan Ji's eccentricities as if they were fact.

The Chinese case is not only valuable in its own right, but makes us think back on the Euro-American case and its peculiar theoretical exclusion of the very popular "Bermuda Triangle discourse" in a regime that admits only truth, falsity, and fiction. One wonders how many of the works in this genre have been collected by university libraries. Even though intellectuals may read such things, they notionally belong to the discourse of rustics. Where does one place such a book in our own system of bibliographical categories, so as to leave decision of veracity in suspension?

The subtitle of this postface invokes "Ripley's Believe It or Not," the wildly popular column/cartoon series, first established in 1919 and spreading into many media venues. The entries included unexpected facts, facts massaged to appear as the unexpected, and material that just perhaps the Ripley establishment believed were indeed facts. It will not do as "gossip," but its large audience suggests the enduring interest in playing on the margins of belief. Ripley's scholars, like their Chinese counterparts, combed the textual tradition (in the New York Library) for interesting accounts to feed an interested audience. I myself remember many Ripley "Believe It or Not" magazines, none of which appear in the Harvard University Library system (there are only a few Ripley books, only one of which is in the main library). The Chinese case reminds us of a neglected history; they made a space for what has been erased in a very different regime of knowledge.

Bibliography

Adachi Kiroku 足立喜六. *Faxian zhuan kaozheng* 法顯傳考證. Translated by He Jianmin 何健民 and Zhang Xiaoliu 張小柳. Shanghai: Shangwu yinshuguan, 1937.
Allan, Sarah, and Alvin P. Cohen, eds. *Legend, Lore, and Religion in China: Essays in Honor of Wolfram Eberhard on His Seventieth Birthday.* San Francisco: Chinese Materials Center, 1979.
Baibu congshu jicheng 百部叢書集成. 4144 vols. Taipei: Yiwen yinshuguan, 1965–68.
Ban Gu 班固, comp. *Han shu* 漢書. 8 vols. Beijing: Zhonghua shuju, 1962.
Bauer, Wolfgang. "Chinese Glyphomancy (*ch'ai-tzu*) and Its Uses in Present-day Taiwan." In *Legend, Lore, and Religion in China,* edited by Sarah Allan and Alvin P. Cohen, 71–96. San Francisco: Chinese Materials Center, 1979.
Beal, Samuel, trans. *Si-yu Ki: Buddhist Records of the Western World.* London: Motilal Banarsidass, 1884.
Bierce, Ambrose. *The Devil's Dictionary.* New York: Oxford University Press, 1999.
Bischoff, F. A. *Le forêt des pinceaux.* Paris: Presses Universitaires de France, 1963.
Bol, Peter K. *'This Culture of Ours': Intellectual Transitions in T'ang and Sung China.* Stanford: Stanford University Press, 1992.
Bossler, Beverly. *Courtesans, Concubines, and the Cult of Wifely Fidelity: Gender and Social Change in China, 1000–1400.* Cambridge, Mass.: Harvard University Asia Center, 2013.
———. "Gender and Entertainment at the Song Court." In *Servants of the Dynasty,* edited by Anne Walthall, 261–79. Berkeley: University of California Press, 2008.
———. "Shifting Identities: Courtesans and Literati in Song China." *Harvard Journal of Asiatic Studies* 62, no. 1 (Jun. 2002): 5–37.
———. "Songdai de jiaji he qie" 宋代的家妓和妾. In *Jiatingshi yanjiu de xinshiye* 家庭史研究的新視野, edited by Zhang Guogang 張國剛, 206–17. Beijing: Sanlian shudian, 2004.

———. "Vocabularies of Pleasure: Categorizing Female Entertainers in the Late Tang Dynasty." *Harvard Journal of Asiatic Studies* 72, no. 1 (Jun. 2012): 71–99.

Bray, Francesca. *Technology and Gender: Fabrics of Power in Late Imperial China*. Berkeley: University of California Press, 1997.

Cai Zong-qi, ed. *Chinese Aesthetics: The Ordering of Literature, the Arts, and the Universe in the Six Dynasties*. Honolulu: University of Hawai'i Press, 2004.

Calhoun, Craig, ed. *Habermas and the Public Sphere*. Cambridge, Mass.: MIT Press, 1992.

Campbell, Mary B. *The Witness and the Other World: Exotic European Travel Writing, 400–1600*. Ithaca: Cornell University Press, 1988.

Cao Xueqin 曹雪芹. *Honglou meng* 紅樓夢. Edited by Zhao Cong 趙聰. 3 vols. Hong Kong: Youlian chubanshe, 1960.

Cao Xueqin 曹雪芹 and Gao E 高鶚. *Honglou meng* 紅樓夢. 4 vols. Beijing: Renmin wenxue chubanshe, 1972.

———. *The Story of the Stone*. Translated by David Hawkes and John Minford. 5 vols. Harmondsworth: Penguin Books, 1973–86.

Cen Zhongmian 岑仲勉. "Ba *Tang zhiyan*" 拔唐摭言. *Guoli Zhongyang yanjiuyuan lishi yuyan yanjiusuo jikan* 9 (1947): 243–64.

Chang, Michael G. "The Good, the Bad, and the Beautiful: Movie Actresses and Public Discourse in Shanghai, 1920s–1930s." In *Cinema and Urban Culture in Shanghai, 1922–1943*, edited by Yingjin Zhang, 128–59. Stanford: Stanford University Press, 1999.

Chen, Jack W. "Blank Spaces and Secret Histories: Questions of Historiographic Epistemology in Medieval China." *Journal of Asian Studies* 69, no. 4 (Nov. 2010): 1071–91.

Chen Menglei 陳夢雷 et al., comps. *Qinding gujin tushu jicheng* 欽定古今圖書集成. Edited by Jiang Tingxi 蔣廷錫 et al. 808 vols. Shanghai: Zhonghua shuju, 1934.

Chen Qinghao 陳慶浩, ed. *Shitou ji Zhiyenzhai pingyu jijiao* 石頭記脂硯齋評語集校. Taipei: Lianjing chuban shiye gongsi, 1985.

Chen Shidao 陳師道. *Houshan tancong* 後山談叢. In Chen Shidao 陳師道, *Houshan tancong* 後山談叢; Zhu Yu 朱彧, *Pingzhou ketan* 萍州可談. Edited by Li Weiguo 李偉國. Beijing: Zhonghua shuju, 2007.

Chen Shiyuan 陳士元. *Mengzhan yizhi* 夢占逸旨. In *Congshu jicheng chubian* 叢書集成初編, vol. 727. Shanghai: Shangwu yinshuguan, 1935–37.

Chen Shou 陳壽, comp. *Sanguozhi* 三國志. 5 vols. Beijing: Zhonghua shuju, 1959.

Chen Shunyu 陳舜俞. *Duguan ji* 都官集. In *Yingyin Wenyuange Siku quanshu* 影印文淵閣四庫全書, vol. 1096. Taipei: Taiwan shangwu yinshuguan, 1983–86.

Chen Zhensun 陳振孫. *Zhizhai shulu jieti* 直齋書錄解題. Edited by Xu Xiaoman 徐小蠻 and Gu Meihua 顧美華. Shanghai: Shanghai guji chubanshe, 1987.

Cheng Junying 程俊英 and Jiang Jianyuan 蔣見元, eds. *Shijing zhuxi* 詩經注析. Beijing: Zhonghua shuju, 1991.
Cheng Shude 程樹德, ed. *Lunyu jishi* 論語集釋. 4 vols. Beijing: Zhonghua shuju, 1990.
Clark, Anthony E. *Ban Gu's History of Early China*. Amherst, N.Y.: Cambria Press, 2008.
Congshu jicheng chubian 叢書集成初編. 3467 vols. Shanghai: Shangwu yinshuguan, 1935–37.
Congshu jicheng xinbian 叢書集成新編. 129 vols. Taipei: Xinwenfeng, 1985.
Cooper, Eugene, and Meng Zhang. "Patterns of Cousin Marriage in Rural Zhejiang and in *The Dream of the Red Chamber*." *Journal of Asian Studies* 52, no. 1 (Feb. 1993): 90–106.
Dai Jianguo 戴建國. "'Zhu pu zhi fen' yu Songdai nubi de falü diwei—Tang Song biange shiqi jijie jiegou yanjiu zhi yi" "主僕之分"與宋代奴婢的法律地位—唐宋變革時期階級結構研究之一. *Lishi yanjiu*, no. 4 (2004): 55–73.
Daoshan qinghua 道山清話. In *Quan Song biji* 全宋筆記, 2nd ser., vol. 1, edited by Zhu Yi'an 朱易安 et al., 83–120. Zhengzhou: Daxiang chubanshe, 2006.
de Groot, J. J. M. "On Chinese Divination by Dissecting Written Characters." *T'oung Pao* 1 (1890): 239–47.
de Souza, Ronald. "In Praise of Gossip: Indiscretion as a Saintly Virtue." In *Good Gossip*, edited by Robert B. Goodman and Aaron Ben Ze'ed, eds., 25–34. Lawrence: University Press of Kansas, 1994.
Dewoskin, Kenneth J., trans. *Doctors, Diviners, and Magicians of Ancient China: Biographies of* Fang-shih. New York: Columbia University Press, 1983.
———. "The Six Dynasties *Chih-kuai* and the Birth of Fiction." In *Chinese Narrative: Critical and Theoretical Essays*, edited by Andrew H. Plaks, 21–52. Princeton: Princeton University Press, 1977.
DiFonzo, Nicholas, and Prashant Bordia. *Rumor Psychology: Social and Organizational Approaches*. Washington, D.C.: American Psychological Association, 2007.
Ding Ruming 丁如明 et al., eds. *Tang Wudai biji xiaoshuo daguan* 唐五代筆記小說大觀. 2 vols. Shanghai: Shanghai guji chubanshe, 2000.
Ditter, Alexei. "Genre and the Transformation of Writing in Tang Dynasty China." PhD diss., Princeton University, 2009.
Dong Gao 董誥, comp. *Quan Tang wen* 全唐文. 11 vols. Beijing: Zhonghua shuju, 1983.
Douglas, Mary. *Implicit Meanings: Essays in Anthropology*. London: Routledge & Kegan Paul, 1975.
Drège, Jean-Pierre. "Clefs des Songes de Touen-houang." In *Nouvelles contributions aux études de Touen-houang*, edited by Michel Soymié, 205–49. Geneva: Librairie Droz, 1981.
———. "Notes d'Onirologie Chinoise." *Bulletin de l'École française d'Extrême-Orient* 70 (1981): 271–89.

Duan Chengshi 段成式, comp. *Youyang zazu* 酉陽雜俎. In *Baibu congshu jicheng*, vol. 46. Taipei: Yiwen yinshuguan, 1965–68.
Ebrey, Patricia Buckley. "Concubines in Sung China." *Journal of Family History* 11, no. 1 (Mar. 1986): 1–24.
———. *The Inner Quarters: Marriage and the Lives of Chinese Women in the Sung Period*. Berkeley: University of California Press, 1993.
Edwards, Louise P. *Men and Women in Qing China: Gender in the Red Chamber Dream*. Leiden: E.J. Brill, 1994.
Egan, Ronald. *The Problem of Beauty: Aesthetic Thought and Pursuits in Northern Song Dynasty China*. Cambridge, Mass.: Harvard University Asia Center, 2006.
Epstein, Maram. *Competing Discourses: Orthodoxy, Authenticity and Engendered Meanings in Late Imperial Chinese Fiction*. Cambridge, Mass.: Harvard University Asia Center, 2001.
Fan Gongcheng 范公偁, comp. *Guoting lu* 過庭錄. Reprinted in Zhang Bangji 張邦基, comp., *Mozhuang manlu* 墨莊漫錄; Fan Gongcheng 范公偁, comp., *Guoting lu* 過庭錄; Zhang Zhifu 張知甫, comp., *Keshu* 可書. Edited by Kong Fanli 孔凡禮. Beijing: Zhonghua shuju, 2002.
Fan Shu 范攄, comp. *Yunxi youyi* 雲谿友議. Beijing: Zhonghua shuju, 1959.
Fan Ye 范曄, comp. *Hou Han shu* 後漢書. 12 vols. Beijing: Zhonghua shuju, 1965.
Fan Ziye 范子燁. *Shishuo xinyu yanjiu* 世說新語研究. Harbin: Heilongjiang jiaoyu chubanshe, 1998.
Fang Xuanling 房玄齡 et al., eds. *Jin shu* 晉書. 10 vols. Beijing: Zhonghua shuju, 1974.
Farrar, James. "'Idle Talk': Neighborhood Gossip as a Medium of Social Communication in Reform Era Shanghai." In *Social Connections in China: Institutions, Culture and the Changing Nature of* Guanxi, edited by Thomas Gold, Doug Guthrie and David Wank, 197–220.
Faxian 法顯. *Faxian zhuan jiaozhu* 法顯傳校註. Edited by Zhang Xun 章巽. Shanghai: Shanghai guji chubanshe, 1985.
Feldherr, Andrew, and Grant Hardy. *The Oxford History of Historical Writing*. Vol. 1, *Beginnings to AD 600*. Oxford: Oxford University Press, 2011.
Gallagher, Catherine, and Stephen Greenblatt. *Practicing New Historicism*. Chicago: University of Chicago Press, 2000.
Gillispie, Charles C., ed. *Dictionary of Scientific Biography*. 18 vols. New York: Scribner, 1970–90.
Gold, Thomas, Doug Guthrie, and David Wank, eds. *Social Connections in China: Institutions, Culture and the Changing Nature of* Guanxi. Cambridge: Cambridge University Press, 2002.
Goodman, Robert B., and Aaron Ben Ze'ed, eds. *Good Gossip*. Lawrence: University Press of Kansas, 1994.
Graham, A. C. *The Book of Lieh-tzŭ*. London: John Murray, 1960.
Gu Shaobo 顧紹柏, ed. *Xie Lingyun ji jiaozhu* 謝靈運集校注. Henan: Zhongzhou guji chubanshe, 1987.

Guo Maoqian 郭茂倩, comp. *Yuefu shiji* 樂府詩集. 4 vols. Beijing: Zhonghua shuju, 1979.

Habermas, Jürgen. *The Structural Transformation of the Public Sphere: An Inquiry into a Category of Bourgeois Society*. Translated by Thomas Burger. Cambridge, Mass.: MIT Press, 1989.

Hall, David L., and Roger T. Ames. *Thinking from the Han: Self, Truth, and Transcendence in Chinese and Western Culture*. Albany: State University of New York Press, 1998.

Han Qi 韓琦. *Anyang ji biannian jianzhu* 安陽集編年箋注. Edited by Li Zhiliang 李之亮 and Xu Zhengying 徐正英. Chengdu: Ba Shu shushe chubanshe, 2000.

Hartman, Charles. *Han Yu and the T'ang Search for Unity*. Princeton: Princeton University Press, 1986.

He Wenhuan 何文煥, ed. *Lidai shihua* 歷代詩話. 2 vols. Beijing: Zhonghua shuju, 1981.

Hegel, Robert E., and Katherine Carlitz, eds. *Writing and Law in Late Imperial China: Crime, Conflict, and Judgment*. Seattle: University of Washington Press, 2007.

Hessler, Peter. *River Town: Two Years on the Yangtze*. New York: HarperCollins, 2001.

Holzman, Donald. "Les Septs Sages de Forêt des Bambous." *T'oung Pao* 44, nos. 4–5 (1956): 317–46.

Hong Mai 洪邁, comp. *Yijian zhi* 夷堅志. Edited by He Zhuo 何卓. 4 vols. Beijing: Zhonghua shuju, 1981.

Hsieh, Andrew C. K., and Jonathan Spence. "Suicide and the Family in Pre-Modern Chinese Society." In *Normal and Abnormal Behavior in Chinese Culture*, edited by Arthur Kleinman and Tsung-yi Li, 29–47.

Hu Houxuan 胡厚宣. *Jiaguxue Shangshi luncong chuji* 甲骨學商史論叢初集. Hong Kong: Wenyoutang shudian, 1970.

Huang, Martin W. *Literati and Self-Re/Presentation: Autobiographical Sensibility in the Eighteenth Century Novel*. Stanford: Stanford University Press, 1995.

Huang Tingjian 黃庭堅. *Huang Tingjian quanji* 黃庭堅全集. Edited by Liu Lin 劉琳, Li Yongxian 李勇先, and Wang Ronggui 王蓉貴. Chengdu: Sichuan daxue chubanshe, 2001.

Huangfu Mi 皇甫謐. *Diwang shiji* 帝王世紀. In *Baibu congshu jicheng* 百部叢書集成, vol. 54. Taipei: Yiwen yinshuguan, 1965–68.

Hucker, Charles O. *A Dictionary of Official Titles in Imperial China*. Stanford: Stanford University Press, 1985.

Huihong 惠洪. *Lengzhai yehua* 冷齋夜話. In *Quan Song biji* 全宋筆記, 2nd ser., vol. 9, edited by Zhu Yian 朱易安 et al., 25–99. Zhengzhou: Daxiang chubanshe, 2006.

Hung, William. "A T'ang Historiographer's Letter of Resignation." *Harvard Journal of Asiatic Studies* 29 (1969): 5–52.

Huntington, Rania. "Chaos, Memory, and Genre: Anecdotal Recollections of the Taiping Rebellion." *Chinese Literature: Essays, Articles, Reviews* 27 (Dec. 2005): 59–91.

Idema, W. L., and E. Zürcher, eds. *Thought and Law in Qin and Han China: Studies Presented to Anthony Hulsewé on the Occasion of His Eightieth Birthday.* Leiden: E. J. Brill, 1990.

Inge, M. Thomas, ed. *Truman Capote: Interviews.* Jackson, Miss.: University of Mississippi Press, 1987.

Ji Qin 冀勤 ed. *Yuan Zhen ji* 元稹集. 2 vols. Beijing: Zhonghua shuju, 1982.

Ji Yun 紀昀 (1724–1805), comp. *Siku quanshu zongmu tiyao* 四庫全書總目提要. *Reprinted in Heyin Siku quanshu zongmu tiyao ji Siku weishou shumu: Jinhui shumu* 合印四庫全書總目提要及四庫未收書目: 禁燬書目, edited by Wang Yunwu 王雲五. 5 vols. Taipei: Taiwan shangwu yinshuguan, 1971.

Jiang Shaoyu 江少虞, comp. *Songchao shishi leiyuan* 宋朝事實類苑. 2 vols. Shanghai: Shanghai guji chubanshe, 1981.

Jiao Xun 焦循, ed. *Mengzi zhengyi* 孟子正義. Beijing: Zhonghua shuju, 1987.

Jin Yizeng 靳義增. "Lun 'Yuanhe ti' de wenxue sixiang" 論元和體的文學思想. *Jiangxi shehue kexue* 6 (2003): 47–49.

Julien, François. *The Propensity of Things: Towards a History of Efficacy in China.* Translated by Janet Lloyd. New York: Zone Books, 1995.

Kempton, Beverly Gary. "Books: Truman Capote." *Playboy* 23, no. 12 (Dec. 1976): 47, 50.

Kleinman, Arthur, and Tsung-yi Li, eds. *Normal and Abnormal Behavior in Chinese Culture.* Dordrecht: D. Reidel Publishing, 1981.

Knechtges, David R. "Poetic Travelogue in the Han Fu." In *Zhongyang yanjiuyuan di 2 jie guoji Hanxue huiyi lunwenji* 中央研究院第2屆國際漢學會議論文集, edited by Zhongyang yanjiuyuan 中央研究院, 127–52. Taipei: Academia Sinica, 1989.

———, ed. and trans. *Wen xuan or Selections of Refined Literature.* Vol. 2, *Rhapsodies on Sacrifices, Hunting, Travel, Sightseeing, Palaces and Halls, Rivers and Seas.* Princeton: Princeton University Press, 1987.

Lanz, Henry. "Metaphysics of Gossip." *International Journal of Ethics* 46, no. 4 (Jul. 1936): 492–99.

Lao Gan 勞榦. "Lun Xijing zaji zhi zuozhe ji qi chengshu shidai" 論西京雜記之作者及其成書時代. *Zhongyang yanjiuyuan lishi yuyan yanjiusuo jikan* 33 (1963): 19–34.

Legge, James, trans. *A Record of Buddhistic Kingdoms, being an account by the Chinese monk Fâ-hien of his travels in India and Ceylon (A.D. 399–414) in search of the Buddhist books of discipline.* 1886; New York: Paragon Book Reprint Corp., 1965.

Levy, Dore J. "Embedded Texts: How to Read Poetry in *The Story of the Stone*." *Tamkang Review* 36, nos. 1–2 (Spring 2006): 210–17.

———. *Ideal and Actual in* The Story of the Stone. New York: Columbia University Press, 1999.

Levy, Marion J., Jr. *The Family Revolution in Modern China.* Cambridge, Mass.: Harvard University Press, 1947.

Lewis, Mark Edward. *The Flood Myths of Early China*. Albany: State University of New York Press, 2006.
———. *Writing and Authority in Early China*. Albany: State University of New York Press, 1999.
Li Fang 李昉 et al., comps. *Taiping guangji* 太平廣記. 10 vols. Beijing: Zhonghua shuju, 1961.
———. *Taiping yulan* 太平御覽. 4 vols. Beijing: Zhonghua shuju, 1960.
Li Jianguo 李劍國. *Tang Wudai zhiguai chuanqi xulu* 唐五代志怪傳奇敘錄. 2 vols. Tianjin: Nankai daxue chubanshe, 1998.
Li Tao 李濤. *Xu zizhi tongjian changbian* 續資治通鑑長編. 12 vols. Beijing: Zhonghua shuju, 1957.
Li Wai-yee. "Dreams of Interpretation in Early Chinese Historical and Philosophical Writings." In *Dream Cultures: Towards a Comparative History of Dreaming*, edited by David Shulman and Guy Stroumsa, 17–42. Oxford: Oxford University Press, 1999.
———. "*Shishuo xinyu* and the Emergence of Aesthetic Self-Consciousness in the Chinese Tradition." In *Chinese Aesthetics: The Ordering of Literature, the Arts, and the Universe in the Six Dynasties*, edited by Cai Zong-qi, 237–76. Honolulu: University of Hawai'i Press, 2004.
Li Zhao 李肇, comp. *Tang Guoshi bu* 唐國史補. In Li Zhao 李肇, comp., *Tang Guoshi bu* 唐國史補; Zhao Lin 趙琳, comp., *Yinhua lu* 因話錄. Shanghai: Shanghai guji chubanshe, 1979.
Liao Yingzhong 廖瑩中, comp. *Jiangxing zalu* 江行雜錄. Edited by Congshu jicheng xubian 叢書集成續編. Taipei: Xinwenfeng, 1985.
Liu Lin 劉琳, Li Yongxian 李勇先, and Wang Ronggui 王蓉貴, eds. *Huang Tingjian quanji* 黃庭堅全集. 4 vols. Chengdu: Sichuan daxue chubanshe, 2001.
Liu Shao 劉劭. *Renwu zhi jiaojian* 人物志校箋. Edited by Li Chongzhi 李崇智. Chengdu: Ba Shu shushe, 2001.
Liu Wenying 劉文英. *Zhongguo gudai de mengshu* 中國古代的夢書. Beijing: Zhonghua shuju, 1990.
Liu Xu 劉昫, ed. *Jiu Tangshu* 舊唐書. 16 vols. Beijing: Zhonghua shuju, 1975.
Liu Yiqing 劉義慶. *Shishuo xinyu jianshu* 世說新語箋疏. Edited by Yu Jiaxi 余嘉錫. Rev. ed. Zhou Zumo 周祖謨, Yu Shuyi 余淑宜, and Zhou Shiqi 周士琦. Shanghai: Shanghai guji chubanshe, 1993.
———. *Shishuo xinyu jiaojian* 世說新語校箋. Edited by Yang Yong 楊勇. 4 vols. Beijing: Zhonghua shuju, 2006.
Liu Zhiji 劉知幾. *Shi tong tongshi* 史通通釋. Edited by Pu Qilong 浦起龍. Shanghai: Shanghai guji chubanshe, 1978.
Loewe, Michael. *A Biographical Dictionary of the Qin, Former Han and Xin Periods (221 BC–AD 24)*. Leiden: Brill, 2000.
———. *Early Chinese Texts: A Bibliographic Guide*. Berkeley: Society for the Study of Early China and Institute of East Asian Studies, University of California, Berkeley, 1993.

Lu Xun 魯迅. *Lu Xun quanji* 魯迅全集. 18 vols. Beijing: Renmin wenxue chubanshe, 2005.

Lü Buwei 呂不韋. *Lüshi chunqiu xinjiaoshi* 呂氏春秋新校釋. Edited by Chen Qiyou 陳奇猷. 2 vols. Shanghai: Shanghai guji chubanshe, 2002.

Luo Dajing 羅大經, comp. *Helin yulu* 鶴林玉露. Edited by Wang Ruilai 王瑞來. Beijing: Zhonghua shuju, 1983.

Ma Qichang 馬其昶, ed. *Han Changli wenji jiaozhu* 韓昌黎文集校注. Shanghai: Shanghai guji chuban she, 1987.

MacCormack, Geoffrey. *The Spirit of Traditional Chinese Law*. Athens: University of Georgia Press, 1996.

Mann, Susan. "The Male Bond in Chinese History and Culture." *The American Historical Review* 105, no. 5 (Dec. 2000): 1600–14.

Mark, Lindy Li. "Orthography Riddles, Divination, and Word Magic: An Exploration in Folklore and Culture." In *Legend, Lore, and Religion in China*, edited by Sarah Allan and Alvin P. Cohen, 43–69. San Francisco: Chinese Materials Center, 1979.

Mather, Richard B., trans. and ed. *Shih-shuo hsin-yü: A New Account of Tales of the World*. 2nd ed. Ann Arbor: Center for Chinese Studies, University of Michigan, 2002.

McMullen, David L. "Han Yü: An Alternative Picture," *Harvard Journal of Asiatic Studies* 49, no. 2 (Dec. 1989): 603–57.

———. *State and Scholars in T'ang China*. Cambridge: Cambridge University Press, 1988.

Meng Erdong 孟二冬. *Zhong Tang shige zhi kaituo yu xinbian* 中唐詩歌之開拓與新變. Beijing: Beijing daxue chubanshe, 1998.

Meyer, Richard J. *Ruan Ling-yu: The Goddess of Shanghai*. Hong Kong: Hong Kong University Press, 2005.

Moore, Oliver. *Rituals of Recruitment: Reading an Annual Programme in the* Collected Statements *by Wang Dingbao (870–940)*. Leiden: Brill, 2004.

Mou Runsun 牟潤孫. *Lun Wei Jin yilai zhi chongshang tanbian ji qi yingxiang* 論魏晉以來之崇尚談辯及其影響. Hong Kong: Chinese University of Hong Kong Press, 1966.

Munro, Donald J., ed. *Individualism and Holism: Studies in Confucian and Taoist Values*. Ann Arbor: Center for Chinese Studies, University of Michigan, 1985.

Naquin, Susan, and Evelyn S. Rawski. *Chinese Society in the Eighteenth Century*. New Haven: Yale University Press, 1987.

Needham, Joseph. *Science and Civilisation in China*. Vol. 2, *History of Scientific Thought*. Cambridge: Cambridge University Press, 1956.

Ning Jiayu 寧稼雨. *Wei Jin mingshi fengliu* 魏晉名士風流. Beijing: Zhonghua shuju, 2007.

Nugent, Christopher M. B. *Manifest in Words, Written on Paper: Producing and Circulating Poetry in Tang Dynasty China*. Cambridge, Mass.: Harvard University Asia Center, 2010.

Ouyang Xiu 歐陽修 and Song Qi 宋祁, comps. *Xin Tangshu* 新唐書. 20 vols. Beijing: Zhonghua shuju, 1975.
Owen, Stephen, ed. and trans. *An Anthology of Chinese Literature: Beginnings to 1911*. New York: W. W. Norton & Company, 1996.
———. *The Late Tang: Chinese Poetry of the Mid-Ninth Century (827–860)*. Cambridge, Mass.: Harvard University Asia Center, 2009.
———. *Readings in Chinese Literary Thought*. Cambridge, Mass.: Council on East Asian Studies, Harvard University, 1992.
———. "A Tang Version of Du Fu: The *Tang shi lei xuan*." *T'ang Studies* 25 (2007): 57–90.
Pei Qi 裴啟. *Pei Qi yulin* 裴啟語林. Edited by Zhou Lengjia 周楞伽. Beijing: Wenhua yishu chubanshe, 1988.
Plaks, Andrew H. *Archetype and Allegory in* The Dream of the Red Chamber. Princeton: Princeton University Press, 1976.
———, ed. *Chinese Narrative: Critical and Theoretical Essays*. Princeton: Princeton University Press, 1977.
———. "Towards a Critical Theory of Chinese Narrative." In *Chinese Narrative: Critical and Theoretical Essays*, edited by Andrew H. Plaks, 309–52. Princeton: Princeton University Press, 1977.
Qi Wei 綦維. "'Yuanhe ti' kaobian" 元和體考辯. *Sichuan daxue xuebao (zhexue shehui kexue ban)* 134, no. 5 (2004): 135–39.
Qiu Zhaoao 仇兆鰲. *Dushi xiangzhu* 杜詩詳注. Beijing: Zhonghua shuju, 1979.
Qu Shouyuan 屈守元 and Chang Sichun 常思春, eds. *Han Yu quanji jiaozhu* 韓愈全集校注. 5 vols. Chengdu: Sichuan daxue chubanshe, 1996.
Qu Tuiyuan 瞿蛻園, ed. *Liu Yuxi ji jianzheng* 劉禹錫集箋證. Shanghai: Shanghai guji, 2005.
Quan Tangshi 全唐詩. 25 vols. Beijing: Zhonghua shuju, 1985.
Ricouer, Paul. *From Text to Action: Essays in Hermeneutics, II*. Translated by Kathleen Blamey and John B. Thompson. London: Athlone Press, 1991.
Rolston, David L. *Traditional Chinese Fiction and Commentary: Reading and Writing Between the Lines*. Stanford: Stanford University Press, 1997.
Ropp, Paul. *Dissent in Early Modern China*. Ann Arbor: University of Michigan Press, 1981.
Rouzer, Paul F. *Articulated Ladies: Gender and the Male Community in Early Chinese Texts*. Cambridge, Mass.: Harvard University Asia Center, 2001.
Ruan Yuan 阮元, ed. *Shisanjing zhushu fu jiaokanji* 十三經注疏附校勘記. 2 vols. Beijing: Zhonghua shuju, 1980.
Sanders, Graham. *Words Well Put: Visions of Poetic Competence in the Chinese Tradition*. Cambridge, Mass.: Harvard University Asia Center, 2006.
Schaberg, David. "Chinese History and Philosophy." In *The Oxford History of Historical Writing*. Vol. 1, *Beginnings to AD 600*, edited by Andrew Feldherr and Grant Hardy, 394–414. Oxford: Oxford University Press, 2011.
Schafer, Edward H. *The Golden Peaches of Samarkand: A Study of T'ang Exotics*. Berkeley: University of California Press, 1963.

Shanghai guji chubanshe 上海古籍出版社, ed. *Han Wei liuchao biji xiaoshuo daguan* 漢魏六朝筆記小說大觀. Shanghai: Shanghai guji chubanshe, 1999.

Shaughnessy, Edward L. "*Shang shu* 尚書 (*Shu ching* 書經)." In *Early Chinese Texts: A Bibliographic Guide,* edited by Michael Loewe, 377–78. Berkeley: Society for the Study of Early China and Institute of East Asian Studies, University of California, Berkeley, 1993.

Shen Chenyuan 沈辰垣, Wang Yiqing 王奕清, and Zhu Yizun 朱彝尊, comps. *Yuxuan lidai shiyu* 御選歷代詩餘. In *Yingyin Wenyuange Siku quanshu* 影印文淵閣四庫全書, vols. 1491–93. Taipei: Taiwan shangwu yinshuguan, 1983–86.

Shen Kuo 沈括. *Mengxi bitan* 夢溪筆談. In *Quan Song biji* 全宋筆記, 2nd ser., vol. 3, edited by Zhu Yian 朱易安 et al., 1–207. Zhengzhou: Daxiang chubanshe, 2006.

———. *Mengxi bitan jiaozheng* 夢溪筆談校證. Edited by Hu Daojing 胡道靜. 2 vols. Shanghai: Shanghai guji chubanshe, 1987.

Shen Yue 沈約, comp. *Song shu* 宋書. 8 vols. Beijing: Zhonghua shuju, 1974.

Shields, Anna M. *Crafting a Collection: The Cultural Contexts and Poetic Practice of the* Huajian ji *(Collection from among the Flowers)*. Cambridge, Mass.: Harvard University Asia Center, 2006.

Shulman, David, and Guy Stroumsa, eds. *Dream Cultures: Towards a Comparative History of Dreaming.* Oxford: Oxford University Press, 1999.

Sima Guang 司馬光, comp. *Sushui jiwen* 涑水紀聞. Edited by Deng Guangming 鄧廣銘 and Zhang Xiqing 張希清. Beijing: Zhonghua shuju, 1989.

———. *Zizhi tongjian* 資治通鑑. 20 vols. Beijing: Zhonghua shuju, 1956.

Sima Tan 司馬談 and Sima Qian 司馬遷. *Shi ji* 史記. 2nd ed. 10 vols. Beijing: Zhonghua shuju, 1962.

Sivin, Nathan. "Shen Kua." In *Dictionary of Scientific Biography,* vol. 12, edited by Charles C. Gillispie, 369–93. New York: Scribner, 1975.

———. "Shen Kua: A Preliminary Assessment of his Scientific Thought and Achievements." *Sung Studies Newsletter* 13 (1977): 31–56.

Slingerland, Edward. *Effortless Action: Wu-wei as Conceptual Metaphor and Spiritual Ideal in Early China.* New York: Oxford University Press, 2007.

Smits, Ivo. *The Pursuit of Loneliness: Chinese and Japanese Nature Poetry in Medieval Japan, ca. 1050–1150.* Stuttgart: F. Steiner, 1995.

Solomon, Bernard S. *The Veritable Record of the T'ang Emperor Shun-tsung.* Cambridge, Mass.: Harvard University Press, 1955.

Song Chuanyin 松傳銀 and Yang Chang 楊昶. *Shenmi de cizi* 神秘的測字. Nanning: Guangxi renmin chubanshe, 2004.

Song Zhenhao 宋鎮豪. "Jiaguwen zhong de meng yu zhanmeng" 甲骨文中的夢與占夢考. *Wenwu* 文物 600 (Jun. 2006): 61–71.

Soymié, Michel, ed. *Nouvelles contributions aux études de Touen-houang.* Geneva: Librairie Droz, 1981.

Stefanovska, Malina. "Exemplary or Singular? The Anecdote in Historical Narrative." *SubStance* 118 (2009): 16–30.

Strassberg, Richard E., trans. *Wandering Spirits: Chen Shiyuan's Encyclopedia of Dreams*. Berkeley: University of California Press, 2008.
Su Che 蘇轍, comp. *Longchuan lüe zhi* 龍川略志; *Longchuan biezhi* 龍川別志. Edited by Yu Zongxian 俞宗憲. Beijing: Zhonghua shuju, 1982.
Su Shi 蘇軾, comp. *Zazuan erxu* 雜纂二續. In Li Yishan 李義山 [Li Shangyin 李商隱] et al., comps., *Zazuan qizhong* 雜纂七種. Edited by Qu Yanbin 曲彥斌. Shanghai: Shanghai guji chubanshe, 1988.
Swann, Nancy Lee. *Pan Chao: Foremost Woman Scholar of China*. New York: Century Co., 1932.
Takigawa Kametarō 瀧川龜太郎. *Shiki kaichū kōshō* 史記會注考證. Taipei: Yiwen yinshuguan, 1976.
Tuotuo (Toghto) 脫脫, ed. *Song shi* 宋史. 40 vols. Beijing: Zhonghua shuju, 1977.
Twitchett, Denis. "Lu Chih (754–805): Imperial Adviser and Court Official." In *Confucian Personalities*, edited by Arthur F. Wright and Denis Twitchett, 84–122. Stanford: Stanford University Press, 1962.
———. *The Writing of Official History Under the T'ang*. Cambridge: Cambridge University Press, 1992.
Waley, Arthur, trans. *The Book of Songs*. Rev. ed. Edited by Joseph R. Allen. New York: Grove Press, 1996.
Walthall, Anne, ed. *Servants of the Dynasty: Palace Women in World History*. Berkeley: University of California Press, 2008.
Waltner, Ann. "Breaking the Law: Family Violence, Gender and Hierarchy in the Legal Code of the Ming Dynasty." *Ming Studies* 36 (1996): 29–43.
Wang Ayling 王瓊玲, ed. *Kongjian yu wenhua changyu: Kongjian yidong zhi wenhua quanshi* 空間與文化場域：空間移動之文化詮釋. Taipei: Hanxue yanjiu zhongxin, 2009.
Wang Dingbao 王定保. *Tang Zhiyan jiaozhu* 唐摭言校注. Edited by Jiang Hanchun 姜漢椿. Shanghai: Shanghai shehui kexueyuan chubanshe, 2003.
Wang Mingqing 王明清, comp. *Huizhu lu* 揮麈錄. Beijing: Zhonghua shuju, 1961.
———. *Yuzhao xinzhi* 玉照新志. In Wang, comp., *Touxia lu* 投轄錄; *Yuzhao xinzhi* 玉照新志. Edited by Wang Xinsen 汪新森 and Zhu Juru 朱菊如. Shanghai: Shanghai guji chubanshe, 1991.
Wang Nengxian 王能憲. *Shishuo xinyu yanjiu* 世說新語研究. Nanjing: Jiangsu guji chubanshe, 2000.
Wang Pijiang 王辟疆, ed. *Tangren xiaoshuo* 唐人小說. Shanghai: Shanghai guji chubanshe, 1978.
Wang Pizhi, *Shengshui yantan lu*. In *Quan Song biji* 全宋筆記, 2nd ser., vol. 4, edited by Zhu Yian 朱易安 et al., 1–107. Zhengzhou: Daxiang chubanshe, 2006.
Wang Renyu 王仁裕, comp. *Kaiyuan Tianbao yishi* 開元天寶遺事. Beijing: Zhonghua shuju, 2006.
Wang Xianqian 王先謙, ed. *Hanshu buzhu* 漢書補注. Taipei: Yiwen yinshuguan, 1955.

———. *Xunzi jijie* 荀子集解. 2 vols. Beijing: Zhonghua shuju, 1988.
Wang Zhi 王銍, comp. *Mo ji* 默記. In Wang Zhi 王銍, comp., *Mo ji* 默記; Wang Yong 王栐, comp., *Yanyi yi mou lu* 燕翼詒謀錄. Edited by Zhu Jieren 朱杰人. Beijing: Zhonghua shuju, 1981.
Wei Tai 魏泰, comp. *Dongxuan bilu* 東軒筆錄. Beijing: Zhonghua shuju, 1997.
———. *Lin Han yinju shihua* 臨漢隱居詩話. In *Lidai shihua* 歷代詩話, edited by He Wenhuan 何文煥. 2 vols. Beijing: Zhonghua shuju, 1981.
Wenying 文瑩, comp. *Xiangshan yelu* 湘山野錄; *Xiangshan yelu, xulu* 湘山野錄, 續錄; *Yuhu qinghua* 玉壺清話. Edited by Zheng Shigang 鄭世剛 and Yang Liyang 楊立揚. Beijing: Zhonghua shuju, 1984.
Wilde, Oscar. *Complete Works of Oscar Wilde*. London: HarperCollins, 1994.
Wright, Arthur F., and Denis Twitchett, eds. *Confucian Personalities*. Stanford: Stanford University Press, 1962.
Wu Jing 吳兢, comp. *Zhenguan zhengyao* 貞觀政要. Shanghai: Shanghai guji chubanshe, 1978.
Wu Zeng 吳曾, comp. *Nenggaizhai manlu* 能改齋漫錄. Shanghai: Shanghai guji chubanshe, 1979.
Xie Weixin 謝維新, comp. *Gujin hebi shilei beiyao: Chubian* 古今合璧事類備要: 初編. Taipei: Xinxing shuju, 1969.
Xu Fuguan 徐復觀. *Liang Han sixiangshi* 兩漢思想史. 3 vols. Shanghai: Huadong shifan daxue chubanshe, 2001.
Xu Yi 許顗, comp. *Yanzhou shihua* 彥周詩話. In *Lidai shihua* 歷代詩話, edited by He Wenhuan 何文煥. 2 vols. Beijing: Zhonghua shuju, 1981.
Yang Bojun 楊伯峻, ed. *Chunqiu Zuozhuan zhu* 春秋左傳注. Rev. ed. 4 vols. Beijing: Zhonghua shuju, 1990.
———. *Liezi jishi* 列子集釋. Beijing: Zhonghua shuju, 1979.
Yang Chang 楊昶 and Song Yinchuan 松傳銀, eds. *Gudai cezi shuping* 古代測字術注評. Guilin: Guangxi shifan daxue chubanshe, 1992.
Yang Jun 楊軍, ed. *Yuan Zhen ji biannian jiaozhu* 元稹集編年校注. Xi'an: San Qin chubanshe, 2002.
Yang Weizhong 楊維中, trans. *Xinyi Foguo ji* 新譯佛國記. Taipei: Sanmin shuju, 2004.
Yang Xianyi and Gladys Yang, trans. *Lu Xun: Selected Works*, 4 vols. Beijing: Foreign Languages Press, 1980.
Yao Zhenzong 姚振宗. *Shishi shanfang congshu* 師石山房叢書. Shanghai: Kaiming shudian, 1936.
Ye Mengde 葉夢得. *Shilin shihua* 石林詩話. In *Lidai shihua* 歷代詩話, edited by He Wenhuan 何文煥. 2 vols. Beijing: Zhonghua shuju, 1981.
Ye Shaoweng 葉紹翁. *Sichao wenjian lu* 四朝聞見錄. Edited by Shen Xilin 沈錫鄰 and Feng Huimin 馮惠民. Beijing: Zhonghua shuju, 1989.
Yingyin Wenyuange Siku quanshu 影印文淵閣四庫全書. 1500 vols. Taipei: Taiwan shangwu yinshuguan, 1983–86.
Yü Ying-shih. "Individualism and the Neo-Taoist Movement in Wei-Chin China." In *Individualism and Holism: Studies in Confucian and Taoist*

Values, edited by Donald Munro, 121–55. Ann Arbor: Center for Chinese Studies, University of Michigan, 1985.

Yuxuan lidai shiyu 御選歷代詩餘. Edited by Shen Chenyuan 沈辰垣 and Wang Yiqing 王奕清 et al. In *Yingyin Wenyuange Siku quanshu* 影印文淵閣四庫全書, vol. 1491–93. Taipei: Taiwan shangwu yinshuguan, 1983–86.

Zhan Xuzuo 詹緒佐 and Zhu Liangzhi 朱良志, eds. *Zhongguo gudai cezishu* 中國古代測字術. Chengdu: Sichuan daxue chubanshe, 1993.

Zhang Bangji 張邦基, comp. *Mozhuang manlu* 墨莊漫錄. Reprinted in Zhang Bangji 張邦基, comp., *Mozhuang manlu* 墨莊漫錄; Fan Gongcheng 范公偁, comp., *Guoting lu* 過庭錄; Zhang Zhifu 張知甫, comp., *Keshu* 可書. Edited by Kong Fanli 孔凡禮. Beijing: Zhonghua shuju, 2002.

Zhao Lin 趙琳, comp. *Yinhua lu* 因話錄. Reprinted in Li Zhao 李肇, comp., *Tang Guoshi bu* 唐國史補; Zhao Lin 趙琳, comp., *Yinhua lu* 因話錄. Shanghai: Shanghai guji chubanshe, 1979.

Zhao Lingzhi, comp. *Houqing lu* 侯鯖錄. Reprinted in Zhao Lingzhi, comp. *Houqing lu* 侯鯖錄; Peng Cheng 彭乘, comp., *Moke huixi* 墨客揮犀; *Xu moke huixi* 續墨客揮犀. Edited by Kong Fanli 孔凡禮. Beijing: Zhonghua shuju, 2002.

Zheng Binglin 鄭炳麟 and Yang Ping 羊萍, eds. *Dunhuangben mengshu* 敦煌本夢書. Lanzhou: Gansu wenhua chubanshe, 1995.

Zhongguo dianyingjia xiehui dianyingshi yanjiubu 中國電影家協會電影史研究部, ed. *Ruan Lingyu* 阮玲玉. Beijing: Zhongguo dianying chubanshe, 1985.

Zhongyang yanjiuyuan 中央研究院, ed. *Zhongyang yanjiuyuan di 2 jie guoji Hanxue huiyi lunwenji* 中央研究院第2屆國際漢學會議論文集. Taipei: Academia Sinica, 1989.

Zhou Guifeng 周桂峰. "Lun Yuanhe ti" 論元和體. *Huaiyin shifan xueyuan bao* 21, no. 5 (1999): 101–105.

Zhou Hui 周煇, comp. *Qingbo zazhi jiaozhu* 清波雜志校注. Edited by Liu Yongxiang 劉永翔. Beijing: Zhonghua shuju, 1994.

Zhou Mi 周密, comp. *Guixin zashi* 癸辛雜識. Edited by Wu Qiming 吳企明. Beijing: Zhonghua shuju, 1988.

———. *Wulin jiushi* 武林舊事. Reprinted in *Dongjing menghua lu: Wai sizhong* 東京夢華錄：外四種, compiled by Meng Yuanlao 孟元老 et al. Beijing: Zhonghua shuju, 1962.

Zhou Xunchu 周勛初, ed. *Tang yulin jiaozheng* 唐語林校證. Beijing: Zhonghua shuju, 1987.

———. *Tangdai biji xiaoshuo xulu* 唐代筆記小說敘錄. Nanjing: Fenghuang chubanshe, 2008.

Zhu Jincheng 朱金城, ed. *Bai Juyi ji jianjiao* 白居易集箋校. 6 vols. Shanghai: Shanghai guji chubanshe, 1988.

Zhu Mu 朱穆. *Gujin shiwen leiju* 古今事文類聚. In *Yingyin Wenyuange Siku quanshu* 影印文淵閣四庫全書, vols. 925–29. Taipei: Taiwan shangwu yinshuguan, 1983–86.

Zhu Qianzhi 朱謙之, ed. *Laozi jiaoshi* 老子校釋. Beijing: Zhonghua shuju, 1984.

Zhu Yian 朱易安 et al., eds. *Quan Song biji* 全宋筆記. 2nd series. 10 vols. Zhengzhou: Daxiang chubanshe, 2006.

Zhu Yu 朱彧, comp. *Pingzhou ketan* 萍州可談. Reprinted in Chen Shidao 陳師道, comp., *Houshan tancong* 後山談叢; Zhu Yu 朱彧, comp., *Pingzhou ketan* 萍州可談. Edited by Li Weiguo 李偉國. Beijing: Zhonghua shuju, 2007.

Contributors

SARAH M. ALLEN is Assistant Professor of Chinese at Wellesley College. She has recently completed a monograph, *Filling the Gaps: Tales and Tale Collections in Tang China,* which is on gossip, hearsay, and ideas of authorship and originality in Tang tales.

BEVERLY BOSSLER is Professor of History at the University of California, Davis. She is the author of articles on gender in the middle period, as well as *Powerful Relations: Kinship, Status, and the State in Song China (960–1279)* (1998) and *Courtesans, Concubines, and the Cult of Female Fidelity* (2013).

JACK W. CHEN is Associate Professor in the Department of Asian Languages & Cultures, UCLA. He has written *The Poetics of Sovereignty: On Emperor Taizong of the Tang Dynasty* (2010) and miscellaneous articles on topics relating to literary culture in medieval China.

RONALD EGAN is the Confucius Institute Professor of Sinology at Stanford University. Most recently, he is the author of *Limited Views: Essays on Ideas and Letters by Qian Zhongshu* (1998) and *The Problem of Beauty: Aesthetic Thought and Pursuits in Northern Song Dynasty China* (2006).

DORE J. LEVY is Professor of Comparative Literature at Brown University. In addition to essays on gardens, comparative literature, and other topics, she is the author of *Chinese Narrative Poetry: The Late Han through T'ang Dynasties* (1988) and *Ideal and Actual in* The Story of the Stone (1999).

STEPHEN OWEN is James Bryant Conant University Professor at Harvard University. Author of many books and articles, he has most recently published *The Making of Early Chinese Classical Poetry* (2006) and *The Late Tang: Chinese Poetry of the Mid-Ninth Century (827–860)* (2007). He is also coeditor of the two volume *Cambridge History of Chinese Literature* (2010).

GRAHAM SANDERS is Associate Professor in the Department of East Asian Studies at the University of Toronto. He is the author of *Words Well Put: Visions of Poetic Competence in the Chinese Tradition* (2006), the coeditor of

The Appropriation of Cultural Capital: China's May Fourth Project (2001), and the translator of Shen Fu's *Six Records of a Life Adrift* (2011).

DAVID SCHABERG is Professor in the Department of Asian Languages & Cultures and Dean of the Division of Humanities at UCLA. In addition to his many articles and book chapters, he is the author of *A Patterned Past: Form and Thought in Early Chinese Historiography* (2001) and cotranslator of the forthcoming new edition of the *Zuozhuan*.

ANNA M. SHIELDS is Associate Professor in the Department of Modern Languages, Linguistics, and Intercultural Communication at the University of Maryland, Baltimore County. She has written *Crafting a Collection: The Cultural Contexts and Poetic Practice of the* Huajian ji *(Collection from Among the Flowers)* (2006) and the forthcoming *One Who Knows Me: Friendship and Literary Culture in Mid-Tang China* (2014).

RICHARD E. STRASSBERG is Professor in the Department of Asian Languages & Cultures at UCLA. He is the author and translator of a number of books, including most recently *A Chinese Bestiary: Strange Creatures from the Guideways through Mountains and Seas* (2002) and *Wandering Spirits: Chen Shiyuan's Encyclopedia of Dreams* (2008). He is currently working on a book about the Kangxi emperor's poems on his estate, the Bishu shanzhuang 避暑山莊.

XIAOFEI TIAN is Professor in the Department of East Asian Languages and Civilizations at Harvard University. Her most recent books are *Beacon Fire and Shooting Star: The Literary Culture of the Liang (502–557)* (2007), *Liubai: Xie zai "Qiushuitang lun Jin Ping Mei" zhihou* 留白：寫在"秋水堂論金瓶梅"之後 (2009), and *Visionary Journeys: Travel Writings from Early Medieval and Nineteenth-Century China* (2011).

Index

Analects (*Lunyu* 論語). *See* Confucius
anecdote, definitions of, 2, 38–39, 89–91, 151, 217–221 passim
"arcane discourse" (*xuantan* 玄談), 52n8
authority, 5, 33–34, 62, 195–96, 198, 200
 and narrative, 7–8, 72, 73, 75, 79

Bai Juyi 白居易, 9, 109, 111–12, 114, 115, 118–19, 123–24, 126, 131n56
Ban Biao 班彪, 31–32
 and "Beizheng fu" 北征賦, 44
Ban Gu 班固, 5, 17, 18, 24, 29–34, 36n35, 36n36, 74, 75, 210, 217
Ban *jieyu* 班婕妤, 32–33, 36n36
 and "Zidao fu" 自悼賦, 33
Ban Zhao 班昭, 33
banquets, 39, 65–67, 138
 and courtesans, 160, 164, 166–67, 172
 and status negotiation, 155–58
Bi Sheng 畢昇, 10, 138–39, 152n10
biji 筆記 ("notebook jottings"), 4, 9–10, 107, 132–33, 136, 139–40, 148–52 passim, 179
 market for, 151–52
Bierce, Ambrose, 90
Big Jiao 焦大 (character), 198

Cai Jing 蔡京, 162, 164
Cai Xiang 蔡襄, 157, 164, 174n7
Campbell, Mary B., 46
Cao Xueqin 曹雪芹, 195, 208–10
Cezi midie 測字密牒. *See* Cheng Xing 程省
chaizi 拆字 ("disassembling graphs"), 178, 190n3. *See also* glyphomancy
Chajiao 茶嬌 (courtesan), 167
Chao Buzhi 晁補之, 163, 166
Chao Zhongzhi 晁冲之, 160
Chen, Jack W., 71
Chen Lie 陳烈, 157
Chen Shidao 陳師道, 163
Chen Shiyuan 陳士元, 12, 179–80, 189
Chen Xiang 陳襄, 159
Chen Xuanyou 陳玄祐. *See* "Lihun ji" 離魂記
Cheng Xing 程省, 12, 182–84
Chu Pou 褚裒, 7, 63–67, 68, 70n21
Chu Shaosun 褚少孫, 22, 23, 33
chuanqi 傳奇 ("transmitted marvels"), 4, 7, 179, 185, 220. *See also* individual *chuanqi* titles
Chunqiu Zuozhuan 春秋左傳 (Spring and autumn annals with the Zuo commentary), 29
Chunyu Yan 淳于衍, 25–28, 30, 36n23

ci 詞 ("song-lyric"), 163–64
civil service examinations, 102, 108, 114–15, 116, 118, 121, 123–24, 126, 155, 188
commoner (*buyi* 布衣), 133, 138, 142, 157, 158
concubines. *See under* courtesans
Confucius, 64–65, 68
courtesans, 11, 154–73 passim
  and calligraphy, 164–65
  commercial, 160–61
  government, 157, 158–60
  household (concubines), 143, 161–62, 163–64, 168–73
  parting from, 11, 165–67, 170, 176n35
  physical appearance of, 143, 158, 161, 165–67, 173
  and poetry, 163–68, 170–71
  released from service (cong liang 從良), 159–60
  as status arbiters, 157–58
  wealth of, 160–61

Dai Yuan 戴淵, 93, 98
Dai Zuo 戴祚 (Dai Yanzhi 戴延之), 45–47
de Souza, Ronald, 194–95, 196, 197
DeWoskin, Kenneth J., 210
distanciation, concept of. *See* Ricoeur, Paul
Diwang shiji 帝王世紀 (Annals of the thearchs and kings), 181–82
Disenchantment (Jinghuan xiangu 警幻仙姑), 186–87, 209, 211
Dou Shen 竇參, 76–79, 83
Dou Xian 竇憲, 33
Du Fu 杜甫, 96
dreams (*meng* 夢), 12, 113, 178–89 passim. *See also* glyphomancy
  and biographical accounts, 183–84, 188–89
  confirmation of (*yan* 驗 or *zheng* 徵), 179
  and dream manuals (mengshu 夢書), 181
  and poetry, 185, 191n13, 208–9
  and skepticism, 178, 180
  typical structure of, 179–81

Elder Sister Sha 傻大姐兒 (Simple) (character), 207–8
Emperor Cheng of the Han 漢成帝, 31, 35n15
Emperor Dezong of the Tang 唐德宗, 77–79, 84n19, 84n20, 111, 117
Emperor Jianwen of the Jin 晉簡文帝, 40
Emperor Ming of the Jin 晉明帝, 59, 70n20, 39–41
Emperor Shenzong of the Song 宋神宗, 170
Emperor Taizong of the Song 宋太宗, 138
Emperor Taizong of the Tang 唐太宗, 74, 86–87n40, 109
Emperor Xianzong of the Tang 唐憲宗, 108, 109, 112, 113, 116, 117, 120, 124, 129
Emperor Xuan of the Han 漢宣帝, 25, 31
Emperor Xuanzong of the Tang 唐宣宗, 86n33, 94, 109, 117, 129n35
Emperor Xuanzong of the Tang 唐宣宗, 117, 121, 129n34, 129n35
Emperor Yuan of the Han, 29
Emperor Yuan of the Jin 晉元帝, 39–41, 53n20
Empress Huo of the Han 漢霍后, 29, 30
Empress Yuan of the Han 漢元后, 24
Empress Xu of the Han 漢許后, 25, 27–30 passim, 35n15, 36n20

Faxian 法顯, 6, 46–51
Fan Shu 范攄, 8–9, 91–92, 100–104
fanyu 反語 ("phonetic recombination"), 184–85. *See also* glyphomancy
Farrar, James, 204
feminine beauty, notions of. *See under* courtesans, physical appearance of
fiction. *See xiaoshuo* 小說

fictionality, 218–22
Foguo ji 佛國記 (*A Record of Buddhistic Kingdoms*). See Faxian 法顯

Gallagher, Catherine, 39
Gao E 高鶚, 208, 209
Gao Wenhu 高文虎, 168, 176n41
Gaoyao 皋陶, 56
gossip, definitions and functions of, 4, 21–22, 29–30, 34n1, 71, 88–90, 149–50, 154, 194–95, 197–98, 204, 219, 221
ghosts and spirits, 71, 99, 108, 113, 133, 150, 183
glyphomancy, 12, 178–88 passim
  as pozi 破字 ("breaking apart graphs"), 178
Gu Kaizhi 顧愷之, 38–39
Gu Shao 顧劭, 60–61
guai 怪 ("unusual"), 9, 111, 114, 115
Guo Jin 郭進, 138
Guo Xiangzheng 郭祥正, 162

Han Qi 韓琦, 172
Han Yu 韓愈, 9, 109, 114, 115–20, 122–23, 124, 126
  and *guwen* 古文 ("ancient-style prose"), 110, 111
  and "Maoying zhuan" 毛穎傳 ("The Biography of Brush-hair"), 115–16
  and *muzhiming* 墓誌銘 for Liu Zongyuan, 119–20
  and *Shunzong shilu* 順宗實錄 (Veritable record of Shunzong's reign), 78–79, 85n27
  and "Yuanhe shengde shi" 元和聖德詩 ("On the Sagely Vitue of the Yuande [Emperor]"), 112
Han Zhen 韓縝, 170
Han Feizi 韓非子, 19
Hanshu 漢書 (History of the Han dynasty), 5, 18, 23–34 passim
historiography, 5, 8, 9, 11, 14, 19–34 passim, 107, 110, 149–50, 210, 218
Historiography Institute (*shiguan* 史館), 91
homosociality, 11, 155
Honglou meng 紅樓夢 (*Dream of the Red Chamber*). See *Story of the Stone*
Holzman, Donald, 62
Huainanzi 淮南子, 19, 35n14
Huan Tan 桓譚, 31, 36n31
Huang Tingjian 廷堅, 162, 173
Huangfu Mi 黃甫謐. See *Diwang shiji* 帝王世紀
Huangfu Shi 皇甫湜, 111, 118, 123, 127n10
Huihong 惠洪, 170
Huo Guang 霍光, 25–30 passim

India, 46–48

Ji Yougong 計有功 (*jinshi* 1121). See *Tangshi jishi* 唐詩紀事
"jixing fu" 紀行賦 ("*fu* recounting travel"), 44
Jia Baoyu 賈寶玉 (character), 186–88, 192n25, 194–95, 197, 199–200, 203–9, 211, 213n25, 214n37, 214n43
Jia Yucun 賈雨村 (character), 196–97, 210
Jia Zheng 賈政 (character), 195–96, 199–201, 203–4
Jinshu 晉書 (History of the Jin dynasty), 38, 40, 44, 63, 75, 84n11, 183–84
Jing Ke 荊軻, 20–21
jiuling 酒令 (drinking game), 95–96
Jiu Tangshu 舊唐書 (Old history of the Tang dynasty), 78–79, 86n31, 86–87n40, 125, 128n20, 131n56

"knowing men" (*zhiren* 知人), 6–7, 55–63 passim, 67
knowledge, private vs. public, 5, 6, 7–8, 17, 21–24, 29, 34, 41, 67–68, 73, 81–82, 89–90, 97, 98, 196–99, 206, 222–23
knowledge, scientific and technical, 10, 132–41 passim, 178
Kou Zhun 寇準, 155–57

Lady Gouyi 鉤弋夫人, 22–23, 25, 35n10, 35n12
Lanz, Henry, 13
Laozi 老子, 31, 69n14
leishu 類書 ("encyclopedia"), 133–34
Leng Zixing 冷子興 (character), 196–97, 212n10
Lewis, Mark Edward, 19
Li Ao 李翱, 111, 118, 122–23, 130n48
Li Gongzuo 李公佐, 86n38, 185, 188, 192n22
Li Gou 李覯, 157
Li Guan 李觀, 122
Li Huizheng 李彙征, 94–104
Li Jie 李誡. See *Yingzao fashi* 營造法式
Li Jifu 李吉甫, 79–83
Li Jing 李璟, 147
Li Linfu 李林甫, 81
Li She 李涉, 8–9, 92–94, 96–104, 105n9, 106n18
Li Shun 李順, 143–45, 149
Li Wan 李紈 (character), 205–6
Li Xianyong 李咸用, 91, 102–3
Li Yi 李益, 115
Li Yunze 李允則, 155–57
Li Zhao 李肇. See *Tang guoshi bu* 唐國史補
Li Zhiyi 李之儀, 162, 171
"Lihun ji" 離魂記 ("The Severed Soul"), 7, 72–73
"Liang Datong guming ji" 梁大同古銘記 ("The Ancient Inscription from the Liang Datong Period"), 7–8, 79–81
Lin Daiyu 林黛玉 (character), 197, 204–9, 214n37
Linghu Chu 令狐楚, 112
Liu Bei 劉備, 61
Liu Chang 劉敞, 167, 170, 176–77n46
Liu Chen 劉晨 and Ruan Zhao 阮肇, story of, 50
Liu Cheng 柳珵. See "Shangqing" 上清傳
Liu Kai 柳開, 110
Liu Shao 劉劭 See *Renwu zhi* 人物志.
Liu Shunü 劉淑女, 165–66
Liu Xiang 劉向, 101
Liu Yiqing 劉義慶, 41, 50, 52n16, 55
Liu Yu 劉裕, 45–46, 47, 74–75, 76, 84n12
Liu Yuxi 劉禹錫, 97–98, 109, 118, 119–20, 123, 129n32
Liu Zongyuan 柳宗元, 109, 118, 119–20, 123
Lu Ji 陸機, 93, 98, 105n10
Lu Xun 魯迅, 2–3, 52n8
Lu Zhao 盧肇. See *Yishi* 逸史
Lu Zhi 陸贄, 76–79, 84n19, 84n20, 85n25, 85–86n30
Lunyu 論語. See Confucius
Lüshi chunqiu 呂世春秋 (*Annals of Master Lu*), 6, 19, 35n14, 57–58

Ma Pan 馬盼 (courtesan), 165
manuscripts and manuscript culture, 89, 100, 103, 105n11, 208, 209, 210
Mei Yaochen 梅堯臣, 164
Mei Zhi 梅摯, 146, 150
Mencius, 75
Meng Jia 孟嘉, 63–64, 67
Meng Jiao 孟郊, 111, 114, 122, 124, 130n48, 130n52
Mengxi bitan 夢溪筆談 (*Chatting with my writing brush at Dreams Creek*), 10, 132–52 passim
  and craftsmen and laborers, 136–39
  and eccentrics, 141–45
  and *fangshi* 方士 ("masters of occult arts"), 142–43
  and lightning, 140–41, 150
  and pole star, 140
  preface of, 135–36
  table of contents for, 133
  See also Shen Kuo 沈括
Mengzhan yizhi 夢占逸旨. See Chen Shiyuan 陳士元
mingshi 名士, 55, 62, 68
Moore, Oliver, 122
Mujing 木經 (*Lumber classic*), 137–38

Nannie Zhao 趙媽媽 (character), 201
narrative subjectivity, 44–46

networks, 2, 6–7, 10, 11, 14, 58, 67–68
novel. See *xiaoshuo* 小說
Nugent, Christopher M. B., 73, 105n11

orality, 14, 44, 72–82 passim, 88–90, 97, 100, 103, 105n11, 124, 149–50, 219
  and dreams, 179–80, 188
Ouyang Xiu 歐陽修, 9, 84n20
Ouyang Zhan 歐陽詹, 122

Pang Tong 龐統, 60–62
Pei Du 裴啟, 111, 120, 129n32
Pei Qi 裴啟. See *Yulin*
pozi 破字 ("breaking apart graphs"), 178, 182–83. See glyphomancy
Prince Dan 太子丹 of Yan 燕, 20–21, 34–35n7
printing and print culture, 73, 138–39, 149, 151, 173–74n1

qi 奇 ("unconventional"), 111, 114, 118, 123
Qin Miaoguan 秦妙觀 (courtesan), 165
Qin Shihuang 秦始皇, 20
Qingyi lu 清異錄 (Records of the pure and unusual), 133
Quan Tangshi 全唐詩 (Complete Tang poems), 97, 185

Renwu zhi 人物志 (The Study of Human Abilities), 6, 58–59
reputation, 6–7, 8, 11, 12, 13, 14, 20, 34n4, 53n22, 55, 62, 66, 71, 79, 80, 92, 98–100, 102, 106n18, 107, 118–19, 120, 122–23, 161, 164, 195, 197–98, 200, 201, 211, 212n5
retributory illness (*yuannie zhi zheng* 原孽之症), 194, 212n3
retributory speech (*yuannie zhi hua* 原孽之話), 194, 195, 205, 208, 211
Ricoeur, Paul, 90
romance, 11, 155–68 passim, 171–73
romance (genre), 34–35n7, 210, 221
Ropp, Paul, 197

Ruan Lingyu 阮玲玉, 1–3

Sanguo zhi 三國志 (Record of the Three Kingdoms), 188–89
"Shangqing" 上清, 7, 76–79, 82, 83, 84n19, 85n23
Shangshu 尚書 (Esteemed documents), 6, 56, 61, 69n4
Shen Chong 沈充, 65–68
Shen Kuo 沈括, 9–10, 132–52 passim
  open-mindedness of, 140–41
  and political awareness, 134–36
  and scientific observation, 139–41
  and waterclock, 140
  and Xining Fengyuan li 熙寧奉元曆 (Xining memorial calendar), 140
  See also *Mengxi bitan* 夢溪筆談
Shengshui yantan lu 澠水燕談錄 (Record of banquet chats by Sheng River), 151
shi yan zhi 詩言志, 90
Shi Yannian 石延年, 10, 143, 145–46, 150, 157
  and drinking postures, 146
shihua 詩話 ("remarks on poetry"), 91, 110, 154, 173–74n1
Shiji 史記 (Records of the historian), 5, 18, 19–23 passim, 24, 30–32, 35n14, 75, 182
Shijing 詩經 (Classic of poetry), 3, 160
Shishuo xinyu 世說新語 (A New Account of Tales of the World), 6–7, 12, 41–44, 50, 51, 52n8, 52n9, 52n16, 55, 59–68, 222
Shuoyuan 說苑 (Garden of legends). See Liu Xiang 劉向
Siku quanshu zongmu tiyao 四庫全書總目提要 (Annotated catalogue of the Imperial Library), 91–92
Sima Qian 司馬遷. See *Shiji* 史記.
Sivin, Nathan, 139, 151
Songshi 宋史 (History of the Song dynasty), 144
Soushen houji 搜神後記 (Later record of searching for spirits), 97

Sri Lanka, 46, 49–50, 54n32
Story of the Stone (*Shitou ji* 石頭記), 5, 12–13, 194–211 passim
Su Che 蘇轍, 155, 174n4
Su Qin 蘇秦, 19–20, 34n4
Su Qiong 蘇瓊 (courtesan), 164
Su Shi 蘇軾, 9, 136
    and courtesans, 159, 163–65, 167, 170, 172–73, 177n55
    and huapan 花判 ("humorous judgments"), 159
Su Song 蘇頌, 159
Su Xiaoxiao 蘇小小, 158
Suo Dan 索紞, 184

Taiping guangji 太平廣記 (Extensive records of the Taiping reign), 108, 126n4
Tang caizi zhuan 唐才子傳 (Biographies of talented Tang poets), 92
Tang guoshi bu 唐國史補 (Supplement to the Tang history of the state), 9, 107, 108, 110, 113–17, 118–24 passim, 128n18, 128n21
Tang tales. See *chuanqi*
Tang yulin 唐語林 (Tang forest of words), 108, 118, 130n41
Tang zhiyan 唐摭言 (Collected sayings from the Tang), 9, 107, 121–25
Tangshi jishi 唐詩紀事 (Anecdotes of Tang poetry), 92, 108, 126n4
Tao Gu 陶穀. See *Qingyi lu* 清異錄
Tao Fan 陶範, 42
Tao Kan 陶侃, 42–44
Tao Yuanming 陶淵明, 97
Tian, Ms. 田氏 (courtesan), 166
Tolstoy, Leo, 13, 17–18
Tiansu 添蘇 (courtesan), 158

Vergil, 17–18

"Waiqi zhuan" 外戚傳 ("Biographies of the In-laws), 24–30
Wang Dingbao 王定保. See *Tang zhiyan* 唐摭言
Wang Dun 王敦, 59–60, 66
Wang Jien 王繼恩, 144
Wang Kui 王逵, 171–72
Wang Mang 王莽, 24, 32
Wang Mingqing 王明清, 161–62, 175n18
Wang Pizhi 王闢之. See *Shengshui yantan lu* 澠水燕談錄
Wang Shao 王韶, 169
Wang Shen 王詵, 165, 172
Wang Wei 王維, 115
Wang Xifeng 王熙鳳 (character), 195–96, 198–99, 201–3
Wang Xiuling 王修齡, 42
Wang Yanzheng 王延政, 147
Wang Yingying 王英英 (courtesan), 164
Wang Yuan 王淵, 161
Wang Zhaoyun 王朝雲 (concubine), 170, 172–73, 177n55
Wang Zhi 王銍, 168
Wei Siming 韋思明 (bandit-recluse), 95–104
Wei Ye 魏野, 158
Wei Yingwu 韋應物, 115
Wen Qiao 溫嶠, 62–63
wuwei 無為 ("nonpurposive action"), 57

Xizheng ji 西征記. See Dai Zuo 戴祚
xiangzi 相字 ("interpreting the forms of graphs"), 178. See also glyphomancy
xiaoshuo 小說
    as fiction, 6, 12, 83n2, 197–98
    as novel, 38, 46, 209
    as "petty discourse," 91–92, 130n42, 209–10
Xie An 謝安, 64–65
Xie Lingyun 謝靈運, 44–46
    and "Zhuanzheng fu" 撰征賦 ("Fu Relating My Journey"), 44–45
Xie Shang 謝尚, 42
Xie Xiao'e 謝小娥, 185
Xin Tangshu 新唐書 (New history of the Tang dynasty), 79, 125, 130n41, 131n56
Xin Wenfang 辛文房. See *Tang caizi zhuan* 唐才子傳

Index / 247

Xinxu 新序 (New accounts). *See* Liu Xiang 劉向
Xu Ganchen 徐幹臣, 171
Xu Zizhi tongjian changbian 續資治通鑑長編 (Continuation of the long version of the comprehensive mirror for aiding government), 144
Xue Baochai 薛寶釵 (character), 186, 200, 206, 207–8
Xunzi 荀子, 56
Yan Shu 晏殊, 171

Yang Guifei 楊貴妃, 94
Yang Lang 楊郎, 59–61, 67
Yang Shu 楊姝 (courtesan), 162, 171
"Yao Hong" 姚泓 (Tang tale), 7, 74–76, 77, 79, 82, 83, 84n10
Ye Mengde 葉夢得, 170, 176–77n46
yeshi 野史 ("unofficial history"), 90–91, 192n20, 210, 221
Yellow Emperor (Huangdi 黃帝), 181–82
Yijing 易經 (Classic of Changes), 184, 191n16
Yishi 逸史 (Uncollected histories), 74
Yingzao fashi 營造法式 (Architectural methods), 137
Yinhua lu 因話錄 (Records of hearsay), 9, 107, 108, 110, 111, 117–21, 129n32, 129n34, 129n35
Youming lu 幽明錄 (Records of worlds of darkness and light), 50
Youyang zazu 酉陽雜俎 (Miscellaneous morsels from Youyang), 184–85
Yu 禹 (sage-king), 56
Yu Hao 喻皓. *See Mujing* 木經
Yu Liang 庾亮, 42–44, 63–65, 70n20, 70n21
Yulin 語林 (Forest of words), 39–41
Yü, Ying-shih, 62
Yuan Zhen 元稹, 109, 111–12, 114–15, 123–24, 127n10, 127n15, 131n56
Yuanhe ti 元和體, 112, 118, 124, 130n41, 131n56
yuefu 樂府 ("Music Bureau") poetry, 95, 105n12, 118, 127n10, 131n56
Yunxi youyi 雲谿友議 (Friendly conversations at Cloudy Creek), 81, 91–104 passim. *See also* Fan Shu 范攄

Zhang Dun 章惇, 169
Zhang Ji 張籍, 111, 114, 118–19, 122–23, 127n11
Zhang Jun 張浚, 162
Zhang Lei 張耒, 165–67
Zhao Feiyan 趙飛燕, 32
Zhao Lingzhi 趙令畤, 159, 165
Zhao Lin 趙璘. *See Yinhua lu* 因話錄
Zhenguan zhengyao 貞觀政要 (Essentials of government during the Zhenguan reign), 4
Zheng Qinyue 鄭欽悅, 79–83
zhiguai 志怪 ("anomaly accounts"), 4, 179, 183
Zhiyan 摭言. *See Tang zhiyan* 唐摭言
Zhongguo 中國, various connotations of, 47–48
Zhou, Mrs. 周嫂子 (character), 202–3
Zhou Shao 周韶 (courtesan), 159, 164
Zhou Xuan 周宣, 188–89, 193n29
zhuan 傳 ("biographical account"), 3–4, 24, 92, 115–16, 180, 209
Zhuan Chunying 囀春鶯 (fl. 11th cent.) (concubine), 165
Zhuang Zhou 莊周 (fl. 4th cent. BCE). *See Zhuangzi* 莊子
Zhuangzi 莊子, 31, 35n14, 178, 180
Zizhi tongjian 資治通鑑 (Comprehensive mirror for aid in governance), 79, 84n18
zongheng jia 縱橫家 (crisscross persuaders), 19
Zou Zhan 鄒湛, 183
Zu Xuan 祖暅 (fl. 5th cent. CE), 140
Zuozhuan 左傳. *See Chunqiu Zuozhuan* 春秋左傳

www.ingramcontent.com/pod-product-compliance
Lightning Source LLC
Chambersburg PA
CBHW021937240426
43668CB00036B/157